Studies in Development Economics and Policy
General Editor: **Anthony Shorrocks**

UNU-WORLD INSTITUTE FOR DEVELOPMENT ECONOMICS RESEARCH (UNU-WIDER) was established by the United Nations University as its first research and training centre and started work in Helsinki, Finland, in 1985. The purpose of the Institute is to undertake applied research and policy analysis on structural changes affecting the developing and transitional economies, to provide a forum for the advocacy of policies leading to robust, equitable and environmentally sustainable growth, and to promote capacity strengthening and training in the field of economic and social policy-making. Its work is carried out by staff researchers and visiting scholars in Helsinki and through networks of collaborating scholars and institutions around the world.

UNU-World Institute for Development Economics Research (UNU-WIDER)
Katajanokanlaituri 6B, FIN-00160 Helsinki, Finland

Titles include:

Tony Addison and Alan Roe (*editors*)
FISCAL POLICY FOR DEVELOPMENT
Poverty, Reconstruction and Growth

Tony Addison, Henrik Hansen and Finn Tarp (*editors*)
DEBT RELIEF FOR POOR COUNTRIES

Ricardo Ffrench-Davis and Stephany Griffith-Jones (*editors*)
FROM CAPITAL SURGES TO DROUGHT
Seeking Stability for Emerging Economies

Basudeb Guha-Khasnobis (*editor*)
THE WTO, DEVELOPING COUNTRIES AND THE DOHA DEVELOPMENT AGENDA
Prospects and Challenges for Trade-Led Growth

Aiguo Lu and Manuel F. Montes (*editors*)
POVERTY, INCOME DISTRIBUTION AND WELL-BEING IN ASIA DURING THE TRANSITION

Robert J. McIntyre and Bruno Dallago (*editors*)
SMALL AND MEDIUM ENTERPRISES IN TRANSITIONAL ECONOMIES

Vladimir Mikhalev (*editor*)
INEQUALITY AND SOCIAL STRUCTURE DURING THE TRANSITION

E. Wayne Nafziger and Raimo Väyrynen (*editors*)
THE PREVENTION OF HUMANITARIAN EMERGENCIES

Matthew Odedokun (*editor*)
EXTERNAL FINANCE FOR PRIVATE SECTOR DEVELOPMENT
Appraisals and Issues

Laixiang Sun (*editor*)
OWNERSHIP AND GOVERNANCE OF ENTERPRISES
Recent Innovative Developments

Studies in Development Economics and Policy
Series Standing Order ISBN 0-333-96424-1
(*outside North America only*)

You can receive future titles in this series as they are published by placing a standing order. Please contact your bookseller or, in case of difficulty, write to us at the address below with your name and address, the title of the series and the ISBN quoted above.

Customer Services Department, Macmillan Distribution Ltd, Houndmills, Basingstoke, Hampshire RG21 6XS, England

---

Debt Relief for Poor Countries

Edited by

Tony Addison, Henrik Hansen and Finn Tarp

in association with the United Nations University–World Institute for Development Economics Research

First published 2004 by
PALGRAVE MACMILLAN
Houndmills, Basingstoke, Hampshire RG21 6XS and
175 Fifth Avenue, New York, N.Y. 10010
Companies and representatives throughout the world

PALGRAVE MACMILLAN is the global academic imprint of the Palgrave Macmillan division of St. Martin's Press, LLC and of Palgrave Macmillan Ltd. Macmillan® is a registered trademark in the United States, United Kingdom and other countries. Palgrave is a registered trademark in the European Union and other countries.

ISBN 1–4039–3482–7 hardback
ISBN 1–4039–3495–9 paperback

This book is printed on paper suitable for recycling and made from fully managed and sustained forest sources.

A catalogue record for this book is available from the British Library.

A catalogue record for this book is available from the Library of Congress.

10 9 8 7 6 5 4 3 2 1
13 12 11 10 09 08 07 06 05 04

Printed and bound in Great Britain by
Antony Rowe Ltd, Chippenham and Eastbourne

For Anja, Grethe, and Lynda, with appreciation

Contents

List of Tables

List of Figures

Foreword

The resources released by debt relief are often seen as crucial for accelerating growth and poverty reduction in poor countries. But despite the heated debate, there has been little in the way of rigorous and independent economic analysis of the debt relief now available through the Heavily Indebted Poor Countries (HIPC) Initiative, launched by the IMF and the World Bank with the support of the international donor community. The economics literature on debt relief is dominated by the experiences of the mainly middle-income countries (mostly in Latin America) which suffered debt crises in the 1980s, but their debt was owed mainly to private creditors, while the debt of the HIPCs (most of whom are in Africa) is mainly owed to official creditors. Consequently, policy-makers in poor countries and their donor partners have had little to guide them in this crucial area of economic policy.

This book fills an important gap in our knowledge. The research reported here – an outcome of a UNU-WIDER conference held in Helsinki in August 2001 – offers a variety of perspectives on the economics of HIPC. It asks why poor countries became indebted in the first place, and what can be done to prevent the problem reemerging. It also provides a valuable menu of techniques for assessing the effects of HIPC debt relief on economic growth and poverty reduction – the latter being especially important in the light of the Millennium Development Goals. The book also highlights the impact of debt relief on the incentives of private and public sector actors, and the role of international forces (such as commodity price instability) as well as domestic factors (such as conflict and weak policy) in causing debt problems. For these reasons, the book makes a timely and welcome addition to the literature on international development economics.

TONY SHORROCKS
Director, UNU-WIDER

Acknowledgements

This book originates in a UNU-WIDER conference on debt relief held in Helsinki in August 2001. The conference was attended by over 150 academics and policy-makers, many from the developing world, in particular Sub-Saharan Africa. The aim of the conference was to bring together researchers to explore the ways in which debt relief impacts on development. We thank all those who attended and presented papers for making the meeting a big success, and for significantly moving the debate on HIPC forward.

The idea for a conference on debt relief originated with the director of UNU-WIDER, Tony Shorrocks, and he has provided much support to the subsequent development of the book. We also thank the Board of UNU-WIDER, and in particular its chairman, Deepak Nayyar, for their encouragement. Liisa Roponen provided invaluable support in the conference logistics, and in the production of this volume. Special thanks are due to Adam Swallow who provided excellent and timely advice at all stages of the publication process and Barbara Fagerman, Lea Hallbäck, Taina Iduozee, Maria Kauppinen, Ara Kazandjian, Dušan Palkovič and Bruck Tadesse were also of great assistance. The book benefited from the editorial services of Keith Povey and Alberta Hagan was of great help in proof-reading.

Chapter 3 previously appeared in the *World Bank Economic Review*, vol. 17, no. 23 (2003). It appears here with the courtesy of Oxford University Press.

UNU-WIDER gratefully acknowledges the financial contributions to its activities of the governments of Denmark, Finland, Norway, Sweden and the United Kingdom. These sponsors are not responsible for any of the information provided or views expressed, which remain those of the editors and contributors alone.

Copenhagen and Helsinki

TONY ADDISON
HENRIK HANSEN
FINN TARP

Notes on the Contributors

Tony Addison is Deputy Director of the World Institute for Development Economics Research (UNU-WIDER) in Helsinki, and was previously on the economics faculty of the University of Warwick.

Jean-Claude Berthélemy is Professor of Economics at the University of Paris 1 Pantheon Sorbonne and consultant for the OECD Development Centre, where he is coordinator of the annual African Economic Outlook report.

Arne Bigsten is Professor of Development Economics at Göteborg University, and has undertaken projects for, among others, the World Bank, United Nations, OECD, ILO, UNU-WIDER and Sida.

Nancy Birdsall, a development economist, is the founding President of the Center for Global Development in Washington, DC, and was previously with the Inter-America Development Bank and World Bank.

Abdur Chowdhury is the Director of the Economic Analysis Division, United Nations Economic Commission for Europe, Geneva.

Stijn Claessens is Professor of International Finance at the University of Amsterdam; from 1987 to 2001 he worked in the World Bank, most recently as Lead Economist, Financial Sector Strategy and Policy Group.

Era Dabla-Norris is an economist with the International Monetary Fund. Her research interests include public finance, institutions and governance, fiscal decentralization and development.

Ishac Diwan is the World Bank's Country Director for Ethiopia and Sudan, and has been Division Chief in the World Bank Institute.

Benno Ferrarini is currently the Director of Economic Research at the World Trade Institute (WTI), Switzerland, and has published in the field of international trade and finance.

Henrik Hansen is Associate Professor, Institute of Economics, at the University of Copenhagen.

Rasmus Heltberg is an economist with the World Bank, and was previously with the University of Copenhagen, specializing in applied poverty analysis.

Jörgen Levin is Research Fellow and Lecturer in the Department of Economics at the Örebro University (Sweden).

John M. Matovu is currently an economist with the International Monetary Fund. His research mainly focuses on tax and expenditure policy and its implications on income distribution.

Oliver Morrissey is Director of the Centre for Research in Economic Development and International Trade (CREDIT), School of Economics, University of Nottingham, and a research fellow in the Overseas Development Institute (ODI), London

Machiko Nissanke is currently Reader in Economics and Head of the Economics Department at the School of Oriental and African Studies (SOAS), University of London. She is an Advisory Committee Member and Chair of the Research Sub-Committee of the AERC.

Catherine Pattillo is a senior economist in the Research Department of the International Monetary Fund. Her research interests include macroeconomic issues in Africa, debt, growth, investment, capital flight and firm behaviour.

Håkan Persson is Associate Professor of Economics at Örebro University, Sweden and has carried out research in CGE modelling, regional science and development economics.

Hélène Poirson is an economist at the International Monetary Fund, and has published on external debt and economic growth.

Aminur Rahman is a PhD candidate in economics at University College, London. He has worked in various capacities at the Centre for Policy Dialogue, the World Bank and the International Food Policy Research Institute.

Luca Antonio Ricci is with the International Monetary Fund, Research Department. His main interests include international macro-economics, growth, exchange rates and international trade.

Kenneth Simler is a Research Fellow in the Food Consumption and Nutrition Division at the International Food Policy Research Institute in Washington, DC, where he conducts research on poverty measurement and public policies to reduce poverty and undernutrition.

Finn Tarp is Professor of Development Economics at the University of Copenhagen and Coordinator of the Copenhagen-based Development Economics Research Group (DERG).

Paul Wade is currently with the World Bank. His main research interests include institutions and governance, and the economics of under-development and South Asia.

List of Abbreviations

ADB	African Development Bank
AERC	African Economic Research Consortium
AGE	Applied general equilibrium
BWI	Bretton Woods Institutes
CCF	Compensatory financing facility
CCL	Contingency credit line
CES	Constant elasticity of substitution
CET	Constant elasticity of transformation
CGE	Computable general equilibrium
CPIA	Country Policy and Institutional Assessment
DAC	Development Assistance Committee
Danida	Danish Agency for Development Assistance
DFI	Direct foreign investment
DFID	Department for International Development (UK)
EDA	Effective development assistance
EIB	European Investment Bank
ERP	Economic reform programme (Zambia)
ESAF	Enhanced structural adjustment facility
FDI	Foreign direct investment
Frelimo	*Frente de Libertação de Moçambique*
G7	Group of Seven
GDP	Gross domestic product
GMM	Generalized method of movements
HDI	Human development indicator
HIC	Heavily Indebted Countries
HIPC	Heavily Indebted Poor Countries
IBRD	International Bank for Reconstruction and Development
ICOR	Incremental capital–output ratio
IDA	International Development Association
IFPRI	International Food Policy Research Institute
IMF	International Monetary Fund
INE	National Institute of Statistics (IAF, Mozambique)
LDC	Least developed country
LES	Linear expenditure system
LSMS	Living Standards Measurement Survey (Ghana)
MDF	Multilateral Debt Fund (Tanzania)

MMD	Movement for Multiparty Democracy (Zambia)
MTEF	Medium-turn expenditure framework
NGO	Non-governmental organization
NPV	Net present value
NTB	Non-tariff barrier
OBA	Overseas development assistance
OECD	Organisation for Economic Co-operation and Development
PAF	Poverty action fund
PPE	Purchasing power parity
PPF	Production possibility frontier
PRGF	Poverty reduction growth framework
PRGS	Poverty reduction growth strategy
PRSP	Poverty Reduction Strategy Paper
Renamo	*Resistência Nacional de Moçambique*
SAL	Structural Adjustment Loan
SAM	Social Accounting Matrix
SAP	Structural Adjustment Programme
SASDA	Secretariat for Analysis of Swedish Development Assistance
SILIC	Severely Indebted Low-Income Country
SSA	Sub-Saharan Africa
SWAP	Sector-wide approach
TFP	Total factor productivity
UNCTAD	United Nations Conference on Trade and Development
UNDP	United Nations Development Programme
VAT	Value-added tax
WDI	World Development Indicators
WTO	World Trade Organization

Part I

Evaluating Debt Relief

1 Introduction*

Tony Addison, Henrik Hansen and Finn Tarp

Introduction

The debt problem of poor countries has attracted considerable public attention, not least through the well-targeted campaigns of Jubilee 2000 and other non-governmental organizations (NGOs) as well as civil society action in developing countries themselves. Unlike the earlier debt crisis of the 1980s (which mainly affected middle-income countries in Latin America), much of the debt of poor countries in Africa and elsewhere is owed to official creditors including the International Monetary Fund (IMF) and the World Bank, a legacy of donor support to structural adjustment programmes (SAPs) in the 1980s. By the early 1990s, debt service was taking a large and rising share of the public budget in poor countries, and donors came under mounting pressure to resolve the issue. In 1996, the Heavily Indebted Poor Countries (HIPC) Initiative was launched with the aim of cutting debt back to sustainable levels, thereby releasing more resources for development spending, including poverty reduction. After further public pressure, this was followed by the Enhanced HIPC Initiative of late 1999 which raised the amount of relief, accelerated the process and tightened the link between debt relief and the objective of poverty reduction. As of September 2003, eight HIPCs had reached their 'completion points' – the point at which they receive their full package of debt relief under the HIPC Initiative process (IMF and World Bank, 2003; World Bank, 2003c).

But the HIPC Initiative raises many issues. Are the Initiative's targets satisfactory and can they be achieved? How did countries become highly indebted in the first place? Was it just bad policy and external shocks, or are deeper political economy forces at work? Will debt relief stimulate significantly more private investment and economic growth? Can we expect much poverty reduction from growth in HIPCs? How can we improve expenditure management to ensure that resources do actually move from debt service to pro-poor spending? How will debt relief affect the relationship between aid donors and poor countries?

These are crucial questions for the development community. But despite the furore, there has been surprisingly little independent and rigorous analysis of debt's development effects in *low-income* countries (as opposed to the work done on middle-income debtors: see, for instance, Sachs 1989a), or the likely impact of debt relief under the HIPC Initiative. Accordingly, this book aims to improve our understanding of the economics of debt relief, including its potential for accelerating growth and reducing poverty. The economics of the HIPC Initiative are especially important because donors and their developing country partners will turn to evaluating the Initiative at some point in the near future. When they look back, they will face a central question: how much did the HIPC Initiative contribute to achieving development goals? An accurate answer to this question in turn requires close attention to the *channels* through which debt relief affects key development variables and an assessment of debt relief's impact relative to other influences (for example, commodity price fluctuations). None of this is easy. Robust methodologies are therefore required, and this book highlights the methodological issues that must be faced.

In putting together this volume, which arose from a major UNU-WIDER conference on debt relief held in August 2001, we have tried to reflect the wide variety of views that exist on HIPC, and our authors come from a broad range of perspectives. The book is divided into three main parts: evaluating debt relief (Part I), the growth effects of debt relief (Part II), and the poverty effects of debt relief (Part III). Each part sets out the main issues and shows, using country examples, how analysis can be done. This introduction sets out the issues and summarizes some of the main themes and results of the book.

Evaluating debt relief

Part I of the volume looks at the rationale for debt relief, including the criteria that have been advanced for providing relief (or not) and for determining its scale. A key concern in this part is to understand and evaluate the rationale for the HIPC Initiative's targets, the attached policy conditionality and to assess whether the Initiative does offer a solid exit for highly indebted countries from their present predicament. This inevitably raises wider issues of what can be expected from the total flow of aid to poor countries and their vulnerability to external shocks, both of which affect the Initiative's chances of success.

The HIPC Initiative's evolution

Mechanisms for restructuring or rescheduling debt have been around for a long time: the most important is the Paris Club which, since the mid-1950s, has been a framework for rescheduling sovereign debt, mainly with Organisation for Economic Co-operation and Development (OECD) creditor governments. The Paris Club provided the initial framework for rescheduling the debts of low-income countries. From the late 1980s onwards, Paris Club creditors granted relief on bilateral official debts on increasingly generous terms as it became clear that the debt problems of poor countries reflected a deep solvency problem that required a reduction in debt levels and not just temporary reductions in debt service. The level of debt forgiveness was raised in two steps: London terms in late 1991 (50 per cent debt reduction), and Naples terms (two-thirds debt reduction) at the end of 1994. Some bilateral donors gave additional, separate, relief by retrospectively converting loans into grants. The grant element of new flows under bilateral aid programmes also increased. As a result, the payment profiles on restructured debt became increasingly longer and lower.

Nevertheless, these mechanisms proved inadequate to the task, especially in the context of the continuing poor economic performance of the indebted countries and the widespread view that the adjustment programmes of the 1980s (which contributed to the build-up of multilateral debt as concessional loans were given to support adjustment) had, at best, delivered only modest gains in growth and poverty reduction. These mechanisms reduced bilateral and commercial debt, but not multilateral debt, and the debt burdens of many low-income countries continued to grow, particularly in sub-Saharan Africa (SSA). Moreover, approaches that had proved successful in resolving the earlier commercial debt crises of the 1980s, in particular the Brady Plan, were by and large not applicable to HIPCs because their debt is overwhelmingly official. In this hiatus, bilateral creditors provided grants to help some countries (e.g. Uganda) to service their multilateral debts. This led some bilateral donors to question why they were effectively compensating multilateral donors for bad lending decisions, thereby facilitating a transfer of the lending risk from the multilateral agencies to their bilateral cousins (see Killick and Stevens, 1997; and Kanbur, 2000; on the early debate).

This unsatisfactory situation led to increasing calls, especially by debtor countries themselves as well as the NGO community, for more thorough action. Proposals also appeared for radical action to write off most or all of the HIPC debt by, for example, a process of international arbitration (Raffer, 2001). Eventually, under pressure, the IMF and the World Bank launched the HIPC Initiative in September 1996. The Initiative aimed to reduce debt servicing to a sustainable level, defined in terms of targets for the ratios of debt to export earnings and public revenues (see below). The Initiative marked a distinct break with the traditional debt relief mechanisms because, for the first time, multilateral debt became eligible for relief.

After much criticism that the Initiative was too limited (and too slow), the Enhanced HIPC Initiative (sometimes called HIPC II) was launched in September 1999 at the G7 Summit in Cologne. It aims to reduce the existing debt stocks of eligible countries by one-half (so that, combined with earlier debt relief efforts, the external debt of HIPCs will fall by 80 per cent). Accordingly, the debt–export ratio target was cut from 250 per cent to 150 per cent. To speed up the process, the fixed three-year period between the decision and completion points was replaced by a floating completion point (with provision of interim relief between the decision point and the completion point). A more explicit focus on poverty reduction was also brought into the framework. In order to qualify, each HIPC must prepare a comprehensive Poverty Reduction Strategy Paper (PRSP) a process that marks the start of a distinctly new phase in aid policy (with implications for non-HIPCs as well). Of the 42 HIPCs, eight have reached their completion points as of mid-2002 (Figure 1.1 shows the position of each country in the process).

In summary, action has been taken on the debt problem of poor countries, but it has been tardy. For a long time it proved difficult to get major donor countries to agree on concrete steps, in particular the modalities for the IMF and the Bank to reduce HIPC debt. This is one facet of the general decline in the rich world's commitment to development issues over the 1990s, also evident in the fall in real aid flows (Tarp, 2000). While progress was eventually achieved it was only after considerable pressure from poor countries as well as international campaigning groups.

Debt sustainability

There are essentially two stages in the HIPC Initiative. In the first three-year stage, the country has to establish a track record in implementing economic reform and poverty reduction policy, including the production of a poverty reduction strategy. At the end of this three-year period the country reaches its decision point; at this stage it is determined whether the debt level is sustainable. Countries whose debt

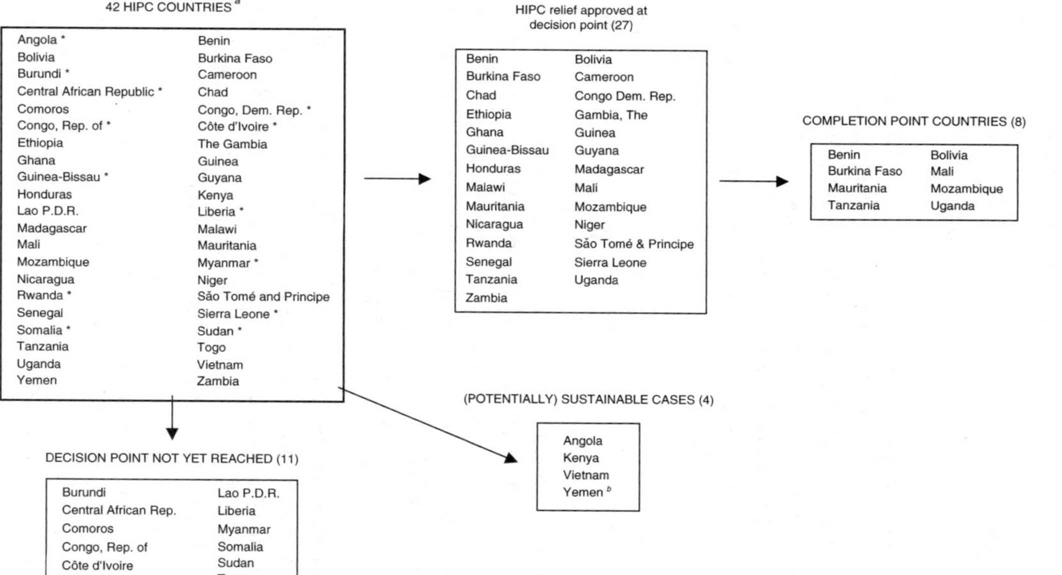

Figure 1.1 . Grouping of the heavily indebted poor countries, as of September 2003

Notes:

* Conflict-affected countries

[a] Comoros has been added to the group, as a preliminary assessment of its debt situation showed a potential needed for debt relief.

[b] Yemen reached decision point in June 2000. Its debt sustainability analysis indicated that it has a sustainable debt burden after the application of traditional debt relief mechanisms. The Paris Club provided a stock-of-debt operation on Naples terms in July 2001.

Source: World Bank (2003c).

remains unsustainable receive debt relief which is committed by the creditors. Countries receive the full package of debt relief once an agreed set of reforms have been implemented; this second stage begins at the completion point (originally a fixed three-year period after the decision point in the original HIPC framework but now a 'floating' completion point), although some countries may receive interim debt relief by the Paris Club between the decision point and the completion point.

Since debt relief has been provided, or will be provided, in a number of steps over time, the IMF and the World Bank calculate and report the net present value (NPV) of debt. Debt stocks in the 27 HIPCs that have reached their decision point (see Figure 1.1) are expected to decline by two-thirds; in 2002 NPV terms, their debt stocks are projected to fall from US$77 billion before traditional relief to US$32 billion after the full delivery of traditional debt relief and HIPC Initiative debt relief, and to US$26 billion after further (committed) bilateral debt relief (IMF and World Bank, 2003: 8). This will, on average, reduce their debt–export ratios from 300 per cent before HIPC relief to 128 per cent by 2005, when most are expected to reach their completion points, and the debt–GDP ratio is expected to decline from 60 per cent before HIPC relief to 30 per cent in 2005 (Table 1.1). While this is very welcome progress, the future external financing requirements of HIPCs will remain high – especially in the context of the ambitious targets for poverty reduction set by the Millennium Development Goals – and mobilizing more aid and external private flows remains an urgent agenda (UNDP, 2003).

However, what matters is not so much the *absolute* value of the debt but whether, after relief, it can be serviced out of export earnings without compromising development goals or imposing an excessive fiscal burden. Therefore at the heart of the HIPC Initiative is the concept of *debt sustainability* that has informed the Initiative's targets.

Debt sustainability has a wide variety of meanings, and can be hard to pin down. Two broad perspectives can be taken (our discussion here follows Hjertholm, 2001). The first relates debt sustainability to the ability or willingness of the debtor to maintain debt service and avoid disruption of debtor–creditor relations: evidence of problems includes the accumulation of payments arrears and debt rescheduling. Note that this perspective on debt sustainability does not address the issue of debt's development effects (either growth or poverty reduction). For example, a country could fully service its debt but this might simultaneously depress its growth. Accordingly, the second perspective looks to

Table 1.1 Debt indicators for developing countries and HIPCs (per cent, weighted averages)

	Developing countries			*HIPCs*[a]		
	Developing country average 2001[b]	*Non-HIPC low-income countries 2001*	*Before enhanced HIPC relief*[c]	*Debt indicators for 2001*	*Debt indicators for 2002*	*After enhanced HIPC relief at the completion point*
NPV of debt –exports ratio[d]	120	143	274	275	214	128[e]
NPV of debt –GDP ratio	38	39	61	65	50	30[e]
Debt service –exports[f]	19	15	16[g]	10	10	8[e]

Notes: Figures represent weighted averages. Former Socialist Federal Republic of Yugoslavia, Liberia, Somalia and Turkmenistan have been excluded because of incomplete data;

[a] HIPCs refers to the 27 countries that had reached the decision point by the end of July 2003 under the enhanced HIPC Initiative.

[b] Developing countries comprise low- and middle-income countries according to the World Bank income classification.

[c] Debt stocks are after traditional Paris Club relief before the decision point. Data refer mostly to end-1998 and end-1999; for the Democratic Republic of Congo, data refer to end-June 2002.

[d] Exports are defined as the three-year average exports of goods and services up to the dates specified.

[e] Data are for 2005.

[f] Exports are defined as exports of goods and services in the current year.

[g] Average over 1998 and 1999.

Sources: World Bank (2003d); HIPC documents; staff estimates.

the development dimensions of debt: a country's debt position is unsustainable if it adversely affects growth and poverty, regardless of whether it is serviced or not. In essence, the history of HIPC is a move from the first, narrow, perspective to the second, more development-focused, perspective. For critics, this movement to a more development-focused view of debt still has some way to go.

In the 1989–90 edition of its *World Debt Tables* (which is now superseded by *Global Development Finance*) the World Bank, for the first time, classified countries according to the severity of their debt problems (see Hjertholm, 2001). Although the Bank discussed the potentially adverse impact of debt on growth, the countries classified as 'problem debtors' were those which had histories of difficulty in servicing their debt, not ones for which the debt burden could be shown to have adversely affected growth (or poverty). Using a selection of 'rule of thumb' debt ratios (to GNP, exports etc.), the Bank identified a group of 27 Severely Indebted Low-Income Countries (SILICs). The methodology was subsequently refined, in 1992, with the adoption of the NPV of debt, in order to account for differences in the time profiles and concessionality of debt across countries. A country was then classified as a SILIC if the NPV of debt–GNP ratio was above 80 per cent, or if the NPV of the debt–exports ratio was above 220 per cent.

Despite its problematic nature, a target threshold of 200–250 per cent for the NPV debt to exports ratio largely determined HIPC I debt relief for three years (1996–99). But the debt–export ratio threshold was then lowered to 150 per cent when the Enhanced HIPC Initiative was introduced in 1999. The rationale for adjusting the criteria was an analysis that showed that the incidence of rescheduling was lowest among countries with debt–export ratios below 150 per cent.

Many commentators have questioned the realism of the HIPC targets. Evidence of the close correlation between external terms of trade shocks and debt servicing problems is set out by Machiko Nissanke and Benno Ferrarini in Chapter 2 in this volume. All countries experienced either a sharp decline or increased volatility in their purchasing power of exports together with their terms of trade. Year-to-year changes in export values have often been as high as 40–50 per cent in the HIPC group. Moreover, for most countries these shocks were worse in the 1990s as compared to the 1980s (the first 'adjustment decade'), and Nissanke and Ferrarini suggest that the negative correlation between the unit value and volume of exports may have resulted from earlier adjustment programmes that pushed up export volumes at the cost of prices (the fallacy of composition argument). The slump in the world coffee price since the mid-1990s is in part due to the expansion in coffee production by low-income countries (including such HIPCs as Uganda) seeking to expand their export revenues; this has resulted in an over-supply in the market, and steep price falls for growers.

Certainly, first-generation reforms either gave insufficient attention to diversifying export bases away from a narrow dependence on primary commodities, or had limited success in diversification (due to the supply-side rigidities characterizing poor economies and/or institutional weaknesses that impeded the effectiveness of market liberalization). Nissanke and Ferrarini argue that debt relief must be set in a broader policy context that provides for better contingency financing to deal with adverse terms of trade shocks. They conclude that the IMF's compensatory financing facility (CCF) and contingency credit line (CCL) are not much help to HIPCs since the CCF is provided on non-concessional terms and the CCL is not available to a country using any other facility such as a PRGF (the most common IMF facility for HIPCs). Instead, and following Krugman (1988), they favour state contingent contracts in which repayment is linked to ability to service debt which is in turn influenced by the country's terms of trade (Berthélemy, Chapter 4 in this volume, also argues that debt relief without indexation on the future state of nature is sub-optimal).

In summary, the fact that HIPCs are subject to wide swings in their terms of trade (due to commodity price fluctuations) and export volumes (due to drought and conflict) exposes the mechanical nature of the Initiative's targets: the impact of *past* external and internal shocks is acknowledged (in the sense that debt relief recognizes that the country cannot realistically repay, in part because of past shocks) but contains no provision for *future* external shocks (i.e. the amount of debt relief is determined at the decision point, whatever subsequently happens to the country's export revenues and fiscal revenues). In this regard, as Berthélemy points out, the HIPC Initiative is crude in comparison to the proposals put forward in the 1980s to resolve the commercial debt crises of that time (and which resulted in such innovations as Brady bonds).

Policy reform

In addition to external shocks, bad policy in debtor countries has undoubtedly contributed to their unsustainable debt positions. Accordingly, countries must establish a track record of reform to qualify for HIPC debt relief.

But what do 'good' policies consist of? Most economists would agree on the need to avoid currency over-valuation and over-taxation of agriculture – policies that prevailed in HIPCs before the first generation of reforms that began in the 1980s (and which undermined the production of tradables, particularly exportables, and thus capacities to service debt). And there is broad agreement that fiscal management must be improved (setting an appropriate target for the fiscal deficit, strengthening public expenditure management and tax reform). Many countries achieved their stabilization targets under the first generation of reforms, and the inflation rate has fallen substantially in most countries – although the measures employed, such as cash budgeting, were often crude and sometimes draconian (Adam and Bevan, 2004).[1]

However, there remain important policy issues which are still open for debate, especially in the second generation of reforms. For instance, what is an appropriate target for the fiscal deficit? Should it be exclusive of aid inflows, or inclusive (as many, including Stiglitz, 1998, have argued)? How effective is the privatization of utilities – in the crucial areas of power generation, water and sanitation and telecommunications – for achieving efficiency and equity goals when state capacities to regulate in the public interest remain unimproved (a factor that in both developed and developing countries has been shown to be critical to achieving the welfare gains promised by privatization)? How can financial sector liberalization be best sequenced with improvements in prudential bank regulation and supervision in countries with only limited institutional capacities (and for the same reason is early capital liberalization desirable – an issue on which the Bretton Woods institutions (BWIs) have back-peddled, following the Asian financial crisis of 1997–98).

Another lacuna is agricultural development, which is crucial for growth and poverty reduction in HIPCs and poor countries more generally. World Bank first-generation conditionality pushed the liberalization of agricultural marketing (to reduce over-taxation of the sector) but the development of private marketing has been patchy at best – and constrained by credit market imperfections and under-investment in transport infrastructure, especially in SSA. Deep and long-standing issues of smallholder agriculture remain to be resolved, for example over the best strategies for resource-poor and remote regions, which often have high poverty levels. Agriculture (and related public goods such as research into smallholder crops) has not seen the kind of investment it so badly needs. The World Bank has largely failed to give these issues the kind of attention they deserve, in contrast to the amount of energy it devoted to promoting agricultural liberalization in the first-generation programmes. This is perhaps one reason why SAPs have been so disappointing in their growth and poverty outcomes (Easterly, 2001)

And broader issues of strategy remain, which touch on the continuing debate on the respective roles of the state and the market in driving development: what, for instance, is the optimal strategy for poor countries in the second-best world of rich-country protectionism? (Alemayehu Geda, 2002; UNCTAD, 2003). The trade policies that the BWIs advocate today to reduce the bias against exporting (eliminate export subsidies and convert import quotas into tariffs which are then reduced) is formally equivalent, but implies a very different role for the state, to the successful East Asian export drive from the 1960s onwards which involved export subsidies counterbalancing the disincentive to exportables arising from quota protection of the home market (a point made by Wood 1997 among others).[2] In summary, the mantra of 'good policy' is often invoked – not least in the debate about aid effectiveness (World Bank, 1998) – but this is a less clear-cut issue than it at first appears (Hansen and Tarp, 2001).

A second and equally important question is: will debt relief increase the government's incentive to pursue the 'right' policies (assuming that some working agreement on these can be reached)? To answer this question, a useful starting point is the debt overhang literature that emerged in response to the (mainly) Latin American debt crisis of the 1980s (Sachs, 1989b). This posits that debt service obligations act as an implicit tax (collected by the creditors) on the resources generated by increased policy reform effort, and accordingly a disincentive (to debtor governments) to increase that effort (Corden, 1988). If this effect exists then debt relief should raise reform effort. There are strong, and contrasting, views on whether the debt overhang argument (which was developed in the context of countries with problems in servicing their *commercial* debt) is applicable to the HIPC countries (for which the debt problem is largely one of *official* debt). Both sides of the debate are represented in this volume.

Birdsall, Claessens and Diwan (Chapter 3 in this volume) argue that the debt overhang argument is not relevant to HIPCs: net transfers to most HIPCs are positive (averaging 12 per cent of gross domestic product (GDP) in Africa) and consequently there is no fear of a 'debt tax' – unlike Latin America in the 1980s when net transfers turned sharply negative and the debt overhang concept entered the debate. Consequently, the HIPC Initiative does not provide positive incentives for better policies in their view. In contrast, Jean-Claude Berthélemy argues in Chapter 4 that the HIPC Initiative does increase incentives to policy reform (i.e. the debt overhang effect exists) in countries with good economic governance (typically the first to reach their decision point) but not in HIPCs with bad economic governance – the ones that most need to change their policies (see Cohen, 2000, who also finds evidence for the debt overhang effect in HIPCs). In the latter group, debt relief will at best act as a multi-year programme of aid flows targeted to poverty reduction, in Berthélemy's view.

In addition to affecting debtor behaviour, the HIPC Initiative will also affect *creditor* behaviour, the other side of what Birdsall, Claessens and Diwan (Chapter 3) call the 'debt game'. They argue that debt relief will enable donors to be more selective in future, concentrating their assistance on countries implementing 'good policy' and drawing back from bad performers after they have provided debt relief. A more efficient allocation of aid will result, and in being able to demonstrate increased success, donors may be able to mobilize more aid for countries with good policy.

Recent analysis of the HIPC problem argues that the short time horizons (high discount rates) of governments lead to bad policy and economic decline (see Easterly, 2002). However, Chapter 5 in this volume, by Tony Addison and Aminur Rahman, argues that this is an incomplete explanation of the HIPC problem. It is necessary to go beyond the HIPC's poor policy performance and into the political economy of the countries to explain why policies were so poor. Addison and Rahman argue that the root cause is institutional decline, resulting in competition between social groups (often along ethnic and regional dimensions) that is increasingly unregulated by rules of the game – the formal rules being weak (or ignored) and the informal rules having buckled under economic and environmental stress. This has two effects on external debt accumulation. The first is to reduce time horizons, leading to bad policy decisions such as real exchange rate over-valuation that discourage tradables production (the effect highlighted in Easterly, 2002). But second, unregulated social competition reduces the time horizons of communities and the larger private sector by raising investor uncertainty. These producers move out of sectors with long-term returns (tropical cash crops, etc.) and switch to activities with more immediate returns (subsistence agriculture and commerce). The former are largely tradables, the latter are non-tradables. The tradables base of the economy, and its capacity to service foreign debt, is therefore squeezed from *two* directions – bad policy and investor uncertainty – both rooted in unregulated social competition.

Addison and Rahman then investigate which of these effects is more important in explaining the probability of becoming a HIPC. The first effect, bad policy, is found to be less important than the second effect, investor uncertainty, in explaining why countries become HIPCs. Therefore efforts to improve policy, while important, are not enough; fundamental political and social reforms, including democratization, are needed to provide new institutional frameworks to govern social competition. This will work to lengthen the time horizons of governments, communities and the private sector, and increase the investment necessary to achieve growth and to avoid future debt crises.

In summary, the overarching issue of governance implies that the HIPC Initiative's criteria may be too narrow and too inflexible. This is especially the case for the 12 HIPCs that are conflict-affected (see Figure 1.1 as well as IMF and World Bank, 2001: 21). Clearly, the conflict dimension of HIPCs cannot be ignored, especially for countries attempting to move from war to post-conflict reconstruction (Addison, 2003). Addison and Murshed (2003) argue that broader political criteria need to be introduced alongside economic criteria in determining countries' eligibility for debt relief. They recommend over-riding economic policy conditionality when there is a reasonable chance that the resources released by debt relief will be used to redress grievances (over the regional pattern of public spending, for example) that have contributed to violent conflict; this will then support political initiatives to secure peace.

Growth effects of debt relief

Part II of the volume examines debt relief's potential to raise economic growth. This is important for two reasons. First, the growth rates of HIPCs have been lamentably low. Consequently, the tax base has stagnated or declined in many cases, and low or declining public revenues have contributed to the under-funding of development spending, including pro-poor spending. Second, growth can reduce income poverty by enhancing livelihood opportunities for the poor – although its effectiveness in doing so depends on complementary action to enhance the human capital and productive assets of the poor which are key determinants of their participation in growth (see Shorrocks and van der Hoeven, 2004, on the relationship between growth and poverty). In fact, growth acceleration could be a key benefit of the HIPC Initiative, although growth is no panacea for deep development problems – and it must be undertaken in ways that ensure environmental sustainability.

Debt–growth linkages

Debt relief can raise growth through three main channels. First, by reducing the debt overhang effect on private investment and economic policies – effects we have already alluded to. Second, by reductions in debt service payments, which in turn make additional resources available for growth-enhancing (and poverty-reducing) public investments. Finally, investment and growth may be spurred by reducing *uncertainty* regarding debt payments and aid flows, where such uncertainty has disruptive macroeconomic effects.

Quantitative assessments of these growth effects can take the form either of econometric estimation or simulations using computable general equilibrium models (CGEs). In this volume there are examples of both methods. We start with the econometric models that are all based on cross-country panel data.

Catherine Pattillo, Hélène Poirson and Luca Ricci (Chapter 6 in this volume) explore the first channel by which debt relief can impact on growth. Through a comprehensive econometric analysis, in which Pattillo, Poirson and Ricci make use of a wide variety of different estimators and model formulations, they look into the impact of external debt in the form of debt–GDP and debt–export ratios on economic growth. The overall conclusion is that high external debt has a statistically significant negative effect on growth. This effect is probably non-linear, supporting the notion of debt overhang effects.

Henrik Hansen (Chapter 7 in this volume) looks at the second channel, which is based on the crowding-out theory by Cohen (1993). In particular, Hansen stresses the necessity of additionality of debt relief resources. By joint analysis of aid flows and debt service payments, Hansen concludes that non-additional debt relief will in all likelihood not lead to increased growth rates in the HIPCs. When he uses a measure of effective aid, developed by World Bank staff, he finds that if decreases in debt service payments are accompanied by falling grant levels, there may even be a negative impact on growth.

Chapter 8 in this volume, by Abdur R. Chowdhury, concludes the chapters on cross-country econometric analyses with a technical appraisal of the robustness of the impact of debt on growth. Chowdhury makes use of the modified extreme bounds analysis by Levine and Renelt (1992) and he finds a robust, negative, relationship between debt and growth, irrespective of the specific debt measure used (debt service–GDP, debt service–exports, total debt–GDP, or total debt–exports). Moreover an analysis of causality shows the causal impact running from debt to economic growth. Chowdhury estimates the effects for two groups of countries, HIPCs and non-HIPCs and, interestingly, he finds detrimental effects of debt in both groups, leading him to argue that debt relief should be extended to those outside the HIPC group as well.

Finally, in Chapter 9 in this volume Arne Bigsten, Jörgen Levin and Håkan Persson use two CGEs to assess the impact of growth in two important HIPCs, Tanzania and Zambia, which both qualified for debt relief in 2001. To capture the impact of the HIPC Initiative it is assumed that debt relief is combined with increased public spending and lower taxes in Zambia, and with increased public spending and accumulation of human capital in Tanzania. In both cases Bigsten, Levin and Persson record a positive impact on growth.

How much extra growth should we expect from the Initiative? Of course, the specific answer depends on the model formulation, among other things. But some common results do emerge. Based on the IMF and IDA (2002) projections for the 26 countries that have reached their decision point, we may translate the debt stock reduction and decline in debt service payments to growth effects using the econometric results presented in Part III of the book. The IMF and IDA expect a cut of about 30 per cent in annual debt service in 2001–05 relative to actual annual debt service payments made in 1998–99. This reduction corresponds to an almost 50 per cent drop in the debt–GDP ratio and an average decline in debt service payments–GDP amounting to about 1.3 percentage points. Interestingly, Pattillo, Poirson and Ricci conclude that halving the 2001 level of debt in the HIPCs is likely to increase the average annual growth rate by 0.5 to 1 percentage point. Hansen finds that if the decline in annual average debt service–GDP amounts to 1.3 percentage points during 2001–05, and if this reduction is additional, then there may be an increase in the average annual growth rate of about 0.2 percentage points. This outcome is surprisingly close to the result reached by Bigsten, Levin and Persson, as they find a 0.2 percentage point increase in the growth rate in both Tanzania and Zambia. Chowdhury (Chapter 8), on the other hand, is closer to Pattillo, Poirson and Ricci as he estimates a growth increase between 0.7 and 1.2 percentage points following the expected decline in debt service to GDP.

Although the empirical work on the growth effect of debt relief is unambiguously positive, the predicted impact of debt reduction is, as seen, often rather small, although the cumulative effect should not be neglected. However, any quantitative examination of the relationship of growth to high indebtedness and debt relief necessarily raises major methodological issues. In particular, whether the growth benefits of debt relief are realized depends on factors, which cannot be included in either econometric models or CGEs. In particular, policy changes are notoriously difficult to predict, which is why none of the above-mentioned studies even attempts to do so. Moreover and perhaps more importantly, as the HIPC Initiative marks a structural break there is a risk that quantitative results based on data and models reflecting past behaviour may not adequately predict what happens after debt relief. Hence the model results do not provide forecasts, but rather they are indicative of potential outcomes whose probability will change if complementary actions are taken (e.g. to stabilize and improve the political situation in HIPCs). But in this case the predicted growth effects of the HIPC Initiative are probably in the lower range, and must be interpreted with care.

Poverty effects of debt relief

If it raises growth, the HIPC Initiative should reduce income poverty (the amount depending on the characteristics of the country concerned, and thus the elasticity of poverty reduction with respect to growth). But the poverty impact of debt relief also depends on the scale of resources released from debt service for pro-poor services and infrastructure, and how effectively the system of public expenditure operates. Such spending can add to the reduction in income poverty resulting from additional growth, but it can also improve the non-monetary dimensions of poverty (showing up in better human development indicators (HDIs)). Moreover, HIPC introduces a new set of dialogue and conditionality processes into the traditional donor–recipient relationship, with poverty reduction being given increased priority under the Enhanced HIPC Initiative and the PRSP process (see Booth, 2001, on the latter). Part III of the volume turns to this crucial issue.

Transforming debt relief into pro-poor services

Identifying who benefits from the resources released by debt relief is crucial for poverty reduction – a point that applies to new aid and public spending in general (see World Bank, 2003a; Reinikka and Svensson, 2004). Accordingly, Part III begins with Chapter 10 by Rasmus Heltberg, Kenneth Simler and Finn Tarp, which focuses on benefit-incidence analysis, an important technique for understanding the distributional effects of public spending. They apply the technique to Mozambique, a major HIPC Initiative beneficiary and one that needs large and effective investment in basic services to achieve poverty reduction, especially in marginalized rural areas. Combining individual client information from survey data with provincial-level data on the cost of service provision, they find that the distribution of public spending in education and health is reasonably progressive (although, as they note, there are also significant variations in service quality across provinces which partly qualify the results). Another important result is that regional and gender imbalances in health and education are more important than income-based differences. This implies that Mozambique's PRSP must deliver on its aims to improve the access of women to basic services (especially to raise the school enrolment of girls and the quality of education they receive) and to narrow the present regional inequalities.

In Chapter 11 in this volume, Era Dabla-Norris, John Matovu and Paul Wade focus on the potential gain to the social sectors from the resources released by debt relief. They report that, on average, debt service is equivalent to 62–71 per cent of total public spending on education and health in HIPCs. They concentrate on education, although their analysis is relevant to health as well. In many HIPCs it is households, not the state, that account for the largest share of total primary education spending (60 per cent in Uganda). Since this is the level of education that has most impact on life-cycle earnings (followed by secondary education), using HIPC relief to raise the public subsidy on primary education can have major effects on the household's decision to forgo the income from child labour and increase school attendance instead. Applying their model to Ghana, Dabla-Norris, Matovu and Wade find significant human capital and growth effects, with poverty falling. They caution, however, that their emphasis on primary and secondary education should not be taken as implying a recommendation to neglect the funding of tertiary education for, in their model, tertiary education has significant long-term growth effects through the formation of skills.

In summary, considerable analytical work is needed to assess the distribution of public spending and the changes in its composition induced by the HIPC Initiative and the PRSP process, as well as to track the additional resources to their final destination, hopefully in increased pro-poor services and infrastructure. If debt relief does raise growth, then analysis must also be undertaken to determine the poverty impact of the growth, in particular whether it reaches the poorest regions, and whether the PRSP has been effective in raising a country's poverty elasticity of growth. This is a demanding agenda.

How can donors best promote and support a pro-poor stance on public spending in recipient governments? This issue is tackled by Oliver Morrissey in Chapter 12 in this volume. In the current approach debt relief, and therefore the resources for pro-poor spending, are released only after a record of policy reform has been demonstrated and after the basis of a pro-poor policy has been set out (the PRSP). Morrissey argues instead for focusing attention on pro-poor expenditures as a first priority rather than on a wide range of policies as at present, the only conditions being the existence of an expenditure strategy, monitoring arrangements and performance indicators (pro-poor policies, while desirable, are a more difficult objective given our limited knowledge of the effects of economic reform on the poor). Morrissey's other proposals are that: debt relief should be initiated only after a PRSP is in place, but that the minimum conditions for eligibility should not be too tight otherwise countries trying to reform in difficult circumstances will be unfairly punished; debt relief can be accelerated when an appropriate package of pro-growth policies is in place, with the country concerned being allowed to establish the level of reform required; and conditions should be part of a negotiating incentive strategy rather than a coercive punishment strategy.

Conclusions

Although the period since 1999 has seen progress on debt relief for poor countries, it is far from clear that the HIPC Initiative will provide a definitive solution to the problem. In particular, the Initiative's targets appear to be too ad hoc and the criteria for debt relief appear to be too narrow. Indeed, the official discourse on debt relief resembles that of the old centrally planned economics: targets are set, growth assumptions are made and little allowance is made for new shocks. This is not the world of commodity price fluctuations, environmental stress and social conflict in which HIPCs exist. In addition, the HIPC Initiative must be seen in the wider context of the stagnation of total external financing for low-income countries, and the continuation of rich-country protectionism (Roland-Holst and Tarp, 2002). Recent estimates indicate that current OECD farm programmes reduce rural incomes in poor countries by US$62 billion annually (Beghin, Roland-Holst and van der Mensbrugghe, 2002), a figure that is over 20 per cent more than even the most ambitious goals for *increased* development assistance.

Turning to the poverty reduction objective, this is laudable but serious questions remain about the ability of poor countries, with weak institutions, to achieve a fast and effective shift of the resources into better services and infrastructure for the poor. Much depends on the quality of the fiscal system (not only public expenditure management but also the ability of revenue institutions to mobilize the necessary additional domestic resources through taxation). However, institutions have degraded – in part because of over-zealous first-generation reforms that neglected the importance of the state – and while some improvement is evident (e.g. in Uganda) institutional recovery is a long haul (Kayizzi-Mugerwa, 2002).

As we emphasized in the Introduction, an extensive evaluation of HIPC will need to be undertaken before 2010, in part because the development community will want to know whether the resources were well spent. Our volume highlights the methodological issues that arise. Our country studies provide templates of how the issues can be approached.

To be successful any future HIPC evaluation must see action on two fronts *now*. First, accelerate efforts to improve data collection, not only at the household level (crucial, for example, in conducting benefit-incidence analysis of the increased public spending arising from debt relief) but also in the reporting of central and local government spending across basic services. Second, national capacities must be built to undertake the evaluation of HIPC's development impact. Given the resources required, and the necessary institutional investment, both actions need to be taken urgently to establish the foundation for future evaluations. It is to be hoped that this volume, and the menu of analytical techniques that it contains, will prove useful in the tasks that lie ahead.

Notes

* The assistance of Heidi Marttila in the preparation of this chapter is greatly appreciated.

1. There is an active debate on how high inflation has to go before it becomes growth-reducing – Bruno and Easterly (1998) estimate the threshold at 40 per cent.
2. This is not to say that such strategies are necessarily appropriate today for poor countries that face difficulties in building state capacity (in a world of World Trade Organization (WTO) rules that constitute a very different set of constraints to those of earlier decades. See Rodrik (1994) on possible trade strategies involving different combinations of the state and the market in allocating resources).

References

Adam, C. and D. Bevan (2004). 'Fiscal Policy Design in Low-Income Countries', in T. Addison and A. Roe (eds), *Fiscal Policy for Development: Poverty, Reconstruction and Growth*, Basingstoke: Palgrave Macmillan for UNU-WIDER.

Addison, T. (ed.) (2003). *From Conflict to Recovery in Africa*, Oxford: Oxford University Press for UNU-WIDER.

Addison, T. and S. M. Murshed (2003). 'Debt Relief and Civil War', *Journal of Peace Research*, 40(2): 159–76.

Alemayehu Geda (2002). 'Debt Issues in Africa: Thinking Beyond the HIPC Initiative to Solving Structural Problems', WIDER Discussion Paper 2002/35, Helsinki: UNU-WIDER.

Beghin, J., D. Roland-Holst and D. van der Mensbrugghe (2002). 'Global Agricultural Trade and the Doha Round: What are the Stakes for North and South?', Paper presented at the OECD–World Bank Forum on Agricultural Trade Reform, Adjustment and Poverty, 23–24 May Paris, and at the Fifth Conference on Global Economic Analysis, June 5–7, Taipei.

Booth, D. (2001). 'PRSP Processes in Eight African Countries: Initial Impacts and Potential for Institutionalization', WIDER Discussion Paper 2001/121, Helsinki: UNU-WIDER.

Bruno, M. and W. Easterly (1998). 'Inflation Crises and Long-Run Growth', *Journal of Monetary Economics*, 41(1): 3–26.

Cohen, D. (1993). 'Low Investment and Large LDC Debt in the 1980s', *American Economic Review*, 83: 437–49.

Cohen, D. (2000). 'The HIPC Initiative: True and False Promises', Technical Paper 166, Paris: OECD Development Centre.

Corden, M. (1988). 'Debt Relief and Adjustment Incentives', *IMF Staff Papers*, 35(4): 628–43.

Easterly, W. (2001). 'The Effect of IMF and World Bank Programmes on Poverty', WIDER Discussion Paper 2001/102, Helsinki: UNU-WIDER.

Easterly, W. (2002). 'How Did Heavily Indebted Poor Countries become Heavily Indebted? Reviewing Two Decades of Debt Relief', *World Development*, 30(10): 1677–96.

Hansen, H. and F. Tarp (2001). 'Aid and Growth Regressions', *Journal of Development Economics*, 64(2): 547–70.

Hjertholm, P. (2001). 'Debt Relief and the Rule of Thumb: Analytical History of HIPC Debt Sustainability Targets', WIDER Discussion Paper 2001/68, Helsinki: UNU-WIDER.

IMF (International Monetary Fund) and IDA (International Development Association) (2002). 'Heavily Indebted Poor Countries (HIPC) Initiative: Status of Implementation', Washington, DC, available at: www.imf.org/external/np/hipc/2002/status/041202.htm.

IMF (International Monetary Fund) and World Bank (2001). 'Assistance to Post-Conflict Countries and the HIPC Framework', Washington, DC, available at: www.imf.org/external/np/hipc/2001/pc/042001.pdf.

IMF (International Monetary Fund) and World Bank (2003). 'Heavily Indebted Poor Countries (HIPC) Initiative – Status of Implementation, Washington, DC: IMF and International Development Association, 12 September.

Kanbur, R. (2000). 'Aid, Conditionality, and Debt in Africa', in F. Tarp (ed.), *Foreign Aid and Development*, London: Routledge, 409–22.

Kayizzi-Mugerwa, S. (ed.) (2002). *Reforming Africa's Institutions: Ownership, Incentives and Capabilities*, Tokyo: United Nations University Press for UNU-WIDER.

Killick, T. and S. Stevens (1997). 'Assessing the Efficiency of Mechanisms for Dealing with the Debt Problems of Low-Income Countries', in Z. Iqbal and R. Kanbur (eds), *External Finance for Low-Income Countries*, Washington, DC: IMF.

Krugman, P. (1988). 'Financing vs Forgiving a Debt Overhang', *Journal of Development Economics*, 29: 253–68.

Levine, R. and D. Renelt (1992). 'A Sensitivity Analysis of Cross-Country Growth Regressions', *American Economic Review*, 82: 942–63.

Raffer, K. (2001). 'Debt Relief for Low-Income Countries: Arbitration as the Alternative to Present, Unsuccessful Debt Strategies', WIDER Discussion Paper 2001/113, Helsinki: UNU-WIDER.

Reinikka, R. and J. Svensson (2004). 'Efficiency of Public Spending: New Microeconomic Tools to Assess Service Delivery', in T. Addison and A. Roe (eds), *Fiscal Policy for Development: Poverty, Reconstruction and Growth*, Basingstoke: Palgrave Macmillan for UNU-WIDER.

Rodrik, D. (1994). 'Getting Interventions Right: How South Korea and Taiwan Grew Rich', *Economic Policy*, 20: 53–101.

Roland-Holst, D. and F. Tarp (2002). 'New Perspectives on Aid Effectiveness', Paper presented at the Annual World Bank Conference on Development Economics, 24–26 June, Oslo.

Sachs, J. D. (ed.) (1989a). *Developing Country Debt and the World Economy*, Chicago: University of Chicago Press.

Sachs, J. D. (1989b). 'The Debt Overhang of Developing Countries', in G. Calvo, R. Findlay, P. Kouri and J. Braga de Macedo (eds), *Debt, Stabilization and Development: Essays in Memory of Carlos Diaz-Alejandro*, Oxford: Basil Blackwell for UNU-WIDER, 80–102.

Shorrocks, T. and R. van der Hoeven (eds) (2004). *Growth, Inequality, and Poverty: Prospects for Pro-Poor Economic Development*, Oxford: Oxford University Press for UNU-WIDER.

Stiglitz, J. E. (1998). 'More Instruments and Broader Goals: Moving toward the Post-Washington Consensus', WIDER Annual Lectures 2, Helsinki: UNU-WIDER.

Tarp, F. (ed.) (2000). *Foreign Aid and Development*, London: Routledge.

UNCTAD (United Nations Conference on Trade and Development) (2003). *Trade and Development Report, 2003: Capital Accumulation, Growth and Structural Change*, New York and Geneva: United Nations Conference on Trade and Development.

UNDP (United Nation Development Programme) (2003). *Human Development Report 2003: Millennium Development Goals – A Compact among Nations to End Human Poverty*, Oxford: Oxford University Press for the United Nations Development Programme.

Wood, A. (1997). 'Openness and Wage Inequality in Developing Countries: The Latin American Challenge to East Asian Conventional Wisdom', *World Bank Economic Review*, 11(1): 33–57.

World Bank (1998). *Assessing Aid: What Works, What Doesn't and Why*, Washington, DC: World Bank.

World Bank (2001). *World Development Report 2000/2001: Attacking Poverty*, Washington, DC: World Bank.

World Bank (2003a). *Debt Relief for the Poorest: An OED Review of the HIPC Initiative*, Washington, DC: World Bank, Operations Evaluation Department.

World Bank (2003b). *World Development Report 2004: Making Services Work for Poor People*, Washington, DC: World Bank.

World Bank (2003c). Progress Summary on the Heavily Indebted Poor Countries, available at: www.worldbank.org/hipc/progress-to-date/progress-to-date.html.

World Bank (2003d). *Global Development Finance (GDF)*, Washington, DC: World Bank.

2
Debt Dynamics and Contingency Financing: Theoretical Reappraisal of the HIPC Initiative*

Machiko Nissanke and Benno Ferrarini

Introduction

As the plight of low-income developing countries in the protracted debt crisis has caught the heart of millions, a worldwide campaign by civil society activists and NGOs for more substantial or total debt cancellation is gathering momentum. In response to the growing demand for effective debt relief measures, governments of G7 and multilateral lending institutions have placed much of their credentials in the HIPC I and II Initiatives. Indeed, by the mid-1990s, it had become clear for creditors of official debt that the repeated debt rescheduling, which has been undertaken through the traditional forum of the Paris Club negotiations since the 1970s, was approaching deadlock. The need for radical measures for writing off bilateral and multilateral official debt finally surfaced as an open agenda on the negotiating table in 1996.

Can the HIPC Initiatives, unlike other measures previously undertaken, deliver a real and durable exit option from the severe debt overhang condition for these HIPCs? An answer to this question depends critically on whether the initiatives are based on the sound diagnosis and deep understanding of the causes of the debt crisis of HIPCs in recent decades.

Naturally, such a complicated situation as the contemporary third world debt crisis cannot be attributed to a single cause. It requires a thorough analysis of a multitude of domestic and external factors that have compounded the current debt overhang stalemate made intractable by traditional debt relief measures. In this context, a provocative thesis on the cause of the debt crisis and overhang, advanced by William Easterly (1999a), deserves a detailed examination from both theoretical and empirical perspectives.

As its analytical basis, Easterly's thesis rests on the intertemporal borrowing/lending model. He argues that a country with an excessive debt is one with a high discount rate against the future and/or a low intertemporal elasticity of substitution. Thus, he views the 'excessive debt' of HIPCs as a reflection of their peculiar order of intertemporal preference (in particular, that of the public sector), exhibiting a tendency to run down country assets. While interpreting the two key parameters of the model in this very specific perspective, his analysis tends to under-play a number of other main structural characteristics of low-income developing economies. Easterly goes on to argue that the granting of progressively more favourable terms of debt and the debt forgiveness without ensuring a switch of economic policies to the ones negotiated with the donor community can have perverse incentive effects. These effects are said to lead both to further debt accumulation of a similar magnitude in anticipation of debt forgiveness and lukewarm efforts in policy reforms.

In our view, Easterly's story of HIPCs' debt dynamics is somewhat misleading, or one-sided at best. The objective of this chapter is to examine debt dynamics of HIPCs and reveal one of the key external conditions responsible for the protracted debt crisis facing HIPCs. The chapter is structured as follows. The next section first discusses the basic features of the intertemporal borrowing model in conjunction with other models such as the growth-cum-debt model and the gap models. In the context of these models, we examine the conditions of debt sustainability. We then review other key concepts of debt dynamics such as the liquidity problem and insolvency condition. Using these concepts, we analyse the conditions under which debt burden becomes unsustainable and debt forgiveness becomes a rational choice for both creditors and debtors to overcome the ensuing 'debt overhang' condition.

In the light of these theoretical expositions, we present empirical evidence as to how debt dynamics has evolved since the 1980s in selected HIPCs and how effective *ex post* debt relief facilities have been in eliminating debt overhang. The penultimate section examines the HIPC facilities and identifies their remaining weaknesses as an effective mechanism for debt crisis prevention. It evaluates the debate on the effectiveness of policy conditionality as applied in the past and the accompanying proposal for raising aid effectiveness by applying the new 'selectivity' rule. The final section presents our proposal to use a *state contingent* debt contract as an *ex ante* debt relief mechanism as opposed to the prevailing *ex post* facilities, in order to stem one of the main conditions engendering an unsustainable debt path.

Models of debt and development

The intertemporal borrowing/lending model, which is used by Easterly to advance his arguments, is an extension of the theory of intertemporal optimization behaviour of the consumer or individual asset holder to the level of a country or nation, with a two-period budget constraint at the given levels of income, y_0 and y_1, and a two-period utility function $U(C_0, C_1)$. Thus, a country's intertemporal utility maximization for the two-periods is usually discussed in a diagram such as Figure 2.1.

In Figure 2.1, an intertemporal production possibility frontier (PPF) represents a trade-off between outputs in the two periods. Point *A* represents autarky position, where a country has no access to international capital markets and both producers and consumers face the domestic interest rate *r*, which exceeds the world interest rate, r^*. The slope of the budget line at point *A* is $-(1+r)$, whereas that of the budget line at points *B* and *C* is $-(1+r)^*$). With opening up to international borrowing, two effects emerge: (i) the country can divert resources to more future production at *B*, as it responds to the lower interest rate, r^*; and (ii) the country enjoys higher current consumption at *C*, as the higher utility indifference curve through point *C* than the one through point *A* indicates.

As Obstfeld and Rogoff (1996) show, this model visually links the current account concept and the domestic investment–saving gap, and illustrates the role of international borrowing and lending to fill

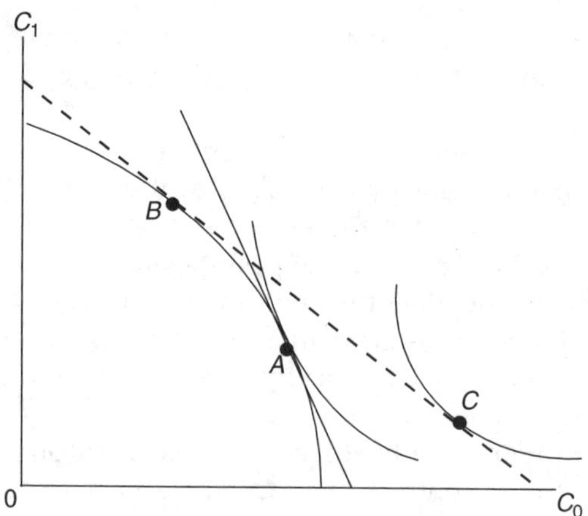

Figure 2.1 Borrowing from abroad

the gap. Thus, accessing the international capital market, i.e. borrowing, allows a country to undertake the extra investment (shown by the horizontal distance between points *A* and *B*) as well as to enjoy the extra first period of consumption (shown by the horizontal distance between points *A* and *C*). The sum of the two horizontal distances (the distance between *B* and *C*) is the first-period current account deficit that reflects its resource gap. At the same time, while a move from *A* to *C* reflects trade gains due to a smoothing of the time path of consumption, further trade gains are realized by the change in the economy's production point from *A* to *B*.

Using this framework, Easterly (1999a) argues that a country's borrowing behaviour is critically influenced by the shape of its intertemporal indifference curve, which in turn is determined by two parameters: the elasticity of intertemporal substitution and the subjective discount rate. The former measures the sensitivity of the intertemporal consumption allocation to an interest rate change, while the latter indicates how much weight the society places in aggregate on current enjoyment against enjoyment in the future. They, in combination, are said to determine the economy's saving and investment schedules. Easterly characterizes HIPCs as countries with a low intertemporal elasticity and a high discount rate.

It is important to note that Easterly interprets the two parameters basically as the society's choice variable, arguing that a country chooses a set of 'wrong' economic policies, which gives rise to a low elasticity of intertemporal substitution and a high discount rate. In particular, the government is seen as having a higher discount rate than private agents, due to the uncertainty of tenure and lower concern for future generations of government. Hence, in his view, first, a country gets into a heavily indebted position out of its own choice. Second, these two key behavioural parameters are assumed to be unchanged after debt relief, unless a country actually implements 'policy reforms', which are packaged by the donor community in the SAPs. According to his thesis, for a country which does not implement the SAPs in full, reduced liability through debt relief could lead to a slower rate of asset accumulation, i.e. a lower investment rate, as it endeavours to maintain its desired net worth as a ratio to consumption. With the constant property of intertemporal preference, the process of debt relief and a progressive substitution of concessional debt for non-concessional debt is seen as keeping the country perpetually heavily indebted, as a result of the possible combination of asset decumulation and liability accumulation.

Thus, Easterly predicts that in the granting of debt relief without ensuring full adherence to policy, the conditionality set by the donor community leads to negative saving and declining investment. This effect of debt relief is supposed to be in addition to other purported negative incentive effects, such as the delay of policy reforms in anticipation of 'selling' reforms for a higher 'price' or the creation of a moral hazard for borrowing in the expectation of debt forgiveness. Easterly presents a number of pieces of disparate empirical evidence to support his thesis of 'high discount behaviour' as the cause of HIPCs' misfortune against the alternative hypothesis suggesting that HIPCs became highly indebted due to external shocks. He concludes that debt relief is futile with unchanged long-run preferences.

However, his arguments stand on rather shaky ground, as a number of serious questions can be raised against his methodology in both its conceptual and empirical aspects. Focusing here on the problems at the conceptual level, Easterly's treatment of the behavioural parameters as a reflection of *permanent* preference order of HIPCs, which could be changed only by adopting SAPs, can be seriously challenged. Indeed, once the structural characteristics of low-income economies, such as the low saving rate and high discount rate, are duly recognized as a manifestation of their stage of economic development rather than that of subjective preference, Easterly's thesis falls apart. Economic development involves many structural changes, including a shift in these behavioural parameters. The real issue here is why SAPs, which have been adopted as conditionality for official aid by most HIPCs since the mid-1980s, have not produced the necessary structural changes.

We shall return later to this critical question raised specifically in relation to SAPs. Here, we continue to discuss the role of external finance for economic development in macroeconomic terms in the context of two other theoretical models, i.e. the *gap* model and the *growth-cum-debt* model. Indeed, the idea that external finance (or foreign savings) could fill the domestic investment–saving gap, illustrated in the intertemporal borrowing model above, is a central discourse in the infamous gap model. In the original gap model, limited domestic savings capacity is regarded as a critically binding constraint to further economic development. Based on the Harrod–Domar growth model, which postulates economic growth to be determined by an incremental capital–output ratio (ICOR) and a fixed domestic savings rate, one of critical roles of official aid or concessional loans is defined as that of filling the gap between the low domestic saving rate and the *desired* investment rate in order to achieve the growth rate.[1]

While foreign and domestic capital are treated as homogeneous in this single gap model, the two-gap models of Chenery and Strout (1966) introduced the *external trade gap* as a qualitatively separate impediment, since foreign exchange availability to meet demand for the imported goods essential for capital formation is recognized as a separate binding constraint on growth. By further distinguishing public saving from private saving, three-gap models, advanced by Bacha (1990), add a third fiscal constraint with a view of the fiscal dimension of the debt crisis and the well-known trade-off between growth and inflation because of the need of attaining fiscal equilibrium with a weak tax base and in the absence of developed financial markets. In these models, external finance availability (i.e. foreign flows netted out of external debt service, private income transfers and changes in foreign exchange reserves) ultimately determines the level of investment, hence the growth rate.

In reality, three gaps identified as a separately distinguishable binding constraint in the model do interact closely with each other endogenously to engender an economy's adjustment path in response to various shocks. For example, *ex ante* adjustments would take place with respect to all the relevant variables and parameters in order to ensure an *ex post* national income accounting identity between the foreign exchange gap and the domestic saving–investment gaps of private and public sectors. As Maizels (1968) notes, contrary to assumptions implied in the original gap models, the parameters should not be considered as fixed, and the *ex ante* domestic resource gap and *ex ante* foreign exchange gap are not truly independent.

The necessary *ex ante* adjustments are by no means either spontaneous or painless, whether achieved through the market mechanism or through government policies. As Chenery and Strout (1966) emphasize, there is no automatic mechanism to equate the gaps, and the process of closing the gaps is, in essence, a disequilibrium adjustment process. In general, the burden of adjustment could fall on one of the variables critical for the prospect of reaching self-sustained growth.[2] Taylor (1988, 1991) shows that while in theory there are several mechanisms according to which the three gaps can be closed in the wake of a widening foreign resource shortfall, the growth rate is an endogenous adjustment variable in all his 18 case-study countries.

High costs occurring in the disequilibrium adjustment process are often related to structural rigidities stemming from the under-developed nature of economic structure. In the case of primary commodity-dependent economies, the absence of resilience and dynamism is most acutely felt in their limited capacity to generate foreign exchange revenues in a sustained manner. Accumulated external debt would easily impose an additional burden on their circumscribed capacity, as foreign exchange gaps would widen over time. Adjustment efforts can easily be undermined and continuously impeded by exogenously driven conditions such as the terms of trade shocks. Application of the three-gap model to SSA economies demonstrates that there is in practice no comfortable adjustment, which would accommodate an external disequilibrium such as the region's 40–50 per cent deterioration in the terms of trade.

In particular, the model implies that when the supply of external finance available to a country is limited or overly inadequate to narrow the gaps, adjustment costs in terms of forgone economic growth can be high. Naturally, private capital is unlikely to be available at the time of gaps emerging in the form of macroeconomic imbalances. Hence, a need arises for official aid assistance. Furthermore, the cost difference between foreign aid and private capital flows can be substantial, as the rate of increase of debt obligation over time varies widely, depending on the degree of concessionality in terms of interest rates charged, the grace period, maturity and other terms of debt conditions. In all cases except grants, the issue of *debt sustainability* poses a potential threat to development. Naturally, debt cannot be sustainable if debt servicing is accompanied by declining income growth and eventually by a reduction in consumption to an unacceptable level, as discussed later.

Thus, it is not surprising to find that the issue of debt sustainability was raised and discussed in the early debt literature, which centres around the growth-cum-debt model. In fact, the debt cycle model, a derivative of the growth-cum-debt model, can be regarded in many respects as tracing a dynamic path generated by intertemporal borrowing over the extended period, and hence as an extension of the intertemporal borrowing/lending model to a multiple period. The possibility of using international borrowing to enhance income over time in the first two stages of the debt cycle is illustrated in Figure 2.2.

In Figure 2.2, the lower curve shows the time path of income Y and absorption A, for a country under capital account autarky, where Y has to be equal to A throughout. In contrast, international borrowing is seen to enhance income over time, by permitting the level of absorption A to exceed income Y by the amount of capital inflow in the first period. However, the country eventually has to cease borrowing and start servicing the debt, forcing it to restrict absorption to a level lower than income. The model assumes that so long as capital inflows finance additional productive investment in the first period, Y grows faster than under the autarky condition, while maintaining absorption at a higher level than under the capital autarky throughout.

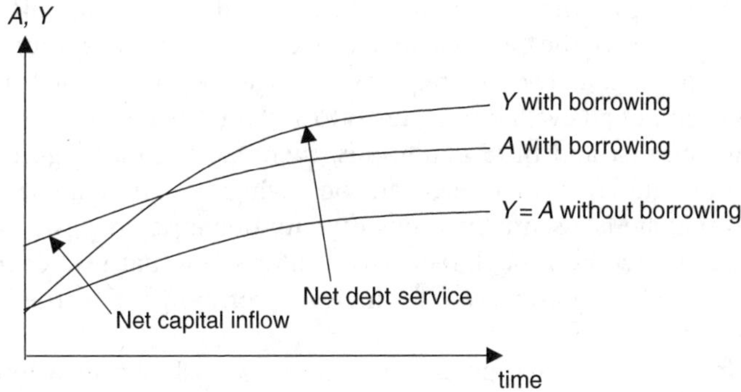

Figure 2.2 The growth-cum-debt model, international borrowing to enhance income
Source: Williamson and Milner (1991: Figure 16.2)

Naturally, such an optimistic scenario of the growth path can be realized under very restrictive conditions only. Earlier debt literature such as Avramovic (1964) is, however, quite positive about the possibility of a country remaining in a capital-importing status with a positive resource transfer for a considerably long period before growth takes off.[3] The conditions for the successful realization of the income-enhancing debt strategy are summarized in the early literature as follows:

(1) Additions to external debt are used for growth-enhancing productive investment
(2) The growth rate targeted by this strategy, g^*, exceeds a stable world interest rate, r^*, i.e. $g^* > r^*$.

The second generation of the growth-cum-debt model, which appeared after the debt crisis in the 1980s (McDonald, 1982; Hernandez-Cata, 1988), notes the following conditions for debt sustainability:

(3) The marginal domestic savings rate, s_d, should exceed the investment ratio required by the target growth rate, I^*, i.e. $s_d > I^*$, so that debt will eventually begin to decline
(4) The marginal product of capital, f_k, should exceed the cost of borrowing, i.e. $f_k > r^*$.

The second and fourth debt sustainability conditions under-score the need for a concessional debt facility for low-income countries, discussed above. Thus, granting concessional debt has a definite economic justification in view of the debt sustainability condition of the poorer countries, whose initial take-off requires a longer period, as well as the mobilization of all available resources to sustain development.

As to the first and third conditions, there has been a long-running debate on the effect of foreign aid on saving and investment.[4] It is argued that aid is essentially a substitute for domestic savings, in particular public savings through reduced tax efforts, and that a large proportion of foreign aid is used to increase consumption rather than investment.

However, the intertemporal borrowing model shown in Figure 2.1 illustrates that increased consumption due to foreign aid flows would be a natural outcome of intertemporal utility maximization. Indeed, as is explicit when the perceived role of aid is to reduce the cost of adjustment to external shocks, one rationale behind the non-investment uses of foreign aid is to smooth consumption over time, which is also welfare-improving. Thus, as Deaton (1989: 91) observes, 'Saving is not only about accumulation, but about consumption smoothing in the face of volatile incomes.'

The crux of the matter in this debate is whether or not foreign aid reduces the domestic saving ratio, not only in the short run as a part of adjustment, but also over the long term.[5] After all, as income is a critical determinant of the saving rate, empirical investigation should concentrate on whether or not aid has contributed to income generation, rather than on the relationship between aid and savings. With regard to the effect of aid on investment, it is argued that the 'superimposed choice' of technology and an investment pattern attached to the flow of foreign aid, together with problems stemming from the fungibility of project aid and tied aid, might lower the marginal efficiency of capital.

A large number of econometric analyses on aggregate relationships between aid, saving and investment have produced inconclusive results so far. However, the debate on the effect of aid on saving and investment has been revived in recent literature dealing with aid effectiveness in SSA, to which we shall return again.

Insolvency, debt overhang and debt forgiveness

The growth-cum-debt literature reviewed above tends to concentrate on the aggregate investment saving gap in discussing the issue of debt sustainability. In contrast, the literature that deals with the issue of liquidity and solvency of external debt focuses attention exclusively on the external performance of the economy in relation to debt service obligations, as the capacity of servicing external debt becomes of paramount importance for creditors and borrowers alike in evaluating the liquidity/solvency condition.

For example, Simonsen (1985) presents the following model to derive a condition for solvency.

The first basic equation describing the dynamics of foreign indebtedness is given by

$$\dot{D} = iD + G$$

where D is the country's net foreign debt outstanding
i is the average nominal interest rate
G stands for the resource gap (+) or surplus (−). (Note that this definition means that a positive resource gap represents a net capital importing position.)

The equation above simply decomposes the net foreign debt increase into: (i) the interest rate payment on debt stock, iD, and (ii) the non-hereditary part, G. Once G is treated as a well-behaved decreasing function of time and interest rate as constant, the assumed time path of these components, shown in Figure 2.3, generates the three phases of the debt cycle through which a country goes from a net debtor position to a net creditor position (i.e. from Phase I through Phase III in Figure 2.3).

In the context of this model, the question is asked as to the condition under which a country can be in a net borrowing position without facing insolvency. To derive the required condition, the above equation is expressed in the form of the ratio of exports as:

$$\dot{z} = (i - x)z + g$$

where $z = D/X$ (debt–export ratio), $g = G/X$ and $x = \dot{X}/X$

Then, if z is to be kept unchanged, i.e. $\dot{z} = 0$, we have an equation for a sustainable resource gap as:

$$g = (x - i)z$$

which is positive for $x > i$. A positive value of g means that a country remains in a net borrowing position.

Thus, we arrive at a widely accepted condition for solvency: for a country to remain solvent, the growth rate of exports must exceed the rate of interest on its outstanding debt, i.e. $x > i$. In this case, resource

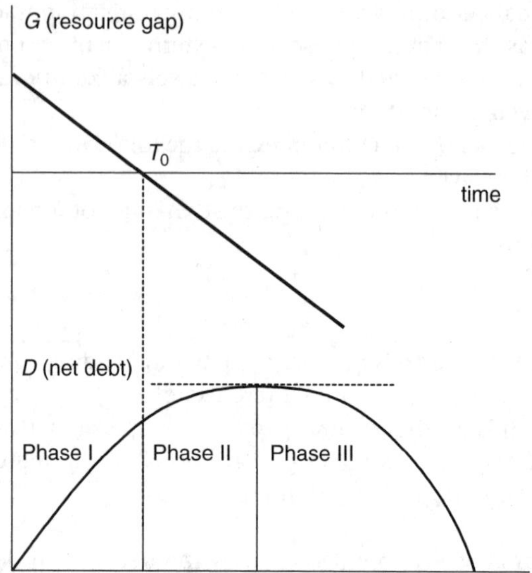

Figure 2.3 The time-path of the debt-cycle model
Source: Simonsen (1995: Figure 4.1).

gaps are sustained indefinitely without pushing the country into relative over-indebtedness.[6]

This solvency condition is less likely to be met in a consistent and stable manner by low-income developing countries dependent on primary commodity exports, even if debt is incurred in concessional terms with very low, predictable interest payment schedules such as International Development Association (IDA) loans. Indeed, the condition confirms the widely accepted reality that these low-income countries would not have access to external finances offered on non-concessional terms, which are prohibitively expensive in relation to their debt servicing capacity. This reality justifying official public debt is ignored by Easterly (1999a), who argues that the 'official lenders should not keep "filling the financial gap" in violation of prudential standards of creditworthiness'.

Furthermore, it is important to note here that this approach to debt dynamics and the solvency condition assumes that all key variables in the model follow a smooth time-path as illustrated in Figure 2.3. In reality, as discussed, variables determining the resource gaps and debt dynamics of HIPCs follow much more complicated and highly volatile time paths. Appendix Table 2A.1 confirms that many HIPCs continuously face an extreme degree of volatility of key variables that engender their debt dynamics.

In the case of primary commodity-exporting countries, the time-path of export earnings, which is the key variable used as a denominator in calculating the debt profile in the model, is highly volatile and largely exogenously driven. While supply-side policies such as exchange rate policy could increase export volume, this may lead to a decline in export earnings through the *fallacy of composition* effects by dampening export prices further (see Appendix Figure 2A.2). Thus, reflecting the high volatility and uncertainty involved in the actual time-path of exports, the debt dynamics of these countries are highly unstable – a condition very different from the one depicted by the theoretical model above.

Maizels (1992) reveals a number of key features of the commodity price movements in the 1970s and 1980s. As shown in Figure 2.4(a),[7] the 1970s were characterized by extremely large short-term price variations with a background of a modest upward trend in real terms. The decade is referred to as one of successive shocks to world commodity markets, driven by fears of shortages and a more general rise in commodity prices. In contrast, commodity prices in the 1980s showed a drastic downward trend with relatively small annual fluctuations. Maizels' study reports several estimates, suggesting that the general commodity terms of trade fell as much as 35 per cent between 1978–80 and 1986–88. Thus, he concludes that 'the commodity price recession of the 1980s has been more severe and considerably more prolonged than that of the Great Depression of the 1930s' (Maizels, 1992: 11). His statement is corroborated by historical data, reproduced here in Figure 2.4(b).[8]

Figures 2.5(a) and 2.5(b) show that many primary commodity prices were highly volatile throughout the 1980s and 1990s. The scale of adjustment required has often far exceeded the capacity of these economies to absorb volatilities through aggregate demand management, while dealing with associated high uncertainty and aggregate risks. Some commodities, such as coffee, cocoa and tin, experienced a price decline of 60–70 per cent between 1980 and 1993.

The implication of this kind of export price movement for a country's external performance is abundantly clear. Appendix Table 2A.1 shows that extremely high volatility continues to characterize all indices throughout the 1990s, affecting external performance of selected HIPC countries (terms of trade adjusted income, purchasing power of exports, export/import price, volume and value indices). For several countries, all measures of their debt payment capacity have continuously and sharply deteriorated. In our view, it is the 'commodity crisis' of this magnitude

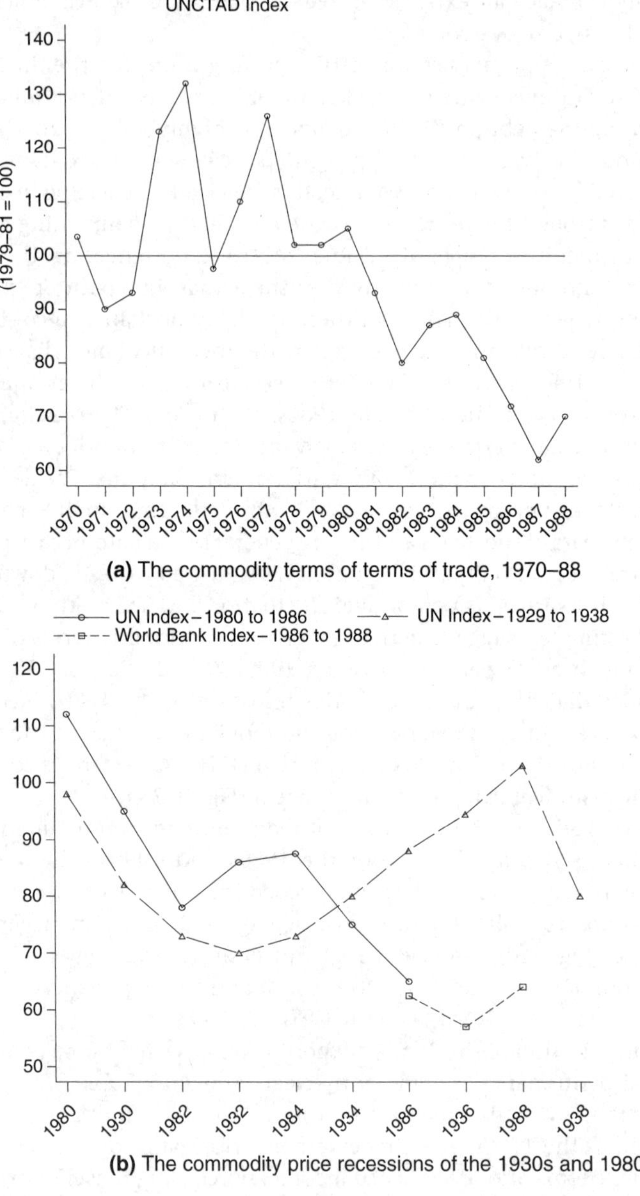

Figure 2.4 Commodities: terms of trade and price recessions

Source:

(a) Maizels (1992: Figure 1.1).

(b) Maizels (1992: Figure 1.2).

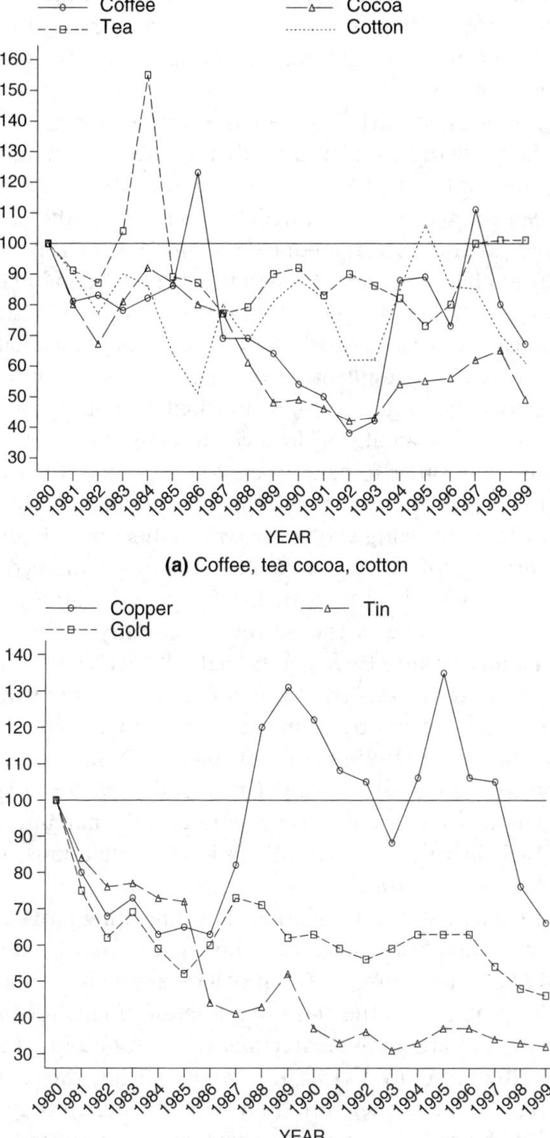

Figure 2.5 Commodity prices, 1980–99

Sources:

(a) IMF (2001b); UNCTAD (2000a).

(b) IMF (2001b); UNCTAD (2000a).

that offers one of the effective explanations for the protracted debt crisis afflicting commodity-dependent low-income countries. This powerful story is often left untold or mentioned as only a marginal contributing factor to the debt crisis.

The beginning of the debt crisis of the poor countries in late 1970 coincided exactly with this 'conveniently forgotten' commodity crisis. A number of commodity-dependent poor countries started experiencing a series of severe liquidity crises for debt payment in the early 1980s. Creditors judged this as a temporary condition, and kept reluctantly financing by rescheduling debt through the Paris and London club negotiations. This was an act of *defensive* lending so that their existing claims were paid at least on a regular basis. Based on the diagnosis that the third world debt crisis was a result of government dirigiste economic policy failure, creditors thought that SAPs attached as policy conditionality would arrest the crisis situation. However, despite acceptance of SAPs by debtor countries in order to gain access to official aid, their debt crises continued to deepen, giving rise to the serious question as to whether the debtor countries were facing a solvency crisis rather than a liquidity crisis.

The *solvency* constraint for the debt dynamics is defined by Eaton (1993) as the condition that 'debt in any period cannot exceed the present discounted value of the borrowing country's stock of wealth, or future income stream'. He suggests that 'all sovereign borrowers are probably solvent in the sense that the discounted present value of their national resources exceeds the value of their national debt (1993: 141). However, as Krugman (1988) notes, in the case of sovereign debt, not all of the future income stream can be made available for servicing debt and some fraction of national income represents the maximum resource transfer, which in turn reflects both rational calculations of the cost default and internal political considerations.

Hence, Krugman points out that there is a bargaining problem between creditors, who would like to maximize the resource transfer, and debtors, who would like to minimize it. The problem is usually compounded by the free-rider problem, as the collective interest of creditors as a whole differs from that of any individual lender. Thus, it becomes increasingly hard for creditors to draw a clear line between a liquidity crisis and an insolvency crisis. The former condition – i.e. the difficulty in attracting voluntary new borrowings to effect repayment of existing debt – arises because of an individual lender's doubts about the solvency of debtors, as a result of her low expectation about their ability to pay.

Indeed, the debt stock has kept increasing over time despite repeated interest amortization and progressive substitution of non-concessional debt for concessional debt, as the debt payment capacity of low-income countries has declined over time. Consequently, a severe *debt overhang,* the condition arising from an excessive amount of debt in relation to debtor's repayment capacity, had arrived by the late 1980s. 'Debt overhang' is defined as the situation where outstanding debt is so large that investment will be inefficiently low without sizeable debt or debt service reduction (Claessens and Diwan, 1989).

Claessens and Diwan (1989) recognize two effects of the debt overhang condition: *liquidity* effects and *incentive* effects. The former refers to the condition in which, given the burden of large external debt with extremely scarce liquidity, both capital formation and consumption reach a minimum level after years of austerity and low income growth. The latter refers to the depressed level of both public and private investment for future growth, as a larger share of the future income stream is expected to be directed for resource transfer abroad. Thus, it is admitted that the two effects combined could push highly indebted countries into a downward spiral, which would further diminish both the debtor's willingness/commitment and capacity for debt payment. This is not the best outcome for creditors either, since both creditors and debtors lose.

Since debt acts as a tax on debtors' resources that deters profitable investment opportunities, the debt overhang condition is usually illustrated in a debt *Laffer curve* such as shown in Figure 2.6 (Krugman, 1988; Cline, 1995). The concave curve traces the value of expected repayment as a function of debt outstanding: as outstanding debt increases beyond the threshold level, the expected repayment begins to fall due to the two effects discussed above. Thus, debt relief through debt service or debt stock reduction becomes a rational choice for both creditors and debtors, when a debtor is said to be on the 'wrong side' of the Laffer curve. For example, a reduction of debt as a result of debt forgiveness is shown in a shift from D_2 to D_1 in Figure 2.6. In contrast, at the lower end of outstanding debt, financing through new money would relieve the country's liquidity problem for some time. Thus, interestingly, a bargaining position tilts further in favour of debt forgiveness as debt stocks increase beyond the threshold where debt overhang begins. A position further right on the Laffer curve, and a major debt stock reduction becomes the only viable solution. The more dominant the disincentive effect of debt overhang, the stronger the case for debt forgiveness in the creditors' own interests as well.

As HIPCs' debt dynamics had evolved since the 1970s creditors were finally forced to recognize this eventuality in taking the HIPC Initiative.

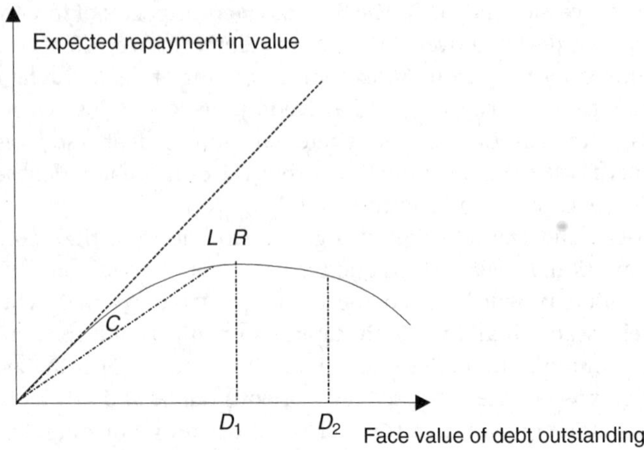

Figure 2.6 The debt relief Laffer curve
Source: Cline (1995: 163).

Debt profiles of selected HIPCs

From the empirical analysis conducted on 11 HIPC countries, of which three representative cases[9] are presented in this section, we observe the following stylized facts:

(i) Saving–investment (S–I), fiscal and foreign exchange gaps were all persistently large in the period 1980–98 and, in part, widened over time.
(ii) Net capital transfers and grants filling these gaps were generally declining, highly volatile and grossly insufficient for initiating a self-sustainable investment–growth–saving cycle.
(iii) External shocks, particularly in the form of persistently declining terms of trade of the HIPCs relying on export proceeds from a small number of primary commodities, make the sustainable accumulation process very difficult.
(iv) As a result, external debt stocks of the HIPCs had been rapidly rising over time, with large shares of new disbursements leaving the debtor countries under the guise of debt service on accumulated external debt. Accumulation of arrears, debt rescheduling and debt forgiveness had so far been inadequate for reducing accumulated debt stocks or making debtors' position sustainable.

Saving–investment, fiscal and current account gaps

Typically, HIPCs' domestic savings fluctuate at extremely low levels, while investment is sustained largely by unstable external financial flows. All countries considered in our sample have registered low, or virtually zero, capacity to generate saving. Negative and volatile S–I gaps for Ghana, Uganda and Zambia are shown in part (a) of Appendix Figure 2A.1. Part (b) shows a pattern in the fiscal budgetary process. While the domestic revenue levels of most HIPCs (including Zambia) as a fraction of GDP were declining over time to levels lower than those of the early 1980s, Ghana and Uganda showed some capacity to raise domestic revenue from a wider tax base.[10]

The S–I, fiscal and foreign exchange gaps were filled by recourse to external finance, as evident from part (a) of Appendix Figure 2A.1, depicting the evolution of current account deficits, including current income transfers and grants, S–I gaps and net resource transfers including grants. In external resources, we observe a pattern common to all 11 HIPCs in our sample:

(i) Current accounts, as defined here, were persistently negative, and there is evidence that neither the foreign exchange gap nor the S–I gap are narrowing over time. Current net resource transfers, almost exclusively from official sources, and also grants have been covering the ensuing capital shortages.
(ii) Official grant flows, the main source of external finance to the HIPCs, declined significantly during the 1990s after a temporary surge in the early years of the decade. Compared to official grants, net transfer payments played a minor role, reflecting a pattern of defensive lending to HIPCs so as to enable the repayment of existing debt, rather than for capital accumulation or as a cushion against external shocks. This fact is further underlined by the more detailed debt-profile analysis given below.

In sum, on all three fronts, gaps were persistent and mostly widening over time, while capital inflows were channelled towards the servicing of debt rather than capital accumulation.

External shocks: deterioration of the terms of trade

With this background of gaps, HIPCs dependent on the exports of a restricted number of primary commodities,[11] become highly vulnerable to any volume or price shocks affecting their export revenues.

Part (c) of Appendix Figure 2A.1 plots the evolution of income adjusted by terms of trade[12] and the purchasing power of exports[13] since 1980. All HIPCs recorded either a severe and persistent downward trend in their terms of trade (e.g. Ghana and Zambia), or a high volatile pattern (as in the case of Uganda). For most HIPCs, both indices had not recovered by 1998 from previous falls. Furthermore, the downturns of these indices were sharper than the upturns, and fluctuations were at considerably deeper levels than those already reached by 1980.[14]

Unsustainable external debt stocks

Debt profiles of the HIPCs suggest that official financial flows were of insufficient magnitude and stability in order to close these countries' widening resource gaps. Appendix Figure 2A.2 shows the evolution of the debt profiles of the three countries reported here.[15] Part (a) of each country's debt profile, plotting disbursements of new debt, total debt service and total net transfers over time, displays a clear trend of declining and volatile transfers since the early 1990s. The volatility of net transfers reflects the volatility of disbursements, rather than actual debt service, which shows a far smoother pattern. In fact, the HIPCs usually appear to service the debt amounts within their capacity to do so, while new disbursements widely depend on the vagaries of donors, and recipients' readiness to accept the burden of conditionalities attached to new loans.

From a comparative analysis of the debt dynamics of the countries reviewed, some significant differences clearly emerge. Ghana and Uganda, the biggest HIPC economies in the sample, have registered higher net transfers–exports ratios over time than other countries. Zambia's debt schedule, on the other hand, shows that net transfers to the country have actually been negative since the early 1990s, and new disbursements mainly served the purpose of rolling over existing debt. Official finance therefore had a defensive character, and detracted from the country's already scarce financial resources, rather than providing much-needed development finance.[16]

Part (b) of Appendix Figure 2A.2 displays the build-up of unsustainable debt burdens for Ghana, Uganda and Zambia. Although a more thorough analysis of the components of net transfers on debt is here omitted, the clearly upward trend of total debt stocks in the case of Ghana and Uganda by itself would suggest the ineffectiveness of past and present debt relief mechanisms in dealing with the HIPCs' debt problem. In the case of Zambia, total external debt stock soared in the second half of the 1980s to a clearly unsustainable level, and has since been fluctuating around that level. A more close analysis of Zambia reveals a typical pattern of the debt unsustainabilty characterizing the HIPCs. In almost two decades Zambia managed to service its debt fully only in 1980. Other years, particularly from 1987 onwards, were characterized by the accumulation of arrears and later, starting in 1990, by rescheduling the principal and interests, largely in excess of debt actually serviced. Only a relatively small portion of debt was actually forgiven. Clearly, debt service had been widely unsustainable long before a substantial new disbursement in excess of US$2.5 billion was eventually granted (in 1995, from bilateral creditors and the IMF, after Zambia had signed a three-year enhanced structural adjustment facility (ESAF) programme with the IMF). This disbursement was earmarked for servicing part of the existing debt stock, obviously respecting the preferential treatment regarding repayment of accumulated arrears on IMF obligations. Certainly, none of the money was used for development purposes, nor did it prove the solution to Zambia's serious external debt stock, which continued to fluctuate at around US$7 billion until 1998. More than 90 per cent of Zambia's debt stock is owed to official (bilateral and multilateral) creditors, and there are certain years during which partial payments of interest and principal falling due were forgiven (1988–94). However, such interventions were far too small to result in any significant amelioration in the sustainability of external debt.

Ghana and Uganda present rather different circumstances. The debt servicing capacity of these two countries has increased over time. The debt service due was largely paid, with a much lesser proportion accumulating into arrears or being rescheduled. Nevertheless, new disbursements were high and, in the case of Uganda, increasing over time. Since debt service by both countries was also rising, actual net transfers were fairly stable in the case of Uganda, and lower and also more volatile in the case of Ghana. New disbursements originated mainly from multilateral lenders' structural adjustment loans (SALs). Although new debt was increasingly on concessional terms, hence raising the share of concessional debt by 1997 to almost 80 per cent for Uganda and to approximately 67 per cent for Ghana, total external debt stock rose to unsustainable levels over time. Uganda has been forgiven interest payments in excess of US$500 million through its involvement in the HIPC Initiative since its first launch in 1996. But the country's total external debt stock has never stopped rising.

In sum, the HIPCs have suffered from a persistent and mounting debt overhang since the mid-1980s, and have been unable – even temporarily – to recover. Debt workouts, particularly those initiated by the Paris Club creditors since the mid-late 1980s, have been far from effective in offering a permanent solution. This is because the rescheduling and forgiven debt stock were only marginal compared to the accumulated debt stocks.

Moreover, facilities were made available *ex post*, and only when debtors were clearly unable to meet obligations. Both the theoretical arguments discussed in the previous sections, and the brief historical account presented in this section, strongly underline the necessity of offering these countries an alternative mechanism to deal with recurrent external shocks.

Evaluation of the HIPC Initiatives

Since the 1980s, debt relief mechanisms have evolved through several stages ranging from short-term non-concessional rescheduling in the post-1982 period, and the refinancing with new loans at more concessional terms in the Toronto and 'enhanced' Toronto terms, relief via some debt reductions in the Naples terms, finally to the HIPC I Initiatives in 1996 and the enhanced HIPC II Initiatives in 1999.[17] These debt relief mechanisms were essentially short-leashed, burdened with inadequacy of the relief and the need for repeated rounds of negotiations. Thus, the main debt indicators deteriorated with a series of convulsions. The question is raised repeatedly as to why the debt burdens of poor countries remain so onerous. In our view, one answer lies in the reluctance of the donor community to grapple effectively with commodity price shocks or terms of trade shocks, one of the critical factors shaping debt dynamics. The HIPC Initiatives addressed many of the drawbacks of traditional debt relief mechanisms.[18]

However, despite significant improvements, the HIPC Initiatives still contain several pitfalls. In our view, the remaining problems are of a quite fundamental nature. Unless these issues are genuinely addressed, the optimism raised initially regarding the HIPC Initiatives' capacity to deliver a durable exit route for the debt burden of most of the HIPCs cannot be justified.

First, the initiatives may easily become under-funded if the debt dynamics of these HIPCs continue to exhibit extreme volatility. In this regard, debt sustainability analyses conducted for forecasting future requirements for debt relief are often based on over-optimistic scenarios regarding future debt servicing capabilities (Killick and Stevens, 1997; UNCTAD, 2000a). Our analysis of the sensitivity of projected targets of debt serving capacity under the HIPC Initiatives against alternative projections based on past export growth records shows that, in most cases, the projected debt path is very close to the alternative estimates based on either the higher end of the export growth rate or the average growth rate achieved since the 1980s. In this sense, as Martin and Alami (2001) note, these projections should be regarded as optimistic targets rather than projections as such.

However, a more serious concern can be raised about the failure of these projections to take into account the very high volatility continuously exhibited by the key variables determining HIPCs' export performance and debt servicing capacities. Thus, the absence of sufficient provisions to deal with external shocks is one of the remaining fundamental weaknesses of the HIPC Initiatives. The lack of financial resources to tackle the emerging shortfalls could lead to a further trade-off in the allocation of donor resources between aid budgets and debt relief financing.

Second, there is considerable tension and potential contradiction between the different components of policy conditionality embedded in the HIPC Initiatives. With the 'eligibility' criteria still firmly in place, the underlying assumption of the HIPC policy conditionality is presumably that complementarities exist between SAPs and additional policies aimed at poverty reduction. However, the economic literature has long recognized that the growth–poverty nexus is rather complicated, and the *pattern* of economic growth and development, rather than the rate of growth *per se*, has significant effects on a country's income distribution and poverty profile. This suggests that the 'growth-enhancing economic policies' of SAPs are not necessarily in agreement with policies targeted to addressing income distribution issues and poverty alleviation targets.

Thus, simply appending the poverty reduction strategy to SAPs without due attention to this complex growth–poverty nexus can be problematic, giving rise to internal inconsistency of the policy package. Furthermore, poverty reduction growth strategy (PRGS) country papers suggest that poverty reduction is to be achieved almost exclusively through an increase in social expenditure. While these policy measures are undoubtedly important elements of any poverty reduction strategy, the unfounded expectation that poverty can be reduced by applying these measures only should not be encouraged, as poverty is the outcome of economic, social and political processes and their interactions, which are mediated through a range of institutions (World Bank, 2000b). The multi-dimensional nature of poverty implies that any poverty reduction strategy should include a set of long-term strategic measures for changing institutional structures and environments.

Third, the effectiveness of the use of policy conditionality in the HIPC Initiatives should be evaluated more carefully, in the wider context of appropriateness of SAPs to effect the structural transformation of the HIPCs' economies that could lead to changes in their disadvantaged form of international linkages. In our view, the conventional way of debating the effectiveness of policy conditionality is too inhibiting, as it is based on the assumption that SAPs are generally appropriate for dealing with the economic problems facing HIPCs. Furthermore, policy conditionality is seen as a means of tying the recipient government to policy reforms designed by the donor community. Therefore, the debate has been conducted largely from a narrow perspective of the moral hazard problem arising from granting debt relief and foreign aid without a firm commitment from the recipient country to reform programmes.

Collier (1998), for example, argues that policy conditionality attached to SAPs can be faulted on the incorrect rationales given to adjustment lending. In his view, none of the three rationales for programme lending – namely the use of aid as an incentive for reform, financing the 'cost of adjustment' and 'defensive lending' to service external debt – is soundly based.

Recognizing this reality, Collier proposes to redesign conditionality from 'incentives' based on promises for policy change to 'selectivity' based on retrospective assessments of performance. That is, instead of using conditionality to induce policy change, Collier proposes that aid be used to target financial flows to governments with good policy environments already in place. His proposal is based on the empirical work by Burnside and Dollar (1997: 30), which suggests that 'when good policy and aid flows happen to coincide the outcome has been very good'. It also originates from Collier's conviction that Africa desperately needs significant 'role models' within the continent. Thus, creating star performers by engineering aid allocation in this way, he argues, would induce many non-reforming governments to change their policies through the pressure of emulation and would result in enhanced overall aid effectiveness.

However, Hansen and Tarp (2001) question the validity of the empirical analysis by Burnside and Dollar, which forms the basis for the 'selectivity' proposal. Their extensive literature survey, extending to three generations of models on aid–growth relationships, confirms that aid enhances growth through its positive effects on domestic savings in the framework of first-generation studies, and on the investment-enhancing effect of aid investigated in second-generation studies. Furthermore, their critical review of the third-generation models based on the new growth theory (which includes the Burnside–Dollar study) shows that the Burnside–Dollar results are the odd-one-out among the other three studies. Overall, in each generation of studies, those arguing for the negative effect of aid on growth are in the minority. Hence, they caution us strongly against basing aid allocation rules on the single-cause explanations.

We argued elsewhere (Nissanke, 2000) that the 'selectivity' proposal in aid allocation requires a critical examination of its possible consequences on aid distribution, as well as the special roles of official bilateral and multilateral aid flows in global finance. While private capital flows by nature move globally in search of higher rates of return, criteria and motivation surrounding aid distribution have historically been much more complex (Maizels and Nissanke, 1984). Noting that 'aid is given for many different purposes and in many different forms', Hansen and Tarp (2001) suggest that the unresolved issue in assessing aid effectiveness is not whether aid works, but how and whether the different kinds of aid instruments available can be made to work better in different country circumstances. Furthermore, unless structural transformation becomes firmly established, the 'star performer' of Africa will continue to shift from one country to another. Ghana found it difficult to maintain its status, attained in the early 1990s, as the 'front-runner of adjustment' (Aryeetey, Harrigan and Nissanke, 2000).

The 'selectivity' proposal should also be examined in relation to the more fundamental question as to who defines (and how to define) good policies for country-specific conditions. We suggest the appropriateness of the design of policy conditionality linked to the HIPC Initiatives be re-evaluated. Stein and Nissanke (1999) suggest that an uneasy mismatch exists between the abstract model on which SAPs are conceived and the reality of the HIPCs. In our view, the slow progress of SAPs in reviving the HIPCs by inducing substantial changes to the structure of trade and production is related more to the fundamental problem of the theoretical construct than to the weak capacity of African states and institutions in implementing and carrying through structural adjustment to completion.

The HIPC Initiatives are praised for being based on improved donor–recipient relationships which involve the recipient governments and civil societies at large in drafting and debating the PRSPs. However, unless genuine debate can be extended to other components of policy conditionality – i.e. the design of SAPs – real ownership of economic reform programmes will not be in the hands of recipient countries.

Instead, given the reality that foreign aid and concessional loans are in short supply, it is more likely that granting debt forgiveness through the HIPC facilities becomes a convenient *de facto* rationing device for aid allocation on the basis of the 'selectivity' principle.

Conclusions

Our theoretical analysis and empirical examination of debt dynamics of HIPCs show that one of the major conditions, which has made their external debt unsustainable and, hence, given rise to the protracted debt crisis over the 1980s and 1990s, is their extreme susceptibility to large-scale external shocks such as terms of trade effects. Above all, there is urgent need to reduce short-term commodity market instability through revitalizing a comprehensive North–South programme (Maizels, 1992). Debt relief measures should be examined in this broad policy context.

Past and existing debt relief mechanisms, including the HIPC Initiatives, have failed to pay sufficient attention to the debilitating condition facing many commodity-dependent developing countries. In particular, the effective and flexible facility of *contingency financing* to deal with external shocks on an *ex ante* basis is absent. Instead, official creditors have continued to apply *ex post* debt relief mechanisms in response to recurrent liquidity crises and the ensuing debt overhang, in the firm belief that the SAPs attached as policy conditionality would bring about the necessary structural transformation to overcome this problem.

The existing contingency financing facilities at the IMF such as the CCF or CCL are not much help to the HIPCs. Apart from the fact that high conditionality has historically been applied to these facilities, CCL is not available to a country using any other facility such as PRGF. CCF is provided on non-concessional terms, and therefore is too expensive (Martin and Alami, 2001).

In our view, it is vitally important to establish truly flexible, *state-contingent* debt relief mechanisms in order to avoid the recurring debt crises that stalled the economic development of low-income countries for so long. Krugman (1988) suggests that the trade-off between debt forgiveness and financing in a typical negotiation can be improved by indexing repayment to the state of nature. His theoretical model shows that debt relief schemes in which repayment is linked to some of measure of the state of nature are much more efficient compared to schemes in which repayment is linked to the ability to pay. This is because the state-contingent schemes could make a distinction between the consequences of a debtor's own efforts and events beyond its control.

Although Cline (1995) dismisses Krugman's proposal of using state-contingent instruments as impractical on a technical ground, devising an efficient, state-contingent debt contract could be made within our technical capability, if we invest sufficient efforts in turning this possibility into reality. What is lacking now is the full recognition and appreciation of one of the key conditions in shaping HIPCs' debt dynamics, and the political will and commitment to realize this possibility.

Appendix

Appendix Table 2A.1 Volatility indicators,[a] 1980–97

	Bolivia			Chad		
	1980–97	*1980–89*	*1990–97*	*1980–97*	*1980–89*	*1990–97*
Terms of trade adjusted income[b]	63.3	31.6	94.7	43.4	22.1	62.8
Purchasing power exp.	14.9	15.9	14.1	29.0	29.5	28.9
Terms of trade	29.5	18.4	10.3	11.6	8.2	10.8
Export volume	29.7	16.5	8.6	30.7	33.6	24.2
Export unit value	21.8	17.7	13.0	16.6	14.9	10.0
Export value	22.21	17.89	18.75	39.7	33.5	30.0
Import volume	32.3	19.8	24.5	31.4	32.4	29.2
Import unit value	12.3	6.3	7.8	23.3	18.4	10.5
Import value	58.19	17.61	53.88	29.9	34.0	22.8
	Ghana			**Malawi**		
	1980–97	*1980–89*	*1990–97*	*1980–97*	*1980–89*	*1990–97*
Terms of trade adjusted income	54.1	19.8	66.5	66.7	37.2	77.4
Purchasing power exp.	103.7	98.0	28.5	18.0	14.5	20.4
Terms of trade	26.8	23.9	5.4	18.1	16.2	13.6
Export volume	83.0	92.2	27.6	18.8	14.2	10.0
Export unit value	39.3	55.9	6.9	15.0	12.8	13.7
Export value	35.9	28.3	30.7	28.7	10.1	19.7
Import volume	79.5	92.9	35.1	21.5	16.6	18.2
Import unit value	46.3	63.3	3.4	19.2	13.7	2.8
Import value	59.5	27.6	37.2	35.9	23.7	18.1
	Mali			**Mozambique**		
	1980–97	*1980–89*	*1990–97*	*1980–97*	*1980–89*	*1990–97*
Terms of trade adjusted income	45.0	16.5	74.1	63.4	40.7	73.3
Purchasing power exp.	37.7	16.5	23.0	46.0	55.0	9.5
Terms of trade	7.3	5.1	7.1	26.3	8.5	21.9
Export volume	43.7	17.6	27.0	38.8	49.2	23.7
Export unit value	11.9	12.6	8.3	18.0	9.6	22.2
Export value	46.0	22.9	21.3	40.8	55.7	11.8
Import volume	22.2	12.9	14.2	15.6	16.6	15.4
Import unit value	13.8	13.7	4.1	16.5	11.9	8.0
Import value	32.4	19.0	16.0	20.1	20.9	11.0
	Rwanda			**Tanzania**		
	1980–97	*1980–89*	*1990–97*	*1980–97*	*1980–89*	*1990–97*
Terms of trade adjusted income	56.2	69.1	42.6	–	–	62.0
Purchasing power exp.	31.2	22.3	40.2	27.4	29.1	26.6
Terms of trade	25.4	29.5	19.5	17.3	10.0	4.6
Export volume	39.2	28.5	46.5	32.8	25.8	27.2
Export unit value	19.9	20.1	17.5	7.6	7.4	8.1
Export value	35.0	16.0	42.3	34.0	29.1	29.2
Import volume	29.0	17.9	36.7	18.7	23.8	11.5
Import unit value	22.7	12.5	27.6	15.7	9.5	5.5
Import value	21.8	15.1	28.1	24.2	21.4	12.9

	Uganda			Zambia		
	1980–97	1980–89	1990–97	1980–97	1980–89	1990–97
Terms of trade adjusted income	73.7	47.9	99.1	47.3	46.3	31.9
Purchasing power exp.	50.7	46.3	56.5	32.2	27.4	21.6
Terms of trade	54.3	38.1	18.5	25.1	29.1	15.3
Export volume	54.0	20.8	51.7	19.4	14.1	15.3
Export unit value	32.6	14.5	19.2	22.8	21.9	17.9
Export value	39.2	19.3	56.9	22.2	24.9	19.5
Import volume	56.4	37.6	59.7	31.3	22.2	27.9
Import unit value	31.4	44.5	3.7	24.6	27.0	8.8
Import value	63.3	34.5	60.5	26.4	29.5	21.8

Memorandum items:

Commodity price (volatilities)	*1980–97*	*1980–89*	*1990–97*
Coffee	27.9	20.7	38.5
Cocoa	27.0	19.7	13.8
Cotton	18.0	18.3	17.5
Tea	18.6	23.3	9.6
Gold	18.4	19.4	6.0
Copper	24.1	26.7	12.4
Tin	42.7	30.3	6.7

Export growth (volatilities)	*1980–97*	*1980–89*	*1990–97*
Zambia	6.5	−2.6	2.9
Rwanda	15.1	5.3	79.9
Chad	5.5	4.7	6.1
Bolivia	2.5	3.3	1.5
Ghana	2.7	11.7	1.1
Malawi	3.4	5.7	2.2
Mali	1.3	1.5	1.3
Mozambique	3.3	−2.6	0.5
Tanzania	–	–	2.2
Uganda	1.7	3.4	1.2

Notes:
[a] Volatility indicators are calculated as the standard deviation/mean ratio of index numbers with base year (1990).
[b] Terms of trade adjusted income series were converted into index numbers for matters of comparability (1990 = 100).
Sources: All data from UNCTAD (2000a), except terms of trade adjustment from World Bank (2000a).

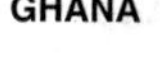

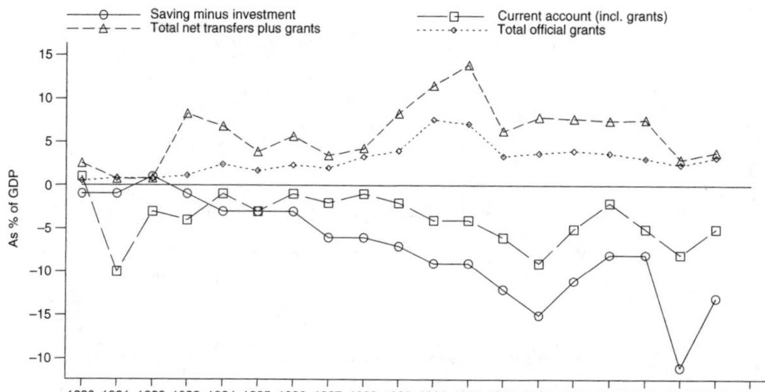

(a) Saving–investment gap and current account deficit with external flows

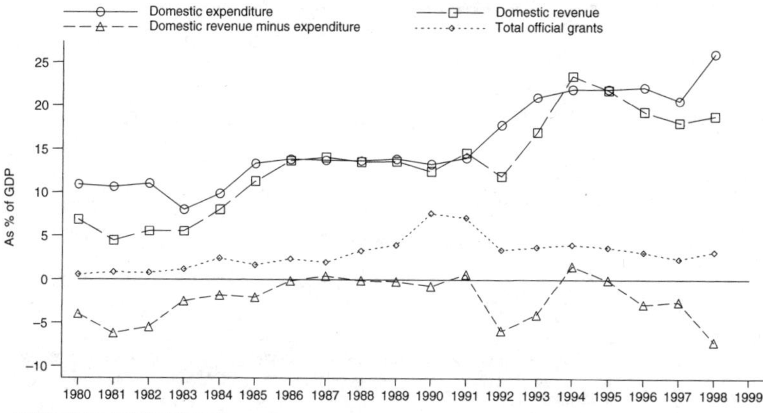

(b) Fiscal gap and official grants

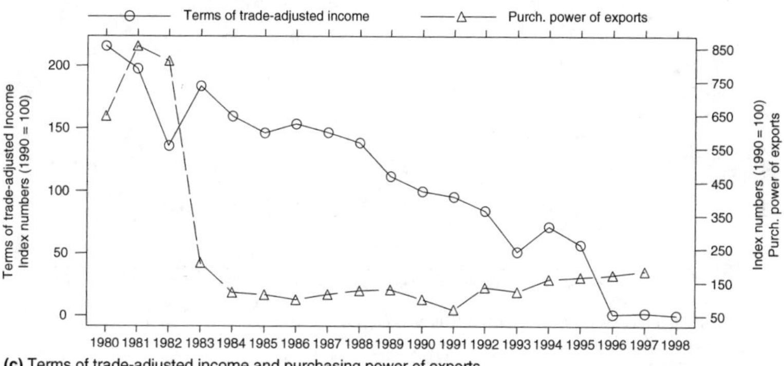

(c) Terms of trade-adjusted income and purchasing power of exports

Appendix Figure 2A.1 Macroeconomic data for Ghana, Uganda and Zambia, 1980–99

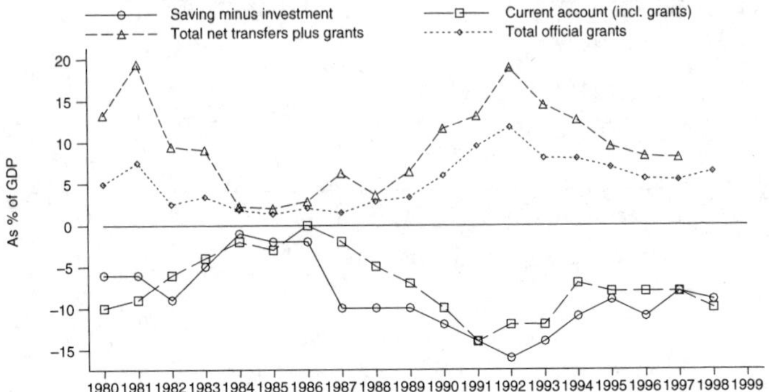

(a) Saving–investment gap and current account deficit with external flows

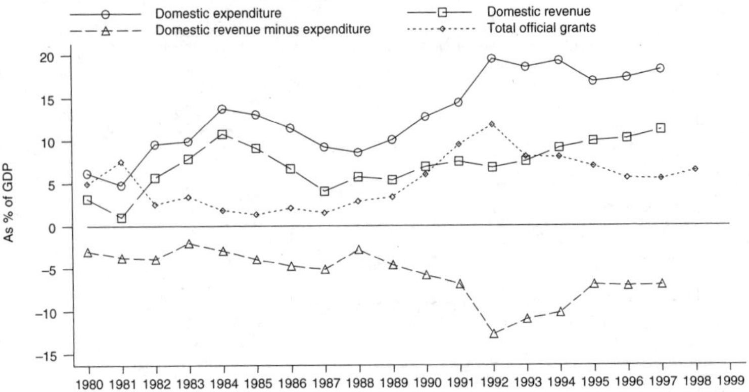

(b) Fiscal gap and official grants

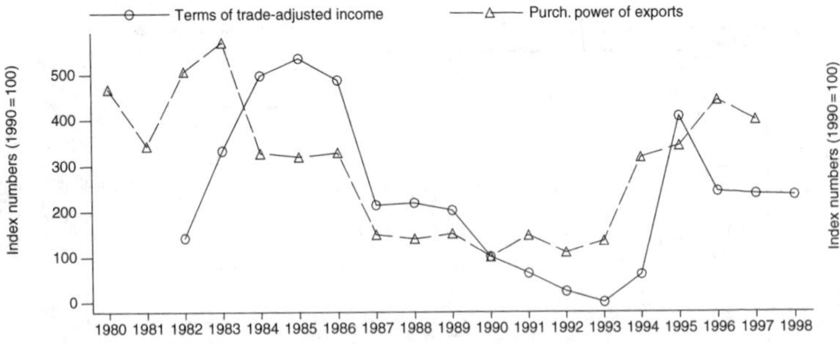

(c) Terms of trade-adjusted income and purchasing power of exports

Appendix Figure 2A.1 (Continued)

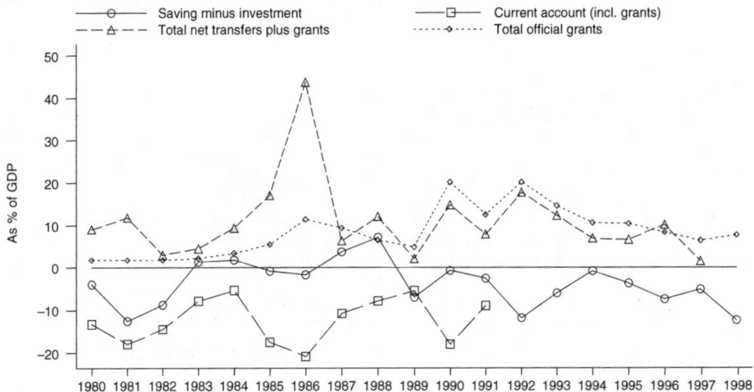

(a) Saving–investment gap and current account deficit with external flows

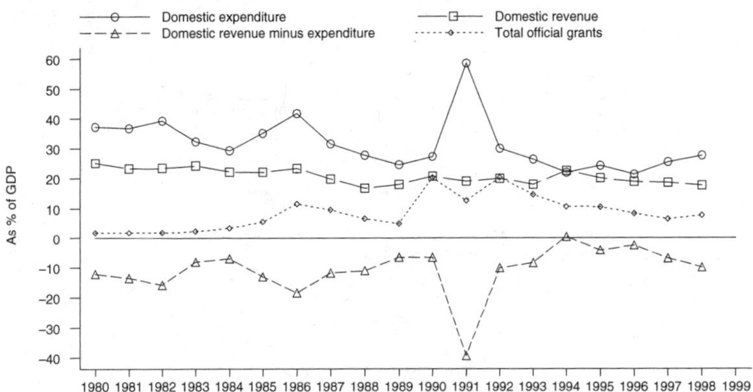

(b) Fiscal gap and official grants

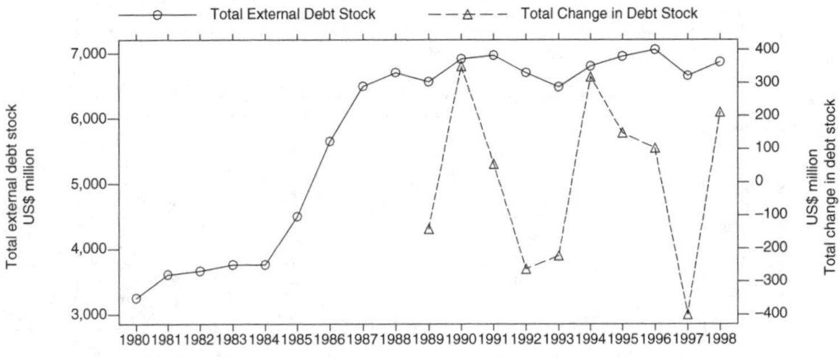

(c) Terms of trade-adjusted income and purchasing power of exports

Appendix Figure 2A.1 (Continued)

GHANA

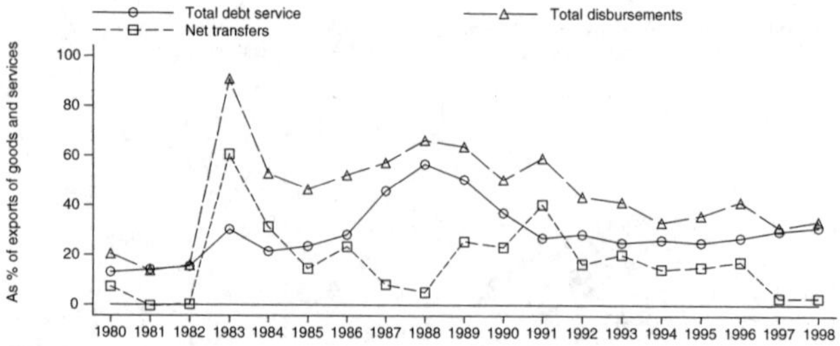

(a) Total debt service, disbursements, net transfers

(b) Total external debt stock

UGANDA

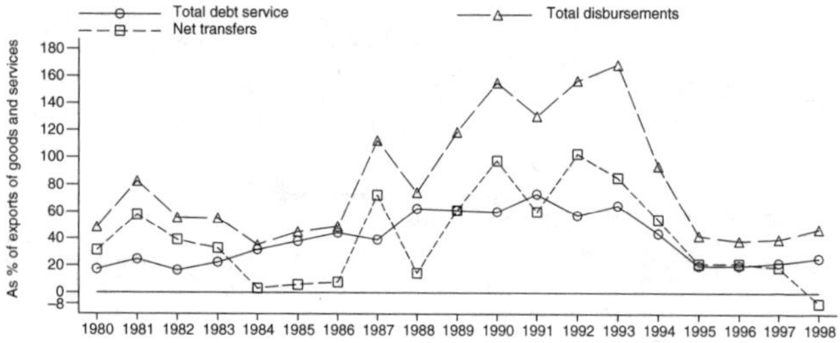

(a) Total debt service, disbursements, net transfers

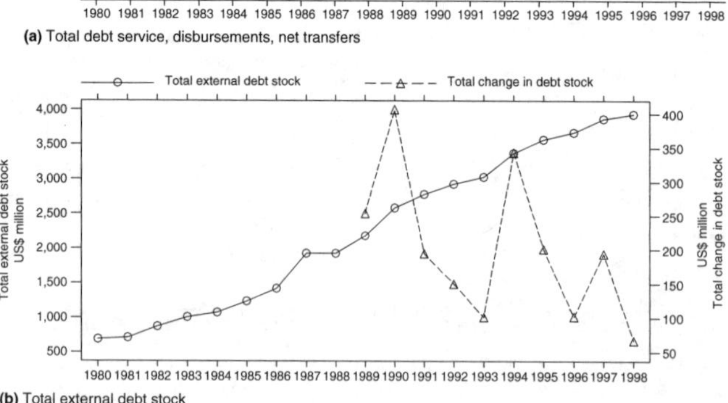

(b) Total external debt stock

Appendix Figure 2A.2 Debt data for Ghana, Uganda and Zambia

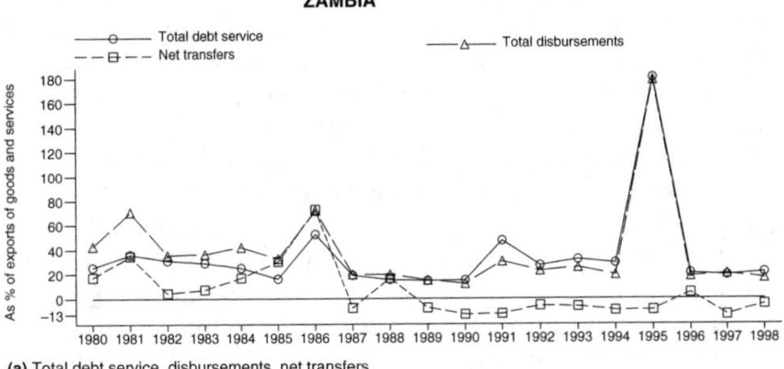

(a) Total debt service, disbursements, net transfers

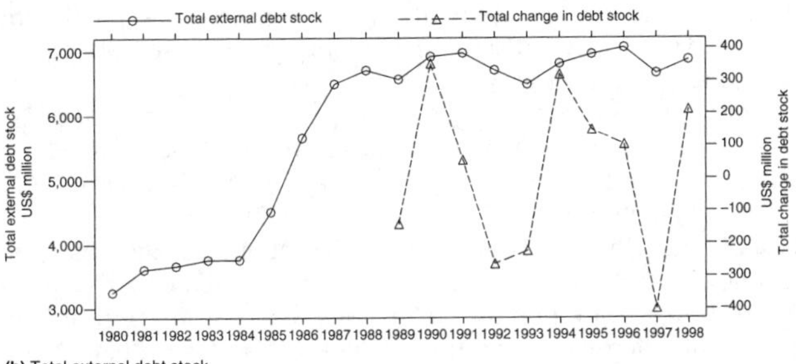

(b) Total external debt stock

Appendix Figure 2A.2 (Continued)

Notes

* The authors are grateful for invaluable comments received from Alfred Maizels and conference participants. This chapter is a shortened version of a WIDER Discussion Paper (Nissanke and Ferrarini, 2001).

1. Easterly's criticism of the financial gap model (1999b) is directed at the gap model's uncritical adoption of the fixed relationships between key parameters as found in the original Harrod–Domar growth model. Indeed, this has been widely recognized as one of the drawbacks of the model, as discussed in our text. However, the gap models, treated as a macroeconomic analysis of the disequilibrium adjustment process (Taylor, 1988, 1991), remain useful as a guide in evaluating the role of external finance in facilitating macroeconomic adjustments. Easterly's criticism against gap calculations as practised at International Financial Institutions (IFIs) is valid and applicable to any other theoretical model, when models are applied mechanically for practical purposes without due calibrations.
2. Chenery and Strout (1966) define 'self-sustaining growth' as growth at a given rate with capital inflow limited to a specified ratio to GNP, which can be sustained without concessional aid.
3. Avramovic (1964), however, warns that progression through the virtuous cycle of debt and growth is by no means automatic and emphasizes the need to fulfil the sustainability conditions presented in the text.

4. Interestingly, for dismissing the usefulness of the financial gap model, Easterly (1999b) treats the following two hypotheses as predictions implied by the model: (i) aid will go into investment one for one; and (ii) there will be a fixed linear relationship between growth and investment in the short run. By testing these predictions with very simple regression analyses, he rejects the financial gap calculations. However, his test does not amount to a rejection of the role of financial aid in economic development as such.
5. Easterly (1999b) emphasizes that there is a moral hazard problem with giving aid on the basis of a 'financial gap', arguing that recipient countries will have an incentive to maintain or increase the financial gap by low saving to get more aid. Our discussion so far provides a different perspective altogether.
6. Kamel (1988) shows that if one applies a stronger solvency criterion, i.e. a country is regarded as solvent if it can ultimately repay its debt and move into a positive net asset position, the solvency condition would become: $x \geq i$ *and* $x > u$. That is, export growth is higher than or at least equal to the interest rate, and export growth is higher than import growth.
7. Figure 2.4(a) shows commodity price indices, which are deflated by UN index of unit values of manufactures exported by developed market economy countries. The graph is reproduced from Figure 1.1 in Maizels (1992).
8. The original graph is Figure 1.2 in Maizels (1992).
9. Bolivia, Chad, Ghana*, Mali, Malawi, Mozambique, Nicaragua, Rwanda, Tanzania, Uganda*, Zambia* (countries marked with an asterisk are reported in this section, and in the Appendixes). See Nissanke and Ferrarini (2001) for a more comprehensive description, including also Mozambique and Tanzania. Useful data are also to be found in IMF (2001a) and IMF (various years).
10. It should be noted, however, that in the case of many HIPCs, fiscal data are notoriously unreliable, with large shares of aid flows often not included in the budgetary accounts.
11. The top three commodities represented the following percentage share of merchandise exports in 1998: Ghana (81.2 per cent), Uganda (68.9 per cent), Zambia (66.9 per cent).
12. The terms of trade effect equals the capacity to import less exports of goods and services in constant prices. Data are in local currency.
13. The value index of exports deflated by the import unit value index.
14. As further documented in Nissanke and Ferrarini (2001), unit value and volume of exports were negatively correlated, suggesting that the *fallacy of composition* may have affected the export revenue of their main commodities. Adjustment programmes designed to push export volumes to higher levels were partly undermined by adverse terms of trade effects over time. Among the countries considered here, Zambia clearly shows the negative price effect. Although the positive volume effect was dominant in the case of Uganda and Ghana, it contributed to an extreme volatility of export proceeds. Year-to-year changes in export values were often as high as 40–50 per cent, contributing in a determinant way to the underlying unsustainability of both current balances and external indebtedness.
15. See Nissanke and Ferrarini (2001) for a more detailed debt profile broken down by creditor type and transfer flows.
16. In the case of Zambia, negative net transfers have been the result of debt service of bilateral and private public and publicly guaranteed debt in excess

of new disbursements, and of repurchases of obligations to the IMF during the 1990s. Negative net transfers were partly offset by positive transfers from multilateral creditors.

17. Killick and Stevens (1997) assess the traditional debt relief mechanisms that are inefficient in terms of adequacy, productivity, transaction cost and transparency.
18. See Killick and Stevens (1997), Killick (2000) and UNCTAD (2000b) for a detailed discussion and critical assessment of the HIPC Initiatives.

References

Aryeetey, E., J. Harrigan and M. Nissanke (2000). *Economic Reforms in Ghana: The Reality and the Mirage*, London: James Currey.

Avramovic, D. (1964). *Economic Growth and External Debt*, Baltimore, MD: Johns Hopkins University Press.

Bacha, E. L. (1990). 'A Three-Gap Model of Foreign Transfers and the GDP Growth Rate in Developing Countries', *Journal of Development Economics*, 32: 279–96.

Burnside, C. and D. Dollar (1997). 'Aid Policies and Growth', Policy Research Department, Macroeconomics and Growth Division, Washington, DC: World Bank.

Chenery, H. B. and A. M. Strout (1966). 'Foreign Assistance and Economic Development', *American Economic Review*, 56(4).

Claessens, S. and I. Diwan (1989). 'Liquidity, Debt Relief and Conditionality', in I. Husain and I. Diwan (eds), *Dealing with the Debt Crisis*, World Bank Symposium volume, Washington, DC: World Bank.

Cline, W. R. (1995). *International Debt Examined*, Washington, DC: Institute for International Economics.

Collier, P. (1998). 'Aid and Economic Development in Africa', Oxford: Centre for the Study of African Economies, University of Oxford.

Deaton, A. (1989). 'Saving in Developing Countries: Theory and Review', Paper presented at the first annual World Bank Conference on Economic Development, Washington, DC, April.

Easterly, W. (1999a). 'How Did Highly Indebted Poor Countries Become Highly Indebted? Reviewing Two Decades of Debt Relief, Washington, DC: World Bank, mimeo.

Easterly, W. (1999b). 'The Ghost of Financial Gap: Testing the Growth Model Used in the International Financial Institutions', *Journal of Development Economics*, 60(2): 423–38.

Eaton, J. (1993). 'Sovereign Debt: A Primer', *The World Bank Economic Review*, 7(2): 137–72.

Hansen, H. and F. Tarp (2001). 'Aid Effectiveness Disputed', *Journal of Development Economics*, 12(3): 375–98.

Hernandez-Cata, E. (1988). 'Issues in the Design of Growth Exercises', IMF Working Paper, Washington, DC: IMF, July.

IMF (International Monetary Fund) (various years). Various country documents (decision point documents, PRSPs) on the HIPC-Debt Relief Initiative, Washington, DC: IMF.

IMF (International Monetary Fund) (2001a). Balance of Payment Statistics (BOPS) CD-ROM.

IMF (International Monetary Fund) (2001b). *International Financial Statistics* (IFS) CD-ROM.

Kamel, N. (1988). 'Criteria for National Solvency', Applied Economics Discussion Paper, University of Oxford.

Killick, T. (2000). 'HIPC II and Conditionality: Business as Before or New Beginning?', Paper presented at the Commonwealth Secretariat Policy Workshop on Debt, HIPC and Poverty Reduction, 17–8 July, London.

Killick, T. and S. Stevens (1997). 'Assessing the Efficiency of Mechanisms for Dealing with the Debt Problems of Low-Income Countries', in Z. Iqbal and R. Kanbur (eds), *External Finance for Low-Income Countries*, Washington, DC: IMF.

Krugman, P. (1988). 'Financing vs Forgiving a Debt Overhang', *Journal of Development Economics*, 29: 253–68.

Maizels, A. (1968). 'Review of A. I. MacBain, Export Instability and Economic Development', *American Economic Review*, 58(3): Part 1.

Maizels, A. (1992). *Commodities in Crisis*, Oxford, Clarendon Press for UNU-WIDER.

Maizels, A. and Machiko Nissanke (1984). 'Motivations for Aid to Developing Countries', *World Development*, 12(9), 879–900.

Martin, M. and R. Alami (2001). 'Long-Term Debt Sustainability for HIPCs: How to Respond to Shocks', London: Development Finance International.

McDonald, D. C. (1982). 'Debt Capacity and Developing Country Borrowing', *IMF Staff Papers*, 29: 603–46.

Nissanke, M. (2000). 'From Aid Dependence to Self-articulated Aspiration: Comparative Analysis of Sub-Saharan Africa and East Asia', *Cambridge Review of International Affairs*, 14(1).

Nissanke, M. and B. Ferrarini (2001). 'Debt Dynamics and Contingency Financing: Theoretical Reappraisal of the HIPC Initiative', WIDER Discussion Paper DP2001/139, Helsinki: UNU–WIDER.

Obstfeld, M. and K. Rogoff (1996). *Foundations of International Economics*, Cambridge, MA: MIT Press.

Simonsen, M. E. (1985). 'The Development Country Debt Problem', in G. W. Smith and J. T. Cuddington (eds), *International Debt and the Developing Countries*, World Bank Symposium volume, Washington, DC: World Bank.

Stein, H. and M. Nissanke (1999). 'Structural Adjustment and the African Crisis: A Theoretical Appraisal', *Eastern Economic Journal*, 25(4): 399–420.

Taylor, L. (1988). *Varieties of Stabilisation Experiences*, Oxford: Clarendon Press.

Taylor, L. (1991). 'Foreign Resource Flows and Developing Country Growth', Research for Action 8, Helsinki: UNU–WIDER.

UNCTAD (United Nations Conference on Trade and Development) (2000a). Handbook of Statistics CD-ROM.

UNCTAD (United Nations Conference on Trade and Development) (2000b). *The Least Development Countries 2000 Report*, New York and Geneva: United Nations.

Williamson, J. and C. Milner (1991). *The World Economy*, London and New York: Harvester Wheatsheaf.

World Bank (2000a). International Bank for Reconstruction and Development (IBRD), World Development Indicators (WDI) CD-ROM.

World Bank (2000b). *Consulting World Development Report 2000*, Washington, DC: World Bank.

3

Policy Selectivity Forgone: Debt and Donor Behaviour in Africa*

Nancy Birdsall, Stijn Claessens and Ishac Diwan

Introduction

A large literature has developed on the country and other factors that influence the effectiveness of aid and the development aid business more generally. Two major findings have emerged (World Bank, 1998). First, aid is more effective when the recipient country's policy and institutional environment satisfies some minimal criteria. Second, aid and debt relief have not been particularly targeted to countries with adequate policies and institutions.[1] In this chapter, we concentrate on understanding the dynamics behind the second finding. To do so, we analyse the donor and official creditor side of the aid process. Our specific hypothesis is that the growing debt of poor countries since the 1980s and its composition has affected the process of granting new loans and grants by donors and official creditors.

Analysing the behaviour of donors and creditors as it relates to the accumulated debt burden is important as it can shed light on a critical policy question. Will the ongoing major programme of debt reduction by the official donor community for poor countries (known as HIPC, for Heavily Indebted Poor Countries) not only reduce debts but also affect future donor behaviour, particularly the ability and willingness of donors to direct aid where it can best be used? Or will more debt reduction simply invite another round of business-as-usual (in the form of new loans and new debt accumulation) of the kind that is implicated in the debt build-up in the first place?

To address these questions, we empirically investigate donor and creditor behaviour using data on net transfers for a panel of 37 Sub-Saharan African (SSA) countries over the 1980s and 1990s. As others have documented, our analysis of past behaviour confirms that the quality of countries' policy framework has mattered little in determining overall net transfers. Importantly, we find that the build-up of debt stocks owed to the multilateral creditors has hindered the targeting of resource flows to those countries that had better policies and improved institutional environments. We find in particular that more indebted countries received more net transfers and that among countries highly indebted to multilaterals, those that had below median quality policies received on average some 2 percentage points of GDP *more* in net transfers over this period. We also find that in low-debt countries, donors are selective with respect to countries' policies, but not so in high-multilateral debt countries. These findings are robust to the use of different estimation techniques and alternative measures for the quality of policy.

These findings suggest that the build-up of debt, especially to multilaterals, has undermined the ability of the donors to be selective with respect to countries' policies – i.e. to transfer less where the policy setting is poor. It implies that debt reduction for high-multilateral debt countries can allow the behaviour of the donor community to shift to a low-debt regime mode, a regime that in the past has allowed selectivity. Debt reduction can in short be interpreted as a way 'out' for a donor community that is otherwise locked into a pattern of non-selectivity in the high-multilateral debt countries.

The chapter is structured as follows. The next section describes the overall setting for development assistance and documents the accumulation of debt of SSA countries over the 1980s and 1990s to different classes of creditors. The following section describes the data we use and provides the major trends and raw statistics. Then we specify our hypothesis, describe the empirical analysis and discuss our major findings. The final section concludes.

Development assistance and debt accumulation in Africa, 1980s and 1990s

Since 1975, SSA countries have been major recipients of overseas development assistance (ODA). Aid in the form of grants and loans from bilateral and multilateral donors has amounted to about US$350 billion (in nominal terms). In some countries, gross aid flows were 60 per cent or more of GDP in some years; in many countries flows often exceeded the government's own tax revenue collection. In the same period, with a few exceptions, countries have had relatively low rates of *per capita* GDP growth. Despite high levels of lending and grant programmes, the growth rate of *per capita* GDP for the region as a whole was negative over the 1980s and 1990s (in the 1980s about –2 per cent per year and in the 1990s about –1 per cent) and average GDP *per capita* at constant prices was lower in 2000 than it was in 1960. The number and proportion of poor people actually increased: 40 per cent of the population of 600 million in SSA in 2000 lived on less than US$1 a day (World Bank, 2000).

Meanwhile, much of the high levels of development assistance took the form of loans and produced a growing stock of debt – from about US$60 billion in 1980 to US$230 billion in 2000. Annual debt service paid also increased, from an average of US$6 billion per annum in the early 1980s, to about US$11 billion in the late 1990s. Growth in debt service was much less than growth in debt, however, due to debt restructuring and increases in the concessionality of resources provided. In the 1990s especially, repeated rounds of debt rescheduling and debt service relief by the official donor community and an increase in the proportion of donor transfers as grants, all kept debt service from rising more.

While many other countries have had external debt problems, two features of the debt problem in Africa are notable. First, because of the preponderant role of official creditors and donors (as opposed to commercial creditors), net transfers have been always positive (and large). Total disbursements in the form of new loans and grants have always exceeded countries' actual debt service; indeed net transfers (the difference between new disbursements and debt service paid) have been 10 per cent or more of GDP for most countries for the two decades. Second, the proportion of total debt owed to the IMF, World Bank and other multilaterals (African Development Bank (ADB), European Investment Bank (EIB)) has been constantly growing as bilateral donors switched from loans to grants and increasing forgave outright portions of debt owed them. Between 1980 and 1998, the share of multilateral debt in total debt increased from about one-seventh to almost one-third of total debt, and the share of the multilaterals in total debt service increased from about one-tenth to one-third.[2]

These features highlight the important differences between the debt problems of the African countries today and those of Latin American and other middle-income countries in the 1980s, which have been extensively analysed (see Eaton and Fernandez, 1995 for a review of this literature). Most debts of the Latin American countries were then due to commercial rather than official creditors. Each of these commercial creditors was individually interested in maximizing the value of its claim on the country. This desire to extract payments led to a 'tax' on the country, a *debt overhang,* where high levels of debt were leading to disincentives to adjust economic policies and where new investors were deterred from committing resources to the country (Diwan and Rodrik, 1992). The literature then stressed the potential beneficial effects of a reduction in the face value of debt for creditors as it could increase the incentives for a debtor to adjust and enhance a country's ability to attract a new (type of) investors and fresh funds. *Ex post*, the debt overhang was resolved through debt reduction (the Brady plan) that seems to have had some of these beneficial effects (Claessens and Diwan, 1994).

The situation of the African countries is quite different (Claessens *et al.*, 1997). Although the debt stocks were rising, they did not impose any actual debt servicing burden as countries received large positive net transfers and did not need to repay their creditors.[3] With debt service payments rising, however, especially to multilaterals, higher and higher disbursements by donors (the multilaterals themselves or the bilaterals) were needed to maintain net transfers. The rising debt levels and the increase in the share of the multilaterals meant that, by the mid-1990s, it was not the indebted countries but the donors and creditors themselves that were caught in a debt trap. The donors wanted to avoid the indebted countries, among the poorest in the world, falling behind in debt service to the multilaterals. Arrears to the multilaterals would have meant the curtailment of future lending by not only the multilaterals but by all other donors as continued aid flows required an active multilaterals' lending programme. Furthermore, from the donors' point of view, arrears would make visible the failure of the past aid transfers.

As debt stock considerations started to drive new disbursements, the quality of policy and the degree of poverty in the countries became increasingly less relevant. The need to maintain high new disbursements in highly indebted countries may have meant that donors no longer had enough freedom to differentiate new disbursements by the quality of policy and the degree of poverty. In other words, indebtedness led the donor community to lose some of its ability to be selective with respect to policy and poverty, and aid flows started to respond more to debt stocks, and less to policy and poverty.[4]

Data and general analysis of donor behaviour

To assess creditor and donor behaviour, we analyse debt indicators and net transfers for a sample of countries in SSA over the period 1977–98. We want to assess donor behaviour to countries in the region independent of whether countries eventually became HIPC-eligible or not, a classification which occurred around 1998, and without the classification itself affecting donor behaviour. We therefore use a sample that includes both HIPC and non-HIPC countries and stop our analysis in 1998. This avoids any sample selection problem. We include in our analysis the 37 SSA countries for which we have all necessary data. Some countries (including Eritrea, Angola, Somalia and Tanzania) are excluded for lack of data on many individual years. Of the 34 African countries eligible for HIPC (in 2002), 29 are included in our sample of 37 (Table 3.1).[5]

The variable of interest for our analysis is the amount of net transfers a country receives from abroad related to debt or grants, i.e. the amount of net movement of real resources to the country from official sources

Table 3.1 Sample countries (37)

HIPCs (29)	*Non-HIPCs (8)*
Benin	Botswana
Burkina Faso	Gabon
Burundi	Lesotho
Cameroon	Mauritius
Central African Republic	Nigeria
Chad	Seychelles
Comoros	Swaziland
Congo	Zimbabwe
Congo, Dem. Rep	
Côte d'Ivoire	
Ethiopia	
The Gambia	
Ghana	
Guinea	
Guinea-Bissau	
Kenya	
Liberia	
Madagascar	
Malawi	
Mali	
Mauritania	
Niger	
Rwanda	
Senegal	
Sierra Leone	
Sudan	
Togo	
Uganda	
Zambia	

Note: HIPC classification as of autumn 2002.

on account of debt or grants. We thus exclude from our analysis flows related to foreign direct, portfolio and other non-debt investments. Net transfers are defined in accordance with the World Bank's Global Development Finance (GDF) as the amount of resources the countries receive in the form of grants and new debt disbursements net of repayments on old debt. Or, in other words,

$$NT = G + NB - (P + R) = G + NB - TDS \tag{3.1}$$

where NT = net transfers, G = the amount of grants (free gifts) the country receives, NB = new debt disbursements, P = principal repayment on existing debt, R = interest payment on existing debt and TDS = total debt service paid, the sum of principal repayment P and interest payments R. We restrict ourselves to those resources that are directed to the government and which mainly come from official, that is non-private, sources. These sources include the World Bank, IMF and other multilaterals as well as bilateral donors and donor agencies.

All data on debt and net transfers are from the World Bank's GDF statistics. This data set, published annually by the World Bank, relies on debtors' reports, cross-verified with creditor sources. It provides the statistics on debt, disbursements and repayments. In accordance with the GDF, all amounts related to debt are on a cash basis, that is, they represent actual payments, and not scheduled amounts, so that arrears or debt and debt service reduction do not confound the data. The GDF does not collect data on grants itself, but rather relies on donors' official development assistance (ODA) and OECD reports (the Development Assistance Committee, DAC) for the grant information. Grants do not give rise to repayment obligations and are thus not affected by the difference between obligations due and actual payments, i.e. arrears. The grants data do include, however, some elements of official debt and debt service reduction as donors have included debt forgiveness in their reported figures. In particular, the amount of grants reported by donors includes some debt forgiveness that may not imply any actual net transfers to the debtor.[6] The quality of the data on official debt reduction is known to be very poor, however, and we cannot correct the grants figure to derive a more accurate actual net resource figure (see further Renard and Cassimon, 2001).

We limit the impact of outliers by dropping observations for years when net transfers to a country as a share of GNP were more than 60 per cent (we also used a lower threshold of 30 per cent but results were not qualitatively different). We also do not always have all the independent variables that we later need in our regressions. This means some country-year observations drop out as well. For our 37 countries, we end up with a total of 848 country-year observations.

We now turn to a systematic analysis of the donors' and creditors' behaviour and try to address a number of specific questions. Were donors' net transfers to countries related to recipient countries' debt stock? Were donors and creditors providing higher net transfers to countries with better policies? For a given policy framework, were donors transferring more to countries with higher levels of poverty? In short, was there selectivity by donors and creditors as a function of countries' (changing) policies and degree of poverty? Or did the mounting debt stock and the resulting debt 'crisis' lock donors into defensive lending to high-debt countries, depriving them of selectivity and leverage with respect to recipient country policies?

We start by dividing our sample of country-year observations into three sub-groups of indebtedness, first distinguishing low- from high-debt countries, and then creating within the high-debt group a further sub-division into a low- and high-multilateral debt group. Specifically, each country-year observation is considered a low- (or high-) debt regime if the country's debt–GDP ratio in that year is below (or above) 62.8 per cent (the median debt–GDP ratio of the whole sample). The high-debt group is further sub-divided into a low- and a high-multilateral debt group, if the share of multilateral debt in total debt for that country and year is below or above 41.2 per cent (the median share of multilateral debt in total debt for the whole sample). In other words, the high-debt, low-multilateral category constitutes those country-year observations where the total debt–GDP ratio is greater than 62.8 per cent, but the share of multilateral debt in total debt is less than 41.2 per cent, while the high-debt, high-multilateral category constitutes those country-year observations where the total debt–GDP ratio is also greater than 62.8 per cent, but the share of multilateral debt in total debt is greater than 41.2 per cent.

Table 3.2 provides the exact classification for each country and each year (note that the total sample in this classification varies slightly, between 34 and 37 as debt data are not available for each year for each country). It shows that the size of the sub-samples varies over time. The number of low-debt countries was 32 in 1977, but dropped to only nine in 1998. For the whole group, the number of high-debt countries grew sharply, from two in 1977 to 27 in 1998. The number of high-multilateral debt countries within the high-debt group increased especially sharply, from 0 in 1977 to 20 in 1998. The number of low-multilateral debt countries within the high-debt group grew from two in 1977 to 14 in 1987 and then dropped to seven in 1998.

Table 3.2 Classification of countries, 1977–98

Country	*1977*	*1978*	*1979*	*1980*	*1981*	*1982*	*1983*	*1984*	*1985*	*1986*	*1987*	*1988*	*1989*	*1990*	*1991*	*1992*	*1993*	*1994*	*1995*	*1996*	*1997*	*1998*
Benin	L	L	L	L	L	L	L	L	ML	L	ML	L	ML	MH	MH	MH	MH	MH	MH	MH	MH	MH
Botswana	L	L	L	L	L	L	L	L	L	L	L	L	L	L	L	L	L	L	L	L	L	L
Burkina Faso	L	L	L	L	L	L	L	L	L	L	L	L	L	L	L	L	L	L	L	L	L	L
Burundi	L	L	L	L	L	L	L	L	L	L	MH	MH	MH	MH	MH	MH	MH	MH	MH	MH	MH	MH
Cameroon	L	L	L	L	L	L	L	L	L	L	L	L	L	L	L	L	L	ML	ML	ML	ML	ML
Central African Republic	L	L	L	L	L	L	L	L	L	L	L	L	L	L	L	L	L	MH	MH	MH	MH	MH
Chad	L	L	L	L	L	L	L	L	L	L	L	L	L	L	L	L	L	MH	L	L	MH	MH
Comoros	L	L	L	L	L	MH	MH	MH	MH	MH	MH	MH	MH	MH	MH	MH	MH	MH	MH	MH	MH	MH
Congo Dem. Rep.	L	L	L	L	L	L	L	ML	ML	ML	ML	ML	ML	ML	ML	ML	ML	ML	ML	ML	ML	ML
Congo Rep.	L	ML	ML	ML	ML	ML	ML	ML	ML	ML	ML	ML	ML	ML	ML	ML	ML	ML	ML	ML	ML	ML
Côte d'Ivoire	L	L	L	ML	ML	ML	ML	ML	ML	ML	ML	ML	ML	ML	ML	ML	ML	ML	ML	ML	ML	ML
Ethiopia	.	.	.	.	L	L	L	ML	ML	ML	ML	ML	ML	ML	ML	ML	ML	ML	ML	ML	ML	ML
Gabon	L	L	L	L	L	L	L	L	L	L	ML	ML	ML	L	ML	ML	ML	ML	ML	ML	ML	ML
Gambia, The	L	L	L	L	MH	MH	MH	MH	MH	MH	MH	MH	MH	MH	MH	MH	MH	MH	MH	MH	MH	MH
Ghana	L	L	L	L	L	L	L	L	L	L	MH	L	L	L	L	MH	MH	MH	MH	MH	MH	MH
Guinea	.	.	.	.	.	.	.	.	.	ML	ML	ML	ML	ML	ML	ML	MH	MH	MH	MH	MH	MH
Guinea-Bissau	L	L	L	.	ML	ML	MH	ML	.	ML	.	.	.	MH	MH	MH	MH	MH	MH	MH	MH	MH
Kenya	L	L	L	L	L	L	L	L	MH	L	MH	MH	MH	MH	MH	MH	MH	MH	MH	MH	L	L
Lesotho	L	L	L	L	L	L	L	L	L	L	L	L	L	L	L	L	L	L	L	L	L	MH
Liberia	L	L	L	L	ML	MH	MH	MH	MH	MH	MH	.	.	.	.	.	.	.	.	.	.	.
Madagascar	L	L	L	L	L	L	L	ML	ML	ML	ML	ML	ML	ML	MH	MH	MH	MH	MH	MH	MH	MH
Malawi	L	L	L	L	MH	MH	MH	MH	MH	MH	MH	MH	MH	MH	MH	MH	MH	MH	MH	MH	MH	MH
Mali	L	L	L	L	L	ML	ML	ML	ML	ML	ML	ML	ML	ML	MH	ML	ML	MH	MH	MH	MH	MH
Mauritania	ML	ML	ML	ML	ML	ML	ML	ML	ML	ML	ML	ML	ML	ML	ML	ML	ML	MH	MH	MH	MH	MH
Mauritius	L	L	L	L	L	L	L	L	L	L	L	L	L	L	L	L	L	L	L	L	L	L

Niger	L	L	L	L	L	L	L	ML	ML	ML	ML	MH	MH	MH	L	L	MH	MH	MH	MH	MH	MH
Nigeria	L	L	L	L	L	L	L	L	L	ML	ML	ML	ML	ML	ML	ML	ML	ML	ML	ML	L	L
Rwanda	L	L	L	L	L	L	L	L	L	L	L	L	L	L	L	L	L	.	MH	MH	L	L
Senegal	L	L	L	L	L	ML	ML	ML	ML	ML	ML	MH	MH	L	L	L	MH	MH	MH	MH	MH	MH
Seychelles	L	L	L	L	L	L	L	L	L	L	L	L	L	L	L	L	L	L	L	L	L	L
Sierra Leone	L	L	L	L	L	L	L	L	L	MH	ML	L	L	ML	ML	ML	MH	MH	MH	MH	MH	MH
Sudan	L	L	L	L	L	ML	ML	ML	ML	L	L	ML	ML	ML	ML	ML	ML	ML	ML	ML	ML	ML
Swaziland	L	L	L	L	L	L	L	L	L	L	L	L	L	L	L	L	L	L	L	L	L	L
Togo	L	ML	ML	ML	ML	ML	ML	ML	MH	MH	MH	MH	MH	MH	MH	MH	MH	MH	MH	MH	MH	MH
Uganda	.	.	.	L	MH	L	L	L	L	L	L	L	L	L	MH	MH	MH	MH	L	L	L	L
Zambia	ML	ML	ML	ML	ML	ML	ML	ML	ML	ML	MH	ML	MH	MH	MH	MH	MH	MH	MH	MH	MH	MH
Zimbabwe	L	L	L	L	L	L	L	L	L	L	L	L	L	L	L	L	L	L	MH	L	L	MH
Number of low-debt	32	30	30	29	26	23	23	19	17	18	13	15	14	15	14	13	11	7	8	9	11	9
Number of low-multilateral debt	2	4	4	5	7	9	8	13	12	13	14	12	12	11	10	11	9	8	8	8	7	7
Number of high-multilateral debt	0	0	0	0	3	4	5	4	6	6	9	8	9	10	12	12	16	20	20	19	18	20
Total for particular year	**34**	**34**	**34**	**34**	**36**	**36**	**36**	**36**	**35**	**37**	**36**	**35**	**35**	**36**	**36**	**36**	**36**	**35**	**36**	**36**	**36**	**36**

Notes: The three debt classifications are constructed as follows: the low-debt regime (L) constitutes those country-year observations where the country's debt–GDP ratio in that year is below 62.8 per cent; the high-debt, low-multilateral (ML) category constitutes those country-year observations where the total debt–GDP ratio is greater than 62.8 per cent and the share of multilateral debt in total debt is less than 41.2 per cent; and the high-debt, high-multilateral category (MH) constitutes those country-year observations where the total debt–GDP ratio is also greater than 62.8 per cent and the share of multilateral debt in total debt is greater than 41.2 per cent.

We next use this classification to compare the behaviour of net transfers across the three different debt regimes. We start by plotting the average ratio of net transfers–GDP for the three debtor classes (Figure 3.1). Net transfers as a share of GDP have been greater in almost all years for the countries in the two high-debt categories, and especially for those in the high-multilateral debt category. Net transfers have declined over time for the countries in all regimes, somewhat more in the high-multilateral debt regime and especially so in the low-multilateral debt regime.

Table 3.3 shows the means (and standard deviations) for the net transfers variable for all countries as well as for the three regimes, averaging over all years. Consistent with Figure 3.1, countries with high-debt ratios and especially debts largely due to multilateral institutions have received larger net transfers. For the period as a whole, high-multilateral debt countries received net transfers equal to some 18 per cent of GDP compared to some 10 per cent of GDP for the low-debt group. The low-multilateral debt cases (a sub-division of the high-debt regime)

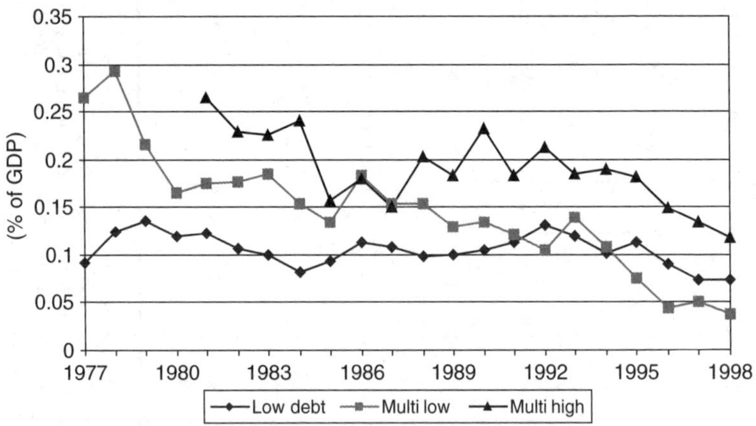

Figure 3.1 Net transfers, 1977–98

Notes: The three debt classification are constructed as follows: the low-debt regime constitutes those country-year observations where the country's debt–GDP ratio in that year is below 62.8 per cent; the high-debt, low-multilateral category constitutes those country-year observations where the total debt–GDP ratio is greater than 62.8 per cent and the share of multilateral debt in total debt is less than 41.2 per cent; and the high-debt, high-multilateral category constitutes those country-year observations where the total debt–GDP ratio is also greater than 62.8 per cent, but the share of multilateral debt in total debt is greater than 41.2 per cent.

Table 3.3 Panel A raw statistics

	All		*Low-debt*		*Low-multi*		*High-multi*	
	mean	*std*	*mean*	*std*	*mean*	*std*	*mean*	*std*
Net transfers/GNP	0.135	0.119	0.104	0.087	0.146	0.151	0.183	0.117
CPIA	2.763	0.813	2.963	0.831	2.488	0.698	2.895	0.670
PVTDSGDP	0.547	0.339	0.323	0.160	0.837	0.308	0.651	0.306
GDPCAP	753	1,082	981	1,314	635	919	321	128
POP	10,824,872	16,612,134	8,527,659	14,559,811	16,741,602	23,105,792	7,601,202	7,240,667
Number of obs.	848		394		239		215	

Notes: The net transfers variable for country *i* in year *j*, NT_{ij}, comes from the World Bank Global Development Finance, in US dollars and is scaled by US dollar GDP. $PVTDSGDP_{ij}$ is the present value measure of all future scheduled debt service payments relative to GDP, where the raw data also come from the World Bank *Global Development Finance*. GDP *per capita*, $GDPCAP_{ij}$, is measured in thousand dollars and comes from the IMF *International Financial Statistics*. Population size, in logarithms, POP_{ij}, comes from the World Bank World Development Indicators. $CPIA_{ij}$ is the policy measure from the World Bank. The three debt classifications are constructed as follows: the low-debt regime constitutes those country-year observations where the country's debt–GDP ratio in that year is below 62.8 per cent; the high-debt, low-multilateral category constitutes those country-year observations where the total debt–GDP ratio is greater than 62.8 per cent and the share of multilateral debt in total debt is less than 41.2 per cent.

received some 15 per cent of GDP, in between the low-debt and the high-multilateral debt cases. This comparison shows that there has been a systemically higher net transfer going to the high-debt countries, especially the high-multilateral debt cases.

Creditor and donor selectivity: empirical analysis

The aggregate statistics indicate that countries that found themselves with higher debts, and especially to multilateral institutions, have received larger net transfers than other countries. Higher net transfers to more-indebted countries need not mean, however, that there was some kind of inefficiency. For one, some unobserved country characteristics such as a high level of poverty or good policies, may have led donors to provide high net transfers. These high net transfers in the past may have been in the form of high lending, resulting in a high debt stock. As a consequence, countries highly indebted today may have been receiving more net transfers in the past and in the current period as well, because they have a higher degree of poverty or better policies. We would call the higher transfers inefficient, however, if they were going to highly indebted countries independent of the quality of their domestic policy, institutional capacity to productively absorb flows and their poverty level. In that case, the high indebtedness, particularly to multilateral creditors, could have been a barrier to selectivity in lending across countries.

We therefore need to control in our net transfers comparisons for country characteristics. For policy, we use an explicit measure of the quality of the policy environment in each country in each year: the World Bank's Country Policy and Institutional Assessment (CPIA). This measure, calculated annually by World Bank country specialists, has 20 different components measuring macroeconomic, sectoral, social and public sector institutions and policies on a scale of 1 to 6. It is determined on the basis of criteria that are standardized across countries. A separate World Bank unit makes a considerable effort to ensure consistency and comparability across countries and over time.[7]

The CPIA has been used by other researchers in investigating the determinants of aid flows, most notably Burnside and Dollar (2000) and Collier and Dollar (2002). As such, it is considered a meaningful measure of the quality of the policy framework in the respective country in each year. The CPIA has also the advantage of including not only criteria related to public policy effort but also to institutional capacity and governance (rule of law, anti-corruption efforts, etc.). Thus it may be more closely related to a country's capacity to absorb transfers effectively than traditional measures of policy effort (such as trade and financial liberalization, privatization, inflation and so on).[8]

A disadvantage of the CPIA index, however, is that it may be influenced by incentives to affect (indirectly) the lending behaviour of the World Bank, including IDA and International Bank for Reconstruction and Development (IBRD). Specifically, country managers may want (and be able) to improve their countries' ratings to justify a larger lending programme for their country. To the extent that this is true, however, the link between policy as measured by the CPIA and lending will be over-stated; and any result showing that policy is not a factor will thus be a stronger result. An additional disadvantage is that the actual CPIA is available to the public only at the country level in more aggregated form, so that our results cannot be replicated except inside the World Bank. We therefore use as a robustness test the policy index created by Burnside and Dollar (2000), which is based on publicly available information. Specifically, the index weights the following three variables: budget surplus as a share of GDP, the rate of inflation and the degree of openness of the economy, as measured by Sachs and Warner (1995).[9] This alternative policy index is a somewhat cruder measure of the quality of policy and institutional environment and we can expect results to be less strong. The policy index can also not be created for all countries and all years as some of the component variables are not always available. Specifically, because of missing data the sample of country-year observations for the policy index is much smaller, only 484 compared to 848 for the CPIA sample.

To investigate the relationship between net transfers and policy by different categories of indebtedness, we first use the CPIA index to classify countries into two groups; those with a CPIA of less than 3, so-called 'bad' policy countries, and those with a CPIA greater than or equal to 3, so-called 'good' policy countries. We do this for the whole group as well as separately for the three debt categorizations. The split for the whole group is 46–54 per cent, that is, about half of the country-year observations are bad policy country-years and half are good policy country-years. We then calculate the mean net transfers as a share of GDP for each sub-classification. We find that there are some statistically significant differences in net transfers between bad and good policy countries (Table 3.4, Panel A). In particular, for all countries combined, bad policy countries receive on average some 1.5 percentage points of GDP more in net transfers than good policy countries do. This difference is also statistically significant.

Table 3.4 Net transfers and GDP

Panel A *T*-test on net transfers/GDP (based on CPIA)

	Difference		*Difference*		*Difference*		*Difference*	
CPIA	*All*	*t-test*	*Low-debt*	*t-test*	*Low-multi*	*t-test*	*High-multi*	*t-test*
All	0.135		0.103		0.146		0.183	
Good	0.127	0.015	0.103	0.001	0.145	0.001	0.163	0.041
Bad	0.142	1.810	0.103	−0.110	0.147	−0.220	0.204	2.610

Panel B *T*-test on net transfer/GDP (based on policy)

	Difference		*Difference*		*Difference*		*Difference*	
Policy	*All*	*t-test*	*Low-debt*	*t-test*	*Low-multi*	*t-test*	*High-multi*	*t-test*
All	0.103		0.084		0.090		0.157	
Good	0.103	0.000	0.080	0.008	0.079	0.016	0.168	−0.025
Bad	0.103	−0.051	0.088	0.868	0.095	0.803	0.143	−1.384

Notes: *t*-test of the difference between the good and bad policy countries.
The net transfers variable for country *i* in year *j*, NT_{ij}, comes from the World Bank *Global Development Finance*, is in US dollar and is scaled by US dollar GDP. *CPIA* is the policy measure from the World Bank. *Policy* is the alternative policy variable. The three debt classifications are constructed as follows: the low-debt regime constitutes those country-year observations where the country's debt–GDP ratio in that year is below 62.8 per cent; the high-debt, low-multilateral category constitutes those country-year observations where the total debt–GDP ratio is greater than 62.8 per cent and the share of multilateral debt in total debt is less than 41.2 per cent; and the high-debt, high-multilateral category constitutes those country-year observations where the total debt–GDP ratio is also greater than 62.8 per cent, but the share of multilateral debt in total debt is greater than 41.2 per cent. The bad policy dummy is if the *CPIA* for that country-year observation was less than 3 or if the alternative policy index was less than its median.

When breaking down the countries further into the three debt groups, we see that there are no statistically significant differences in net transfers between bad and good policy countries for the groups of low-debt and low-multilateral debt countries. The difference in net transfers for the overall sample seems to be caused by the behaviour of net transfers to the high-multilateral debt countries, where there is a difference between bad and good policy countries of 4.1 percentage points of GDP. This difference is statistically significant, with a *t*-statistic of 2.6. In other words, countries highly indebted to multilaterals received more net transfers when their policies were worse than average.

When we use the sample for which we have the alternative policy index, we find similar effects for the debt breakdowns, but different for the further breakdown by the policy index (Table 3.4, Panel B). The comparisons in net transfers between the debt groups are qualitatively similar to the overall comparisons: the low-debt group receives net transfers equal to 8.4 percentage points of GDP and the low-multilateral debt group equal to 9 percentage points, while the high-multilateral debt group receives 15.7 percentage points, a difference of 7 percentage points with the low-debt group. But the breakdown between good and bad policy countries does not indicate the same results. For the high-multilateral debt group, bad policy countries actually receive some 2.5 percentage points less in net transfers. For none of the debt classifications, however, is there a statistically significant difference between the bad and good policy countries, possibly because the sample is smaller and the index cruder, or because we have not yet controlled for other variables.

So far, the analysis has investigated only the simple interrelationships between the quality of policy, indebtedness and net transfers. While the raw statistics suggest that the degree and nature of indebtedness affects the relationship between policy and net transfers in case of the CPIA, although not in case of the alternative index, the data remain suggestive as they do not yet control for other country characteristics and vary by policy index and sample. The data of Table 3.3 already indicate that it can be important to control for other country characteristics as there are large differences in GDP *per capita* and population size between the three groups of indebtedness countries. To assess properly the relationship between net transfers on the one hand and the quality of policy on the other hand, we therefore extend our analysis. Specifically, we perform a multi-variate regression, where we control for a number of country characteristics.

The first control variable is the degree of indebtedness. Since the stock of debt is simply a transformation of accumulated past borrowing, it could be that high debt reflects country circumstances or policies that explain large net transfers in the past. These characteristics could include former colonial ties (Alesina and Dollar, 2000), strategic interests of donors, openness of the economy, policy stance, or other country factors. These country characteristics may lead countries that received high net transfers in the past and thus have high debt stocks, to continue to receive net transfers today. Including past indebtedness will control for some of this tendency.

Second, we want to control for the degree of poverty in the country as donors may provide net transfers in relationship to a country's degree of poverty irrespective of policy, indebtedness and other country factors. To control for the incidence of poverty is difficult, however, as poverty data are not available for long time periods. We have only a small, cross-country sample of poverty data for the 1990s. We therefore use instead GDP *per capita* (in dollars) as a proxy for the incidence of poverty (as well as the overall level of development of the country). *Per capita* income varies more greatly between the groups of countries. The high-multilateral debt countries are much poorer on average than the low-debt countries, US$320 *per capita* versus US$980 *per capita* (see Table 3.3). Perhaps they receive more net transfers simply because they are poor, and the relationship between net transfers and indebtedness arises because of greater poverty levels in high debt countries.

Third, we want to control for the size of the countries' economy since there is a tendency of smaller countries to receive relatively more aid, as reported among others by Burnside and Dollar (2000). (This relationship may arise because small countries tend to be more open and thus more exposed to international shocks, because donors expect greater influence on policy in smaller countries, or for other reasons.) In our specification, we use the logarithm of population as a control variable for size.

Finally, to control for any other country differences and possible endogeneity in the relationships, we use a fixed-effects estimation technique. Fixed effects allow us to control for any unobserved country characteristics and to take care of any (remaining) endogeneity issues. We also employ ordinary least squares as a robustness test. We estimate the following model:

$$NT_{ij} = \alpha + \beta_1^* \, PVTDSGP_{ij} + \beta_2^* \, GDPCAP_{ij} + \beta_3^* \, LNPOP_{ij} + \beta_4^* \, CPIA_{ij} + \beta_5^* (\textit{Debt classification interacted with policy dummies}_{1,2,3} \; \textit{for country i and year j}).$$

The net transfers variable for country *i* in year *j*, NT_{ij}, is scaled to GDP. $PVTDSGDP_{ij}$ is the present value measure of all future scheduled debt service payments relative to GDP, which thus takes into account the concessionality of debt. This measure is preferred to such measures as the total debt stock–GDP, which ignores the degree of concessionality of debt, or annual debt service–GDP, which does not provide a measure of the full future debt burden. *PVTDSGDP* is taken from the database for the *Global Development Finance*. GDP *per capita* in thousands of dollars, *GDPCAP*, is used as a proxy for the overall level of development of the country and the incidence of poverty. Data on GDP *per capita* are from the IMF *International Financial Statistics*. Population size, in logarithms, *LNPOP*, is to control for the size of the country and comes from the World Bank. *CPIA* is our policy measure variable already introduced (which we also substitute by the alternative policy index). The three debt dummies interacted with good/bad policy dummies are constructed consistent with Tables 3.2 and 3.4: for all three debt groups (low-debt, high-debt low-multilateral and high-debt high-multilateral) we created a separate bad policy dummy if the CPIA for that country-year observation was less than 3 (or if the alternative policy index was less than its median).

Table 3.5 provides the basic regression result. We find that net transfers are positively related to debt stocks, consistent with Figure 3.1 and the raw statistics of average net transfers by country indebtedness classification (Table 3.3). This relationship may reflect the defensive lending of donors, with high debt stocks triggering more net transfers to prevent arrears. This is possible, although to prevent arrears it would be necessary only to 'roll over' debt service due by providing an equal amount of new disbursements (i.e. keep net transfers at zero), and not be necessary to provide additional net transfers as debt burdens become larger. The positive coefficient is also possible because some country characteristics not included in the regression may be correlated with past and current net transfers, but the fixed-effects regression technique should control for most of these characteristics. The positive relationship is not likely due to the fact that the net transfers figures we use are not corrected for any official debt reduction included by donors in the grant figures they report to the OECD, as that would lead to a downward bias.[10] Our preferred interpretation for the positive coefficient is that when debt stocks are large, countries manage to 'bargain' for larger net transfers, perhaps as donors are more eager to prevent the possibility of arrears or default which would increase the visibility of any failures of past lending programmes.

We also find that countries tend to receive larger net transfers when they are poor; the coefficient on GDP *per capita* is statistically significant and negative.[11] Finally, there is evidence of a small-country effect as the coefficient for population (in logs) is statistically significant and negative.

Surprisingly, we find no direct effects of the policy variable on net transfers as the coefficient for *CPIA* is statistically insignificant.[12] It seems as if the quality of a country's policy does not affect the relative amount of net transfers it receives. When we analyse the effects of bad policy for the three debt groups, however, we find that the high-multilateral

Table 3.5 Basic result (net transfer)

	(1)		(2)		(3)	
	Fixed-effect, with CPIA		*OLS, with CPIA*		*Fixed-effect, with alternative policy variable*	
	Coef.	*t*	*Coef.*	*t*	*Coef.*	*t*
PVTDSGDP	0.097	8.26	0.101	9.47	0.107	6.23
GDPCAP	−0.022	−4.01	−0.058	−17.26	−0.011	−1.75
LNPOP	−0.114	−7.97	−0.041	−17.12	−0.091	−4.95
CPIA or *POLICY*	0.003	0.63	0.004	0.60	0.000	0.04
BPL	0.000	0.00	0.012	1.13	−0.004	−0.56
BPLM	0.009	1.01	−0.001	−0.09	−0.008	−0.76
BPHM	0.026	2.86	0.030	2.54	0.017	1.77
CONSTANT	1.834	8.42	0.735	16.33	1.480	5.21
Obs.	848		848		484	
F-value	22.53		89.44		11.52	
R-squared			0.422			
(adjusted)						
within	0.17				0.155	
between	0.28				0.156	
overall	0.17				0.046	
χ^2						

Notes: The net transfers variable for country *i* in year *j*, NT_{ij}, comes from the World Bank *Global Development Finance*, is in US dollars and is scaled by US dollar GDP. $PVTDSGDP_{ij}$ is the present value measure of all future scheduled debt service payments relative to GDP, where the raw data also come from the World Bank *Global Development Finance*. GDP *per capita*, $GDPCAP_{ij}$, is measured in thousand dollars and comes from the IMF *International Financial Statistics*. The coefficients for *GDPCAP* are multiplied by 1,000. Population size, in logarithms, $LNPOP_{ij}$, comes from the World Bank *World Development Indicators*. *CPIA* is the policy measure from the World Bank. *Policy* is the alternative policy variable. The three debt classifications are constructed as follows: the low-debt regime constitutes those country-year observations where the country's debt–GDP ratio in that year is below 62.8 per cent; the high-debt, low-multilateral category constitutes those country-year observations where the total debt–GDP ratio is greater than 62.8 per cent and the share of multilateral debt in total debt is less than 41.2 per cent; and the high-debt, high-multilateral category constitutes those country-year observations where the total debt–GDP ratio is also greater than 62.8 per cent, but the share of multilateral debt in total debt is greater than 41.2 per cent. The bad policy dummy is if the *CPIA* for that country-year observation was less than 3 or if the alternative policy index was less than its median.

debt countries with bad policy receive about 2.5 percentage points *more* in net transfers as a share of GDP. For the other two groups, the coefficient for the bad policy dummy is not statistically significant. The 2.5 percentage points more in net transfers is itself less than the

4 percentage points reported earlier (Table 3.4). Since the earlier comparisons did not control for country characteristics, it suggests that some of the control variables partly explain the higher net transfers. The large remaining difference, equal to about one-fifth of the average net transfers all countries received over this period, nevertheless implies that in the high-multilateral debt countries, bad policy is associated with more, not fewer, net transfers. This result confirms our hypothesis that for countries highly indebted to the multilaterals, donors have not been able to practise selectivity with respect to the policies countries have adopted (and with respect to their institutional capability). Indeed, they have provided more, not fewer resources where policy has been worse. Our interpretation is that, because of the large multilateral debts, donors have allowed poor policy to continue in these countries and actually provided more resources to accommodate the larger macro-imbalances which in turn caused the higher debt stocks.

We confirm this result using a number of robustness tests. We start by reporting the ordinary least squares (OLS) regression results (Table 3.5, column (2)). The regression results have the same signs, but somewhat different statistical significance for the various control variables. The OLS results generally show stronger statistical results for the country control variables, not surprisingly since the fixed effects results control more for country differences. Again, the present value of debt–GDP has a positive statistically significant coefficient and the level of GDP *per capita* and the population size (in logs) has a statistically significant negative coefficient. The policy variable itself, *CPIA*, is again not statistically significant, suggesting that the fixed-effects estimator does not hide permanent characteristics related to the quality of countries' policy. The bad policy dummy remains statistically significant, again only for the high-multilateral debt group, and has a size implying a 3.0 percentage point difference in net transfers. Our finding is thus robust to the particular estimation technique used.

We next investigate whether using the alternative policy index changes our results. We do so again using the fixed effects regression techniques (Table 3.5, column (3)). We find that our results are weaker in terms of statistical significance, possibly because the sample is more than halved, from 884 to 484 country-year observations. The coefficient on the dummy for the countries highly indebted to multilaterals with bad policy now indicates that these countries receive some 1.7 percentage points more in net transfers and is still statistically significant at the 10 per cent level. All other policy dummies and the policy variable itself are not significant while the control variables retain their sign and significance. This result suggests that the use of a cruder policy index does not qualitatively change our main result.

As another robustness test, we investigate whether the relationship between debt and net transfers may have been affected by the occurrence of shocks and the role of arrears. Many of the countries in the sample have been faced with large terms of trade shocks, and these have been frequently cited as one of the reasons for the poor economic performance of the countries, the need for continued aid flows and the poor policy records. If GDP were to decline on a systematic basis because of these shocks, this would not be a problem in our regressions. There could be a bias in our regression results, however, if there is a relationship between shocks and debt build-up. The argument would be as follows. Say that a country faces a surprise drop in GDP and is not able to pay its debt service due. The debt–GDP ratio would rise because of the drop in GDP and the rise in debt (as arrears are being capitalized into the debt stock). The net transfers–GDP ratio will also be high because GDP is low and net transfers are possibly high due to arrears that reduce debt service paid and increases in new disbursements by creditors and donors to mitigate the impact of the shock. Since there have been quite big shocks to GDP for many of the countries in our sample, this pattern of net transfers to GDP being higher for countries and years when debt to GDP is also high could bias our coefficients. There could also be a bias through the policy response, at least as measured. If countries adjust poorly to shocks and end up with larger fiscal deficits and higher inflation, policy (as measured) could be worse when net transfers are higher. This is possible particularly for the alternative policy index that relies heavily on the budget surplus and inflation for its construction. Furthermore, donors may be more willing to accommodate poor policies when countries are faced with adverse shocks, creating a similar bias.

To check for this possibility, we estimated a trend measure of annual GDP by running for each country a simple regression of actual GDP on a time trend.[13] We then replaced actual GDP in the various ratios (NT–GDP, PVTDS–GDP and GDP *per capita*) by trend GDP as predicted by this regression. This way the ratios are not affected by any short-run shocks to GDP. We also included the deviation of GDP from trend as an additional independent variable in the regression to investigate whether net transfers respond to short-run shocks to GDP, possibly confounding the results on the policy and other variables. Table 3.6 reports the results, using again the fixed-effects regression technique.

We find that the use of the permanent level of GDP in the ratios and adding the departure from trend in each year does not change our main

Table 3.6 Net transfer regression on fitted GDP and using gross flows on actual GDP

	(1)		(2)		(3)	
	Net transfers, fixed-effect		*Gross flows, fixed-effect*		*Gross flows, OLS*	
	Coef.	*t*	*Coef.*	*t*	*Coef.*	*t*
PVTDSGDP	0.134	14.68	0.196	16.41	0.187	19.31
GDPCAP	−0.039	−6.55	−0.015	−2.71	−0.052	−17.01
LNPOP	−0.135	−9.67	−0.123	−8.4	−0.037	−17.11
RESIDUAL	0.000	1.26	na	na	na	na
CPIA	0.009	1.86	0.006	1.23	0.010	1.75
BPL	0.003	0.36	0.003	0.38	0.012	1.22
BPLM	0.012	1.43	−0.003	−0.34	−0.016	−1.5
BPHM	0.021	2.33	0.015	1.59	0.015	1.38
CONSTANT	2.125	9.98	1.939	8.76	0.655	16.11
Obs.	848		848		848	
F-value	51.55		50.22		141.96	
R-squared (adjusted)					0.538	
within	0.342		0.307			
between	0.341		0.337			
overall	0.238		0.224			

Notes: The net transfers variable for country i in year j, NT_{ij}, comes from the World Bank *Global Development Finance*, is in US dollars and is scaled by US dollar GDP. Gross flows, *GF*, is new disbursements and grant, comes from the World Bank *Global Development Finance*, is in US dollars and is scaled by US dollar GDP. $PVTDSGDP_{ij}$ is the present value measure of all future scheduled debt service payments relative to GDP, where the raw data also come from the World Bank *Global Development Finance*. GDP *per capita*, $GDPCAP_{ij}$, is measured in thousand dollars and comes from the IMF *International Financial Statistics*. The coefficients for *GDPCAP* are multiplied by 1,000. Population size, in logarithms, $LNPOP_{ij}$, comes from the World Bank *World Development Indicators*. *CPIA* is the policy measure from the World Bank. The three debt classifications are constructed as follows: the low-debt regime constitutes those country-year observations where the country's debt–GDP ratio in that year is below 62.8 per cent; the high-debt, low-multilateral category constitutes those country-year observations where the total debt–GDP ratio is greater than 62.8 per cent and the share of multilateral debt in total debt is less than 41.2 per cent; and the high-debt, high-multilateral category constitutes those country-year observations where the total debt–GDP ratio is also greater than 62.8 per cent, but the share of multilateral debt in total debt is greater than 41.2 per cent. The bad policy dummy is if the *CPIA* for that country-year observation was less than 3. In column (1) trend-fitted GDP is used to calculate the various ratios and residual is the actual deviation of GDP from trend GDP.

result. The coefficient on the bad policy dummy for the countries highly indebted to multilaterals indicates that these countries receive some 2.1 percentage points more in net transfers, which remains statistically significant at the 5 per cent level. The coefficients on the control variables *PVTDSGDP, GDPCAP* and *LNPOP* do not change much in magnitude and actually become somewhat more significant. Interestingly, the deviation from trend GDP itself, while positive, is not statistically significant. This suggests that net transfers are not being adjusted much in response to short-run shocks to GDP, and even if they are, this pattern does not affect the overall relationship that we stress – i.e., from a combination of high indebtedness and poor policy to larger net transfers. In other words, donors do not necessarily adjust net transfers in response to shocks, but rather are more willing to accommodate poor policy when multilateral debts are large. In that sense, our conclusions are reinforced.

We further confirm the importance of debt stocks in determining donors' behaviour by investigating the behaviour of gross flows, instead of net transfers. We can rewrite the left-hand side variable of (3.1) as $NT = NB + G - DS$, i.e. net transfers being new debt disbursements plus grants minus debt service. Taking into account that debt service is necessarily quite strongly related to the outstanding stock of debt, it is likely that gross flows, $NB + G$, are much more sensitive to debt stocks than net transfers are. To check for the role of debt stocks in gross flows, we replace in the base regression the dependent variable net transfers by the variable gross flows, also scaled by GDP, and rerun the regression. Table 3.6, columns (2) and (3) reports these results using fixed-effects and OLS regression techniques, respectively.

We find, as expected, that debt stocks, *PVTDSGDP*, are a very important determinant of gross flows, with a coefficient on debt stocks of 0.20, compared to 0.1 in the base regression for net transfers. This confirms that creditors and donors provide gross flows in response to debt service due – i.e. roll over gross claims, which itself is closely related to debt stocks. But there is an additional effect related to debt classification and policy that adds to this tendency to provide gross flows. While the coefficient on the bad policy dummy is less significant, it still indicates that gross flows are 1.5 percentage points higher to those countries highly indebted to multilaterals with poor policies. Again, the results suggest that donors respond perversely to debt stocks, disbursing regardless of policy and other country circumstances, and actually provide more to countries with poor policies highly indebted to multilaterals.

Finally, we show the perverse relationships between net transfers and policy in the countries highly indebted to multilaterals by plotting the simple, univariate scatter of net transfers and *CPIA* for each of the three indebtedness groups (Figure 3.2; the results of simple univariate regressions are also reported). As can be seen, only in the case of the countries highly indebted to multilaterals is there a negative relationship

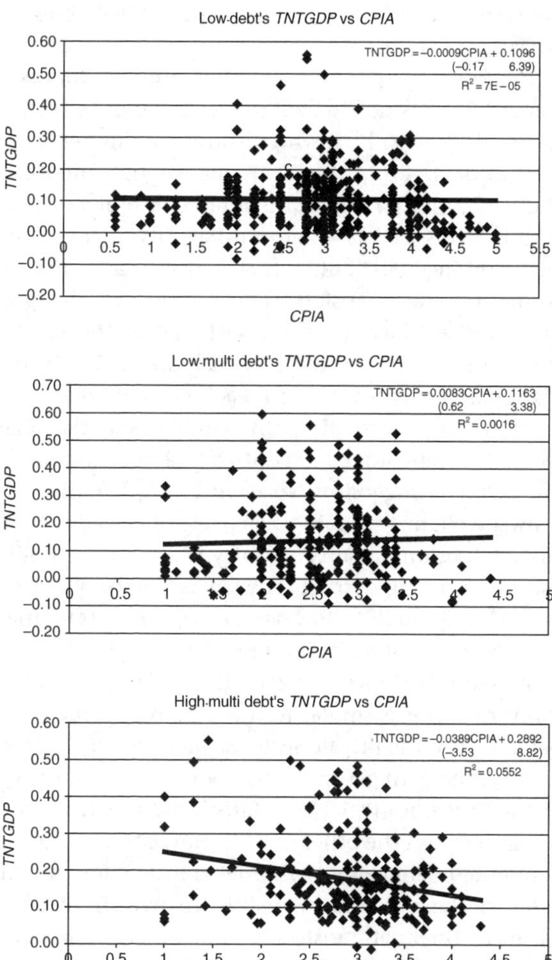

Figure 3.2 Net transfers and policy, by debtor classification

Notes: The three debt classification are constructed as follows: the low-debt regime constitutes those country-year observations where the country's debt–GDP ratio in that year is below 62.8 per cent; the high-debt, low-multilateral category constitutes those country-year observations where the total debt–GDP ratio is greater than 62.8 per cent and the share of multilateral debt in total debt is less than 41.2 per cent; and the high-debt, high-multilateral category constitutes those country-year observations where the total debt–GDP ratio is also greater than 62.8 per cent, but the share of multilateral debt in total debt is greater than 41.2 per cent.

between net transfers and *CPIA*. For the other indebtedness groups, the relationship is non-existent.

We also address the question whether among donors and creditors some are more sensitive to debt stocks and more selective to policy than others are. We do so by distinguishing among net transfers of six classes of donors or creditors: the IDA (concessional) and IBRD windows of the World Bank, the IMF, all multilaterals combined (which comprise IDA, IBRD and IMF as well as other multilaterals such as ADB and EIB), all bilaterals combined (including grants as well as loans) and private creditors (only the net transfers they provide to the governments are included). Table 3.7 shows the results, using the same regression specification as in Table 3.5 and employing the fixed-effects estimator, but running separately regressions for each class of creditor.

For the net transfers from the IDA window and the bilaterals, the coefficients for the debt stock (*PVTDSGDP*) variable are statistically significant and positive, suggesting an element of defensive lending and bargaining by the country. (Again, the effects of lagged net transfers due to some unknown or unmeasured country characteristic leading to both high debt stocks and high current transfers is less likely as we used fixed effects.) For the IBRD and IMF, however, the coefficients for the debt stock variable are statistically significant and negative, suggesting their greater concern with creditworthiness, thus cutting back new lending to more indebted countries. This is similar to the negative coefficient for the net transfers behaviour of the private sector, which can safely be assumed to be mostly concerned with getting repaid. For all multilaterals combined, the sign for the debt stock variable is statistically significant and positive, suggesting that IDA and the other multilaterals compensate for the more repayment-oriented behaviour of the net transfers for the IMF and the IBRD. Combined, these donors are mainly involved in defensive lending or otherwise relate their net transfers to some other country characteristic not controlled for yet. The coefficients for the control variables, *GDPCAP* and *LNPOP*, are generally the same as for the overall net transfers regressions, although not always statistically significant. The exception appears to be IDA, where there is a large-, rather than small-country effect.

The coefficients on the policy variable *CPIA* are statistically insignificant for the net transfers from the IBRD and bilaterals, as well as for the net transfers from the private sector. Net transfers from IDA and the IMF, and all multilaterals combined, relate in a positive way to the quality of policy, with the coefficients also statistically significant. The positive relationship for IDA may be expected as the allocation of IDA resources is explicitly linked to the quality of the policy framework. In contrast, for

Table 3.7 Fixed-effect regression (net transfer)

	IDA		*IBRD*		*IMF*		*All multilateral*		*Bilateral plus grant*		*Memo: private*	
	Coef.	*t*	*Coef.*	*t*	*Coef.*	*t*	*Coef.*	*t*	*Coef.*	*t*	*Coef.*	*t*
PVTDSGDP	0.027	12.83	−0.003	−2.38	−0.008	−3.12	0.025	5.99	0.085	9.30	−0.013	−2.57
GDPCAP	0.000	0.10	−0.001	−1.29	−0.001	−0.98	−0.003	−1.66	−0.020	−4.71	0.001	0.57
LNPOP	0.010	3.85	−0.013	−7.81	−0.013	−4.22	−0.033	−6.42	−0.048	−4.26	−0.034	−5.67
CPIA	0.002	2.54	0.001	1.30	0.003	2.46	0.006	3.59	−0.003	−0.89	0.000	0.12
BPL	−0.001	−0.62	−0.001	−1.40	0.001	0.54	−0.001	−0.18	0.002	0.35	−0.002	−0.50
BPLM	−0.004	−2.38	0.000	−0.51	0.003	1.51	0.003	1.08	0.005	0.72	0.001	0.15
BPHM	−0.001	−0.50	0.001	0.74	0.003	1.64	0.003	0.99	0.021	3.07	0.001	0.29
CONSTANT	−0.156	−4.05	0.191	7.85	0.200	4.21	0.491	6.36	0.812	4.80	0.531	5.79
Obs.	848		848		848		848		848		848	
F-value	45.93		14.62		7.12		13.95		23.53		8.98	
R-squared												
within	0.29		0.11		0.06		0.11		0.17		0.07	
between	0.00		0.09		0.00		0.21		0.34		0.07	
overall	0.07		0.02		0.00		0.05		0.27		0.01	

Notes: The net transfers variable for country *i* in year *j*, NT_{ij}, comes from the World Bank *Global Development Finance*, is in US dollars and is scaled by US dollar GDP. $PVTDSGDP_{ij}$ is the present value measure of all future scheduled debt service payments relative to GDP, where the raw data also come from the World Bank *Global Development Finance*. GDP *per capita*, $GDPCAP_{ij}$, is measured in thousand dollars and comes from the IMF *International Financial Statistics*. The coefficients for *GDPCAP* are multiplied by 1,000. Population size, in logarithms, $LNPOP_{ij}$, comes from the World Bank *World Development Indicators*. *CPIA* is the policy measure from the World Bank. *Policy* is the alternative policy variable. The three debt classifications are constructed as follows: the low-debt regime constitutes those country-year observations where the country's debt–GDP ratio in that year is below 62.8 per cent; the high-debt, low-multilateral category constitutes those country-year observations where the total debt–GDP ratio is greater than 62.8 per cent and the share of multilateral debt in total debt is less than 41.2 per cent; and the high-debt, high-multilateral category constitutes those country-year observations where the total debt–GDP ratio is also greater than 62.8 per cent, but the share of multilateral debt in total debt is greater than 41.2 per cent. The bad policy dummy is if the *CPIA* for that country-year observation was less than 3 or if the alternative policy index was less than its median.

the bilaterals, high indebtedness to multilaterals when combined with bad policy has perverse effects. The bad policy effect in case of the high-multilateral debt category for the bilaterals is economically large, some 2.1 percentage points of GDP. In the case of the IMF, there is also a positive effect on net transfers from belonging to the bad policy, high-multilateral debt countries, but it is only 0.3 percentage points and just significant at the 10 per cent level. The IDA and the IBRD, as well as all multilaterals combined, have no significant bad policy effect, and IDA actually provides fewer net transfers to bad policy countries with high debt, but a low share of multilateral debts. Since the bilaterals increase net transfers to GDP for the bad policy, high-multilateral debt countries by some 2.1 per cent, close to the total 2.5 per cent effect for all net transfers (as reported in Table 3.4), it seems that the higher net transfers going to bad policy countries is almost entirely due to the bilateral donors.[14] While we found the quantitative effects of the IMF to be small, the IMF is very important (as in the Paris Club reschedulings and donors' meetings an IMF programme is almost always required). Seemingly, the IMF provides the signal of accommodating bad policy more easily for those countries that have high debts to the multilaterals.

As a last robustness test, we ran separately for each class of indebtedness the base regression, but without the policy–debt interaction dummies, to investigate the behaviour of each creditor or donor with respect to policy for each type of country (not reported). The sample sizes vary (394 for the low-debt group, 239 for the high-debt, low-multilateral and 215 for the high-debt, high-multilateral group). We find net transfers from IDA to be significant positively related to policy for the low-debt and the high-multilateral debt group (although for the latter only at the 10 per cent level). For the net transfers from the IMF, the policy variable is only statistically significant positive for the low-multilateral debt group, while for the bilaterals the policy variable is actually statistically significant negative for the low-multilateral debt group. For all multilaterals combined, the policy variable is positive and significant for the low-debt and the low-multilateral debt groups, but not for the high-multilateral debt group. This confirms again that donors have greater difficulty being selective with respect to policy for the high-multilateral debt countries, actually act perversely, but have been able to be selective in low-debt countries.

Conclusions and implications

Net transfers remained positive over two decades in most countries of SSA, and fell only somewhat in the 1990s. With low growth in recipient countries, however, continued net transfers meant a rising stock of debt relative to output. The bilateral donors tried to minimize the resulting burden of debt service by shifting to grants and by repeated rounds of debt service relief.[15] The multilateral institutions were more restricted in ensuring repayments to themselves via new loans, since new loans would only further increase the debt burden. At the same time, the multilaterals could not accept arrears. It was the bilateral donors that were ensuring repayments to the multilaterals. Bilateral donors in effect were ensuring that some of the poorest countries would not, despite poor policy, be pushed into arrears to the multilaterals. Countries 'benefited' from this need to avoid arrears since they were able to bargain for more net transfers as their debt stocks increased. The core reason was that arrears to the multilaterals are a problem for all donors as they halt not only multilateral lending but signal the end of 'business as usual' for the other donors as well and may be seen as a failure of the development assistance business in that country. Importantly, this need to maintain net transfers came at the cost of losing selectivity with respect to country policy, especially for those countries highly indebted to multilaterals with bad policy. For these countries, the development community actually accommodated poor policies through higher net transfers.

This interpretation has important policy implications. It suggests that if debt levels are reduced enough in high-multilateral debt countries, then the behaviour of the donor community can shift into a low-debt regime mode for those countries – a regime that in the past has allowed selectivity for multilaterals, at least for IDA. Debt service reduction under HIPC (and now further enhanced under HIPC II) can thus be interpreted as a way 'out' for the donor community otherwise locked into non-selectivity in the high-multilateral debt countries.[16] Debt relief, by encouraging selectivity and changing donor behaviour for the better, can ensure more funds for countries currently indebted but with good policies. As shown by others, additional resources for countries with good policies would help enhance their growth and lead to more poverty reduction. Without additional overall donor resources, selectivity would of course imply fewer funds for countries with bad policies.[17] Ironically, the return to more selective transfers may avoid the full costs of the debt reduction programme. That will be the case if the HIPC programme is 'paid for' out of traditional donor financing, leading to lower future transfers to HIPCs or other poor countries. The fact that some of the 'grants' figures today already include official debt reduction suggests that donors see grants and debt reduction to some extent as substitutes.

At the same time, though necessary, debt reduction is far from sufficient to ensure donor selectivity. There is a need, particularly following what may become 'non-selective' debt relief, for greater emphasis on selectivity in future grants making and lending. This will require deep institutional changes on the part of the donors, in both their own bilateral programmes and in their influence on the multilaterals. Fortunately, our analysis of the past behaviour of creditors suggests that with debt reduction, this is at least possible. Donors can make the necessary break with past practice – and thus increase their contribution to the tremendous development challenges in Africa. Better donor behaviour would also set the stage for more effective development assistance in the long run and make it politically possible to convince the public in donor countries to maintain and even raise development assistance budgets.

Notes

* This chapter previously appeared in the *World Bank Economic Review*, vol. 17, no. 3 (2003). It appears here with the courtesy of Oxford University Press.

1. Burnside and Dollar (2000). The first finding is not without controversy, however, particularly regarding the robustness of the connection between 'good policy' and aid effectiveness. See, for example, Hansen and Tarp (2001). Hansen and Tarp (2000) review the literature. See further World Bank (1998) on aid effectiveness.
2. Total debt service paid also increased, from about 7 to 15 per cent of the value of exports.
3. The fact that net transfers have generally been positive has not been sufficiently taken into account in the oft-heard arguments that countries are spending more on debt service than on social programmes. Birdsall and Williamson (2002) point out that it may, however, still be true that the local taxes needed to pay debt service are not really offset by the often-tied aid transfers for specific projects.
4. Easterly (1999) develops a model to explain why countries with certain characteristics end up with high debt. His model has the strong implication that countries pursue bad policies to receive future debt reduction. The model does not examine the behaviour of the creditors to these countries, however, in relations to the debt composition.
5. The HIPC sample includes mainly SSA countries. Since also the bulk of aid flows has been going to SSA countries, we focus on the behaviour of donors in these countries.
6. This could lead to a negative relationship between net transfers and the stock of debt, since debt stocks are reduced by some amount while grants are higher, which would bias downward the coefficients on debt stock in our regression analysis of net transfers reported below. As we find positive coefficients, any misreporting only strengthens our results.
7. Obviously the ratings have an element of judgement that may be affected by specialists' separate knowledge of a country's actual or likely overall prospects;

this makes them potentially endogenous to, for example, growth, though probably less to net transfers in a particular year.

8. In the absence of any good argument for alternative weighting of the components, we use the average. Collier and Dollar (2002) show that their results regarding aid allocation and poverty are not sensitive to reweighting the components.
9. The specific equation as developed by Burnside and Dollar (2000) is: Policy = 1.28 + 6.85* Budget Surplus − 1.40* Inflation + 2.16* Openness.
10. To correct the net transfers for debt reduction is difficult, as Renard and Cassimon (2001) have documented. They write: 'We have no strong basis to suggest a percentage by which the DAC figures must be reduced to give a correct expression of the costs of debt reduction to the donors'. Still, as also noted by Renard and Cassimon, the inclusion of official debt reduction in aid would bias upward the net transfers countries actually received. At the same time, the total debt reduction figure is reported in the GDF and the debt stock is reduced by the official debt reduction. This would upward bias net transfers and downward bias *PVTDSGDP*, which would mean that the coefficient on *PVTDSGDP* would be biased downward, weakening the relationship. Besides biasing the coefficient on the debt stocks, there could be some other bias in our regression results as well. We therefore investigated whether the estimated relationship between net transfers and policy is affected in a systematic way by degree of debt reduction. Regression results (not reported) show that all estimated coefficients are robust to the inclusion of the GDF-reported debt reduction figures as another independent variable.
11. We multiply the coefficients on *GDPCAP* by 1000 for presentational purposes. As noted, poverty data are not available for long time periods, but we do have a small, cross-country sample of poverty data. When substituting poverty for *GDPCAP* for that sample, we find that countries with relatively greater poverty counts have larger net transfers.
12. While this appears to contradict other findings, this insignificance of the policy variable mainly results from the fact that we do not use the non-linear specification others have used. Collier and Dollar (2002) show that transfers (to all recipient countries) are non-monotonic with respect to the *CPIA*; they rise for a low and moderate level of *CPIA* and then decline as *CPIA* improves further. When we also allow for this non-linearity, we find that about half of the countries lie on the upward sloping and another half on the downward sloping part of the curve. This means one cannot make a general statement on the effects of policy on net transfers.
13. We thank the editor of the *World Bank Economic Review* for suggesting this methodology.
14. Similarly to the overall net transfers regression, we also conducted OLS regression. The results were essentially the same. When using our alternative policy index, we find that policy is no longer significant for any creditor or donor class. Bilaterals and IMF still transfer some 1.3 and 0.4 percentage points, respectively, more to bad policy, high-multilateral debt countries, while IDA transfers less to bad policy countries in all three indebtedness classes and IBRD transfers somewhat less to the bad policy, high-multilateral debt countries. When using the trend GDP to calculate

the ratios and adding the deviation from trend GDP as another regression variable, we find that the bilaterals transfer 1.9 percentage points more to the bad policy, high-multilateral debt countries while IDA transfers less to bad policy countries in the high-debt, low-multilateral indebtedness class. We also find some evidence of smoothing of income shocks for net transfers from IDA and IMF as the coefficients on the residual GDP are positive for these two classes. Policy remains insignificant for all classes, however, except for net transfers from private creditors, where it is positive. Finally, regression results for gross flows (instead of net transfers) as a dependent variable show that the coefficient for the debt stocks is the highest for the bilaterals and that the bilaterals provide 1.7 percentage points more in gross flows to the bad policy, high-multilateral debt countries. IDA gross flows are less to bad policy, low-multilateral debt countries, but respond positively to policy, as do IMF gross flows. All these results are not reported, but are available from the authors.

15. As some countries' GDP *per capita* fell (e.g., Côte d'Ivoire, Nigeria), some countries became eligible for cheaper IDA loans from the World Bank and concessional loans from the ADB. That also helped minimize the burden of increasing debt service.
16. The HIPC programme of debt relief will be unlikely directly to free resources in high-debt countries for spending on the poor. It has not been high-debt burdens that have constrained resources transfers: on the contrary, high-debt countries have been receiving more net transfers relative to other poor countries. In addition, of course debt reduction by itself also does not free up resources for countries when debt was effectively not being serviced to begin with. On the other hand, it is likely that in some countries transfers in the form of multiple donor projects, often tied to donor supplied services, were not a good substitute for the direct increase in revenues (via a decrease in tax-financed debt service) that debt relief provides, as discussed in Birdsall and Williamson (2002). They make a case, in well-managed countries, for the greater efficiency of debt relief as a form of aid compared to donor-financed projects.
17. The latter group could end up with reduced net transfers simply because the debt reduction will make it easier for donors and creditors to reduce what our evidence suggests is now forced defensive lending. Debt reduction can also more effectively create a virtuous circle by crowding in private flows to good policy/low debt countries (Birdsall and Williamson, 2002).

References

Alesina, A. and D. Dollar (2000). 'Who Gives Foreign Aid to Whom and Why?', *Journal of Economic Growth*, 5(1): 33–63.

Birdsall, N. and J. Williamson, with Brain Deese (2002). *Delivering on Debt Relief: From IMF Gold to a New Aid Architecture*, Washington, DC: Center for Global Development and Institute for International Economics.

Burnside, C. and D. Dollar (2000). 'Aid, Policies, and Growth', *American Economic Review*, 90(4): 847–68.

Claessens, S., E. Detragiache, R. Kanbur and P. Wickham (1997). 'Heavily-Indebted Poor Countries' Debt: Review of the Issues', *Journal of African Economies*, 6(2): 231–54.

Claessens, S., and I. Diwan (1994). 'Recent Experience with Commercial Debt Reduction: Has the "Menu" Outdone the Market?', *World Development*, 22(2): 201–13.

Collier, P. and D. Dollar (2002). 'Aid Allocation and Poverty Reduction', *European Economic Review*, 46(9): 1475–500.

Diwan, I., and D. Rodrik (1992). 'External Debt, Adjustment, and Burden Sharing: A Unified Framework', Princeton Studies in International Economics, 73, Princeton University.

Easterly, W. (1999). 'How Did Highly Indebted Poor Countries Become Highly Indebted? – Reviewing Two Decades of Debt Relief', Policy Research Working Paper 2225, Washington, DC: World Bank, Development Research Group.

Eaton, J. and R. Fernandez (1995). 'Sovereign Debt', in G. M. Grossman and K. S. Rogoff (eds), *Handbook on International Economics*, 3, North-Holland: Elsevier.

Hansen, H. and F. Tarp (2000). 'Aid Effectiveness Disputed', *Journal of International Development*, 12(3): 375–98.

Hansen, H. and F. Tarp (2001). 'Aid and Growth Regressions', *Journal of Development Economics*, 64(2): 545–68.

Renard, R. and D. Cassimon (2001). 'On the Pitfalls of Measuring Aid', WIDER Discussion Paper 2001/69, Helsinki: UNU-WIDER.

Sachs, J. and A. Warner (1995). 'Economic Reform and the Process of Global Integration', *Brookings Papers on Economic Activity*, 1: 1–118.

World Bank (various years). *Global Development Finance*, Washington, DC: World Bank.

World Bank (1998). *Assessing Aid – What Works, What Doesn't Work, and Why*, New York: Oxford University Press.

World Bank (2000). *Can Africa Claim the 21st Century*?, Washington, DC: World Bank.

4

HIPC Debt Relief and Policy Reform Incentives

Jean-Claude Berthélemy

Introduction

Towards the end of the debt crisis decade, a vast literature on the issue of debt overhang emerged, which significantly influenced policy thinking and decisions concerning debt relief programmes in favour of developing countries. In a nutshell, the argument of this literature was that too heavy a debt burden was creating disincentives in the indebted countries, which in turn impeded adjustment and reform policies. According to this analysis, debt service obligations acted as an implicit taxation on all future returns on investments and reforms, therefore limiting the willingness of governments to implement the appropriate policies needed to promote economic growth. As a consequence, high debt implied low growth and, in the absence of a major debt relief initiative, heavily indebted countries were meant to stay trapped in a low equilibrium.

In 1996, the G7, the IMF and the World Bank proposed a comprehensive debt relief approach in favour of the highly indebted poor countries (HIPCs), known as the first phase HIPC Initiative (HIPC I). It was then enhanced in 1999 at the G7 summit in Cologne (HIPC II). Enhancement not only increased its size and coverage, but also changed its nature somewhat, because of the strong emphasis put on poverty reduction policies rather than on debt relief only.

The question posed in this chapter is the following: Will the HIPC Initiative provide the incentives to implement the reform policies that are necessary to improve development prospects in HIPCs? To answer this question, I first focus on the incentive effects of pure debt relief, but it is also necessary to take into account the fact that the HIPC Initiative now includes two components: debt relief and obligations for the debtor to implement a poverty reduction programme.

Despite the emphasis put on the issue of debt overhang by the G7 in Cologne in 1999, there are some negative answers to our question. Birdsall, Claessens and Diwan (Chapter 3 in this volume), in particular, argue that the assumption of an implicit taxation effect due to debt overhang is not relevant for HIPCs, because very often these countries have received positive net transfers from creditors, rather than negative ones. Consequently, they propose a different perspective, stating that the initiative would not provide direct incentives to invest and implement reform policies in the HIPCs, but would introduce favourable incentives on the creditor side. More precisely, the HIPC Initiative, after debt relief, would permit more efficient aid policy by donors, because aid agencies could concentrate on selective financial assistance to countries implementing 'good' policies. In their words, the HIPC would end the 'debt game'.

This suggests that it is necessary to introduce into our analysis a discussion of the interaction between debt relief and good economic governance. Thus, our question has two dimensions; the first is whether the programmes proposed in the context of the HIPC Initiative can, for a given governance, improve incentives towards better adjustment and reform policies, as was explained earlier in the debt overhang literature. The answer to this first question depends on the initial quality of governance. The second dimension concerns the influence of HIPC programmes on governance. On this issue, notwithstanding the indirect impact through aid selectivity considered by Birdsall, Claessens and Diwan, I suggest that HIPC programmes contain a number of elements that may improve governance and policy-making.

The next section provides a brief discussion of the initial literature on the adverse incentives introduced by debt overhang. We go on to describe the main features of the HIPC Initiative, and discuss the differences between this initiative and pure debt relief. Then the next section elaborates on previous discussions and provides an analysis of the likely outcomes of HIPC programmes, with some emphasis on their impact on social expenditure.

The 'old' debt overhang literature revisited

In the 1980s Sachs introduced the notion that debt reduction could create favourable incentives in an indebted country (Sachs, 1989). His theory was based on the idea that too heavy a debt service burden would imply that all efforts to improve future revenues through investment and reforms would only increase future payments to the creditors, thus creating a bias towards immediate consumption of all available income and against adjustment efforts.

Several analytical models of the debt overhang effect have been proposed, in particular by Corden (1988) and Helpman (1989). Corden (1988) considers the impact of debt and debt relief on adjustment efforts by a government, supposed to be able to make welfare-maximizing decisions on the domestic allocation of resources. Implementing adjustment policy implies immediate costs such as public consumption reductions and only uncertain future benefits. A two-period framework, in which adjustment or reform policy defined in a broad sense as policies implying short-term sacrifices leading to longer-term benefits, is considered in first the period. The cost of adjustment is equivalent to an investment, which increases future (second-period) output. With very high debt service obligations, such an improvement of future output will result only in increased debt service payments rather than in more income available for consumption in the second period. Conversely, in the absence of adjustment, second-period output will remain low, which means only more arrears (or rescheduling) on debt service obligations.

Under such circumstances, debt service obligations act as an implicit tax on the proceeds of the first-period investments, collected by creditors. Consequently, no adjustment policy is implemented or it is delayed for a long time, and the economy stays trapped in a high debt–low growth equilibrium. However, if debt service obligations are reduced, at least part of the new income generated by first-period investments will be available for second-period consumption. This means that debt relief may create positive incentives to implement adjustment and reform policies. The implicit marginal taxation on the proceeds of first-period investment efforts falls to zero. This outcome, favourable to the debtor country, may be beneficial to the creditors as well if adjustment policies improve growth performance and thus the future debt service capacity of the debtor.

Following Corden, this framework can easily be expanded by introducing stochastic shocks on available income. For instance, one may assume that during good states of nature, the debtor country may be able to fully pay its debt service, while in bad states of nature it may not. If a country invests in the first period and if the second-period state of nature is favourable, then it can keep all the benefits generated by its investment. Conversely, if the second-period state of nature is unfavourable, such benefits will accrue to its creditors. Therefore, the expected implicit marginal rate of taxation of investment returns in favour of creditors is somewhere between 0 and 1. It goes down to zero only when debt service obligations, even in bad states of nature, are equal or below payment capacity. Conversely, under good states of nature, creditors, after debt relief, get fewer payments than the available maximum debt service capacity.

This discussion of the outcomes of debt relief in the presence of external shocks suggests that a once-for-all debt reduction, without indexation on the future state of nature, is sub-optimal. It would be preferable to provide higher debt relief under bad states of nature when the creditors cannot in any event collect much debt service, and less under good states of nature. I revert to this issue of the consequences of external shocks for the design of a debt relief programme in my discussion of the HIPC Initiative outcomes.

The previous framework assumes that the government can control domestic resource allocation, which is a strong assumption. However, similar properties are obtained in a framework where the private sector makes strategic decisions on resource allocation through its investment. For instance, Helpman (1989) proposed a framework where private investment is negatively influenced by future income taxation, which in turn depends on future debt service obligations.

This amounts to expanding the previous framework by considering a second-best world, where government policy instruments are minimal (the rate of taxation on private sector income). Under such circumstances, the implicit taxation effect considered by Corden becomes explicit taxation of the private sector. When government debt service obligations are high, private sector income is heavily taxed. This leads to low investment.

In this framework, the consequences of debt overhang will depend on the structure of the tax system. Economic activities that are highly taxed will be affected the most. In the case of the usual African HIPCs, these are the formal sector firms and, in some cases, primary export activities. Consequently, debt overhang in such countries may particularly discourage economic modernization as well as outward orientation.

Some authors (e.g. Borensztein, 1990, in the case of the Philippines, or Cohen, 1993, for a cross-section study) have attempted successfully to test the impact of debt stock on private investment performance by introducing a debt overhang effect in an econometric investment equation.

Reduced form estimates of the debt overhang effect have been also attempted, which relate indirect observations of debt service capacity to the debt burden borne by debtors. In this vein, Krugman (1989) has proposed considering a debt relief 'Laffer' curve, as shown in Figure 4.1.

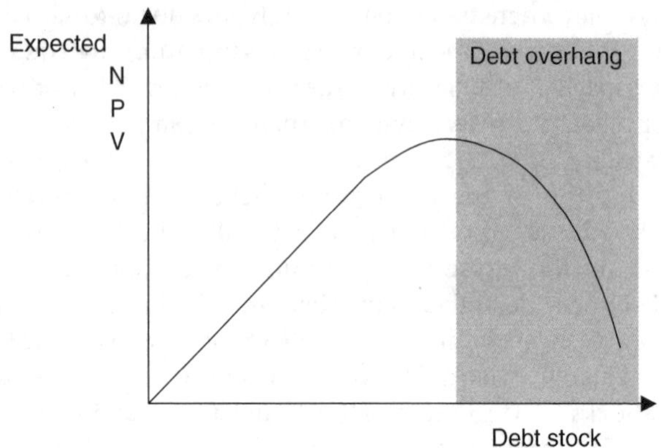

Figure 4.1 The debt relief 'Laffer' curve

In this figure the actual value of the debt stock owed by a country, defined as the present value of expected future debt service payments, becomes smaller when debts (i.e. the NPV of future debt service actually due to creditors) increase after a certain threshold. This threshold, which defines the debt overhang, corresponds to the point where adjustment/ investment disincentives created by more debt service obligations are high enough to reduce future expected debt service payments.

The emergence of a secondary market for commercial debts owed by intermediate income countries in the 1980s has provided information to test such a curve. Several authors (e.g. Cohen, 1990) have estimated equations where the secondary market price of debt (which is equivalent to the slope between the origin and any point of the debt relief 'Laffer' curve) is declining with debt indicators such as the debt–export ratio. It depends also on the country's rescheduling and arrears history. However, the data on which such equations have been estimated are very fragile, because the secondary market liquidity was in several cases very low, with only a few actual deals. Moreover, by definition, such tests can be performed only for countries owing significant debts to commercial creditors, while HIPCs are principally (when not exclusively) indebted *vis-à-vis* official creditors.

Notwithstanding these practical issues, Cohen (2000) has applied his previous secondary market price equation to an analysis of the possible outcomes of the HIPC Initiative. To this end he has computed 'notional' secondary market debt prices for countries eligible for the HIPC Initiative by simulating his equation based on pre-Brady plan Latin American debt prices. His point is that at the current level of HIPCs' debt ratios, their notional debt prices are very low. He concludes that the significance of the HIPC Initiative should, to a large extent, be scaled down in the sense that the actual cost for creditors will be very small: they will forgive debts that would have not been repaid anyhow.

Nevertheless, Cohen's computations also suggest that the HIPC Initiative should be very significant in terms of incentives for the individual debtor countries: low implicit debt prices are equivalent to very high debt overhang. Under such circumstances, the incentive impact of debt relief should be maximal.

This view is somewhat contrary to the one proposed by Birdsall, Claessens and Diwan (Chapter 3 in this volume), who argued that HIPCs, which receive on average positive net transfers from creditors, cannot suffer an implicit taxation due to their debt obligations. However, their argument is not entirely convincing. The matter of the fact is that, even though HIPCs enjoy positive net transfers, this is because they receive new aid flows corresponding to projects financed by donor agencies. In the previous analytical framework borrowed from Corden and Helpman, what counts is the amount of resources that a government can discretionarily allocate, and not the total aggregate resources that it receives. The central issue is whether projects financed by donors are truly 'owned' by the debtor government – i.e. whether this government would have decided on such an expenditure in the absence of aid flow. Recent discussions on the necessity to improve the ownership of reforms and development policies by governments in African countries suggest that the answer to this question is too often negative. As a consequence, project aid does not always add resources to the budget a debtor government can discretionarily allocate. This implies that, notwithstanding project aid flows which have reversed net transfers in favour of HIPCs, their debt service obligations may have actually created a taxation effect as assumed in earlier literature.

The Birdsall, Claessens and Diwan analysis points to another major issue, namely whether the government in place tries to implement 'good' economic policies. In the initial debt overhang literature, it was assumed that the government's objective was to maximize the nation's welfare. Within this framework, only the debt overhang disincentives can prevent implementation of the right economic policies. If the government has different objectives (e.g. protecting vested interests), the policies implemented may be the wrong ones, whatever its debt obligations. This discussion suggests that the impact of HIPC debt relief programmes cannot be assessed independently of the quality of economic governance in the debtor countries.

The HIPC Initiative

The current HIPC Initiative takes stock of previous developments in debt relief and growth literature by acknowledging that unsustainable debt and debt service obligations are counter-productive. It builds also on the experience gained in the early 1990s with the Brady initiative, which proposed an ambitious debt relief plan in favour of the heavily indebted middle-income countries and had been instrumental in the resolution of the Latin American debt crisis.

The Brady approach of the early 1990s was not adapted to the HIPCs, because their debts were principally due to multilateral and bilateral official creditors, and could not be handled the same way as commercial debts. The Paris Club provided more and more generous debt relief on bilateral official debts, but this – for lack of a comprehensive treatment of debt obligations – was not sufficient to eliminate their debt overhang. A large part of HIPCs' debts had been contracted after the Paris Club cut-off dates and in several countries most of the debts were due to multilateral rather than to bilateral institutions. By comparison, resolving the commercial debt issue in the Brady plan countries was very close to providing a comprehensive debt relief programme.

In 1996, the G7, the IMF and the World Bank proposed a comprehensive debt relief approach, known as the first phase HIPC Initiative (HIPC I). The initiative was then reinforced and accelerated in 1999 at the G7 summit in Cologne (HIPC II).

The objective of the current HIPC Initiative is to cut the total debt stock (in net present value) owed by eligible countries to 150 per cent of their exports. A second threshold is considered for economies that are very open to external trade, where the maximum sustainable debt is considered equivalent (in NPV) to 250 per cent of fiscal revenue.

These thresholds are defined at the decision point, and determine the amount of debt relief received during an interim period and at the completion point, whatever the future evolution of export and fiscal incomes of the beneficiary country. By comparison, in a few instances, debt relief programmes proposed in the early 1990s in the context of the Brady initiative introduced a somewhat more sophisticated approach, which made the final size of debt relief conditional on future exogenous events. This was the case for Mexico, whose debt reduction plan contained a 'recapture clause', stating that Mexico would have to increase payments to its former creditors in the event of a future improvement in oil prices. This kind of recapture clause may play a useful role in adapting the post-relief debt service to future external shocks. By comparison, under the HIPC Initiative, the existence of future external shocks is ignored, while eligible countries are usually subject to very wide variations in their terms of trade, and in their agricultural primary export volumes as well.

Under the enhanced HIPC Initiative, a HIPC programme means not only debt reduction, it also implies that the beneficiary government must agree to allocate the amount of money saved on debt service to well-specified projects. With this obligation, the HIPC Initiative directly imposes the issue of good economic governance: before granting debt relief to a specific country, one first wants to ensure that the country in question will use the proceeds of debt relief for the 'right' objectives. Such a concern was already present in the first phase of the HIPC Initiative, insofar as countries had (and still have) to show a good track record before reaching the decision point, as well as the completion point. Now, however, it plays a much greater role.

This policy conditionality is specified in the PRSP that the government has to prepare in consultation with the various stakeholders before reaching the completion point of the HIPC debt reduction programme (and a preliminary PRSP is required before the decision point). In some countries (e.g. Uganda, Chad), the proceeds of debt relief are registered in a 'virtual account', which finances commitments specified in the PRSP. These expenditures usually cover education, health services and basic infrastructure.

At this stage, two particular features of the current HIPC Initiative need to be stressed. First, it specifically introduces distributional policy objectives that go beyond the mere conditioning of the decision and completion points on good economic governance. This point must not be overdone, however, insofar as investment for the future will, in many cases, create positive outcomes for the poor. In analytical terms, such conditionality on a poverty reduction programme is not much different from the one on good economic policy making. As a matter of fact, many PRSPs mention strong economic growth as the first and essential condition for poverty reduction. It has, however, practical consequences in focusing public spending programmes on social expenditure and other policy measures aimed at fighting poverty.

In this sense, the HIPC Initiative is comparable more to the 'debt for development' swaps introduced, usually by NGOs, in the 1990s than to pure debt relief. In such deals, debt was repurchased to private or official creditors (at a price below its face value) and then cancelled in exchange for government expenditure commitments to favour identified development goals (such as environment protection projects). The major difference, however, is that the HIPC Initiative is comprehensive, while debt swaps were implemented on a small scale and thus could not be considered as possible solutions to a debt overhang.

Second, HIPC programmes may, particularly through the preparation of PRSPs, have a positive institutional development impact. In several countries, the PRSP has created the first opportunity for dialogue between the government and citizens on development objectives. They may also facilitate time-consistent efforts towards development objectives, insofar as they represent irreversible long-term aid commitments, and stronger ownership of development policies by debtor governments. HIPC programmes also play a useful role in capacity-building. In some cases, the budgetary procedures set up for allocating proceeds from debt service relief have a positive influence on a government's fiscal rules and procedures. In addition, the preparation of the PRSP has, in many instances, led to new initiatives to launch poverty surveys, which had been overlooked for a long time.

To sum up, the HIPC Initiative is not simply a comprehensive debt relief programme, it also creates new development policy commitments and, occasionally, new budgetary rules for beneficiary governments.

Will the HIPC Initiative create the right incentives?

The answer to this question depends critically on the initial policy stance of the government. If already committed to poverty reduction or to good economic governance before the HIPC programme, at least some of the poverty alleviation expenditures identified in the PRSP will already have been budgeted. In these 'virtuous' countries, HIPC programmes would release resources for free utilization in the government budget because some poverty reduction projects would, in any event, have been implemented. Thus, the consequences of HIPC programmes can be analysed along the lines of our previous discussion of the policy incentive impacts of pure debt relief.

In these cases, one can predict the consequences of debt relief on the structure of public expenditure to be minimal, or at least less dramatic than in countries not initially committed to poverty alleviation. In view of the poverty reduction emphasis of the HIPC programmes, looking at their expected impact on social expenditure could provide a relevant proximate indicator of such consequences.[1]

To test the hypothesis that the impact of HIPC programmes will depend on the quality of initial economic governance also requires identifying the 'virtuous' countries, not a straightforward task.

However, a good proxy can be found in the dates when the different countries reached their HIPC decision point. Early programmes were granted to countries implementing good policies; the lengthy negotiations before reaching the decision point can be linked mostly to situations where economic governance initially was not considered entirely satisfactory.[2]

In Figure 4.2, I have grouped the countries reaching decision point before April 2001 into three sub-sets: (i) first-phase countries, i.e. countries entering the HIPC Initiative in its first phase before the 1999 enhancement decision;[3] (ii) countries reaching their decision point between January and June 2000;[4] and (iii) other countries.[5] Figure 4.2 shows clearly that on average late-comers are committed – or at least are expected by the IMF and the World Bank – to increase their social expenditure much more than others. For the three country groups, the average rate of change in social expenditure is 37, 45 and 63 per cent, respectively.

Moreover, as suggested by Figure 4.3, the implicit elasticity of social expenditure to debt service reduction is expected to be much higher in late-comers than in other countries. On average, debt service will decline by 34, 26 and 19 per cent, respectively, in the first, second and

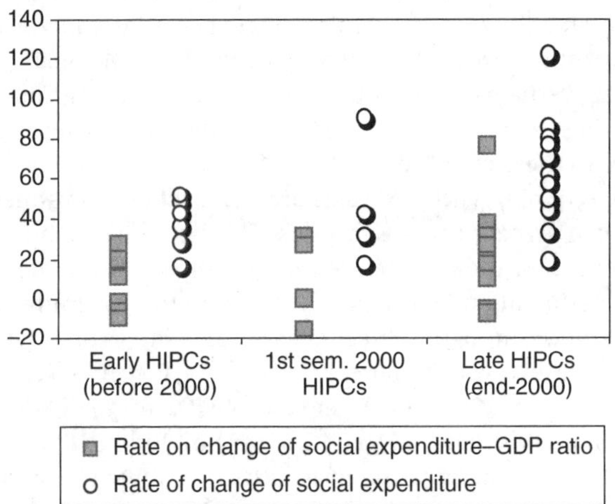

Figure 4.2 Expected growth of social expenditure, 1999–2002

Note: 'Early HIPCs' are countries which reached the decision point of the HIPC Initiative before 1 January 2000; '1 sem. 2000' are countries who reached the decision point during the first semester of 2000; 'Late HIPC'= after 31 June 2000.

Sources: Based on IMF and World Bank (2001b).

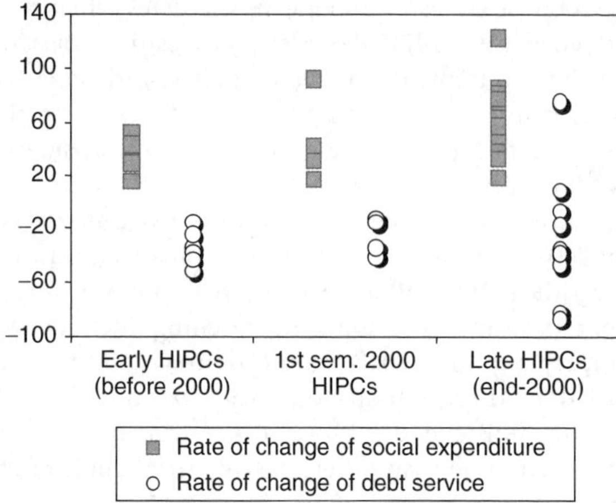

Figure 4.3 Expected growth of social expenditure vs decline of debt service, 1999–2002
Sources: Based on IMF and World Bank (2001b).

third group of countries, while the ranking of their social expenditure rates of growth will be the other way round. This confirms that a higher proportion of debt relief proceeds will be earmarked to social expenditure in countries with initially worse economic governance.[6]

These observations tend to confirm our expectation that the impact of HIPC programmes on public spending depends on the quality of initial economic governance, with 'virtuous' countries having much greater free will. This suggests that our standard debt overhang theory may apply only to these countries.

But precisely put, 'virtuous' cases are those where adjustment incentive issues are perhaps the least serious. The fact remains, however, that in such countries, the debt burden is still, or was before debt relief, a drag on investment and growth, be it through the government budgetary constraint or through indirect negative incentives on private investments. Private investment rates are still very low in several of these countries; between 12.5 and 13 per cent of GDP for Mali, Mozambique and Uganda in 2000 (and below 11 per cent in Burkina Faso), while the average rate of private investment for Africa as a whole was close to 14 per cent. This suggests that these countries should be able to reap some indirect benefits from the HIPC Initiative in the future. In fact, recent estimates show that private investment increased after implementation of the HIPC debt relief – in Uganda, the private investment rate was close to 14 per cent in 2002.[7]

Conversely, in countries lacking a previous political commitment to good economic governance and poverty reduction, no adjustment and reform incentives will be created by the HIPC debt relief as such. Moreover, no reduction of taxes on the formal sector will be feasible in the short to medium term (the poor are usually outside the formal sector), which means that it will continue to bear a heavy tax load. This may create future disillusion, which will later impact negatively on private sector behaviour. In Chad, for instance, private sector representatives expected the principal outcome of the HIPC programme would be a reduction in taxation, but this is very unlikely, given that it will not ease the budget constraint of the government.

If these countries were exempt from external shocks, this would not be a big issue. In any event, be it through debt relief incentives or through the PRSP implementation, development expenditure would be realized more readily after HIPC programmes than before.

However, external shocks will affect the outcome of the HIPC programmes. This issue, already mentioned, will be particularly sensitive for countries with poor initial economic governance. In bad states of nature, the government will have to continue to spend debt relief proceeds on projects identified in the PRSP, even though the country will be in no better position to pay its remaining debt service – no more than prior to the HIPC programme was it able to pay its full debt service in bad states of nature. Temporary fiscal difficulties leading to high risks of domestic or external arrears will reemerge, and the debtor government will need some form of exceptional financial assistance. Therefore, in many instances, aid agencies may be faced with the obligation of providing new finance again or rescheduling at concessional conditions to avoid failure of the HIPC programme.

In good states of nature, debtor policy makers will have money available for investments and adjustment measures that could protect them later during occurrences of bad states of nature. But if they do not implement such policies and simply consume their windfall gains, they may receive more exceptional financing in bad states of nature. Again, for all practical purposes, the return on investment and fiscal adjustment measures will be implicitly taxed during future occurrences of bad states of nature.

One solution to this issue would be to make HIPC debt reduction conditional on the state of nature; during bad states, debt service obligations should be reduced or cancelled, or increased during good states of nature, or both. This would require, however, advance definition of the circumstances which would constitute good or bad states of nature. For oil-exporting countries, a proxy could be based on the evolution of oil prices (and possibly oil output), similar to the recapture clause of the Mexican Brady deal. But it would be impossible to foresee all possible circumstances for all countries that could be considered as good or bad states of nature. Furthermore, such clauses would be politically difficult to implement, because they could be interpreted by public opinion as a sort of confiscation of windfall gains by the donors to the detriment of poor debtors.

Another, albeit second-best, solution would be to earmark windfall gains obtained during good states of nature to PRSP projects, in order to ascertain that such incomes were not wasted. Therefore, the PRSP virtual account or its equivalent would receive more than the mere proceeds of debt relief in good states of nature, and it could receive less in bad states of nature. This kind of scheme can be found partially in the case of Chad, where in the context of its negotiations to reach the HIPC decision point at the end of 2000, the government agreed to earmark all its future income generated by oil production[8] to poverty reduction projects identified in the PRSP. More specifically, the HIPC decision point was reached only after the creation of the 'Collège de Contrôle et de Surveillance des Revenus Pétroliers', which was given the authority to ensure that all Chad's future oil income (and not only debt service relief proceeds) be spent on poverty eradication as specified in the PRSP.

Conclusion

The HIPC Initiative is a major improvement in the treatment of debt issues in poor countries. It recognizes that comprehensive debt reduction is a necessary condition for economic and social progress in HIPCs.

The HIPC Initiative also recognizes that not all debtor governments are initially committed to good economic governance. If for this reason only, pure debt relief is far from being the panacea for the countries concerned. Taking this into account, a major feature of the HIPC Initiative is that it combines debt relief with conditionality on poverty reduction policies.

In countries with good economic governance, the HIPC programme will work more or less as expected in the debt overhang theory, so that debt relief creates positive incentives for more investment and reform. But these are the good cases, not the countries where such positive changes are needed the most.

In countries with dismal economic governance, poverty reduction conditions linked to the HIPC Initiative change its nature. It will work much less as debt relief than as a multi-year programme of aid flows targeted to poverty reduction projects. This may have favourable outcomes, because it will avoid debt relief proceeds being wasted, and will increase social expenditure. However, the indirect incentive gains of HIPC programmes will be minimal in such countries. To solve this issue at least partially, more attention should be paid to the treatment of external shocks: debt service and public expenditure obligations of the debtor governments should be made conditional on the state of nature. Original and politically feasible institutional arrangements that would mimic this could be founded in procedures set up to earmark windfall gains enjoyed in good states of nature to the PRSP virtual account.

The HIPC programmes also contain a number of elements that may strengthen, through the preparation and implementation of PRSPs, institutional-building. Such institutional improvements should be a major long-term positive outcome of HIPC programmes, beyond the medium-term adjustment and investment consequences considered in this chapter.

Notes

1. As shown by IMF/World Bank (2001a), tracking the impact of HIPC programmes on public spending policies within the existing budget management systems is almost impossible, and one has to rely on crude approximations to get an idea of this impact.
2. A counter-example is Ghana, because this country decided only lately to apply for HIPC debt relief. Since Ghana had not yet reached the decision point in 2001, this does not affect results shown.
3. Bolivia, Burkina Faso, Guyana, Mali, Mozambique and Uganda. Côte d'Ivoire is excluded because after having reached an early decision point in the first phase of the HIPC initiative, it was unable to reach either a completion point in the first phase or a decision point in the second phase until 2002.
4. Honduras, Mauritania, Senegal and Tanzania.
5. Benin, Cameroon, Gambia, Guinea, Guinea Bissau, Madagascar, Malawi, Nicaragua, Niger, Rwanda, São Tomé and Zimbabwe.
6. Only an elasticity approach, rather than a direct comparison of debt relief and social expenditure increase is relevant since (i) the definition of social expenditure differs among countries and (ii) the new priority given to poverty reduction implies that social expenditure increases more than the debt relief proceeds.
7. *Sources*: *African Economic Outlook 2002/03*, African Development Bank and OECD.
8. Due to start in 2003 or 2004, thanks to the development of the Doba oil field.

References

Borensztein, E. (1990). 'Debt Overhang, Debt Reduction and Investment: The Case of the Philippines', IMF Working Paper WP/90/77, Washington, DC: IMF.

Cohen, D. (1990). 'Debt Relief: Implications of Secondary Market Discounts and Debt Overhangs', *World Bank Economic Review*, 4: 43–53.

Cohen, D. (1993). 'Low Investment and Large LDC Debt in the 1980s', *American Economic Review*, 83: 437–49.

Cohen, D. (2000). 'The HIPC Initiative: True and False Promises', OECD Development Centre Technical Paper 166, Paris: OECD.

Corden, W. M. (1988). 'Debt Relief and Adjustment Incentives', *IMF Staff Papers*, 35(4): 628–43.

Helpman, E. (1989). 'Voluntary Debt Reduction – Incentives and Welfare', *IMF Staff Papers*, 36(3): 580–611.

IMF (International Monetary Fund) and World Bank (2001a). 'Tracking of Poverty-Reducing Public Spending in Heavily Indebted Poor Countries (HIPCs)', Washington, DC: IMF and World Bank, March.

IMF (International Monetary Fund) and World Bank (2001b). 'Heavily Indebted Poor Countries (HIPC) Initiative: Status of Implementation', Washington, DC: IMF and World Bank, April.

Krugman, P. (1989). 'Market-Based Debt-Reduction Schemes', in J. Frenkel (ed.), *Analytical Issues in Debt*, Washington, DC: IMF, 258–78.

Sachs, J. D. (1989). 'The Debt Overhang of Developing Countries', in G. Calvo, R. Findlay, P. Kouri and J. Braga de Macedo (eds), *Debt, Stabilization and Development: Essays in Memory of Carlos Diaz-Alejandro*, Oxford: Basil Blackwell for UNU-WIDER, 80–102.

5

Resolving the HIPC Problem: Is Good Policy Enough?*

Tony Addison and Aminur Rahman

Introduction

Unless we understand, and act upon, the causes of the present HIPC problem, its recurrence is almost certain.[1] Poor countries, and poor people, will be condemned to live through repeated cycles of borrowing, default and recession. But this is easier said than done. The voluminous literature on debt relief emphasizes everything from bad policy to terms of trade shocks to political instability to globalization. Depending on one's personal preferences (and biases) you can 'pick and mix' virtually any combination of explanatory factors.

One way to start cutting through this jumble of potential causes is to return to a fundamental idea, namely that the decision to borrow, and the choice of what to do with the loan, is intimately linked to the rate of *time preference* of the borrower (or, put another way, the rate at which the future is *discounted* relative to the present). This in turn drives resource exchanges across time, and thus the current account position and other macroeconomic identities (Buiter, 1981; Obstfeld and Rogoff, 1996: 1).

This is the approach taken by Easterly (2002) in seeking to explain why debt problems occur, and why they persist:

> A country that has gotten an 'excessive' external debt may be one with a high discount rate against the future ... After receiving debt relief, the high discount rate country would like to accumulate the same amount of external debt again.
>
> (Easterly, 2002: 1680)

But what causes such a high discount rate? Easterly (2002) offers a number of possibilities, ranging from high rates of pure time preference (rooted in the shorter expected lifetimes of the populations of poor countries) to politicians with very short time horizons, leading to excessive (debt-financed) current spending without concern to future debt service. He finds that average policies in HIPCs were generally worse than those of other LDCs, controlling for income, over the period 1980–97. Easterly (2002) concludes that governments impose their high discount rates on the rest of society through bad macroeconomic policy, leading to debt service problems. This result supports the IMF and World Bank focus on a country's track record of policy reform, and the use of 'good policy' as a key criterion for eligibility for debt relief.

Building on Easterly's framework this chapter offers a somewhat different explanation of how time horizons shorten and how this causes debt problems. We argue that the root cause is a decline in the formal and informal institutions – 'rules of the game' in the sense of North (1997) – which govern competition between social groups (which may be formed along ethnic, regional or other dimensions). Opportunistic behaviour then becomes rife, encompassing both high- and low-state actors. This manifests itself in a shortening of the government's time horizon (the bad policy effect in Easterly, 2002).

But in addition we argue that opportunistic behaviour also rises within and between communities together with the larger private sector. Rising uncertainty then affects their investment decisions as their time horizons shorten. They move out of sectors that yield their returns in the longer term (for instance, tropical cash crops) and switch into sectors with more immediate returns (subsistence agriculture and commerce). The former are largely tradables, the latter are largely non-tradables.

The tradables base of the economy, and its capacity to produce foreign exchange to service external debt, is therefore squeezed from *two* directions. It is squeezed by real exchange rate over-valuation and other bad policy (the consequence of the government's rising discount rate) *and* the direct investor uncertainty effect (the consequence of a rising discount rate among communities and the private sector). Our empirical analysis finds that this investor uncertainty effect is more important in explaining whether a country is a HIPC or not than bad policies (which are only weakly significant once investor uncertainty and the tropical nature of HIPC tradables is controlled for). Bad policy and investor uncertainty arise from the same cause, unregulated social competition.

Hence, rectifying policy failure is insufficient to resolve the HIPC crisis (our conclusion). Fundamentally, it requires institution-building, including democratization, to provide a better framework of rules for social competition (in particular to take the 'edge' off ethnic conflict). If this is successful, then the time horizons of communities, the private sector and governments will lengthen, contributing to a recovery of tradables production, growth and the avoidance of debt crisis. This alone will not solve the HIPC crisis – constraints such as limited infrastructure and low human capital must be overcome – but it is an essential prerequisite.

A conceptual framework

Competition between social groups – differentiated along ethnic, religious, class and regional lines – occurs within all societies. Societies that are stable today invested heavily in institutions (rules of the game) that resolve competition (over resources, employment and markets) in a peaceable manner (Addison and Murshed, 2001). With few exceptions, the HIPCs are young nations (32 of the 41 achieved independence after 1957). Many inherited institutional weakness at independence. Their subsequent institutional investment was characterized by repeated setbacks, and undermined by negative economic growth. As a result, many areas of economic life are increasingly unregulated by any proper rules of the game. The formal rules are weak (e.g. ineffective legal systems) and the informal rules have buckled under prolonged recession and environmental stress (examples include Côte d'Ivoire, Guinea-Bissau, Kenya and Nigeria).[2] And in 11 of the 41 HIPCs, unregulated social competition eventually degenerated into outright civil war – the case in the DRC, for instance.[3]

With weak formal rules, and opportunistic behaviour rising, individuals increasingly depend on their 'ethnic capital' (Azam, 2001). Evidence exists that ethnic fragmentation can lead to poor policies (Easterly and Levine, 1997), adversely affect public goods provision (Alesina, Baqir and Easterly, 1999; Miguel, 1999), and encourages corruption (Mauro, 1995). State actors, both high- and low-level, look to their ethnic capital and reduce their investment in maintaining government institutions, including the policy making apparatus. Still, the effect of ethnic fragmentation is tempered when democracy and other formal rules constrain behaviour. Thus Collier (2001) finds that ethnic diversity does not reduce growth in full democracies, but it reduces growth by up to 3 percentage points in dictatorships. The former appears to be better than the latter at regulating social competition along ethnic lines.

It is not only the discount rates of state actors that rise as social competition becomes unregulated, this is also true for communities and the larger

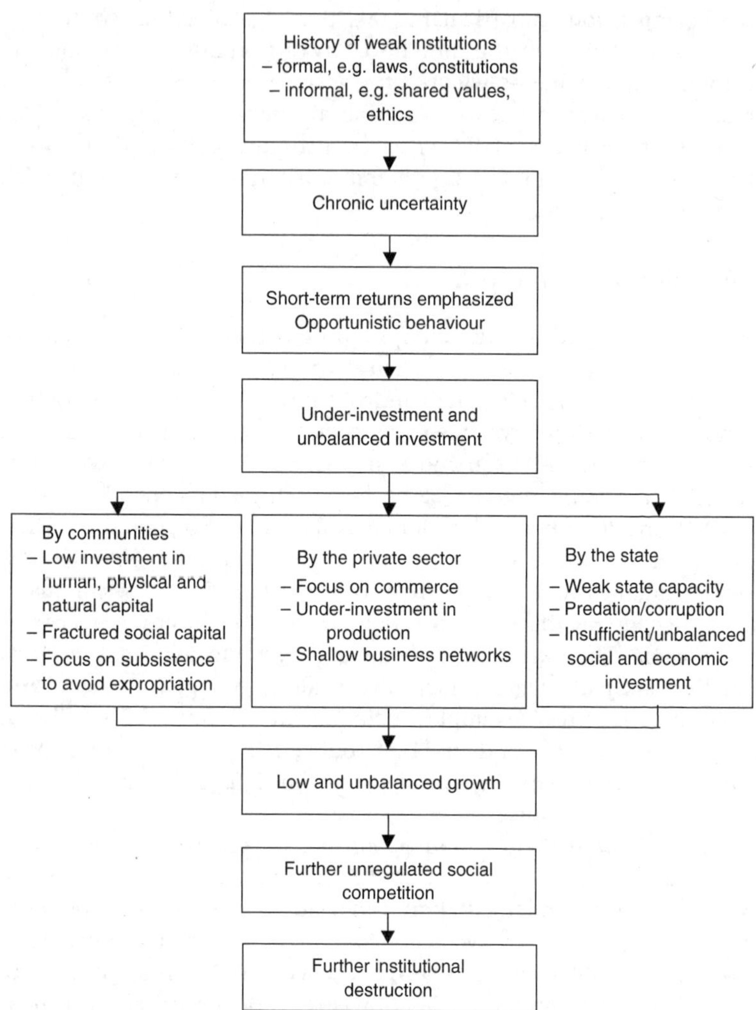

Figure 5.1 The investor uncertainty effect
Source: Addison (2003: 7).

private sector (see Figure 5.1 adapted from Addison, 2003). Uncertainty raises their discount rates and lowers their rates of investment. And it also distorts their pattern of investment (we refer to the latter as the *investor uncertainty* effect of unregulated social competition).

To see why consider the following from Addison and Murshed (2001). The net present value (*NPV*) of a private investment project in sector *i*, producing an output Q_i selling at a price P_i is given by (5.1). Rising and unregulated social competition raises transactions costs (σ) due to the increasing difficulty of enforcing contracts, either formally or informally.[4] It also raises production costs (C) due to reduced sanctions on theft. And unregulated social competition raises uncertainty about the future, and therefore increases the private discount rates of potential investors (r):

$$NPV_i = \frac{\sum_t Q_i(P_i - \sigma_i) - C_i}{(1+r)^t} \tag{5.1}$$

All three effects reduce aggregate investment. But the rise in r also has a larger effect on investment in tradables as compared to non-tradables.[5] This arises from the difference in the time-profile of private benefits and costs associated with each activity. HIPC non-tradables consist of subsistence food crops and services, while tradables typically consist of 'permanent' crops such as cocoa, coffee, tea and bananas. Non-tradables yield their returns in a year, requiring little or no fixed capital beyond working capital. In contrast, permanent crops 'embody large amounts of capital per worker because of the time needed to grow them from seeds to fruit-producing plants' (Leamer and Schott, 1999: 11). Therefore the tradables producer faces a much longer time horizon (5 years for tree crops) than in non-tradables, and a larger initial physical capital investment (whereas non-tradables require mostly working capital). Accordingly, any rise in the private rate of discount will reduce investment in tradables by proportionately more than non-tradables.[6]

The interaction between investor uncertainty and the decision to produce agricultural tradables throws further light on the apparent role of a tropical location in explaining poor economic performance, particularly in SSA, as found by Sachs and Warner (1995). The literature on this issue emphasizes the impact of a high incidence of disease, high transport costs and the high costs of developing new technologies for tropical agriculture on the economic performance of tropical countries (Hausmann, 2001). Investor uncertainty, rooted in rising social competition – particularly over valuable natural resources – may be another reason for this poor performance (39 out of 41 HIPCs are in the tropical category).

In summary, rising investor uncertainty associated with unregulated social competition shifts production incentives in favour of non-tradables, an effect that is entirely independent of the fall in the relative price of tradables to non-tradables associated with an over-valued real exchange rate and other policy failure. Foreign exchange generation, and the ability to service debt, is according squeezed from *two* sides; bad policy and investor uncertainty, both rooted in the same fundamental cause – rising and unregulated social competition. We now turn to estimating the relative weight of these two sets of effects on the probability of becoming a HIPC.

The determinants of indebtedness: an empirical investigation

The empirical model

Our sample includes all the developing countries for which relevant data are available.[7] The potential explanatory variables fall into two broad categories. First, macroeconomic and policy variables such as: the inflation rate; a measure of the black market foreign exchange premium; a measure of financial repression/development; government consumption; and the fiscal deficit (excluding grants). These are the variables most often used by the 'getting policies right' paradigm.[8] The second set of variables are social and structural, to capture the investor uncertainty effects. These are: ethno-linguistic fragmentation; polity (autocratic to democratic political systems); geographical location (whether or not the country lies in the tropical zone); the share of trade in GDP, and the terms of trade (to capture vulnerability to adverse terms of trade shocks, etc.).[9]

We estimate probit models to see how different variables contribute to the probability of becoming a HIPC over the period 1960–99. We use the mean value of different explanatory variables over the period, as we are interested in the long-run fundamentals rather than mere short-run fluctuations.

Macroeconomic and policy variables

Poor policies are frequently identified as the key to becoming a HIPC (and they were similarly cited as critical to Latin America's debt crisis in the 1980s). We therefore start with this issue. Table 5.1 provides a summary and comparison of the mean values of the main macroeconomic and policy indicators of HIPC and non-HIPC developing countries and developed countries since 1960.

This shows a mixed picture. Government consumption over 1960–99 was lower in HIPCs compared to developing and developed countries.

Table 5.1 Macroeconomic and policy indicators of HIPC vs non-HIPC developing and developed countries, 1960–99

Variable	*HIPC*	*Non-HIPC developing countries*	*Developed countries*
Government consumption (% of GDP)	14.77	17.38	17.64
Average rate of inflation	114.52	84.95	7.5
Fiscal deficit (excluding capital grants)	−7.90	−4.82	−2.76
Openness	57.75	80.09	85.77
Official exchange rate to parallel exchange rate ratio	0.89	0.90	1.00
M2 as a % of GDP	13.17	21.88	53.30

And the ratio of the official exchange rate to the parallel exchange rate in HIPCs was not significantly different from other countries. On the other hand, the inflation rate was higher and the level of financial development/liberalization and openness (proxied by the share of trade in GDP) were lower in HIPC economies than in non-HIPC developing economies.

We now examine whether the divergence in these policy variables affects a developing country's probability of becoming a HIPC. The probit estimates of the marginal effect of each and all of these macroeconomic and policy variables, with the corresponding level of statistical significance, are presented in Table 5.2.

As can be seen from Table 5.2, most of the policy indicators highlighted in the 'good policy' paradigm do not significantly affect the probability of being a HIPC country. Among the various policy variables, only the effect of fiscal deficit and a measure of financial development/liberalization seem to be statistically significant (Model 7 in Table 5.2). Quantitatively, an infinitesimal increase in the fiscal deficit will increase the probability of being a HIPC by 0.045 points, while the increase in the level of financial development will reduce the corresponding probability by 0.065 points. When entered together, none of the other policy variables seem to be significant determinants in explaining the probability of being a HIPC, although when each of these variables is entered separately in the probit Models 1–6, openness – even though it appears as a statistically significant variable – has virtually nil economic significance. Although government consumption appears to be significant at the 10 per cent level (Model 1) it has a negative sign.

Table 5.2 The marginal effects of policy variables (evaluated at corresponding sample mean) on the probability of a developing country being a HIPC

Dependent variable: HIPC dummy, 1 = HIPC country, 0 = non-HIPC developing country

Explanatory variables	*Model 1*	*Model 2*	*Model 3*	*Model 4*	*Model 5*	*Model 6*	*Model 7*
Government consumption	−0.011*						0.027
	(−1.79)						(1.36)
Inflation rate		0.00					0.00
		(0.61)					(1.17)
Fiscal deficit (excluding grants)			−0.015**				−0.045***
			(−2.39)				(−2.60)
Official exchange rate to parallel exchange rate ratio				−0.047			0.559
				(−0.27)			(1.52)
M2 % of GDP					−0.036***		−0.065***
					(−3.33)		(−3.50)
Openness						−0.004***	0.003
						(−3.43)	(0.94)
No. observations	144	126	116	140	73	147	65
Wald χ^2	3.22	0.38	5.73	0.79	11.09	11.76	21.71

Note: Heteroscedasticity-corrected *Z*-statistics are in parentheses:

* Significant at 10% level.

** Significant at 5% level.

*** Significant at 1% level.

Table 5.3 Ethno-linguistic fractionalization and polity score of HIPC vs non-HIPC developing and developed countries

Variable	*HIPC*	*Non-HIPC developing countries*	*Developed countries*
Ethno-linguistic fractionalization, 1960	60.95	38.35	21.55
Polity score, average 1960–99	−4.55	−0.85	6.71
Tropical dummy	39 tropical countries (out of 41)	56 tropical countries (out of 115)	16 tropical countries (out of 53)

Ethnic fragmentation, polity and tropical location

As discussed previously, investor uncertainty, associated with increasingly unregulated social competition, can reduce tradables production and undermine debt service. And poor policies can be a symptom or outcome of this deeper social problem. We therefore investigate to what extent factors such as ethnic fragmentation, polity and a tropical dummy – all factors associated with investor uncertainty – influence the probability of becoming a HIPC.

Table 5.3 presents the mean value of ethno-linguistic fractionalization in 1960 (which measures the probability that two randomly selected people from a given country will not belong to the same ethno-linguistic group). Table 5.3 also includes the polity score average for 1960–99 (ranging from −10 (implying strongly autocratic) to 10 (implying strongly democratic)). Finally, the number of tropical countries for each category – HIPC, non-HIPC developing and developed countries – is presented.

The ethnic fragmentation index is much higher, while the polity score is much lower, in HIPCs as compared to the non-HIPC developing countries (and the corresponding values for the non-HIPC developing countries are also unfavourable compared to the developed countries). Moreover, while 56 out of 115 non-HIPC developing countries are tropical, 39 out of 41 HIPCs belong to the tropical category. Only 16 countries out of 53 developed countries belong to the tropical category.

Thus it is reasonable to assume that the problems associated with ethnic fragmentation, poor polity and tropical location are much worse in HIPCs as compared to non-HIPC developing and developed countries. To investigate further we estimate probit models to see how these factors affect the probability of a developing country being a HIPC. The marginal effects, along with the corresponding level of statistical significance, are presented in Table 5.4.

From Models 1–3, we can see that the effect of each of these factors on the probability of a being a HIPC is highly significant. Quantitatively, an infinitesimal increase in the ethnic fragmentation index will increase the probability of being a HIPC by 0.01 points, while the probability of being a HIPC decreases by 0.03 points due to an infinitesimal increase in the polity score. If a developing country is a tropical country, then its probability of being a HIPC will increase by 0.38 points. The interaction between social competition (ethnicity) and tropical location – through the impact of investor uncertainty on the production of agricultural tradables – may be the more important link between a tropical location and HIPC status than weakness in the terms of trade of producers of tropical tradables (which we find is insignificant, as does Easterly, 2002).

In Model 4, when we enter all these three factors, each of them still remains significant. However, the level of statistical significance of the ethnic fragmentation coefficient goes down at the 10 per cent level after controlling for the polity and tropical dummy. This finding is consistent with more recent studies on ethnic fragmentation (Collier, 2001) that the adverse effect of ethnicity is reduced in democracies, while it rises in autocracies. In order to explore this issue further, we interact ethnic fragmentation with the polity score in Model 5. We now find that ethnic fragmentation is no longer a statistically significant determinant and we could not reject the null hypothesis that both ethnic fragmentation and its interaction with the polity score are zero. This is consistent with the recent studies on the effect of ethnic fragmentation. On the other hand, the polity score still remains significant at the 10 per cent level and also the joint test of hypotheses that both the polity score and its interaction with ethnic fragmentation is not different from zero were not accepted at the 10 per cent level. This finding suggests that at a given level of ethnic fragmentation, an increase in democratization reduces the probability of being a HIPC.

Finally, in Model 6, we also include two policy indicators, a measure of financial development/liberalization, money and quasi-money as a percentage of GDP and the fiscal deficit, which appear as statistically significant policy indicators (see Table 5.2, Model 7). While the result of Model 6 remains similar, only now does the fiscal deficit appear as the significant policy factor, while M2 as a percentage of GDP reduces its level of statistical significance. This in turn supports our argument that

Table 5.4 The marginal effects of ethnicity, polity and tropicality (evaluated at corresponding sample mean) on the probability of a developing country being a HIPC

Dependent variable: HIPC dummy, 1 = HIPC country, 0 = non-HIPC developing country

Explanatory variables	*Model 1*	*Model 2*	*Model 3*	*Model 4*	*Model 5*	*Model 6*
Ethnic fragmentation, 1960	0.007***			0.004*	0.002	0.003
	(3.25)			(1.74)	(0.83)	(0.99)
Polity score, average 1960–99		−0.031***		−0.063***	−0.036*	−0.052*
		(−4.24)		(−3.82)	(−1.61)	(−1.82)
Tropical dummy			0.378***	0.569***	0.584***	0.493***
			(4.77)	(4.63)	(4.83)	(3.23)
Ethnic fractionalization × polity Score					−0.001	−0.000
					(−1.20)	(−0.10)
Budget deficit						−0.063***
						(−2.82)
M2 % of GDP						−0.018
						(−1.31)
No. of observations	83	129	156	82	82	63
Wald χ^2	10.57	17.95	22.78	37.92	33.74	29.37

Note: Heteroscedasticity-corrected *Z*-statistics are in parentheses:
* Significant at 10% level.
** Significant at 5% level.
*** Significant at 1% level, the marginal effect is for discrete change of dummy variable from 0 to 1.

successful resolution of HIPC problem requires more than just good policy.

We also find good news, which is that the adverse effects of ethnicity can be resolved by more democratization. As a number of HIPCs are war affected (see the Appendix), we also investigated the effect of total duration of war on the probability of being a HIPC, but it did not appear as significant and hence is not reported (also the finding of Easterly, 2002). Unregulated social competition, rather than outright violent conflict, is more important in explaining debt service problems for HIPCs as a whole (although of course war remains individually important for 11 of the 41 HIPCs).

Conclusions and policy implications

Following Easterly (2002), this chapter has focused on the importance of time preference, and thus the discount rate, in determining debt problems. We find that the chances of becoming an HIPC are raised when competition among social groups raises the discount rates of state actors, communities and the private sector. Short-term horizons among state actors do cause debt problems (through bad policy) but so too does investor uncertainty among communities and entrepreneurs. Our empirical results suggest that the investor uncertainty effect is more pronounced in explaining HIPC status than policy failure. Both effects are rooted in the breakdown of informal and formal rules of the game, taking place in countries that are already institutionally weak.

What do these results imply for policy? At least three policy conclusions can be drawn. First, resolving the HIPC problem is going to be a lot tougher than donors and countries presently expect. 'Deep interventions' to change the rules of the game, so that competition between social groups is regulated and peaceful, are essential (Dixit, 1999). The introduction of multi-party politics made strong progress in the HIPC group during the 1990s. But other institutions of a democracy (independent judiciaries, transparent party financing and a free press) still remain underdeveloped.

Second, and following from the first conclusion, there are high economic returns from preventing and reversing the erosion of institutions in HIPCs, especially in SSA. Donor assistance to HIPCs in the area of governance must be stepped up. The provision of a system of international criminal justice to fill the gap left unfilled by national justice systems is also critical in holding all social actors, not just those in the state, to account, (including their use of foreign borrowing).

Third, a reduction in unregulated social competition, and in particular strengthening property rights, will improve the attractiveness of HIPC countries to international commercial lenders and to direct foreign investment (DFI). At present DFI to SSA is very much concentrated on the mining sector. While mining generates much-needed foreign exchange, diversifying the export base must be a priority (UNCTAD, 2001). Moreover, mining has a low employment multiplier, and the use of resource rents for development is constrained by weak and non-transparent fiscal systems. Increased private capital flows into agricultural tradables will assist countries to move up the value chain of tropical products (and to develop manufacturing through more processing of agricultural products) and to diversify their export bases. This will avoid a recurrence of the HIPC problem.

Appendix: list of HIPCs used in the analysis

1. Angola*
2. Benin
3. Bolivia
4. Burkina Faso
5. Burundi*
6. Cameroon
7. Central African Republic*
8. Chad
9. Congo*
10. Congo, Dem Rep.*
11. Côte d' Ivoire
12. Ethiopia**
13. The Gambia
14. Ghana
15. Guinea
16. Guinea-Bissau*
17. Guyana
18. Honduras
19. Kenya
20. Lao PDR
21. Liberia*
22. Madagascar
23. Malawi
24. Mali
25. Mauritania
26. Mozambique
27. Myanmar*
28. Nicaragua
29. Niger
30. Rwanda*
31. Sierra Leone*
32. Sãó Tome and Principe
33. Senegal
34. Somalia*
35. Sudan*
36. Tanzania
37. Togo
38. Uganda
39. Vietnam
40. Yemen, Rep. of
41. Zambia

Note: * = War-affected. ** = Cessation of hostilities signed on 18 June 2000, peace talks are under way.
Sources: IMF and World Bank (2001).

Notes

* We are grateful to the participants in the 17–18 August 2001 Helsinki meeting for their comments, especially to Ernest Aryeetey, Jean-Claude Berthélemy, Léonce Ndikumana, Gordon Menzies and Charles Okeahalam. We thank Bill Easterly for discussions and assistance. All errors remain our own.

1. There are 41 HIPCs according to the World Bank and IMF classification. Papers on all aspects of the HIPC issue can be found at the UNU-WIDER web site. www.wider.unu.edu, from the conference on Debt Relief held on 17–18 August 2001 in Helsinki.
2. For instance, in SSA inappropriate policy and environmental degradation (due in part to population growth and adverse climate changes) have contributed to the weakening of what were previously effective informal rules governing access to natural capital (soils, water, forests, etc.) resulting in an increase in local disputes, especially between resident and migrant communities.
3. IMF and World Bank (2001) classifies 11 HIPCs as conflict (war)-affected. All of the HIPC wars are civil wars, with the exception of Ethiopia, and its recent war with Eritrea. See Addison and Murshed (2001b) on the potential of debt relief to reduce civil war.
4. Transactions costs (σ) resulting from rising unregulated social competition drive a wedge between producer and consumer prices.
5. We use the standard definitions, namely that tradables are goods and services whose prices are influenced by world prices (importables and exportables) while non-tradables are goods and services whose prices are purely determined by domestic supply and demand (see World Bank 1990 for a discussion of this framework).
6. Similarly, the rising discount rate will affect investment in mineral tradables (important in Angola, DRC, Zambia, etc.). However, production in these sectors is geographically concentrated (often as an enclave) and is therefore more immune to the rise in transactions costs (σ) and production costs (C) than is the case for agricultural tradables. For instance many of the oil wells in West Africa are offshore.
7. See the Appendix for a list of countries from the HIPC class.
8. The data for macropolicy variables are from the Global Development Network Database.
9. The value of the ethnic fragmentation index is for 1960. By now a substantial number of studies have used this variable; the original source of the data is *Atlas Narodov Mira* (1964). Polity data are from Marshall and Jaggers (2000). The polity score ranges from –10 (strongly autocratic) to 10 (strongly democratic). The data on duration of war since 1955 are from Sambanis (2000).

Bibliography

Addison, T. (2003). 'Communities, Entrepreneurs, and States', in T. Addison (ed.), *From Conflict to Reconstruction in Africa,* Oxford: Oxford University Press for UNU-WIDER.

Addison, T. and S. M. Murshed (2001). 'From Conflict to Reconstruction: Reviving the Social Contract', WIDER Discussion Paper DP2001/48, Helsinki: UNU–WIDER.

Addison, T. and S. M. Murshed (2002). 'On the Economic Causes of Contemporary Civil Wars', in S. M. Murshed (ed.), *Issues in Positive Political Economy*, London, Routledge, 22–38.

Addison, T. and S. M. Murshed (2003). 'Debt Relief and Civil War', *Journal of Peace Research*, 40(2), 159–76.

Alesina, A., R. Baqir and W. Easterly (1999). 'Public Goods and Ethnic Divisions', *Quarterly Journal of Economics*, 114(4): 1243–84.

Atlas Narodov Mira (1964). Miklukho-Maklai Ethnological Institute at the Department of Geodesy and Cartography of the State Geological Committee of the Soviet Union, Moscow.

Azam, J.-P. (2001). 'The Redistributive State and Conflicts in Africa', *Journal of Peace Research*, 38: 429–44.

Buiter, W. H. (1981). 'Time Preference and International Lending and Borrowing in an Overlapping-Generations Model', *Journal of Political Economy*, 89(4): 769–97.

Collier, P. (2001). 'Implications of Ethnic Diversity', *Economic Policy* 32: 129–55.

Dixit, A. K. (1999). 'Some Lessons from Transaction-Cost Politics for Less-Developed Countries', Princeton University, unpublished manuscript.

Easterly, W. (2002). 'How Did Highly Indebted Countries become Highly Indebted? Reviewing Two Decades of Debt Relief', *World Development*, 30(10): 1677–96.

Easterly, W. and R. Levine (1997). 'Africa's Growth Tragedy: Policies and Ethnic Divisions', *Quarterly Journal of Economics*, 112(4): 1203–50.

Hausmann, R. (2001). 'Prisoners of Geography', *Foreign Policy*, 122: 45–53.

IMF (International Monetary Fund) and World Bank (2001). 'Assistance to Post-Conflict Countries and the HIPC Framework'. Washington, DC: IMF and World Bank, available at: www.imf.org/external/np/hipc/2001/pc/042001.pdf.

Leamer, E. E. and P. K. Schott (1999). 'Natural Resources as a Source of Latin American Income Inequality', World Development Report Memorandum, Washington, DC: World Bank, processed, available at: www.worldbank.org/poverty/wdrpoverty/background/leamer.pdf.

Marshall, M. J. and K. Jaggers (2000). 'Polity IV Project: Political Regime Characteristics and Transitions, 1800–1999', College Park: Center for International Development and Conflict Management, University of Maryland.

Mauro, P. (1995). 'Corruption and Economic Growth', *Quarterly Journal of Economics*, 110(3): 681–712.

Miguel, T. (1999). 'Ethnic Diversity and School Funding in Kenya', Cambridge, MA: Harvard University, mimeo.

North, D. C. (1997). 'The Contribution of the New Institutional Economics to an Understanding of the Transition Problem', WIDER Annual Lectures 1, Helsinki: UNU–WIDER.

Obstfeld, M., and K. Rogoff (1996). *Foundations of International Macroeconomics*, Cambridge, MA: MIT Press.

Sachs, J. D. and A. M. Warner (1995). 'Natural Resource Abundance and Economic Growth', NBER Working Paper 5398, Cambridge, MA: National Bureau of Economic Research.

Sambanis, N. (2000). 'Partition as a Solution to Ethnic War: An Empirical Critique of the Theoretical Literature', *World Politics*, 52: 437–83.

UNCTAD (United Nations Conference on Trade and Development) (2001). *Trade and Development Report 2001*, Geneva: UNCTAD.

World Bank (1990). *Making Adjustment Work for the Poor: A Framework for Policy Reform in Africa*, Washington, DC: World Bank.

Part II
Growth Effects of Debt Relief

6

External Debt and Growth: Implications for HIPCs*

Catherine Pattillo, Hélène Poirson and Luca Ricci

Introduction

Excessive external indebtedness has plagued numerous developing countries since the 1980s. In the 1980s, a number of middle-income countries – especially in Latin America – experienced high indebtedness, and most of them have since managed to reduce it, partly through international efforts such as the Brady plan. However, in the second half of the 1990s, policy-makers around the world began to recognize that very high large debt levels were a contributing factor to the extreme poverty of many low-income countries, despite the fact that a sizeable share of the lending to these countries had occurred at concessional rates.

In September 1996, the IMF and the World Bank jointly created the Initiative for the Heavily Indebted Poor Countries (HIPC Initiative), which provides conditional financial assistance from the international community – in addition to traditional debt relief mechanisms – to countries that meet specific policy and performance criteria.[1] The aim was to reduce external debt of qualifying countries to sustainable levels. Determining what levels of debt are sustainable for low-income countries is very difficult, as the analysis involves projections of overall economic performance, in particular of future export and fiscal revenue earnings. The main target level for the net present value (NPV) of debt was initially set at 200–250 per cent of exports, and then lowered in 1999 to 150 per cent of exports.

The objective of this chapter is to make use of recent empirical contributions on the relation between debt and growth to provide an assessment of the potential impact of debt reduction on the economic performance of HIPCs. The results suggest that the HIPC debt relief initiative may contribute to increases in *per capita* growth by about

1 per cent for countries that are scheduled to receive assistance, provided that these economies sufficiently reduce macroeconomic and structural distortions, as well as high economic and political risks that might otherwise constrain growth.

The remainder of the chapter is divided in four sections: a survey of the literature; a description the data employed; an outline of the estimation methods and report of the results; and then finally some conclusions.

Theoretical considerations and related literature

From the literature, what do we know about the effect of debt on growth for developing countries and why would we expect the effect to be non-linear? Traditional neoclassical models suggest that 'reasonable' levels of borrowing by a developing country are likely to enhance its economic growth (Eaton, 1993). Countries at early stages of development have small stocks of capital and are likely to have investment opportunities with rates of return higher than in advanced economies. As long as they use the borrowed funds for productive investment and they do not suffer from macroeconomic instability, policies that distort economic incentives, or sizeable adverse shocks, growth should increase and allow for timely debt repayments.

Why do large levels of accumulated debt lead to lower growth? The most well-known explanation comes from 'debt overhang' theories, which show that if there is some likelihood that in the future debt will be larger than the country's repayment ability, expected debt service costs will discourage further domestic and foreign investment, and thus harm growth (Krugman, 1988; Sachs, 1989). Potential investors will fear that the more is produced, the more will be 'taxed' by creditors to service the external debt, and thus they will be less willing to incur costs today for the sake of increased output in the future.

Some considerations thus suggest that at reasonable levels of debt, further borrowing would be expected to have a positive effect on growth, while others stress that large accumulated debt stocks may be a hindrance to growth. Both these elements together imply that debt is likely to have non-linear effects on growth. Although the debt overhang theories have not explicitly traced the effect on growth, it may be possible to extend and translate the debt Laffer curve posited by these models into a Laffer curve for the effect of debt on growth. Since the peak of the debt Laffer curve shows the point where rising debt stocks begin acting as a tax on investment, or other activities that require up-front costs in exchange for future benefits, this may relate to the point at which debt begins to have a negative marginal impact on growth.

What aspects of these general theories may be particularly relevant for HIPCs? First, some authors have argued that the debt overhang theories may have broader implications. In addition to effects on investment levels, the incentive effects associated with the need to service large debt stocks will tend to reduce the benefits to be expected from policy reforms that would enhance efficiency and growth, such as trade liberalization and fiscal adjustment (see Corden, 1989). The government would be less willing to incur current costs if it perceived that the future benefit in terms of higher output would partly accrue to foreign lenders. Given the poor policies of HIPCs, any potential deterrent to policy reform could be especially detrimental for growth.

Second, another channel pointed to in the literature is that large debt stocks may have negative effects on economic performance because of the uncertainty about what portion of the debt will actually be serviced with the country's own resources.[2] It may not be clear what terms debt will be rescheduled, whether there will be additional lending, what changes in government policies the rescheduling will entail, etc. High levels of debt and the associated uncertainties could lower growth through reduced levels of investment – or, more speculatively, through the efficiency of capital accumulation, as the investment that does take place may be poorly allocated to activities with quick returns rather than longer-term irreversible investment. Again, given continual changes in debt rescheduling and debt relief efforts, uncertainty related to debt is likely to be high for HIPCs.

There may also be special considerations that imply that the relationship between debt and growth is different for HIPCs. Debt overhang theories were originally developed for countries heavily indebted to private commercial creditors; the debt of HIPCs is primarily owed to official creditors. Even though debt levels are extremely high, these countries continued to receive large net transfers of resources during the 1990s, primarily concessional assistance from official creditors. Claessens *et al.* (1997) argue that if creditors allocate aid independently of debt, then standard debt overhang theory would apply. Otherwise, it depends on the criteria determining aid flows. For example, if HIPCs are more likely to be dependent on aid in the future and creditors reduce aid when economic conditions improve, then the adverse incentive effects of debt are even worse. Conversely, if aid increases as policies and growth improve, then debt overhang effects will tend to be weakened. Finally, some argue that it is unlikely that there are significant negative debt overhang effects on investment in HIPCs, given that more fundamental constraints, such as weaknesses in their domestic investment climate, may be the more important factors (World Bank, 2001).

Turning to previous empirical work not specific to HIPCs, two existing studies specifically relate to the non-linear effects of debt. Cohen (1997) finds that the probability of debt rescheduling – which depends positively on external indebtedness – significantly lowers growth. He finds that debt becomes excessive when it reaches levels of the order of 50 per cent of GDP or 200 per cent of exports. Elbadawi, Ndulu and Ndung'u (1997) is the only empirical study we are aware of that directly considers non-linear effects of debt on growth. Their results imply a growth maximizing debt–GDP ratio of 97 per cent, which is quite high considering that the average debt–GDP ratio in our sample is 70 per cent.

In a recent work, we find evidence of a non-linear relation between external debt and growth (Pattillo, Poirson and Ricci, 2002). We identify a range of values (specific to the type of debt indicator) after which the 'average' impact of debt on growth becomes negative. For the NPV of the debt–exports indicator, such a range is very close to the debt target (150 per cent of exports) of the current HIPC Initiative. We also identify ranges of values for the optimal level of debt – i.e. the level after which the 'marginal' impact of further debt accumulation becomes negative – which are approximately half of the ranges in which the average impact of debt turns negative. Interestingly, for the average developing country in the sample, the effect of doubling debt is to reduce growth by half to a full percentage point, suggesting that the average country is already on the 'wrong' side of a hypothetical debt Laffer curve. Finally, and somewhat surprisingly, the results in the 2002 paper suggest that that most of the effect of debt on growth takes place through the efficiency of investment, rather than just its level.

Methodology

The methodology in this chapter follows Pattillo, Poirson and Ricci (2002). We employ a growth regression *à la* Mankiw, Romer and Weil (1992), controlling for standard determinants of growth (lagged income *per capita*; the investment rate; secondary schooling; population growth rate (all in logs)); differences in policies (openness and the fiscal balance), and external shocks (terms of trade growth). The analysis uses three-year average panel data for 93 developing countries over the period 1969–98. We also use 10-year averages to check the robustness of our findings to cyclical effects.

For our debt variable, we use various debt stock indicators, including a World Bank data set that measures the NPV of debt (see Easterly, 2001a). Specifically, we use four different indicators: debt ratios (debt–exports and debt–GDP), in nominal terms and in NPV terms. This is important because most studies have simply considered debt ratios in nominal terms, whereas most countries sampled have contracted debt at concessional rates – meaning that the NPV is less than the face value of the debt. In order to properly identify the debt overhang effect (reduced or distorted incentives for investment due to high anticipated future debt service payments) through the above debt stock indicators, we also included debt-service to exports, to control for any contemporaneous crowding-out effects arising from resources being spent on debt service instead of investment or other growth-enhancing domestic spending.

We employ four estimation methodologies for robustness: (i) ordinary least squares (OLS); (ii) instrumental variables using lagged values as instruments to correct for potential endogeneity of the debt, investment, schooling, openness and fiscal balance variables; (iii) fixed effects to control for unobserved country-specific factors, such as institutional quality and history; and (iv) system-GMM to correct for endogeneity and for the bias introduced by the lagged income variable in the presence of fixed effects. In addition, to ensure that our results are not driven by time-specific effects or the presence of outliers, we estimate most regressions with and without time dummies, as well as with the full sample and with a reduced sample from which outliers are eliminated.

We use two alternative non-linear specifications: a quadratic and a spline function. We estimate a quadratic (inverted U-curve) specification, where the debt variable is entered in both linear and quadratic terms, and then a spline (inverted V-shaped curve) specification, where the impact of debt can have a structural break, endogenously determined as the break that maximizes the fit of the regression.

Results

Our results can be used to shed some light on the potential growth impact of debt relief for the average HIPC country. Official documents show that the NPV of debt in the year 2000 was on average about 300 per cent of exports and 80 per cent of GDP for HIPCs.[3] As the objective of the Initiative is to eventually reduce the NPV of debt of HIPC s to 150 per cent of exports, we can evaluate the effect of halving the debt from its 2000 level using each of the four debt indicators.[4] This exercise then also assumes that NPV of debt–GDP and the two ratios of nominal debt–exports and debt–GDP would be halved by HIPC debt relief. Note also that, by reducing the NPV of debt to 150 per cent of exports, the HIPC Initiative would eliminate the negative *average* effect of debt on growth (according to estimates by Pattillo, Poirson and Ricci (2002) based on a model with debt dummies, countries with debt levels beyond 160–170 per cent of exports tend to have significantly slower growth than the average, everything else being equal).

We consider the impact of halving debt using both the quadratic and spline specification, as well as providing the estimate from the linear model. The impact of halving the debt based on the linear models and spline functions would be the same as that for the overall sample. Here we noted that for the average country in the regression, halving the extent of indebtedness generally implies an increase in growth of half to a full percentage point, and that the estimates are surprisingly similar across all debt ratio indicators, specifications, and methodologies (see Pattillo, Poirson and Ricci, 2002).

However, it may be more reasonable to try to determine the effects of halving debt using a method that takes into consideration the differential starting point of the HIPCs, in terms of their current debt levels. Table 6.1 summarizes the results for the quadratic estimation, where it is also necessary to consider the starting point (average current level of debt of HIPCs).[5] In general, halving the debt from the levels borne by HIPCs in 2000 is estimated to raise *per capita* growth by about 1 percentage point. Consistent with the HIPCs' higher initial indebtedness, this estimate is at the high end of the effects of halving debt for the average country in the sample.

However, the above results may not automatically apply to the case of HIPCs, given the standard results of the second-best theory, and the fact that the regression holds for the average country in the sample. That is, even though in the quadratic specification we are taking account of the differential average debt levels (for HIPC vs non-HIPCs), the regressions still hold for average values of the additional explanatory variables, including investment and policies. For HIPCs, the disincentive to invest and the skewness in the allocation of resources to economic activities with short-run horizons might not improve much when debt is reduced, as other macroeconomic and structural distortions as well as political factors might still be binding.[6] It should be noted, nonetheless, that the policy conditionality associated with the HIPC debt relief will

Table 6.1 Effects of halving debt on growth (for HIPCs that reached the decision point) based on a quadratic specification[a]

	Nominal debt to:		*NPV of debt to:*	
	Exports	*GDP*	*Exports*	*GDP*
OLS	0.42	**0.83**	0.45	**0.93**
with time dummies	0.29	**0.78**	0.28	**0.78**
without outliers	**0.69**	**0.89**	0.69	0.94
with time dummies and without outliers	**0.53**	**0.83**	0.47	**0.81**
IV	**0.62**	0.71	0.39	**0.79**
with time dummies	**0.56**	**0.71**	0.14	0.66
without outliers	0.37	0.41	0.21	0.43
with time dummies and without outliers	0.37	0.47	0.57	0.42
Fixed effects	0.43	**0.97**	0.43	**0.89**
with time dummies	0.68	**1.66**	0.57	**1.41**
without outliers	**0.88**	**1.13**	0.63	**1.10**
with time dummies and without outliers	**1.34**	**1.83**	0.88	**1.62**
System-GMM with time dummies and without outliers	0.44	10.19	0.21	**0.48**

Notes: Bold denotes significance at the 10 per cent level.

[a] Computed at the average, that is as Log (2) * β_D + [Log (2)]^2 * β_{D2} + 2 * Log (2) * β_{D2} * Log (average D for 22 HIPCs).

The averages are 1999 figures for 22 HIPCs that reached their decision point by 2002: debt–exports, 625; debt–GDP, 169; NPV of debt–exports, 300; NPV of debt–GDP, 80.

Sources: NPV ratios are from Easterly (2001a), nominal debt ratios from World Bank (2001).

contribute to bringing the macroeconomic situation of the HIPCs closer to that of the average country in the sample. Further study would be necessary to investigate the case of HIPCs in particular.

Other arguments that are sceptical of a potential positive growth effect from a debt reduction in HIPC cases are less convincing. First, it could be argued that a positive effect on growth is unlikely as countries will still continue to have a substantial debt service burden. It should be noted, though, that HIPCs generally receive grants and official financing which reduce the problem of *current* negative resource transfers (which would otherwise limit the amount of economic resources that can be currently devoted to investment activities). It is true, however, that the uncertainty about the extent of *future* grants and official aid could still contribute to distortions in the incentives to invest and to allocate resources efficiently. Second, one may think that the potential growth benefit is likely to be small as the debt reduction under the HIPC Initiative might have been already anticipated by the investors. (That is, that HIPCs have not had a debt overhang problem recently as it was not expected that they would repay their debts anyway). However, this point relates to *when* the growth effect may take place, and not whether it may take place. If one were to believe that HIPC debt reduction from 300 to 150 per cent of exports is already fully anticipated by investors (a questionable assumption), then economic incentives might have already improved and might already be contributing to better growth prospects.

Conclusions

This chapter attempts to investigate the potential impact of debt reduction on the economic performance of HIPCs. Following Pattillo, Poirson and Ricci (2002), it employs a standard growth framework augmented with various indicators of debt, in nominal and in NPV terms, measured as a ratio to both exports and to GDP. We use several econometric specifications (quadratic debt terms, a model with debt dummies, and a spline function, in addition to a simple linear specification) to capture the non-linearity of the relation between debt and growth. The chapter also employs several different methodologies (OLS, instrumental variables, fixed effects, and system-GMM). Additional robustness tests are provided by estimating regressions which eliminate outliers and include time dummies, and by using decade-average data instead of three-year average data to eliminate any possible business-cycle effects.

The results provide tentative insights in assessing the potential impact of the HIPC debt relief initiative on countries that are scheduled to receive assistance:

- Debt relief may contribute to increases in *per capita* growth by about 1 per cent for these countries, and should eliminate the debt-related growth shortfall of HIPCs relative to other developing countries (in fact, by reducing the NPV of debt to 150 per cent of exports, debt reduction would eliminate the negative *average* effect of debt on growth). However, the second-best theory may suggest that such a growth dividend might not arise as these economies are often severely affected by other macroeconomic and structural distortions, as well as by high economic and political risks.

- If it were to arise, the increase in growth might initiate a *virtuous growth cycle* which, in the absence of additional increases in debt levels, would contribute to further reducing debt ratios.
- However, the results reported above also indicate that the *target debt level* of the HIPC Initiative remains close to the estimated threshold above which the impact of debt on growth is likely to be on average negative, and well above the estimated growth-maximizing level of debt. In other words, the HIPC Initiative might reduce the level of indebtedness just to a level where a new increase in debt (which may be likely, given the level of development and poverty of these countries) would have a negative impact on growth.
- It should also be noted that the *economic and political situation* of these countries makes them a non-typical sub-sample, and further research is therefore necessary to provide a more definitive assessment of the relation between debt and growth for HIPCs.

Appendix: list of countries

HIPCs

Benin, Bolivia, Burkina Faso, Cameroon, *Chad, Côte d'Ivoire, Ethiopia,* Gambia, *Ghana,* Guinea, Guinea-Bissau, Guyana, Honduras, Madagascar, Malawi, Mali, Mauritania, Mozambique, Nicaragua, Niger, Rwanda, Senegal, *Sierra Leone,* Tanzania, Uganda, Zambia

Note: HIPC countries that had not reached decision point by end-2001 are in italic.

Other countries

Algeria, Argentina, Bahrain, Bangladesh, Botswana, Brazil, Burundi, Cambodia, Cape Verde, Central African Rep., Chile, China P. R.: Mainland, Colombia, Comoros, Congo Dem. Rep. of, Congo Republic of, Costa Rica, Cyprus, Djibouti, Dominican Republic, Ecuador, Egypt, El Salvador, Fiji, Guatemala, Haiti, India, Indonesia, Iran, Jamaica, Kenya, Korea, Lao PDR, Lebanon, Lesotho, Libya, Malaysia, Mauritius, Mexico, Morocco, Myanmar, Namibia, Nepal, Nigeria, Pakistan, Panama, Papua New Guinea, Paraguay, Peru, Philippines, Somalia, South Africa, Sri Lanka, Sudan, Suriname, Swaziland, Syrian Arab Republic, Thailand, Togo, Trinidad and Tobago, Tunisia, Turkey, Uruguay, Venezuela, Vietnam, Yemen Republic of, Zimbabwe.

Notes

* The authors would like to thank Bill Easterly for sharing his data set on NPV of external debt; Eduardo Borensztein, Peter Clark, Daniel Cohen, Kenneth Kletzer, Paul Masson, Ashoka Mody, Sam Ouliaris, Eswar Prasad, Robert Powell and Xavier Sala-i-Martin for useful discussions; participants in the WIDER Debt Relief Conference (Helsinki, 2001); and Grace Juhn for excellent and invaluable research assistance.

1. For a description, see http://www.imf.org/external/np/exr/facts/hipc.htm.
2. See Servén (1997) for a general overview of the literature on investment under uncertainty.
3. IDA and IMF (2001: Annex Table 3a, column 1 and Annex Table 5, column 1). These figures are actually likely to under-estimate the extent of indebtedness, as they are calculated only for countries that reached a decision point.
4. Note that the historical variability present in the debt data is driven by both decreases and increases in the debt stocks (see, for example, Figure 1 in Pattillo, Poirson and Ricci, 2002), implying that it is reasonable to use the estimated relationships to assess the impact of lowering as well as increasing debt levels.
5. For underlying regression results and robustness tests, see Pattillo, Poirson and Ricci (2002).
6. See, for example, Easterly (2001b) for a discussion of why debt forgiveness may not improve economic performance if the domestic incentive structure is poor.

References

Claessens, S., E. Detragiache, R. Kanbur and P. Wickham (1997). 'Analytical Aspects of the Debt Problems of Heavily Indebted Poor Countries', in Z. Iqbal and R. Kanbur (eds), *External Finance for Low-Income Countries*, Washington, DC: International Monetary Fund.

Cohen, D. (1997). 'Growth and External Debt: A New Perspective on the African and Latin American Tragedies', Centre for Economic Policy Research Discussion Paper, 1753.

Corden, W. M. (1989). 'Debt Relief and Adjustment Incentives', in J. A. Frenkel, M. P. Dooley and P. Wickham (eds), *Analytical Issues in Debt*, Washington, DC: International Monetary Fund.

Easterly, W. (2001a). 'Growth Implosions, Debt Explosions, and My Aunt Marilyn: Do Growth Slowdowns Cause Public Debt Crises?', World Bank Policy Research Working Paper, 2531, Washington, DC: World Bank.

Easterly, W. (2001b). *The Elusive Quest for Growth*, Cambridge, MA: MIT Press.

Eaton, J. (1993) 'Sovereign Debt: A Primer', *World Bank Economic Review*, 7(2): 137–72.

Elbadawi, I., B. Ndulu and N. Ndung'u (1997). 'Debt Overhang and Economic Growth in Sub-Saharan Africa', in Z. Iqbal and R. Kanbur (eds), *External Finance for Low-Income Countries*, Washington, DC: IMF.

IDA (International Development Association) and IMF (International Monetary Fund) (2001). 'The Challenge of Maintaining Long-Term External Debt Sustainability', Washington, DC: IDA and IMF.

Krugman, P. (1988). 'Financing vs. Forgiving a Debt Overhang', *Journal of Development Economics*, 29: 253–68.

Mankiw, N. G., D. Romer and D. Weil (1992). 'A Contribution to the Empirics of Economic Growth', *Quarterly Journal of Economics*, 107(2): 407–37.

Pattillo, C., H. Poirson and L. Ricci (2002). 'External Debt and Growth', IMF Working Paper 02/69, Washington, DC: IMF.

Sachs, J. (1989). 'The Debt Overhang of Developing Countries', in G. A. Calvo *et al.* (eds), *Debt Stabilization and Development: Essay in Memory of Carlos Diaz Alejandro,* Oxford: Basil Blackwell for UNU-WIDER.

Servén, L. (1997). 'Uncertainty, Instability, and Irreversible Investment: Theory, Evidence, and Lessons for Africa', World Bank Policy Research Working Paper, 1722, Washington, DC: World Bank.

World Bank (2001). *Global Development Finance,* Washington, DC: World Bank.

7

The Impact of External Aid and External Debt on Growth and Investment*

Henrik Hansen

Introduction

Additionality, in the sense that debt relief should supplement, not replace, the flow of development aid is a key concept underlying the HIPC Initiative. But assessing the additionality of HIPC debt relief is extremely difficult, if not outright impossible. Some writers (e.g. Birdsall and Williamson, 2002), expect only modest additionality from bilateral donors while they doubt that debt relief from the World Bank can be additional. This leaves the IMF as the main contributor of additional resources.

If additionality is unlikely, it becomes relevant to look into the question of what happens to growth and investment when both debt service and aid flows decrease. In the present study we make a first pass at answering this question. That is, we wish to assess the possible outcome of HIPC debt relief without additionality.

At first sight, the question is rather naïve. If the net flow is unchanged, there seems little scope for improvements in growth performance. However, looking at the two strands of literature – one dealing with aid effectiveness and the other with the impact of debt problems – the question becomes more pertinent. For more than 30 years there have been intensive discussions about the macroeconomic impact of development aid and, even today, many scholars and politicians are convinced that, on average, aid is wasted if not downright harmful to economic growth. In contrast, the analyses of the impact of debt problems following the 1980s Latin American debt crisis seldom discussed whether external debt had negative effects on investment and growth. A negative impact was taken for granted which is why the focus was instead on the specific link from external debt to investment. Usually, the debt overhang theory of Krugman (1988) and Sachs (1989) was held up against the pure crowding-out theory advocated by Cohen (1993).

Based on the discussions of aid effectiveness and debt problems, one is inclined to conclude that if there is a large (overhang) effect of external debt on investment and economic polices while aid is wasted, debt relief along the lines of the HIPC Initiative could be beneficial for growth even without additionality. Birdsall and Williamson condense this idea in the assumption that 'an assured dollar of debt relief is probably more efficient in generating development than a promise of a dollar of new aid' (Birdsall and Williamson, 2002: 72).

But the aid effectiveness debate is still open, and the World Bank perception that aid is effective only in a good policy and institutional environment is far from universal. In addition, the disincentive effect of the debt overhang may be modest in many HIPCs because they, in contrast to the heavily indebted countries of the 1980s, have official instead of private debt and net inflows of funds. Taken together, this means that there is another scenario, in which debt relief without additionality has little or no impact on growth and investment.

Assessing the possible outcome of non-additional debt relief may be of more than academic interest. 'Aid fatigue' – a term now present in every politician's glossary – which is to a large extent generated by unfulfilled expectations may be replaced by 'debt relief weariness' if the HIPC Initiative fails to live up to the high hopes in terms of increased growth and poverty alleviation. To avoid new disappointments, and never-ending discussions of what went wrong and who to blame, it is important to be realistic with respect to the projected results of the HIPC Initiative.

In this chapter we look at the recent past in 50 developing countries. The idea is to quantify the joint impact of debt service payments and aid flows on growth and investment. The sample of 50 countries includes some of the HIPCs and a large group of non-HIPCs. The main reason for looking at many non-HIPCs is that if we concentrate on the HIPCs there is a serious risk that our predictions will be biased because of endogenous sample selection with respect to debt performance. This is also the reason why we have chosen to look at a period before the HIPC Initiative was launched in 1996. Needless to say, using both HIPC and non-HIPC countries to assess the importance of debt service and aid flows implies strong assumptions of (conditional) similarity and linearity. But these are underlying assumptions in all cross-country studies.

The main result of the analysis is that decreasing debt service payments have a (small) positive impact on growth and investment. But decreasing debt service payments in combination with decreasing aid flows has no significant growth effects while there may even be a negative impact on investment. This means that additionality appears to be important for a successful outcome of the debt relief initiative. In the analysis, we concentrate on the impact of debt service payments and aid flows, conditional on macroeconomic policies. Therefore, if the main channel of HIPC-generated growth is through improvements in policies and institutions, there may well be a positive result of non-additional debt relief. But in this case successful debt relief arrangements, in some sense, are more the results of successful conditionality and selectivity than the results of debt forgiveness.

We begin with a brief description of some macroeconomic trends in the 50 countries in our sample (next section). The main purpose is to compare the trends across the heavily indebted countries (HICs) of the 1980s, the HIPCs of the 1990s and countries that are neither HIC nor HIPC (non-HI(P)C). The next section resumes our econometric results. First we look at debt service payments, aid flows and growth followed by an analysis of the impact on investment. Then we try to assess the likeliness of simultaneous changes in debt service and aid flows, concentrating on the experience in the HIC countries. Interestingly, we find that while official assistance is only weakly related to debt service payments, the composition of loans in terms of the size of the grant element does respond to changes in debt service payments, in the sense that the grant element decreases after debt service payments drop. This means that there is a (recent) historical record of non-additionality in relation to debt relief, but this non-additionality cannot be found directly in the official statistics. We discuss this issue and some limitations of the present study in relation to assessing the possible success or failure of the HIPC Initiative in the concluding section.

A comparison of some macroeconomic trends in HIC, HIPC and other developing countries, 1974–93

In this section we briefly present the patterns of some macroeconomic indicators that have attracted attention in studies of external debt problems and aid effectiveness. Data for 50 developing countries are analysed in the present study (see Table 7.1). The country sample includes 15 of the 'Baker 17' heavily indebted middle-income countries (HIC) and 17 of the current HIPCs.[1] In the time series dimension, the sample covers the years 1974 to 1993, whereby the analysis is based on observations prior to the HIPC Initiative, while the 1980s debt crisis is included.

Table 7.1 Sample countries (50)

Argentina*	Ethiopia**	Malawi**	Sri Lanka
Bolivia*(**)	Gabon	Malaysia	Syrian Arab Republic
Botswana	Gambia, The**	Mexico*	Thailand
Brazil*	Ghana**	Morocco*	Togo**
Cameroon**	Guatemala	Niger**	Trinidad and Tobago
Chile*	Guyana**	Nigeria*	Tunisia
Colombia*	Haiti	Pakistan	Turkey
Congo, Dem. Rep.**	Honduras**	Paraguay	Uruguay*
Costa Rica*	India	Peru*	Venezuela*
Dominican Republic	Indonesia	Philippines*	Zambia**
Ecuador*	Jamaica*	Senegal**	Zimbabwe
Egypt, Arab Rep.	Kenya**	Sierra Leone**	
El Salvador	Madagascar**	Somalia**	

Notes:
* Countries classified as heavily indebted countries (HIC).
** Countries classified as heavily indebted poor countries (HIPC).

Following common practice in cross-country growth studies, we transform the annual observations into period averages of the flow variables and initial observations of the stock variables. In the present analysis, four-year epochs are used whereby the time series dimension is reduced to five periods.[2] Table 7.2 reports the development over time of the macroeconomic indicators, the levels of external debt, debt service payments and aid flows. Data sources are given in the Appendix (p. 153). The data presented are median levels in each of the five periods for the 19 non-HI(P)Cs, the 15 HICs and the 17 HIPCs, respectively.

The median growth rates in real *per capita* GDP vary substantially across time and between country groups, however, the worldwide decrease in growth rates after 1975 is evident. The mid-1970s were characterized by relatively high growth rates in most of the countries. During the late 1970s growth rates declined, turning negative in the early and mid-1980s in most HIC and HIPC countries. In the late 1980s and early 1990s, most HIC countries returned to positive growth rates but, in general, did not return to the levels of the early 1970s. Throughout the 1970s and 1980s, there is a clear ranking of the country groups as the median growth rate in the HIPCs is far below the median growth rates in the non-HI(P)C and HIC groups (with the exception of the period 1982–85). As seen, the growth rates in most of the HIPCs in the sample were not only low, but also negative already from the late 1970s and onwards.

Gross domestic investment as a share of GDP was more or less constant for the non-HI(P)C group (though with a peak in the late 1970s)

Table 7.2 Median levels of major economic indicators, 1974–93

		Periods				
		1974–77	*1978–81*	*1982–85*	*1986–89*	*1990–93*
Real *per capita* GDP growth (%)	Non-HI(P)C	4.25	4.02	1.77	1.08	2.46
	HIC	2.49	1.22	−2.16	1.00	1.40
	HIPC	0.34	−0.90	−1.98	−0.55	−1.09
Gross domestic investment (% of GDP)	Non-HI(P)C	23.32	26.10	23.96	22.29	23.50
	HIC	24.35	25.06	19.60	21.71	19.15
	HIPC	20.78	26.44	15.35	15.78	16.12
Institutional quality	Non-HI(P)C	4.42	4.42	4.42	4.42	4.42
	HIC	5.12	5.12	5.12	5.12	5.12
	HIPC	4.35	4.35	4.35	4.35	4.35
Budget surplus (% of GDP)	Non-HI(P)C	−2.73	−3.69	−5.30	−2.97	−2.14
	HIC	−2.56	−2.02	−5.22	−2.46	−1.14
	HIPC	−3.57	−6.53	−6.68	−4.05	−3.71
Inflation (%)	Non-HI(P)C	11.48	11.33	9.36	9.46	12.76
	HIC	18.89	21.57	26.60	33.95	24.73
	HIPC	13.87	11.82	13.60	18.36	15.36
Sachs–Warner openness	Non-HI(P)C	0.00	0.00	0.00	0.00	0.75
	HIC	0.00	0.00	0.00	0.25	1.00
	HIPC	0.00	0.00	0.00	0.00	0.25
External debt (% of GDP)	Non-HI(P)C	15.54	24.10	29.11	45.12	51.10
	HIC	20.95	35.70	45.32	67.00	70.76
	HIPC	24.50	42.48	63.45	87.01	92.70
NPV of debt (% of GDP)	Non-HI(P)C	14.84	18.02	27.05	43.41	48.99
	HIC	17.96	31.70	39.96	59.18	65.41
	HIPC	21.91	38.87	54.31	63.29	72.10
Debt service (TDS–GDP, %)	Non-HI(P)C	2.15	2.80	5.32	6.05	5.12
	HIC	3.35	6.73	9.25	8.52	7.25
	HIPC	2.65	5.20	6.88	8.27	6.76
Official development assistance (ODA–GDP,%)	Non-HI(P)C	1.70	1.41	2.09	2.83	2.09
	HIC	0.55	0.26	0.22	0.45	0.77
	HIPC	3.67	7.21	6.73	9.62	13.25
Effective development assistance (Real EDA–GDP, %)	Non-HI(P)C	0.42	0.68	0.78	0.83	0.61
	HIC	0.24	0.13	0.12	0.13	0.17
	HIPC	2.15	2.93	2.96	3.30	3.40
Average grant element (%)	Non-HI(P)C	49.33	48.58	54.35	48.62	43.99
	HIC	23.20	25.71	28.83	17.67	25.25
	HIPC	72.05	69.73	69.69	76.00	83.43
ODA–Debt service (% of GDP)	Non-HI(P)C	−0.12	−0.37	−2.29	−1.91	−2.53
	HIC	−2.88	−5.85	−8.12	−7.52	−5.91
	HIPC	0.37	0.80	0.95	2.94	4.88

while it declined in most HIC and HIPC countries from the early 1970s to the early 1990s. A rather sharp break occurred in the mid-1980s with typical investment ratios falling to new levels, just below 20 per cent in the HIC group, and not exceeding 15–16 per cent in most of the HIPCs.

Variations in cross-country growth and investment performance are frequently explained by differences in institutions and macroeconomic policies. In Table 7.2 we list four measures of institutions and macroeconomic policy outcomes. The first is a measure of institutional quality constructed by Knack and Keefer (1995). Although institutional quality is not independent of *per capita* income or growth (see Chong and Calderón, 2000), differences in this measure are often used to explain variations in growth rates across countries. Here, the measure of institutional quality is constant over time (and actually based on data for 1982 or later), but the variation across the country groupings is informative: the median HIC country has better institutions than the median non-HI(P)C, while most HIPC countries have institutions of (slightly) poorer quality.

Fiscal balance has also been stressed as a growth-enhancing factor in many studies. Looking at the time trends in Table 7.2, it is clear that the median budget surpluses dropped sharply from the 1970s to the early 1980s, followed by gradual improvements. In fact, most of the countries in the non-HI(P)C and the HIC groups had better fiscal balances in the 1990–93 period compared to the mid-1970s. Again, there is a clear ordering across the country groupings. The median HIPC country has consistently a larger budget deficit relative to GDP than the median non-HI(P)C country whereas the median HIC country has a lower deficit.

Looking at the pattern of inflation rates, the cross-country variation is rather different compared to the fiscal balance, with extreme inflation rates being a relatively common problem in Latin America. Inflation rates in most HIPC countries are actually close to the median non-HI(P)C inflation rate in the early periods, whereas most countries in the HIC group have inflation rates which by far exceed the median rate in the two other country groups. Hence, part of the relatively good record for fiscal balance in the HIC group may be explained by inflation taxes.

Openness to trade is another recurrent theme in growth and development discussions. In the present study we make use of the indicator for openness constructed by Sachs and Warner (1995).[3] Table 7.2 reveals that most of the 50 countries in the sample were closed until the early 1990s according to the Sachs–Warner indicator. The typical HIC country changed to more open trade policies just around 1990 and in the last period in the sample most of the HIC countries had completed the change in trade policies. This is not so for the non-HI(P)C and the HIPC groups, in which most countries were closed until the early 1990s. (The value 0.25 for openness indicates that the median HIPC country was open in the last year of the final period.)

Next, turning to external debt, we report three measures. The total external debt as a percentage of GDP is given both in nominal and NPV terms.[4] The medians of both measures show a sharply rising trend over the sample period. In 1974–77 the median of the nominal debt–GDP was just above 15 per cent in the non-HI(P)C group with the NPV debt–GDP being only slightly lower. In 1990–93 the median debt level in this group had exploded to 50 per cent (just above in nominal terms and just below in NPV terms). The rather constant difference between the nominal and the NPV ratios implies that a large fraction of the loans to these countries was non-concessional. For the HIC and in particular the HIPC countries the gap between the nominal and the NPV ratios was widening over the period. This means that an increasing fraction of the loans were on (increasingly) concessional terms. The difference between the nominal and NPV ratios was around 20 percentage points in the last period for the median HIPC country, while it was a modest 5 percentage points for the median HIC country. Still, the median HIPC country had the highest debt–GDP ratios throughout, closely followed by the median HIC country. However, as is well known, a direct comparison of the debt–GDP levels across the country groups is not relevant because of the marked differences in the composition of the debt. This difference is in part reflected in the levels of debt service payments. Debt service payments as a percentage of GDP are consistently higher for the median HIC country compared to the median HIPC country. Yet, at the end of the sample period, median debt service payments were substantial in all three country groups and the share of debt service payments to GDP was of the same order of magnitude in the HIC and HIPC groups.

The measurement of aid flows has been discussed as part of the analytical background for the World Bank Report *Assessing Aid* (World Bank, 1998). In particular, Chang, Fernandez-Arias and Servén (1998) discuss several methodological shortcomings of the DAC statistic 'official development assistance' (ODA) and they propose a new measure denoted 'effective development assistance' (EDA).[5] There are several important differences between the two statistics. First of all, the EDA measure includes only the sum of grants and grant equivalents of official loans, where the grant equivalents are based on all official loans regardless of the level of the grant component. (In contrast, ODA includes all loans with a grant component above 25 per cent.) Moreover, grant components of loans are based on donor and time varying discount rates. The second important difference is that the EDA measure excludes technical assistance and debt forgiveness.[6]

In the present analysis, we look at both aid measures as percentages of GDP. ODA is given as the current US$ inflow to current US$ GDP. In contrast, EDA is given as real effective aid flows to real PPP-adjusted GDP (see Burnside and Dollar, 2000). Official aid flows as a percentage of GDP to the non-HI(P)C countries increased slightly from the 1970s onwards. Yet a simple rule of thumb seems to be that the typical non-HI(P)C country received transfers around 2 per cent of GDP. Effective aid to this group also increased over the sample period, but effective aid was always well below 1 per cent of real GDP. Official aid to the HIC group was quite low and appears to have undergone a cyclical movement over the sample period. The median of effective aid to the HIC group was more constant, fluctuating around 0.12–0.13 per cent of GDP in the three middle periods, but increasing to 0.17 per cent in the last period. Finally, using both measures of aid, the median HIPC country received increasing inflows. However, the two aid measures also show divergence for this group. The increase in the median of ODA flows from the first to the last period is almost 10 percentage points; in contrast the increase in the median EDA is only 1.25 percentage points.

The discrepancy between the time-paths of ODA and EDA can, to a large extent, be explained by the treatment of debt forgiveness and by variations in the grant elements of the official loans. To illustrate the latter point, Table 7.2 reports medians of the average grant elements in EDA loans. As seen, the average grant elements fluctuate over time, and for the median non-HI(P)C country the grant element is actually lower at the end of the sample compared to the beginning. Once more, there is a marked difference between the country groups, as the grant element has a somewhat cyclical pattern for the median non-HI(P)C and median HIC country while it is trending upwards for the median HIPC country. The time pattern for the two first groups is interesting, as there appears to be a peak around the debt-crisis years followed by a sharp decline in the succeeding period. This is worth a thought in relation to the HIPC Initiative because it shows that ODA transfers may increase while at the same time aid – in terms of grant elements – may actually decrease.

The last rows of Table 7.2 report the median difference between ODA inflows and debt service payments. Most countries had debt service payments in excess of ODA inflows throughout the sample period. But this is not the case for the HIPC countries, for which most had larger ODA inflows than debt service outflows. The fact that ODA inflows exceeded debt service payments has led Birdsall, Claessens and Diwan (Chapter 3 in this volume), among others, to question if the debt overhang theory of Krugman and Sachs is relevant for the HIPC countries. Sachs *et al.* (1999), however, argue that the debt burden falls heavily on the budget, while grants frequently finance the extra-budgetary activities established by donors, resulting in a deinstitutionalization of public activities. The latter effect may induce poorer policies and this may be interpreted as a debt overhang effect.

Summing up, it is evident that most of the HIPC countries (in this sample) had significantly lower growth rates and investment ratios; poorer institutions; higher budget deficits; slower movement towards open trade policies and higher aid inflows compared to the HIC countries in Latin America and other developing countries in our sample. They also had higher debt–GDP ratios (in both nominal and NPV terms), but they did not, in general, have high debt service payments compared to the HIC countries and, throughout, the ODA exceeded debt service payments in most of the countries in this group.

In what follows we focus on the impact of debt service payments and aid flows on growth and investment, conditional on the policy variables discussed above. The central question is whether reducing debt service payments is beneficial to growth at constant or decreasing levels of aid inflows.

Econometric results

In this section we look at cross-country regressions to assess the statistical significance and economic impact of external debt and aid. On p. 143 we present the results of growth regressions, before turning to investment regressions. Later we make an attempt to assess whether debt service payments and aid flows are correlated (both in good times and in bad times). Throughout, debt service payments and aid flows are included as endogenous regressors.[7] There are several reasons why we consider debt service payments to be endogenously determined. First of all, a country may be forced, or may choose, to postpone debt service, either formally through negotiations or *de facto* as arrears. In any event, postponing debt service is in all likelihood a function of the growth rate. One particular link, noted by Easterly (2001), is that GDP growth interacted with the debt–GDP ratio is a good predictor of debt servicing problems if these problems arise because of insolvent public sectors. Second, endogeneity of aid implies endogeneity of debt service because part of the debt service, which is actually paid, may have been financed through new loans or grants. Finally, we wish to focus on the predictable part of the debt service payments, as this is what governments and investors include in development plans and projects.[8]

In all regressions we condition on the macroeconomic policy and institutional variables as discussed. In addition to these controls, we also include time dummies to capture the worldwide changes in growth rates and a dummy for Sub-Saharan Africa (SSA).

Growth regressions

Table 7.3 presents results of cross-country growth regressions using the 50 countries given in Table 7.1. To take account of the endogeneity of

Table 7.3 Growth regressions

Dependent variable	*Growth rate in real GDP per capita (%)*					
Sample	*50 countries, 5 periods (1974–77 to 1990–93)*					
Regression	*(1)*	*(2)[a]*	*(3)[b]*	*(4)[c]*	*(5)[d]*	*(6)[e]*
Budget surplus	0.040	0.003	0.075**	0.072**	0.027	0.014
(% of GDP)	(1.17)	(0.09)	(2.56)	(2.38)	(0.73)	(0.38)
Inflation	−0.017**	−0.018**	−0.014**	−0.014**	−0.016**	−0.015**
	(4.15)	(4.37)	(3.27)	(3.32)	(3.65)	(3.62)
Sachs–Warner	2.085**	2.221**	1.899**	1.791**	2.267**	2.256**
openness	(4.40)	(4.83)	(4.12)	(4.03)	(4.83)	(4.96)
Institutional quality	0.573**	0.606**	0.660**	0.618**	0.666**	0.653**
	(3.67)	(4.12)	(4.34)	(4.14)	(4.40)	(4.35)
Sub-Saharan Africa	−1.549**	−1.598**	−2.131**	−2.137**	−2.476**	−2.777**
	(3.21)	(3.42)	(3.94)	(3.94)	(4.18)	(4.25)
Debt service		−0.092			−0.145*	−0.161**
(TDS–GDP, %)		(1.15)			(1.98)	(2.28)
Official aid			0.115**		0.140**	
(ODA–GDP, %)			(2.93)		(2.73)	
Effective aid				0.281**		0.440**
(real EDA–GDP, %)				(2.60)		(2.84)
Observations	226	226	226	226	226	226
RMSE	2.92	2.84	2.91	2.87	2.87	2.83
Hansen *J*-test		0.14	0.17	0.28	0.31	0.50

Notes: Time dummies are included in all regressions. Robust *t*-statistics in parentheses. * Significant at 10%, ** significant at 5%.

Regression (1) is an OLS regression; regressions (2)–(6) are two-step GMM regressions. Instruments common to regressions (2)–(6): Initial real GDP *per capita*, Initial external debt, Initial external debt squared.

[a] Additional instruments: Lagged debt service and lagged debt service squared.

[b] Additional instruments: Lagged official aid and lagged official aid squared.

[c] Additional instruments: Lagged effective aid and lagged effective aid squared.

[d] Additional instruments: Instruments in regressions (2) and (3).

[e] Additional instruments: Instruments in regressions (2) and (4).

debt service payments and aid flows, all results in which these variables are used as regressors are based on instrumental variable GMM regressions (see, e.g., Hayashi, 2000: Chapter 3).

Regression (1) is the baseline formulation that includes only the control variables. The results of the baseline regression are in accordance with other studies. The impact of a budget surplus appears positive, but highly imprecisely determined. Inflation has a significantly negative impact on growth, yet the importance in terms of economic significance appears modest. If the median HIC had experienced an annual inflation rate of roughly 15 per cent in the 1990–93 period instead of 25 per cent, the result would have been an increase of less than 0.2 percentage points in the growth rate. However, the extreme inflation rates experienced in some of the countries in the sample do seem to have a measurable impact on growth. (Decreasing inflation by 1 standard deviation, 36 percentage points, leads to about a 0.6 percentage point increase in growth.) An open trade policy does seem to have both statistically and economically significant impact on growth. Closed economies (say, Malawi, Nigeria and Pakistan) give up 2 percentage points of annual growth compared to open economies (say, Bolivia, Ghana and Indonesia), so the movement towards more open trade polices should have resulted in increased growth – everything else being equal. Institutional quality is also both statistically significant and economically important. If the median HIPC were able to change the institutional quality rating to achieve the rating of the median HIC country, this would lead, according to the regression results, to just above a 0.4 percentage point increase in annual growth. Finally, it appears that the growth rates of the 18 SSA countries in the sample were on average more than 1.5 percentage points lower than the countries outside this region – conditional on policies and institutions.

Regressions (2), (3) and (4) in Table 7.3 append debt service payments, official aid and effective aid to the baseline regression one at a time. The results are that debt service payments have a negative, but quite insignificant, impact on growth while aid has a significantly positive impact regardless of the aid measure. The insignificance of debt service payments is slightly surprising in light of other recent empirical analyses of debt and growth. In particular, Chowdhury (Chapter 8 in this volume) explores the impact of debt service payments on growth using the modified extreme bounds analysis of Levine and Renelt (1992). Chowdhury finds debt service payments to have a robust negative impact on growth in both a sample including only HIPCs and a sample including only non-HIPCs.[9]

Regressions (5) and (6) give the central results of our analysis. In these regressions debt service payments and aid inflows are added jointly to the baseline regression.[10] In both regressions, debt service payments and aid are statistically significant, so we may address the question: what is the average impact on growth if both debt service payments and aid flows are reduced? In regression (5) the positive impact of official aid and the negative impact of debt service payments are of the same order of magnitude, and the sum of the coefficients is not significantly different from zero. Hence, if debt service payments are reduced while official aid is kept constant (one form of additionality) there will be a positive impact on growth, amounting to roughly 15 basis points for each 1 percentage point decrease in debt service payments to GDP. According to IMF and IDA (2002) for the 26 countries that have reached their decision points under HIPC II, the decline in average annual debt service to GDP during 2001–05 is expected to be 1.3 percentage points lower compared to 1998–99. Using regression (5) this will lead to an increase in annual growth of just below 0.2 percentage points. For comparison we may note that the effect corresponds to a 12 percentage point decrease in annual inflation or one-tenth of the drop in average growth rates from 1974–78 to the later periods. But note that if official aid is reduced one for one with the debt service payments, there will be no gain in terms of growth. Hence, according to the regression results, the small positive effect of debt relief disappears if there is no additionality – unless there is an indirect effect working through policies.

Comparing regressions (5) and (6) we find that effective aid has a much larger impact compared to official aid, as the coefficient on effective aid is more than three times larger than the coefficient on official aid. Yet, this corresponds well to the ratio of official aid to effective aid in the sample. The overall average ratio is 4, with a sharp increase in the final period – probably because of debt forgiveness; the median ratio is 3 throughout. The interesting difference is that official aid may be constant and even increase slightly while effective aid decreases. Recall, from Table 7.2, that official aid to the median HIC doubled from 1982–85 to 1986–89 while at the same time effective aid was constant.[11] There was also an increase in official aid to the median HIPC country of more than 3.5 percentage points from 1986–89 to 1990–93 while effective aid was roughly constant.[12] If the HIPC Initiative goes together with a decrease in effective aid, the HIPCs may well experience a negative effect on growth even though there is additionality in the form of constant official aid.

When official and effective aid are included jointly in the growth regression, the result is a significant impact of effective aid while the impact of official aid becomes insignificant.[13] This implies that regression (6), i.e. using effective aid, seems to be preferred when the two aid flows are compared. Interestingly, this points towards the importance of the level of grants, not the level of official aid flows, in the discussion of additionality.

At this point it must be stressed that the results are partial. In the regressions we condition on macroeconomic policies and institutional quality. If the removal of the debt overhang and the (increased) donor pressure lead to changing policies and institutions, this will counteract the direct impact of changes in debt service payments and aid flows. The result may be an overall positive impact on growth following non-additional debt relief.

Investment regressions

Most of the recent studies on debt problems and aid effectiveness concentrate on the impact on growth. But in the early and mid-1990s, interest was centred on investment rates because the debt overhang theory was linked directly to investment. (See, e.g., Greene and Villanueva, 1991; Savides, 1992; Warner, 1992; Cohen, 1993; Servén and Solimano, 1993; and Oshikoya, 1994.) With the exception of Warner, all studies conclude that debt (either debt stock or debt service payments, or both) had a negative impact on investment rates. In order to complete our analysis of debt service payments and aid, we follow these authors and estimate investment regressions. We make no attempt in the direction of formulating a structural investment relation; instead we condition on the initial level of real GDP *per capita* and the policy controls used in the growth regressions. However, in contrast to the growth regressions, we apply an estimator that takes account of unobserved country specific effects. This is quite common in cross-country investment regressions.[14] Using a fixed-effects estimator implies that we may drop time constant regressors. Hence, the measure of institutional quality and the SSA dummy are left out from the investment regressions in Table 7.4.

Regression (1) in Table 7.4 is the baseline regression. The following regressions (2)–(4) append debt service payments and the two aid variables one by one. Finally, regressions (5) and (6) jointly include debt service payments and each of the aid variables.

Looking first at the control variables we find, not surprisingly, that the initial level of GDP *per capita* has a strong positive impact on investment in all regressions. The elasticity of the investment ratio with respect to initial GDP *per capita* evaluated at the mean varies between

Table 7.4 Investment regressions

Dependent variable	*Growth domestic investment (% of GDP)*					
Sample	*50 countries, 5 periods (1974–77 to 1990–93)*					
Regression	*(1)*	*(2)*[a]	*(3)*[b]	*(4)*[c]	*(5)*[d]	*(6)*[e]
Initial real GDP	0.108**	0.112**	0.171**	0.182**	0.175**	0.202**
per capita (log)*100	(3.54)	(3.49)	(4.68)	(4.72)	(4.40)	(4.83)
Budget surplus	−0.179	−0.175	−0.215**	−0.240**	−0.233**	−0.282**
(% of GDP)	(1.54)	(1.49)	(1.99)	(2.13)	(2.30)	(2.75)
Inflation	−0.028**	−0.027*	−0.028*	−0.026*	−0.031**	−0.030**
	(2.37)	(1.92)	(1.69)	(1.70)	(2.62)	(2.63)
Sachs–Warner	2.034	1.917	2.123*	1.586	2.425*	1.807
openness	(1.49)	(1.45)	(1.69)	(1.24)	(1.91)	(1.32)
Debt service		0.161			−0.389*	−0.583**
(TDS–GDP, %)		(0.96)			(1.94)	(2.42)
Official aid			0.668**		0.817**	
(ODA–GDP, %)			(3.05)		(2.99)	
Effective aid				2.252**		3.265**
(real EDA–GDP, %)				(2.64)		(3.49)
Observations	176	176	176	176	176	176
RMSE	4.13	4.16	4.21	4.30	4.24	4.44
Hansen *J*-test		0.99	0.10	0.21	0.44	0.21

Notes: All regressions are based on orthogonal deviations (see Arellano and Bover, 1995). Time dummies are included in all regressions. Robust *t*-statistics in parentheses. * Significant at 10%; ** significant at 5%. Regression (1) is an OLS regression; regressions (2)–(6) are two-stage least squares (2SLS) regressions.

Instruments common to regressions (2)–(6): Initial external debt, Initial external debt squared.

[a] Additional instruments: Lagged debt service and lagged debt service squared.

[b] Additional instruments: Lagged official aid and lagged official aid squared.

[c] Additional instruments: Lagged effective aid and lagged effective aid squared.

[d] Additional instruments: Instruments in regressions (2) and (3).

[e] Additional instruments: Instruments in regressions (2) and (4).

0.5 (regression (1)) and 0.9 (regression (6)). We record a negative effect of the budget surplus in all regressions, although it is not always statistically significant. The negative impact of improvements in the fiscal balance may seem surprising in light of the importance of reductions in budget deficits in many of the structural adjustment programmes (SAPs) in the sample period. However, this result is nicely explained in Servén and Solimano (1993) and Easterly (1999); fiscal adjustment (frequently forced) is often implemented by cutting public investment. Unless this reduction in public investment is counteracted by an increase in private investment, gross domestic investment will decrease, and Servén and Solimano (among others) actually find complementarity between public and private investment leading to an even larger drop in gross domestic investment. Inflation has also a negative impact on investment, which is a more anticipated result. A 10 percentage point increase in inflation appears to lead to a drop in the investment ratio in the neighbourhood of 0.3 percentage points. Finally, open trade policies have a positive impact, but in our regressions the effect is not well determined. This may be due to the binary nature of the Sachs–Warner openness variable in combination with the fixed-effects estimator.

Turning to the variables of primary interest, we find no significant effect of debt service payments when this variable is added separately. In contrast, both aid measures are statistically significant and the impact of effective aid is roughly three times higher than the impact of official aid. This corresponds to the results of the growth regressions. When debt service payments and the aid variables are included jointly, we find significant effects of both flows with opposite signs. If official aid is kept constant while debt service payments increase by 1 percentage point, there will be a decrease in the investment rate of just above 0.33 of a percentage point. Interpreting this experiment as a change in net outflows, we find the result to correspond well with the finding in Cohen (1993) given the differences in data and analytical methods. Yet, in regression (5) it is possible to look at a counteracting change in official aid flows that keeps net flows unchanged, and we find that this experiment leads to a significant increase in the investment ratio by roughly 0.4 percentage points. Given the HIPC Initiative, the experiment should be reversed – i.e. lack of additionality in the form of equally reduced debt service payments and aid inflows seems to have a negative impact on investment. This result is somewhat stronger than the result for growth where equal changes in official aid and debt service payments balance exactly.

The results in regression (6) also support the corresponding growth regression, as the impact of effective aid is four times larger than the impact of official aid. Moreover, we find effective aid to be significant and official aid insignificant also for investments in a regression including both variables. Again, a probable conclusion is that debt relief accompanied by changes in the composition of aid flows leading to constant official aid and decreasing effective aid has a negative impact on both growth and investment – unless policy changes counteract the effect.

Co-movements in debt service payments and aid

Having looked at the possible effect of (non-)additionality, the question remains as to whether it is a valid experiment to decrease debt service payments and aid simultaneously.[15] There is little doubt that the increasing debt in SSA (of which 34 countries are HIPCs) was accompanied by increasing aid flows. Sachs *et al.* (1999), Kanbur (2000) and Birdsall, Claessens and Diwan (Chapter 3 in this volume) all stress this point.[16] But this does not necessarily imply that decreasing debt service payments goes along with decreasing aid flows. Going beyond SSA by looking at the three country groups introduced earlier, we may give a partial answer to the question by looking at the correlations between debt service payments and the two aid statistics. Another, perhaps more interesting, partial answer can be given by looking at reduced form relations for debt service and aid flows to the HICs.

Table 7.5 presents the correlations between contemporaneous debt service payments and aid flows. The relationship between debt service and aid is positive and quite strong when we focus on the HICs, and for this group of countries the correlations with the two aid measures are practically identical (0.39 vs 0.38). The HIPC group has a lower correlation between debt service payments and official aid compared to the HIC group, whereas the correlation with effective aid is higher. The correlations between debt service payments and the aid variables are statistically significant for both of the two aforementioned groups. This is not the case when we focus on the non-HI(P)C countries. The correlations are negative for these countries, but highly insignificant.

One problem with the simple correlations is that the average increases over time in debt service payments and aid inflows in particular in the HIPCs may result in spurious correlations. Therefore we also report conditional correlations between debt service payments and aid in which time effects are partialled out by regression on time dummies. There is no significant impact on the HIC and non-HI(P)C group

Table 7.5 Correlations between debt service payments and aid

	Debt service and official aid			*Debt service and effective aid*		
	HIC	*HIPC*	*Non-HI(P)C*	*HIC*	*HIPC*	*Non-HI(P)C*
Raw data	0.39	0.30	−0.11	0.38	0.44	−0.11
Conditional on time dummies	0.43	0.21	−0.08	0.41	0.37	−0.13

correlations while the HIPC correlations decrease as expected. However, the latter correlations are still high and significant between debt service payments and effective aid in particular.

Overall, the correlations show that debt service payments and aid flows did not vary independently in the HIC and HIPCs, but on the other hand there is no evidence of tight co-movements. Needless to say, there are many factors causing debt service and aid flows hence the conclusion from the correlations is just that there is a historical record of simultaneous changes in debt service and aid.

In order to dig a bit deeper into the question of co-movements between debt service and aid flows, we look at reduced form regressions for aid and debt service flows focusing on the HIC group. The HICs are interesting because all 15 countries have experienced both increasing and decreasing debt service payments as a percentage of GDP in the sample period.

Table 7.6 reports results for three pairs of regressions, each pair being a system of debt service payments and a measure of aid. The three systems

Table 7.6 Reduced form regressions for aid and debt service in HICs

Dependent variable	*Official aid*	*Debt service*	*Effective aid*	*Debt service*	*Average grant element*	*Debt service*
Regression	*(1a)*	*(1b)*	*(2a)*	*(2b)*	*(3a)*	*(3b)*
Lagged real *per capita* GDP growth	−0.134** (2.00)	−0.087 (0.93)	−0.044** (2.31)	−0.087 (0.93)	−1.180* (1.88)	−0.018 (0.17)
Initial real GDP *per capita* (log)	−0.497 (1.64)	−0.569** (1.96)	−0.139 (1.44)	−0.550* (1.79)	−5.850* (1.85)	−1.140** (2.17)
Lagged debt service	0.045 (1.42)	0.746** (11.5)	0.031** (2.96)	0.738** (12.65)	1.044** (2.04)	0.745** (7.29)
Lagged official aid	0.962** (5.86)	0.123 (0.83)				
Lagged effective aid			0.898** (7.58)	0.466 (0.88)		
Lagged avg. grant element					0.692** (7.48)	0.003 (0.15)
Observations	75	75	75	75	60	60
R^2	0.84	0.69	0.83	0.69	0.68	0.63
Residual correlation	0.01		−0.09		−0.16	

Notes: Time dummies are included in all regressions. Robust *t*-statistics in parentheses.
* Significant at 10%, ** significant at 5%.

include only lagged regressors in order to avoid endogeneity issues. This means that the regressions should not be interpreted as structural in any way, but merely as simple forecast models. The systems share a very limited set of control variables, as only time dummies, the lagged growth rate and the initial value of real GDP *per capita* are included in the regressions.[17]

Looking first at the system of official aid and debt service payments in regressions (1a)–(1b) it appears that the model for official aid is really about the changes in *aid flows*. The coefficient to lagged aid is 0.96 and not significantly different from 1. The only other significant variable in the regression for official aid is the lagged growth rate, which has a negative impact on the changes in aid. In other words, countries with a history of relatively high growth rates have decreasing levels of official aid to GDP. Conditional on lagged aid and growth there is no significant link from lagged debt service payments to official aid.[18] Moreover, the residual correlation given in the last row of Table 7.6 reveals that, conditional on the past, there is no contemporaneous relationship between debt service and official aid flows. The regression for debt service (1b) has also only two significant regressors. But here it is the lagged debt service and the initial level of real *per capita* GDP. This means that there was no (robust) direct link between debt service payments and official aid flows in the HIC countries in the 1980s and early 1990s. However, in Table 7.3 it is established that official aid and debt service payments both had an impact on growth, which means that there was an indirect link.

The picture is different for effective aid and debt service payments reported in regressions (2a)–(2b). The two debt service regressions (1b) and (2b) are practically identical, in particular neither official aid nor effective aid has any impact on the debt service flows, once lagged debt service and initial income are conditioned upon. But, there is a link from debt service payments to effective aid. As the coefficient is positive, we find that periods with relatively high debt service payments are followed by periods with relatively high effective aid inflows – and vice versa – which is an important observation in the present context: decreasing debt service is followed by decreasing effective aid. The impact of debt service seems quite low, but this is because effective aid as a percentage of GDP is low in the HIC countries (see Table 7.2). In fact, the elasticity of effective aid with respect to lagged debt service is exactly 1 when evaluated at the HIC group median. Thus, a 1 per cent decrease in debt service payments is followed by a 1 per cent decrease in effective aid flows.[19] Since the model is dynamic, with a high coefficient to lagged aid, there seems to be a high cumulative effect of changes in debt service payments.

We end the analysis of the HIC countries by looking slightly differently at the aid flows. Specifically, in the third system in Table 7.6 we use the average grant element as a dependent variable. As noted in Table 7.2 the grant element for the median HIC country showed a mildly cyclical behaviour somewhat similar to the debt service payments, and the results in regressions (3a)–(3b) demonstrate that there is a statistically significant link between the average grant element and debt service payments. The average grant element of EDA loans is decreasing in the lagged growth rate and the initial real GDP *per capita*, although both effects are only weakly significant. Furthermore, the link between debt service payments and effective aid is confirmed, as there is a significant positive link from lagged debt service to the average grant element. So when the debt service payments fell, the average grant elements followed, and it appears to be of the order of 1 percentage point drop in debt service to GDP leading to a 1 percentage point drop in the average grant element. Again, we find causation from debt service to aid but not the other way round.

Needless to say the analysis of co-movements must be interpreted with caution in relation to the HIPC Initiative. We look at 15 HICs over a very interesting but fairly short period of time, and these countries were never promised anything in terms of additional inflows. However, the results of the divergence of official and effective aid are interesting. By varying the interest rate and the maturity or the grace period on a loan, it is easy to change the grant element in a way that will not be recorded in the ODA statistics. And it appears that the HICs did experience such changes in the composition of aid flows.

Discussion

In this study we have focused on the additionality issue of the HIPC Initiative. The question of whether or not the debt relief resources are supplementing conventional aid flows is important for at least four reasons. First of all, it is impossible to measure whether aid flows are in fact additional. Second, it is highly unlikely that the sum of all debt relief resources can ever be additional. Some bilateral donors have fixed aid budgets given as percentages of their gross national income, and for these donors (say, Denmark, the Netherlands, Norway, Sweden) debt relief has not been, and will not be, additional. For other countries (say, the United States and Japan) it is questionable whether it is the HIPC Initiatives or foreign policy that (may) generate increases in the foreign aid budgets. For the international financial institutions (IFIs), it has been argued that the World Bank (IDA) is unable to make debt relief resources additional, while it should be possible for the IMF, at least to some extent. Third, the desirability of additionality on a country-by-country basis has been questioned. Authors like Kanbur (2000), Birdsall and Williamson (2002), and Birdsall, Claessens and Diwan (Chapter 3 in this volume) all call for non-additionality in order to strengthen policy conditionality and country selectivity in future aid allocations. According to their view, a major argument in favour of the HIPC Initiative is that donors can give up defensive lending to HICs and reallocate aid to countries with good policies and institutions. Finally, it may be questioned whether additionality is really necessary for a successful outcome of the HIPC Initiative. If the negative incentive effects of debt overhang and the uncertainty in debt service payments are substantial, then HIPC debt relief may actually generate increasing growth and development even though the net transfers are kept constant.

The main result of our study is that additionality is actually important. If debt service payments and ODA are reduced one for one, there is no impact on growth, while there may be a drop in investment rates. Moreover, even if the level of official assistance is kept constant, there may be a negative impact on growth if the lending terms get harder, i.e. if the grant element of the loans decreases. This form of non-additionality is interesting because it is difficult to detect from (aggregated) official statistics and because it appears that changes in the grant element were actually related to changes in debt service payments in the Baker plan group of heavily indebted countries in the late 1980s and early 1990s.

When changes in EDA in the HIC group and the World Bank emphasis on policy conditionality and country selectivity in aid allocations – which seem to have broad support among US scholars and politicians – are coupled with our regression results, it emerges that not all HIPCs are sure to benefit from the HIPC Initiative in terms of higher economic growth.

Appendix A: data sources

Real *per capita* GDP growth (per cent)	World Bank, World Development Indicators (WDI)
Gross domestic investment (per cent of GDP)	World Bank, World Development Indicator (WDI)
Initial real GDP *per capita* (1985-PPP$)	Penn World Tables, Mark 5
Institutional quality	Knack and Keefer (1995)

Budget surplus (per cent of GDP)	IMF, IFS and World Bank, WDI
Inflation (per cent)	IMF, IFS (log differences of CPI)
Sachs–Warner openness	Sachs and Warner (1995)
External debt (per cent of GDP)	World Bank, WDI
NPV of debt (per cent of GDP)	Easterly (2001)
Debt service (TDS/GDP, per cent)	World Bank, WDI
Official aid (ODA/GDP, per cent)	OECD, DAC
Effective aid (EDA/GDP, per cent)	Burnside and Dollar (2000)
Average grant element	Chang, Fernandez-Arias and Servén (1998)

Notes

* I am grateful to Carl-Johan Dalgaard for numerous discussions that turned an idea at large into the present study, to Peter Hjertholm for his encyclopaedic knowledge about external debt in developing countries and to Jens Kovsted and John Rand for their sharp comments.

1. Bolivia is classified both as HIC and HIPC.
2. The epochs are: 1974–77; 1978–81; 1982–85; 1986–89 and 1990–93. Initial income and the debt stock variables are observations for the years 1973, 1977, 1981, 1985 and 1989.
3. Sachs and Warner (1995) define a country as having a closed trade policy if it has (at least) one of four characteristics: (i) Non-tariff barriers (NTBs) covering 40 per cent or more of trade; (ii) a black market exchange rate that is depreciated by 20 per cent or more relative to the official exchange rate; (iii) a socialist economic system or (iv) a state monopoly on major exports.
4. The data for NPV of external debt are from Easterly (2001).
5. Renard and Cassimon (2001) provide another methodological discussion of aid measurements and discuss the relative merits of ODA and EDA.
6. Prior to 1989, debt forgiveness was negligible but in the period 1990–93 a total of US$7.4 billion was classified as debt forgiveness by DAC.
7. Endogeneity of aid has been discussed in depth elsewhere therefore we do not pursue this issue here. See, e.g., Papanek (1972), Burnside and Dollar (2000) and Hansen and Tarp (2001).
8. The importance of uncertainty in aid flows and debt service payments has been analysed elsewhere. See Lensink and Morrissey (2000) on aid flows, Claessens *et al.* (1997) for a survey of results about the debt burden and uncertainty and Dijkstra and Hermes (2001) for an analysis of growth and uncertainty in debt service payments.
9. There are many possible explanations for the different results: country coverage, time periods and estimation methods. With respect to the last point we may note that when regression (2) is estimated using OLS with a standard co-variance estimator, the impact of debt service payments is significant.
10. In other studies we have advocated decreasing returns to aid in the form of adding aid squared to the regressions (Dalgaard and Hansen, 2001; Hansen and Tarp, 2000, 2001). For the sake of completeness we may add that squared terms of aid and debt service payments are statistically insignificant in regressions (5) and (6).

11. A more concrete observation is that effective aid to Argentina was halved (0.03 to 0.015 per cent of real GDP) while official aid more than tripled (0.04 to 0.14 per cent of current GDP) from 1982–85 to 1986–89.
12. Here the example could be Sierra Leone for which official aid almost doubled (9 to 17 per cent of GDP) from 1986–89 to 1990–93 while effective aid remained constant (2.3 per cent of real GDP).
13. A regression including both official and effective aid makes no sense in terms of economics; therefore we do not report the regression results in Table 7.3. But such a regression is the artificial model nesting regressions (5) and (6) in Table 7.3. See Atkinson (1970) for the original idea for this kind of nesting and Gourieroux and Monfort (1994) for a survey of testing non-nested hypotheses.
14. We have chosen to apply the orthogonal deviation transformation proposed by Arellano and Bover (1995).
15. The examples of deviations between official aid and effective aid in Table 7.2 are illuminating but they do not 'prove' a systematic tendency, which is what we need in assessing the historical validity of the experiment.
16. UNCTAD (2000) extend the country coverage slightly as they find a close correlation between gross official disbursements and debt service in the 48 least developed countries in 1997 and 1998; 18 of the LDCs are outside Africa.
17. This means that we are actually looking at a trivariate auto regression in (log) real *per capita* GDP, aid and debt service. However, the GDP regressions are of no interest in the present context, which is why they are not reported.
18. The insignificance of lagged debt service payments is driven by one observation; Jamaica 1990–93. If this observation is excluded (or all observations for Jamaica) there is a significant positive impact from debt service payments. However, it is difficult to explain why Jamaica should be excluded from the analysis except for the fact that Jamaica is the HIC country with the highest debt service payments–GDP in all periods.
19. When Jamaica 1990–93 is excluded from the system with official aid, the elasticity of official aid with respect to debt service payments is 0.76. So, whether or not we record a significant link from debt service to official aid, the impact on effective aid is larger than on official aid.

References

Arellano, M. and O. Bover (1995). 'Another Look at the Instrumental Variables Estimation of Error-Components Models', *Journal of Econometrics*, 68: 29–51.

Atkinson, A. C. (1970). 'A Method for Discriminating between Models', *Journal of the Royal Statistical Society*, Series B, 32: 323–53.

Birdsall, N. and J. Williamson (2002). 'Delivering on Debt Relief: From IMF Gold to a New Aid Architecture', Washington, DC: Center for Global Development and Institute for International Economics.

Burnside, C. and D. Dollar (2000). 'Aid, Policies, and Growth', *American Economic Review*, 90: 847–68.

Chang, C. C., E. Fernandez-Arias and L. Servén (1998). 'Measuring Aid Flows: A New Approach', Policy Research Working Paper 2050, Washington, DC: World Bank.

Chong, A. and C. Calderón (2000). 'Causality and Feedback Between Institutional Measures and Economic Growth', *Economics and Politics*, 12: 69–81.

Claessens, S., E. Detragiache, R. Kanbur and P. Wickham (1997). 'Analytical Aspects of the Debt Problems of Heavily Indebted Poor Countries', in Z. Iqbal and R. Kanbur (eds), *External Finance for Low-Income Countries*, Washington, DC: International Monetary Fund, 21–48.

Cohen, D. (1993). 'Low Investment and Large LDC Debt in the 1980s', *American Economic Review*, 83: 437–49.

Dalgaard, C.-J. and H. Hansen (2001). 'On Aid, Growth and Good Policies', *Journal of Development Studies*, 37: 17–41.

Dijkstra, G. and N. Hermes (2001). 'The Uncertainty of Debt Service Payments and Economic Growth of HIPCs: Is There a Case for Debt Relief?', WIDER Discussion Paper DP2001/122, Helsinki: UNU–WIDER.

Easterly, W. R. (1999). 'How Did Highly Indebted Poor Countries Become Highly Indebted? Reviewing Two Decades of Debt Relief', Development Research Group, Washington, DC: World Bank.

Easterly, W. R. (2000). 'When Is Fiscal Adjustment an Illusion?', *Economic Policy*, 28: 57–86.

Easterly, W. R. (2001). 'Growth Implosions and Debt Explosions: Do Growth Slowdowns Cause Public Debt Crises?', *Contributions to Macroeconomics*, 1: Article 1.

Gourieroux, C. and A. Monfort (1994). 'Testing Non-Nested Hypotheses', in R. F. Engle and D. L. McFadden (eds), *Handbook of Econometrics, IV*, Amsterdam Elsevier Science, 2583–37.

Greene, J. and D. Villanueva (1991). 'Private Investment in Developing Countries', *IMF Staff Papers*, 38: 33–58.

Hansen, H. and F. Tarp (2000). 'Aid Effectiveness Disputed', *Journal of International Development*, 12: 375–98.

Hansen, H. and F. Tarp (2001). 'Aid and Growth Regressions', *Journal of Development Economics*, 64: 547–70.

Hayashi, F. (2000). *Econometrics*, Princeton: Princeton University Press.

IMF (International Monetary Fund) and IDA (International Development Association) (2002). 'Heavily Indebted Poor Countries (HIPC) Initiative: Status of Implementation', available at: www.imf.org/external/np/hipc/2002/status/ 041202.htm.

Kanbur, R. (2000). 'Aid, Conditionality and Debt in Africa', in F. Tarp (ed.), *Foreign Aid and Development: Lessons Learnt and Directions for the Future*, London and New York: Routledge, 409–22.

Knack, S. and P. Keefer (1995). 'Institutions and Economic Performance: Cross-Country Tests Using Alternative Institutional Measures', *Economics and Politics*, 7: 207–27.

Krugman, P. (1988). 'Financing vs. Forgiving a Debt Overhang: Some Analytical Notes', *Journal of Development Economics*, 29: 253–68.

Lensink, R. and O. Morrissey (2000). 'Aid Instability as a Measure of Uncertainty and the Positive Impact of Aid on Growth', *Journal of Development Studies*, 36: 31–49.

Levine, R. and D. Renelt (1992). 'A Sensitivity Analysis of Cross-Country Growth Regressions', *American Economic Review*, 82: 942–63.

Oshikoya, T. W. (1994). 'Macroeconomic Determinants of Domestic Private Investment in Africa: An Empirical Analysis', *Economic Development and Cultural Change*, 42: 573–96.

Papanek, G. F. (1972). 'The Effect of Aid and Other Resource Transfers on Savings and Growth in Less Developed Countries', *Economic Journal*, 82: 934–50.

Renard, R. and D. Cassimon (2001). 'On the Pitfalls of Measuring Aid', WIDER Discussion Paper DP2001/69, Helsinki: UNU–WIDER.

Sachs, J. D. (1989). 'The Debt Overhang of Developing Countries', in J. B. de Macedo and R. Findlay (eds), *Debt, Growth and Stabilization: Essay in Memory of Carlos F. Diaz Alejandro*, Oxford: Basil Blackwell for UNU-WIDER.

Sachs, J. D., K. Botchwey, M. Cuchra and S. Sievers (1999). 'Implementing Debt Relief for the HIPCs', Center for International Development Working Paper, Cambridge, MA: Harvard University.

Sachs, J. D. and A. M. Warner (1995). 'Economic Reform and the Process of Global Integration', *Brooking Papers on Economic Activity*, 1: 1–118.

Savides, A. (1992). 'Investment Slowdown in Developing Countries during the 1980s: Debt Overhang or Foreign Capital Inflows?', *Kyklos*, 45: 363–78.

Serven, L. and A. Solimano (1993). 'Debt Crisis, Adjustment Policies and Capital Formation in Developing Countries: Where Do We Stand?', *World Development*, 21: 127–40.

UNCTAD (United Nations Conference on Trade and Development) (2000). *The Least Developed Countries 2000 Report*, New York and Geneva: UNCTAD.

Warner, A. M. (1992). 'Did the Debt Crisis Cause the Investment Crisis?', *Quarterly Journal of Economics*, 107: 1161–86.

World Bank (1998). *Assessing Aid, What Works, What Doesn't, and Why*, World Bank Policy Research Report, Oxford: Oxford University Press.

8
External Debt, Growth and the HIPC Initiative: Is the Country Choice Too Narrow?

Abdur R. Chowdhury

Introduction

The external debt burden of many low- and middle-income developing countries has increased significantly since the 1980s.[1] This prompted the multilateral Paris Club and other official bilateral and commercial creditors to design a framework in 1996 to provide special assistance for heavily indebted poor countries (HIPCs) for whom traditional debt relief mechanisms (provided under the Paris Club's Naples terms) are not sufficient.[2] In return, these countries agreed to pursue IMF- and World Bank-supported adjustment and reform programmes and meet specific policy and performance criteria.

The HIPC Initiative has been considered a major breakthrough mainly due to its key goal of reducing the debt of poor countries to sustainable levels that would allow them to avoid the process of repeated debt rescheduling. As of April 2003, 41 countries, mostly in Africa, have been classified as being eligible for debt relief under the HIPC Initiative (IMF, 2003).[3] Of this group, 26 countries have debt relief agreements in place, with relief already flowing in. Two countries (Bolivia and Uganda) have already reached their completion points under the enhanced HIPC Initiative of 1999 (HIPC II), which replaced the original HIPC Initiative of 1996 (HIPC I) (IMF, 2001, 2003).

Nevertheless, major concerns have been raised by policy makers and academics about the capacity of the enhanced HIPC Initiative to provide long-term debt sustainability, mainly because (i) the growth assumption is too optimistic; (ii) debt sustainability analysis is inappropriate; and (iii) country selection is too narrow (Gunter, 2001).[4] It is the third issue that is the main focus of this chapter.

A large number of studies on external debt have concentrated only on the countries included in the HIPC Initiative (Sachs *et al.*, 1999; Cohen, 2001; Gunter, 2001, 2002; Abrego and Ross, 2002). If our intention is to analyse the overall relationship between debt and growth, then such concentration could lead to a sample selection bias.[5] Abrego and Ross (2002) have shown that while the overall debt level of the 41 HIPCs tripled from 1980 to 1995, it declined somewhat in the late 1990s. In contrast, the debt level of all developing countries, and even of all low-income countries, continued to rise throughout the same period.

Should the debt retirement initiative thus be limited to the 41 HIPC countries, or should more countries be included under the debt reduction initiative? The answer to this question has important policy implications as a significant number of countries that have been presumed to have a sustainable debt burden also suffer from ever-increasing debt service payments. This has led to a cancellation of many domestic development projects thereby compromising long-term poverty-reducing growth prospects.[6]

This chapter addresses this concern by comparing the impact of foreign indebtedness on economic growth in two separate groups of countries to see if the effect varies across these two groups.[7] One group consists of countries that are currently eligible to participate in the HIPC Initiative, while the other group consists of severely and moderately indebted countries that have not yet qualified for the HIPC programme. The first group has 35 countries,[8] the second group 25.[9]

The findings in this study show that the economic malaise due to foreign indebtedness is not limited to the HIPC group. Other low- and middle-income countries suffering from either severe or moderate indebtedness have also experienced a similar adverse effect on long-term economic growth. From the policy perspective, the findings have important implications. If the objective of the debt debate is to enhance the long-term growth prospects of the indebted countries, it may not be enough to limit the debt reduction initiatives only to the 41 HIPC group. Countries outside the HIPC initiative are also finding themselves in a vicious cycle of debt, low growth, poverty and still higher debt. Hence the issue of debt reduction, retirement, or write-off should not be limited to the HIPC group and should be extended to other countries that are in dire need of assistance.[10]

Methodologically, the chapter suggests two improvements over the existing studies in this area. First, most of the studies in the cross-sectional debt–growth literature have assumed that observed data are random outcomes of a controlled experiment. However, if the data are not random draws from a homogeneous population, ignoring heterogeneity among the cross-sectional units will result in biased or meaningless estimates (Balestra and Nerlove, 1966; Hsiao, 1986). In this chapter, following Hsiao *et al.* (1989) and Weinhold (1999), we employ a specification consistent with the dynamic partial adjustment principle. We initially explore the issue of homogeneity across different countries. Initial estimations show a high degree of heterogeneity across countries. Next, we control for the country-specific differences by assuming that the coefficients of country-specific factors are fixed and different while the coefficients of the other variables are random draws from a common population.

Second, most studies in this area consider only a small number of explanatory variables in trying to establish a statistically significant relationship between debt and growth. However, economic theory does not provide a complete specification of which variables are to be held constant when statistical tests are performed on the relation between debt and growth (Cooley and LeRoy, 1981). It is thus likely that many candidate regressions may have an equal theoretical basis, but the coefficient estimates on the debt variable may depend on the conditioning set of information. The study uses a variation of Leamer's (1983) extreme bounds analysis, as suggested in Levine and Renelt (1992), to test the robustness of coefficient estimates to changes in the conditioning set of information.

The chapter is organized as follows. The next section briefly looks at the debt–growth nexus. We then introduce the concept of causality in panel data, and go on to report the results from the causality tests. Findings from the sensitivity analysis are then given and concluding remarks are included in the final section.

The debt–growth nexus and the HIPC Initiative

Worldwide events in the 1970s and 1980s – particularly the oil price shocks, high interest rates and recessions in the developed countries, and then weak primary commodity prices – are usually referred to as the major contributors to the debt explosion in the developing countries (IMF, 2000). A number of studies in the literature have summarized these factors to include, but not limited to, (i) exogenous factors, such as adverse terms of trade shocks; (ii) the absence of sustained adjustment policies, e.g. inadequate progress with structural reform for promoting sustainable growth in exports and output, which gave rise to sizeable financing needs and failed to strengthen the capacity to service debt;

(iii) the lending and refinancing policies of creditors, particularly lending on commercial terms with short repayment periods in the late 1970s and early 1980s and non-concessional rescheduling terms for most of the 1980s; (iv) the lack of prudent debt management by debtor countries, driven in part by excessive optimism among creditors and debtors about the prospects of increasing export earnings and thereby building debt servicing capacity; (v) lack of careful management of the currency composition of debt; and (vi) political factors, such as civil war and conflict (see Afxentiou and Serletis, 1996 and Brooks *et al.*, 1998 for a detailed discussion on these issues).

Whatever the reasons that may have led to the unprecedented surge in the debt volume, developing countries are faced with a mounting problem that severely constrains economic performance. Some poor countries increasingly resort to new borrowing simply to service debt (IMF, 2000; Easterly, 2002).

A major motivation for debt relief arises from the presumption that a deleterious interaction exists between a heavy debt burden (or a debt overhang) and economic growth (Serieux and Samy, 2001). The widely discussed 'debt overhang theory' suggests that a heavy debt burden creates a disincentive for private investment due to concerns for future taxes and/or debt-induced crises (Krugman, 1988). This reduces investment spending leading to a slowdown in economic growth. The cycle continues with further reduction in investment following the economic slowdown, an increase in the debt–income ratio, and a reinforcement of the disincentive effect which ultimately leads to stagnation.

A heavy debt burden can also affect growth through other avenues, such as the crowding-out effect. The debt servicing cost of the public debt can crowd-out public investment expenditure, thus reducing total investment directly and also indirectly by reducing complementary private expenditure (Diaz-Alejandro, 1981). It can also reduce the productivity of investment due to lost externalities from certain types of public investment, such as physical infrastructure (Serieux and Samy, 2001).

In a number of theoretical models, however, reasonable levels of current debt inflows are expected to have a positive effect on growth. In traditional neoclassical models, allowing for capital mobility, or the ability of a country to borrow and lend, increases transitional growth. There is an incentive for capital-scarce countries to borrow and invest as the marginal product of capital exceeds the world interest rate.

Since the early 1980s, the international financial community has developed a number of mechanisms to alleviate the problems of debtor countries in fulfilling their external obligations. During most of the

1980s, Paris Club creditors provided rescheduling for low-income countries on non-concessional terms and on market-related interest rates. Subsequently, these rescheduling continued, conditional on the adoption of an IMF adjustment programme, under the Toronto terms (1988), London terms (1991) and Naples terms (1994).[11]

More recently, as a result of rising concerns about the debt service capacity of some severely indebted countries, the World Bank and IMF launched the HIPC Initiative in 1996. At the outset, the Initiative identified 41 countries as potentially eligible for debt relief. But it soon became clear that the original HIPC framework was not a sufficient solution for many poor countries to reach debt sustainability. Consequently, in 1999 the Initiative was enhanced to provide faster, broader and deeper debt relief (Marchesi, 2003).[12]

The debt reduction initiative is part of a larger effort by the international donor community to redefine the external assistance strategy toward the poorest countries (Birdsall, Claessens and Diwan, Chapter 3 in this volume).[13] The question that naturally arises here is the choice of the 41 countries. Is it prudent to limit the HIPC Initiative only to these 41 countries, or should it be expanded to other poor countries who share a similar economic malaise? The primary focus of this chapter is to investigate this issue by considering two country groupings – HIPC and non-HIPC.

Causality in panel data

In the existing literature on panel data, most of the standard causality tests are performed using the following model:

$$y_{it} = a_0 + \sum_{j=1}^{m} a_j y_{it-1} + \sum_{j=1}^{m} b_j x_{it-1} + f_i + u_{it} \tag{8.1}$$

where $i = 1 \ldots n$, and f_i is the fixed effect.[14] The fixed effect can be eliminated by taking the first difference of (8.1) which gives:

$$y_{it} - y_{it-1} = \sum_{j=1}^{m} a_j (y_{it-1} - y_{it-j-1}) + \sum_{j=1}^{m} b_j (x_{it-1} - x_{it-j-1}) + (u_{it} - u_{it-1}) \tag{8.2}$$

However, in (8.2), the error term $(u_{it} - u_{it-1})$ is correlated with the regressor $y_{it-j} - y_{it-j-1}$. To take care of this correlation problem, (8.2) is estimated using a two-stage least squares (2SLS) method with instrumental variables procedure with a time varying set of instruments. The issue of causality from x to y is, then, tested using the joint hypotheses $b_1 = b_2 = \cdots = b_m = 0$.

The problem with this estimation process is the assumption that the coefficient on the explanatory variables is equal across all the units in the panel data. In other words, these models are based on the underlying assumption of homogeneity of the relationships in question across countries in the panel. However, given the diverse nature of different developing countries, a degree of heterogeneity in the dynamic structure as well as the relationships between different macroeconomic variables is likely to exist, especially in a panel data set. Estimating such dynamic heterogeneous models by imposing homogeneous parameter values can potentially lead to misspecification biases in the estimation process. In fact, Monte Carlo simulations have shown that these estimates will be biased and inconsistent, and that the bias will increase as the sample size gets larger (Pesaran and Smith, 1995; Weinhold, 1999). As Nair-Reichert and Weinhold (2001) have shown, this restriction of a single coefficient on the causal variable implies that either causality occurs everywhere or it occurs nowhere in the panel. In other words, the assumption eliminates the possibility that the data set can be heterogeneous.[15]

Hence in a panel data set, a more flexible criterion would be desirable. An alternative specification would be the Mixed Fixed and Random (MFR) model as suggested by Hsiao *et al.* (1989) in a non-dynamic setting. Weinhold (1999) and Nair-Reichert and Weinhold (2001) have considered a variation of the MFR model as an alternative specification for panel data causality testing in the presence of heterogeneous dynamics.

In particular, they consider the model:

$$y_{it} = \alpha_i + \delta_i y_{it-1} + \beta_{1i} x^*_{1it-1} + \cdots + \beta_n x_{2it-1} + u_t \qquad (8.3)$$

where x^*_{it-1} denote the orthogonalized candidate causal variable after the linear influences of the remaining right-hand side variables have been taken into account. Orthogonalization provides for appropriate interpretation of the estimated variances by making sure that the coefficients are independent.

The advantage of the MFR model is that it can be used to control for the effects of both the fixed and random country-specific factors so that parameters characterizing common behaviour across countries and over time can be consistently estimated. As shown in Hsiao *et al.* (1989), this model allows improved predictions for any one country by combining the information on all the countries through a Bayes procedure.

Unlike the other panel data estimators in the literature, e.g. the Standard Fixed Effects Estimator, a Random Coefficient Estimator and the Pooled Mean Group Estimator, the MFR model allows for complete heterogeneity of the long-run coefficients by using information on the distribution of the estimates on the lagged exogenous variables to get the required information. As a result, it is much less sensitive to outliers.[16] Weinhold (1999) shows that the MFR model also performs well compared to the instrumental variables (GMM) approach.

Two features of the MFR model make it ideally suited for testing the presence of causality in heterogeneous panel data sets in this chapter. First, by allowing for a distribution of causality across the panel, we do not have to assume – erroneously, in some cases – that causality occurs everywhere, or nowhere, in the panel. Second, the combination of a less-biased mean estimate and an idea of the degree of heterogeneity provides a better understanding of the underlying process than the traditional panel causality tests.

Estimation results from the MFR model

The sample period covers 1982–99. The starting point of the sample corresponds to the beginning of the debt crisis. For each variable, three-year averages are calculated in order to net out the effects of short-run fluctuations, while maintaining the ability to utilize the time series dimension of the data.[17] Data on the debt variables are collected from the *Global Development Finance* data set of the World Bank, while the data on all the other variables are taken from the *International Financial Statistics*. There are 210 observations for the HIPC group and 150 observations for the non-HIPC group.

Table 8.1 presents the results for the 35 countries in the HIPC group from the following regression equation using a non-dynamic fixed effects panel:

$$PCGDP_{it} = a_i + a_1 X_{it} + INITIALGDP_i + a_3 INV_{it} + a_4 EXP_{it} + a_5 GOVTEX_{it} + a_6 M2_{it} + u_{it} \tag{8.4}$$

The dependent variable is the *per capita* real GDP (*PCGDP*). The independent variables include the initial level of *per capita* real GDP (*INITIALGDP*). A negative coefficient on this variable would support the view of conditional convergence which is consistent with neoclassical growth models as well as some endogenous growth models.[18] Following the empirical growth models, the investment–GDP ratio (*INV*) is included.

The next variable is the export–GDP ratio (*EXP*) which measures the degree of openness in a country. The ratio of government expenditures to

Table 8.1 Contemporaneous OLS fixed-effects panel regressions for 35 countries in the HIPC group

Variables	*(1)*	*(2)*	*(3)*	*(4)*
TDS/GDP	−0.780 (3.69)			
TDS/EXP		0.025 (1.06)		
DEBT/GDP			−0.057 (2.06)	
DEBT/EXP				−0.003 (1.44)
INITIALGDP	−1.246 (3.22)	−1.875 (4.10)	−1.567 (3.65)	−2.006 (4.54)
INV	0.769 (3.88)	0.610 (2.81)	0.875 (2.94)	0.591 (2.49)
EXP	2.104 (3.65)	1.022 (2.85)	1.359 (3.10)	0.942 (2.08)
GOVTEX	0.709 (4.06)	0.366 (2.01)	0.070 (1.40)	0.085 (1.55)
M2	1.802 (4.20)	0.780 (3.86)	1.603 (4.85)	0.743 (2.34)
R^2	0.36	0.39	0.31	0.37

Note: The dependent variable is the growth rate of real *per capita* GDP. The column headings (1)–(4) represent the four debt measures, *TDS/GDP, TDS/EXP, DEBT/GDP* and *DEBT/EXP*, respectively. Fixed effects are not shown. The figures in parentheses are the absolute values of the heteroscedasticity-consistent *t*-statistics.

GDP (*GOVTEX*) is included as fiscal policy is used to promote economic growth in the developing countries. These two variables help to control for differences in total factor productivity (TFP). The M2–GDP ratio (*M2*) measures the degree of financial deepening. The assumption is that an increase in financial deepening would enhance growth. In a 'cash-in-advance' theory of money a higher anticipated inflation rate is predicted to reduce capital formation (Stockman, 1981; Widmalm, 2001).[19]

In (8.4), X_i represents the four debt variables – *TDS/GDP, TDS/EXP, DEBT/GDP*, and *DEBT/EXP*, respectively. In the empirical literature, the external debt stock and total debt service have been the most popular measures of external debt employed. In order to make this study comparable to previous studies, four variables using these two measures of external debt are generated – total debt service–GDP ratio (*TDS–GDP*), total debt service–exports ratio (*TDS/EXP*), debt–GDP ratio (*DEBT/GDP*), and debt–exports ratio (*DEBT/EXP*). The use of these two measures will also help to isolate the debt overhang effect (which can be captured with a variable representing the burden of future debt service, such as the debt stock) from the potential crowding-out effect (proxied by a contemporaneous debt service ratio) (Pattillo, Poirson and Ricci, Chapter 6 in this volume).

Columns (1)–(4) in Table 8.1 show the results from estimating (8.4) for the four debt variables. The results are not consistent across the debt variables. Two of the variables – *TDS/GDP* and *DEBT/GDP* – have a statistically significant negative sign while the remaining two debt variables are statistically insignificant. The initial level of *per capita* GDP has the expected negative sign and is statistically significant. The remaining four variables – *INV, EXP, GOVTEX* and *M2* – have a statistically significant positive impact on the growth of *per capita* income. One possibility for the differing results for the foreign debt variable may be that debt variables have an impact only on those countries that have reached a particular threshold of openness.

We, therefore, test to see if the coefficients on the debt variables depend on the level of openness in a country:

$$b_k = b_{k0} + b_{k1} OPEN_{it} \tag{8.5}$$

By substituting the value of b_k in (8.4), we get:

$$\begin{aligned} PCGDP_{it} = {} & a_i + a_1 X_{it} + a_2 INITIALGDP_i + a_3 INV_{it} + a_4 EXP_{it} \\ & + a_5 GOVTEX_{it} + a_6 M2_{it} + a_7 INTER_{it} + u_{it} \end{aligned} \tag{8.6}$$

where $a_7 = b_{k1}$ and *INTER* is the interaction term of each of the debt variables, *TDS/GDP, TDS/EXP, DEBT/GDP* and *DEBT/EXP* with the level of openness. These interaction variables are denoted as *OPEN1, OPEN2, OPEN3*, and *OPEN4*, respectively.

Table 8.2 presents the results for each debt variable after taking into account the possibility of interaction. These results are significantly different from those reported in Table 8.1. Once the four debt variables are allowed to vary with the level of openness in the country, all of them become statistically significant and are negative irrespective of the level of openness. These results indicate that the economic growth returns of additional foreign aid actually decrease with increased openness.

For countries with non-traded currencies, external debt service payments require the purchase of foreign currency which must be earned from exports, capital inflows, or drawing down reserves. In the absence of substantial reserve coverage, rising exports, or sizeable capital inflows, higher debt service means reduced import capacity (Serieux

Table 8.2 Contemporaneous OLS fixed-effects panel regressions with interaction term for 35 countries in the HIPC group

Variables	*(1)*	*(2)*	*(3)*	*(4)*
TDS/GDP	−0.159			
	(3.77)			
TDS/EXP		−0.310		
		(5.77)		
DEBT/GDP			−0.619	
			(7.40)	
DEBT/EXP				−1.135
				(6.08)
INITIALGDP	−2.683	−2.769	−3.844	−1.504
	(3.20)	(3.99)	(4.09)	(2.68)
INV	0.997	1.054	1.399	1.086
	(4.20)	(5.87)	(5.96)	(4.02)
EXP	4.166	2.960	1.008	0.602
	(7.25)	(6.32)	(3.78)	(2.95)
GOVTEX	2.004	1.306	0.576	0.085
	(3.88)	(4.77)	(3.90)	(2.01)
M2	0.365	0.195	0.720	0.565
	(2.95)	(1.98)	(3.66)	(2.65)
OPEN1	−0.642			
	(4.95)			
OPEN2		−0.409		
		(7.35)		
OPEN3			−1.044	
			(5.76)	
OPEN4				−3.042
				(5.31)
R^2	0.49	0.47	0.41	0.39

Note: *OPEN1, OPEN2, OPEN3* and *OPEN4* are the interaction terms of the four debt variables and the export–GDP ratio, respectively. See notes to Table 8.1.

and Samy, 2001). This usually leads to import compression that is effected either through price rationing (currency devaluation) or non-price rationing (import restrictions). This may lead to reduced imports of capital goods that can eventually lead to reduced investment and thus lower economic growth (Moran, 1990).

The coefficient estimates for the other variables in the equation are as expected. The initial level of *per capita* GDP has a statistically significant negative impact supporting the convergence hypothesis. The remaining four variables, *INV, EXP, GOVTEX* and *M2* have a statistically significant positive impact on the growth of *per capita* GDP.

Table 8.3 reports similar results for the 24 countries in the non-HIPC group. The coefficient estimates for the debt variables are all negative and statistically significant suggesting the adverse effect that foreign indebtedness is having on these economies. It also shows that the growth-retarding impact of external debt is not limited to the HIPC

Table 8.3 Contemporaneous OLS fixed-effects panel regressions for 24 countries in the non-HIPC group

Variables	*(1)*	*(2)*	*(3)*	*(4)*
TDS/GDP	–0.256 (2.49)			
TDS/EXP		–0.199 (3.76)		
DEBT/GDP			–0.033 (1.99)	
DEBT/EXP				–0.176 (4.32)
INITIALGDP	–3.375 (3.94)	–2.291 (2.85)	–3.416 (4.71)	–3.501 (6.05)
INV	0.825 (4.43)	0.571 (3.81)	1.323 (5.16)	0.985 (3.25)
EXP	0.333 (2.61)	0.610 (4.25)	1.004 (4.50)	0.778 (2.20)
GOVTEX	4.590 (5.14)	3.166 (6.24)	3.090 (6.71)	2.059 (3.52)
M2	0.622 (1.98)	0.513 (2.06)	0.890 (2.13)	0.056 (2.88)
OPEN1	–0.095 (1.77)			
OPEN2		0.008 (2.15)		
OPEN3			–0.128 (1.85)	
OPEN4				–0.063 (3.80)
R^2	0.24	0.19	0.31	0.25

Note: See notes to Tables 8.1 and 8.2.

group. Other low- and middle-income countries are also suffering from similar economic malaise.

The initial level of *per capita* GDP has the expected negative sign and is statistically significant. The coefficient estimates for *INV, EXP, GOVTEX* and *M2* have the anticipated positive sign and are statistically significant. However, the coefficient estimates for the interaction variables are not similar to those reported earlier. In the case of the ratio of the two debt variables to *GDP, OPEN1* is insignificant while *OPEN3* is negative but significant only at the 10 per cent level. The interaction term in the *TDS/EXP* equation is statistically significant but positive, while in the *DEBT/EXP* equation the term is significant but negative.

Next, we test for the presence of a causal relationship between the four debt variables and the growth of *per capita* income in the context of dynamic panel models. Here, the growth of *per capita* GDP is modelled as a function only of lags of itself and other independent variables. Thus the model shown in (8.4) now becomes:

$$PCGDP_{it} = a_i + PCGDP_{it-1} + a_1 X_{it-1} + a_2 GDP_{it} + a_3 INV_{it-1} + a_4 EXP_{it-1} + a_5 GOVTEX_{it-1} + a_6 M2_{it-1} + u_{it} \qquad (8.7)$$

As shown by Nair-Reichert and Weinhold (2001), the inclusion of the lagged dependent variable provides a proxy for many omitted variables. Due to data constraint, the lag length is limited to one.

Tables 8.4 and 8.5 provide the causality test results for the two groups of countries. These results are derived from an MFR estimation of the basic model (8.4) in which the coefficient on the lagged dependent variable is country-specific and the coefficients on the other independent variables are allowed to have a normal distribution. The mean and variance of each of the independent variables are given in the tables. The variance estimates in both tables indicate the presence of heterogeneity across the two panels.

Table 8.4 shows the results for the HIPC group. Both the government expenditure and M2 variables, expressed as a ratio of GDP, have a statistically significant positive causal impact on *per capita* income growth. Interestingly, the variance of the government expenditures variable, while large, is much smaller relative to the mean than the variance of the M2 variable. This indicates that the degree of heterogeneity across the countries in the sample is smaller for government fiscal policy than for monetary policy. As the M2 variable measures the degree of financial deepening in a country, the results suggest that the degree of financial deepening has varied significantly across countries.

Table 8.4 Causality tests in a mixed, fixed effects random model for 35 countries in the HIPC group, 1982–98

Variables	*(1)*	*(2)*	*(3)*	*(4)*
TDS/GDP	−0.714 (3.67) [1.46]			
TDS/EXP		−1.190 (4.70) [2.16]		
DEBT/GDP			−2.440 (7.66) [8.15]	
DEBT/EXP				−6.355 (12.14) [8.32]
GDP	−1.491 (3.12) [17.34]	−1.282 (3.40) [20.76]	−1.508 (5.32) [35.18]	−1.611 (5.18) [32.10]
INV	1.265 (3.90) [20.16]	1.452 (4.37) [23.08]	1.710 (5.10) [37.20]	0.952 (2.55) [19.44]
EXP	1.375 (2.90) [8.55]	2.411 (6.25) [15.76]	4.400 (7.85) [20.16]	0.785 (3.95) [40.02]
GOVTEX	2.076 (3.15) [16.21]	1.992 (7.12) [24.60]	0.988 (3.76) [19.05]	0.342 (3.10) [28.66]
M2	0.108 (2.19) [21.43]	0.394 (4.70) [18.35]	0.480 (5.13) [16.44]	0.990 (4.29) [17.77]

Note: The figures in parentheses ( ) are the absolute values of the *t*-statistics while the figures in brackets [ ] are the coefficient variance. For a description of the table, see notes to Tables 8.1 and 8.2.

Exports also have a significantly positive causal impact on *per capita* income growth. This represents the positive impact that export-oriented growth strategy, embraced by many of these low-income countries, has had since the early 1980s. Initial level of *per capita* GDP has the anticipated negative sign while the investment–GDP ratio has the anticipated positive sign. Both are statistically significant.

As for our main variable of interest, debt, the result is consistent irrespective of the debt measure employed. Debt has a statistically significant

Table 8.5 Causality tests in a mixed, fixed effects random model for 24 countries in the non-HIPC group

Variables	*(1)*	*(2)*	*(3)*	*(4)*
TDS/GDP	−0.311 (2.88) [1.99]			
TDS/EXP		−1.774 (3.89) [1.76]		
DEBT/GDP			−1.856 (3.54) [6.10]	
DEBT/EXP				−2.040 (2.64) [1.34]
GDP	−3.371 (3.20) [20.78]	−3.380 (3.75) [28.24]	−2.265 (2.98) [34.10]	−3.229 (3.04) [38.90]
INV	1.044 (4.98) [12.76]	1.050 (4.65) [14.20]	1.420 (5.16) [22.40]	1.772 (5.62) [30.66]
EXP	0.242 (2.16) [5.10]	0.056 (2.05) [8.22]	0.128 (3.11) [6.24]	0.317 (3.63) [10.56]
GOVTEX	0.410 (2.99) [20.18]	0.585 (3.84) [33.81]	0.281 (2.06) [40.16]	0.699 (4.28) [35.90]
M2	0.166 (1.98) [29.71]	0.078 (1.88) [38.30]	0.132 (2.06) [24.77]	0.095 (1.80) [40.26]

Note: The figures in parentheses ( ) are the absolute values of the *t*-statistics while the figures in brackets [ ] are the coefficient variance.

negative causal impact on *per capita* real GDP growth in the HIPC group. Not only is the mean impact negative, but the relatively small value of the variances indicates that this relationship is universal across the panel.

Interestingly, Table 8.5 also reports similar results for the non-HIPC group. All four debt measures have a statistically significant negative causal impact on *per capita* real GDP growth. The results are universal across the panel, as indicated by the small variances. The findings for the remaining variables are not significantly different from those reported in Table 8.4.

Finally, in Table 8.6, following the method suggested in Nair-Reichert and Weinhold (2001), we check for the robustness of the results. From a theoretical standpoint, the MFR estimation has built-in diagnostics in the form of the estimated variances that show whether the results are influenced by a few outlier countries. To make sure that this has not been the case, a cross-validation leverage check is performed in which one country from each panel is dropped from the data set and the model is reestimated with the remaining countries. For instance, for the HIPC group, the model is reestimated by dropping one of the 35 countries at a time. This process is repeated 35 times so that any undue effects of an outlier country will be reflected by significantly different results for the sample omitting that country. Similar procedure is employed for the 24 non-HIPCs.

Table 8.6(a) shows that, for the HIPCs, the standard deviation of the mean estimate is quite low at 0.0362 and the range varies from 0.311 to 0.402. The level of significance of the mean estimate is very high, with the average *t*-statistics significant at least at the 5 per cent level.

Table 8.6(b) reports the results for the non-HIPC group. The results are similar to Table 8.6(a). The mean estimate is highly significant and the range varies from 0.5175 to 0.7004. Again, the standard deviation of the mean estimate is only 0.0561 and the mean is statistically significant. These results indicate the robustness of our findings and the absence of any outlier country in the sample.

Table 8.6(a) Cross-validation check of the results for 35 countries in the HIPC group

Variable	*Mean*	*Std dev.*	*Minimum*	*Maximum*
a	0.3527	0.0362	0.3117	0.4025
t-stat.	3.710	0.383	2.412	4.926

Table 8.6(b) Cross-validation check of the results for 24 countries in the non-HIPC group

Variable	*Mean*	*Std dev.*	*Minimum*	*Maximum*
a	0.6224	0.0561	0.5175	0.7004
t-stat.	4.051	0.443	3.455	3.016

Sensitivity analysis

In this section, we explore whether the relationship between various measures of foreign indebtedness and economic growth, as reported in the previous section, are robust or fragile to small changes in the conditioning information set. The reliability and the robustness of the relationship are evaluated using a version of Leamer's (1983) extreme bounds analysis as developed in Levine and Renelt (1992).

In particular, the following regression is estimated:

$$PCGDP = a + b_m\mathbf{D} + b_i\mathbf{I} + b_z\mathbf{Z} + u \tag{8.8}$$

where *PCGDP* is the growth of *per capita* GDP, *D* is a particular debt variable, **I** is the set of base variables included in all regressions and **Z** is a sub-set of variables selected from a pool of variables identified by past studies as potential important explanatory variables of economic growth.[20]

We first select the debt variable (*D*), and run a base regression that includes only the **I**-variables and the debt variable. Then we compute the regression results for all possible linear combinations of up to three **Z**-variables and identify the lowest and highest values for the coefficient of the debt variable, b_m, that cannot be rejected at the 5 per cent level of significance. If the estimated coefficient of debt variable remains significant over this procedure, the correlation is said to be 'robust'. The 'extreme bounds' are the highest estimated correlation plus two standard errors and the lowest minus two standard errors. If the coefficient fails to be significant in some regression, the correlation is termed as 'fragile'. Widmalm (2001) has suggested that, to reduce multicollinearity, no pair of variables in **I, Z**, or **D** should measure the same underlying phenomenon.

Following Levine and Renelt (1992) and Widmalm (2001), the set of variables in the **I** set include the lagged value of *per capita* GDP, investment–GDP ratio and average annual growth rate of population. The pool from which the set of three control variables **Z** is drawn includes variables that are considered to be potential sources of economic growth. These include the export–GDP ratio, ratio of government expenditures to GDP, the M2–GDP ratio, inflation rate, years of education, dependency ratio and ratio of foreign direct investment (FDI)–GDP.

First, the robustness of different measures of external debt is examined. Equation (8.8) is estimated, using a pooled cross-section time series approach, where different measures of debt are, in turn, substituted for **D**. One advantage of this pooled cross-sectional data is that it can allow for time-specific effects as the worldwide conditions for growth may not be equally advantageous over time.[21] The extreme bound results for the 35 HIPC countries are reported in Table 8.7 while those for the low- and middle-income countries are reported in Table 8.8.[22]

In Table 8.7, the correlation between each of the four measures of indebtedness and growth in the HIPC group turns out to be robust. The coefficients are negative and statistically significant, suggesting that

Table 8.7 Results from the extreme bound analysis of the various debt measures in 35 countries in the HIPC group

M-variable	*Bound*	b_m	R^2
TDS/GDP	high	−0.548 (2.01)	0.41
	base	−0.663 (2.61)	0.42
	low	−0.918 (3.16)	0.47
TDS/EXP	high	−0.022 (3.10)	0.38
	base	−0.31 (3.66)	0.41
	low	−0.36 (3.79)	0.44
DEBT/GDP	high	−0.681 (2.07)	0.49
	base	−0.873 (2.55)	0.50
	low	−0.910 (3.31)	0.51
DEBT/EXPORT	high	−0.104 (3.81)	0.33
	base	−0.098 (3.50)	0.35
	low	−0.084 (2.87)	0.35

Note: The base '*b*' is the estimated coefficient of the *M*-variable in (8.1) when *per capita* GDP growth is regressed, using 2SLS, on the *M*- and *I*-variables. The high '*b*' is the estimated coefficient from the regression with the extreme high bound ($b_m + 2$ standard deviations); the low '*b*' is the coefficient from the regression with the extreme lower bound. The *I* variables are the lagged value of the log of *per capita GDP, Investment/GDP* and population growth rate. The conditioning set of *Z*-variables includes three variables from a group of seven.

Table 8.8 Results from the extreme bound analysis of the various debt measures in 24 countries in the non-HIPC group

M-variable	*Bound*	b_m	R^2
TDS/GDP	high	−0.093	0.39
		(2.34)	
	base	−0.104	0.39
		(3.01)	
	low	−0.119	0.37
		(3.00)	
TDS/EXPORT	high	−0.210	0.27
		(4.37)	
	base	−0.169	0.28
		(2.20)	
	low	−0.155	0.28
		(2.16)	
DEBT/GDP	high	−0.366	0.40
		(3.77)	
	base	−0.344	0.39
		(3.22)	
	low	−0.219	0.34
		(4.15)	
DEBT/EXPORT	high	−0.055	0.41
		(2.77)	
	base	−0.076	0.42
		(2.89)	
	low	−0.070	0.38
		(2.95)	

Notes: See notes to Table 8.7.

external indebtedness retards economic growth in the HIPC group. This finding is consistent with the World Bank–IMF view that unless drastic actions are taken by these countries to reduce their external indebtedness, economic growth will suffer.

Table 8.8 provides similar statistics for the 24 countries in the non-HIPC group. Interestingly, the results are similar to those reported in Table 8.7. Irrespective of the debt measure employed, a robust negative correlation between the debt variable and economic growth suggests that foreign indebtedness has reduced the potential growth of *per capita* income in these countries. One policy implication of this result is that, when it comes to seriously tackling the issue of debt and providing adequate debt relief, our attention should not be focused only on the

HIPC group. Low economic growth in other severely and moderately indebted countries can also be traced to their foreign debt problem. And hence debt relief policies should also be devised for these countries.

Conclusions

The multilateral donor institutions have identified 41 countries to be eligible for the enhanced HIPC Initiative and are seeking a solution to their debt problems by combining substantial debt reduction with policy reforms to raise long-term growth and reduce poverty. The findings here show that the economic malaise due to foreign indebtedness is not limited to the HIPC group. Other low- and middle-income countries suffering from either severe or moderate indebtedness have also experienced a similar adverse effect on long-term economic growth.

The chapter aims to enhance the existing literature on the debt–growth nexus by analysing the relationship in two separate country groups using the mixed, fixed and random coefficient approach that allows for heterogeneity in the causal relationship between debt and growth. The results show a statistically significant negative causal impact running from each of the four debt measures to economic growth in both country groups. Further, the extreme bounds analysis shows that the relationship between a debt measure and economic growth is robust to changes in the conditioning set of information included in the regression equations. Irrespective of the debt measure used, the results are robust across the two separate country groups, HIPC and non-HIPC, as well as two different testing procedures.

From a policy perspective, the findings have important implications. If the objective of the debt debate is to enhance the long-term growth prospects of the indebted countries, it may not be enough to target the debt reduction initiatives only to the 41 countries of the HIPC group. Countries outside the HIPC Initiative are also finding themselves in a vicious cycle of debt, low growth, poverty and still higher debt. Without going into the merits of the proposals for debt write-off for all countries, it can be safely asserted that the HIPC Initiative has to be extended to all the indebted countries, and not only to a selected few. Only then can the fruits of economic growth be enjoyed by all people. Otherwise, the debt debate will continue without any net tangible improvement as new countries would inevitably join the ranks of countries that find their debt unsustainable.

Notes

1. Developing (including middle-income) country debt rose from US$500 billion in 1980 to US$1 trillion in 1985 and more than US$2 trillion in 2003 (IMF, 2000, 2003). For a history of the debt crisis see, among others, Daskeking and Powell (1999).
2. The Paris Club is the name given to the meetings between government creditors, mainly OECD countries, and debtor countries under the auspices of the French government.
3. These countries saw their total indebtedness increase from US$60 billion in 1980 to a peak of about US$190 billion in 1995, then decline somewhat to about US$170 billion by 1999 (IMF, 2000, 2001; Abrego and Ross, 2002).
4. Other major critiques of the enhanced HIPC Initiative can be grouped into overall problems with the HIPC framework and specific problems related to HIPC debt relief. See Gunter (2002) for a discussion of these issues.
5. Hansen (Chapter 7 in this volume) makes a similar point.
6. Anwar (2002) analyses the case of unsustainable debt burden in a non-HIPC (e.g. Pakistan).
7. Birdsall, Claessens and Diwan (Chapter 3 in this volume) also look at a group of HIPC and non-HIPC countries in Africa. However, they concentrate on the donor and official creditor side, exploring how the growing debt in these countries has affected the provision of new resources by the donor community.
8. The 35 HIPC countries included in the sample are Benin, Bolivia, Burkina Faso, Burundi, Cameroon, Central African Republic, Chad, Congo, Côte d'Ivoire, Democratic Republic of the Congo, Ethiopia, Gambia, Ghana, Guinea, Guinea-Bissau, Guyana, Honduras, Liberia, Madagascar, Malawi, Mali, Mauritania, Mozambique, Myanmar, Nicaragua, Niger, Rwanda, Senegal, Sierra Leone, Somalia, Sudan, Tanzania, Togo, Uganda, and Zambia. Of the original list of 41 countries that were considered for HIPC Initiative assistance, several countries were dropped from analysis for a number of reasons. A debt sustainability analysis showed that Angola, Kenya, Vietnam and Yemen have a sustainable debt burden after the application of the traditional debt relief mechanisms. The Lao PDR indicated its intention of not requesting assistance under the HIPC Initiative (IMF, 2001). São Tomé and Principe was dropped from the sample due to the lack of consistent data.
9. The non-HIPC countries included in the sample are Algeria, Argentina, Bangladesh, Brazil, Chile, Colombia, Costa Rica, Dominican Republic, Ecuador, Egypt, El Salvador, Guatemala, India, Indonesia, Jamaica, Morocco, Nigeria, Pakistan, Paraguay, Peru, the Philippines, Sri Lanka, Venezuela and Zimbabwe. These countries are moderately to severely indebted. Six of these countries (Bangladesh, India, Indonesia, Nigeria, Pakistan and Zimbabwe) have *per capita* GDP (at 1999 prices) less than US$755. The remaining countries have a *per capita* GDP (at 1999 prices) between US$756 and $9265 as calculated by the World Bank. All 24 countries are covered by the World Bank's *Global Development Finance* (GDF) and report to the World Bank Debtor Reporting System.

10. There is an ongoing debate on the merits of debt retirement and write-off in the developing countries. While organizations like Jubilee Plus have spoken forcefully for complete debt write-off, many organizations, such as the IMF, have taken an opposite stand. Interested readers are referred to, among others, the web sites www.jubileeplus.org and www.imf.org for a discussion of their respective viewpoints. See also Roodman (2001).
11. See Easterly (2002) for a brief history of debt relief provided under these terms.
12. For a discussion of the logic behind the HIPC Initiative, its current progress and the debt sustainability outlook after HIPC relief see, among others, IMF (2000, 2001, 2003); Abrego and Ross (2002) and Berthélemy (Chapter 4 in this volume).
13. Besides explicit debt relief, substitution of concessional debt for non-concessional debt has been going on throughout the period (Easterly, 2002).
14. See Nair-Reichert and Weinhold (2001) for a detailed discussion on this issue.
15. In addition, Nair-Reichert and Weinhold (2001) have suggested that in a heterogeneous data set it is possible that the mean coefficient could have statistically significant values of either sign but still not reflect much of the underlying economic condition.
16. For a more detail discussion, see Nair-Reichert and Weinhold (2001).
17. As pointed out in Pattillo, Poirson and Ricci (Chapter 6 in this volume), the time series dimension of the data is as important for understanding how debt affects economic growth over time (the within-country variability of the panel data) as it is for understanding how countries with different levels of debt experience different growth patterns (the between-country variability of panel data).
18. See, for example, Quah (1993).
19. Although few empirical studies in the growth literature include all of these variables, most studies control for some sub-set. Levine and Renelt (1991) survey 41 studies on economic growth and provide a list of variables included in these studies. Moreover, these variables are consistent with new growth models that depend on constant returns to reproducible inputs or endogenous technological change (Barro, 1990; Romer, 1990).
20. The explanatory variables in (8.8) are assumed to be independent and linear (Kormendi and Meguire 1985).
21. Following Widmalm (2001), a fixed-effects test of whether growth rates in these country groups as a whole are influenced in a common direction in different time periods was conducted. The hypothesis of no time specific effects was strongly rejected. This is similar to the findings given in Easterly *et al.* (1993) who reported that country characteristics influenced the relative levels of income rather than differences in growth rates.
22. To conserve space, the sensitivity results for the base variables (included in the **I**-set) are not reported here. In general, the lagged *per capita* GDP growth and investment–GDP ratio have been found to be robust, while the population growth rate has been found to be fragile. These results are available from the author.

References

Abrego, L. and D. Ross (2002). 'Debt Relief Under the HIPC Initiative: Context and Outlook for Debt Sustainability and Resource Flows', WIDER Discussion Paper DP2002/44, Helsinki: UNU–WIDER.

Afxentiou, P. and A. Serletis (1996). 'Growth and Foreign Indebtedness in Developing Countries: An Empirical Study Using Long-Term Cross Country Data', *Journal of Developing Areas*, 31: 25–39.

Anwar, T. (2002). 'Unsustainable Debt Burden and Poverty in Pakistan', WIDER Discussion Paper DP2002/53, Helsinki: UNU–WIDER.

Balestra, P. and M. Nerlove (1966). 'Pooling Cross-Section and Time Series Data in the Estimation of a Dynamic Model: The Demand for Natural Gas', *Econometrica*, 34: 585–612.

Barro, R. (1990). 'Government Spending in a Simple Model of Endogenous Growth', *Journal of Political Economy*, 98(2): 103–25.

Brooks, R., M. Cortes, F. Fornasari, B. Ketchekmen, Y. Metzgen, R. Powell, S. Rizavi, D. Ross and K. Ross (1998). 'External Debt Histories of Ten Low-Income Developing Countries: Lessons from Their Experiences', IMF Working Paper Series WP/98/72, Washington, DC: IMF.

Cohen, D. (2001). 'The HIPC Initiative: True and False Promises', *International Finance*, 4(3): 363–80.

Cooley, T. and S. LeRoy (1981). 'Identification and Estimation of Money Demand', *American Economic Review*, 71: 825–44.

Daskeking, C. and R. Powell (1999). 'From Toronto Terms to the HIPC Initiative: A Brief History of Debt Relief for Low Income Countries', IMF Working Paper WP/99/142, Washington, DC: IMF.

Diaz-Alejandro, C. (1981): 'Southern Cone Stabilization Plans', in W. Cline and S. Weintraub (eds), *Economic Stabilization in Developing Countries*, Washington, DC: Brookings Institution.

Easterly, W. (2002). 'How did Highly Indebted Poor Countries Become Highly Indebted? Reviewing Two Decades of Debt Relief', *World Development*, 30(10): 1677–96.

Easterly, W., M. Kremer, L. Pritchett and L. Summers (1993). 'Good Policy or Good Luck? Country Growth Performance and Temporary Shocks', *Journal of Monetary Economics*, 32: 459–83.

Gunter, B. (2001). 'Does the HIPC Initiative Achieve its Goal of Debt Sustainability?', WIDER Discussion Paper DP2001/100, Helsinki: UNU–WIDER.

Gunter, B. (2002). 'What's Wrong with the HIPC Initiative and What's Next?', *Policy Development Review*, Spring.

Hsiao, C. (1986). *Analysis of Panel Data*, New York: Cambridge University Press.

Hsiao, C., D. Mountain, M. Chan and K. Tsui (1989). 'Modeling Ontario Regional Electricity System Demand Using a Mixed Fixed and Random Coefficients Approach', *Regional Science and Urban Economics*, 19: 565–87.

IMF (International Monetary Fund) (2000). 'The Logic of Debt Relief for the Poorest Countries', Washington, DC: IMF, mimeo.

IMF (International Monetary Fund) (2001). 'The Impact of Debt Reduction under the HIPC Initiative on External Debt Service and Social Expenditures', Washington, DC: IMF, mimeo.

IMF (International Monetary Fund) (2003). 'Debt Relief under the Heavily Indebted Poor Countries (HIPC) Initiative: A Fact Sheet', Washington, DC: IMF, mimeo.

Kormendi, R. and P. Meguire (1985). 'Macroeconomic Determinants of Growth: Cross-Country Evidence', *Journal of Monetary Economics*, 16: 141–63.

Krugman, P. (1988). 'Financing vs. Forgiving a Debt Overhang', *Journal of Development Economics*, 29: 253–68.

Leamer, E. (1983). 'Let's Take the Con out of Econometrics', *American Economic Review*, 73: 31–43.

Levine, R. and D. Renelt (1991). 'Cross-Country Studies of Growth and Policy: Some Methodological, Conceptual, and Statistical Issues', WB Working Paper Series 608, Washington, DC: World Bank.

Levine, R. and D. Renelt (1992). 'A Sensitivity Analysis of Cross-Country Growth Regressions', *American Economic Review*, 82: 942–63.

Marchesi, S. (2003) 'Adoption of an IMF Programme and Debt Rescheduling: An Empirical Analysis', *Journal of Development Economics*, 70(2): 403–23.

Moran, C. (1990). 'Imports under a Foreign Exchange Constraint', *World Bank Economic Review*, 3(2), 279–95.

Nair-Reichert, U. and D. Weinhold (2001). 'Causality Tests for Cross-Country Panels: A New Look at FDI and Economic Growth in Developing Countries', *Oxford Bulletin of Economics and Statistics*, 63(2): 153–71.

Pesaran, H. and R. Smith (1995). 'Pooled Mean Group Estimation of Dynamic Heterogeneous Panels', *Journal of Econometrics*, 68: 79–113.

Quah, D. (1993). 'Galton's Fallacy and Tests of the Convergence Hypothesis', *Scandinavian Journal of Economics*, 95: 427–43.

Romer, P. (1990). 'Endogenous Technological Change', *Journal of Political Economy*, 98(2): 71–102.

Roodman, D. (2001). 'Still Waiting for the Jubilee: Pragmatic Solutions for the Third World Debt Crisis', Worldwatch Paper, 155, Washington, DC: Worldwatch.

Sachs, J., K. Botchway, M. Cuchra and S. Sievers (1999). 'Implementing Debt Relief for the HIPCs', Cambridge, MA: Center for International Development, Harvard University, available at: www.cid.harvard.edu/.

Serieux, J. and Y. Samy (2001). 'The Debt Service Burden and Growth: Evidence from Low Income Countries', Paper presented at the WIDER Development Conference on Debt Relief, 17–18 August, Helsinki: UNU–WIDER.

Stockman, A. (1981). 'Anticipated Inflation and the Capital Stock in a Cash-in-Advance Economy', *Journal of Monetary Economics*, 8: 387–93.

Weinhold, D. (1999). 'A Dynamic Fixed Effects Model for Heterogeneous Panel Data', London: London School of Economics, mimeo.

Widmalm, F. (2001). 'Tax Structure and Growth: Are Some Taxes Better than Others?', *Public Choice*, 107: 199–219.

9

Debt Relief and Growth: A Study of Zambia and Tanzania

Arne Bigsten, Jörgen Levin and Håkan Persson

Introduction

The issue of debt relief was hotly debated during the 1990s, and extensive debts have been considered to cripple the growth prospects of particularly the poorest least developed countries (LDCs). The Heavily Indebted Poor Countries (HIPC) Initiative is an attempt to provide comprehensive debt relief to the poorest and most indebted countries. The World Bank and the IMF launched the first version (HIPC I) in 1996. In 1999 it was enhanced following global consultations in Cologne, where it was considered necessary to provide more extensive and faster debt relief with clearer links to poverty reduction (HIPC II).[1]

The purpose of this chapter is to contribute to the debate on the evaluation of the impact of debt relief on the LDCs. We will sketch what factors need to be taken into account in the analysis, explain why computable general equilibrium (CGE) models may be useful for this type of analysis and then use such models to simulate some policy impacts for Tanzania and Zambia. The models used are neoclassical equilibrium models, which fail to take some potentially important disequilibria into account. Some of the parameters that are used in the analysis are hypothetical, which means that future analyses need to be refined to provide more reliable answers as to how large the effects could be, but we still believe that our analysis throws light on the issues involved.

The chapter is structured as follows: in the next section we outline the framework we use to analyse the impact of debt relief. Then we provide brief reviews of the economies of our two country cases, Tanzania and Zambia. The next section discusses the use of computable equilibrium models and presents the two CGE models that are used in the analysis, before we present the results of the analysis. The final section summarizes the main results and suggests ways forward for the analysis of debt relief impacts.

Evaluating the impact of debt relief

To analyse the economic impact of debt relief one needs to take account of at least two issues. We must ask how much resources are released under the HIPC Initiative.[2] When the overall size of the HIPC assistance is identified, one must determine how the allocation of resources changes as a result of the new resources. A baseline is required to assess the changes in government spending. For example, a baseline medium-term expenditure framework (MTEF) prepared before the receipt of HIPC assistance could be compared with one that includes HIPC assistance. The evaluation of the impact of HIPC assistance is complicated by the fact that it is not possible to track HIPC funding perfectly. The link between aid and the recipient's budgetary allocation is not straightforward because much aid is fungible (Adam *et al.*, 1994, 1994).[3]

When it comes to debt relief, there are in principle – as with budget support – two options: it can be used either to increase government spending or to reduce taxes. Public expenditures are clearly one of the main channels through which foreign aid influences development outcomes. During periods of debt relief the government faces a difficult intertemporal choice with regard to the setting of the overall target for public expenditures. Should it spend all the money immediately or 'save' some of the resources for the future?

The most difficult question for the evaluation of the impact of debt relief concerns the effect of government expenditures on growth, productivity and overall economic welfare. All poverty reduction strategy papers (PRSPs) aim to shift the composition of public spending towards poverty-reducing programmes. Most strategies aim at enhancing the access of the poor to primary education and to primary and preventive health care services, and to develop the infrastructure. While increased access to education and health services would have a positive impact on the stock of human capital and productivity of individuals, investment in infrastructure would primarily lower transaction costs, which would have a positive impact on production activities and investment and hence income. Thus while expansion of both social and economic infrastructure should increase income in the longer term, the short-term benefits might be larger through investments in economic infrastructure.

Furthermore, it might be the case that low incomes are a binding constraint limiting the household's use of public services such as education and health.

Another choice is whether the government really should spend all additional resources. An alternative would be to reduce taxes, which could stimulate economic growth and hence increase revenue and expenditures in the longer term. These tax measures could take several forms, but essentially this use of the extra resources puts more money into the private sector and shifts the spending decisions to private firms or individuals. The benefit of reducing taxes in terms of additional private investment could be higher than the benefit from increased spending on public services.[4]

Thus, the view taken in this chapter is that the HIPC Initiative releases extra government resources, which can be used either to increase government expenditures or to reduce taxation. Increased government expenditures can be in the form of increased public consumption or increased public investment, while lower taxes may lead to higher private investment or higher private consumption. These various choices and their impacts are the focal point of this chapter.

Tanzania and Zambia: two HIPCs

Macroeconomic developments in Tanzania

Tanzania is one of the poorest countries in the world with a large external debt. Tanzania's external debt is about US$7.3 billion, equivalent to 101 per cent of GDP in December 1999. The debt burden has grown rapidly despite generous treatment of Tanzania in Paris Club negotiations. Since 1995 the government of Tanzania has improved the management of the economy and the late 1990s witnessed major progress in stabilizing the economy. There has been progress toward a market-based economy and movement away from the previous reliance on direct controls and government ownership of the means of production.

Since the mid-1990s the macroeconomic performance has improved. Compared to the early 1990s real GDP growth has increased and the average growth rate for the 1995–2000 period was about 4.1 per cent or 1.4 per cent in *per capita* terms (Table 9.1).

The government has been quite successful in its attempt to stabilize the economy. One of the major issues has been to cut down on government activities and there has been a remarkable contraction.

Table 9.1 Tanzania: growth rates of sector output and GDP, 1992–2000

	1992	*1993*	*1994*	*1995*	*1996*	*1997*	*1998*	*1999*	*2000*
Agriculture	1.2	3.1	2.1	5.8	3.9	2.4	1.9	4.1	3.4
Mining	7.7	8.2	15.0	11.7	9.6	17.1	27.4	9.1	13.9
Manufacturing	−4.0	0.6	−0.2	1.6	4.8	5.0	8.0	3.6	4.8
Electricity and water	−1.3	0.9	2.0	6.1	11.1	2.2	5.5	3.9	5.0
Construction	5.8	−14.4	1.4	−14.7	7.6	8.2	9.9	8.7	8.4
Trade	−0.7	−0.4	1.1	3.5	3.5	5.0	4.7	6.0	6.5
Transport	14.2	0.1	0.9	5.9	1.1	4.9	6.2	5.8	6.1
Finance	−0.9	−7.1	−5.2	6.0	10.4	−15.8	−3.0	0.7	3.3
Public administration and other services	5.6	−3.9	−0.1	−2.7	1.6	3.2	2.7	3.5	3.6
GDP at factor cost	1.8	0.4	1.4	3.6	4.2	3.3	4.0	4.7	4.9

Source: IMF (2000).

Since the peak in 1992 when government expenditure was about 26 per cent of GDP, it has now been reduced to a mere 11 per cent (Table 9.2). However, the tight fiscal policy has not, so far, produced the intended boost in private investment. Indeed, since the peak in 1993, private investment as a share of GDP has seen a steady decline, reaching 12 per cent of GDP in 1998. This might suggest that an excessive shake-out of some public investment categories, such as investment in

Table 9.2 Tanzania: use of resources and external account, 1991–98 (% of GDP at market prices)

	1991	*1992*	*1993*	*1994*	*1995*	*1996*	*1997*	*1998*
Private consumption	74.6	75.1	85.0	78.9	82.0	82.7	78.1	85.4
Private investment	15.9	16.3	17.8	17.5	16.0	13.1	11.0	12.4
Government expenditures	25.5	26.3	27.3	21.7	18.3	15.0	10.9	10.8
Government consumption	17.3	17.8	19.7	16.1	15.0	11.5	8.1	7.5
Government investment	8.2	8.4	7.7	5.7	3.3	3.5	2.7	3.3
Exports of goods and services	9.0	11.1	18.2	19.5	23.5	20.3	14.4	18.2
Imports of goods and services	25.0	28.8	48.3	37.7	39.8	31.1	14.5	26.9
Resource balance	−16.0	−17.7	−30.1	−18.2	−16.4	−10.8	0.0	−8.7
Net factor income	−3.4	−4.7	−3.5	−2.8	−2.1	−1.0	−1.5	−1.8
Net transfers	15.2	18.7	17.1	15.5	6.3	5.2	3.8	4.8
Current account deficit	−4.2	−3.6	−16.5	−5.5	−12.1	−6.6	2.3	−5.7

Source: Bank of Tanzania.

Table 9.3 Tanzania: internal balance, 1991–98 (% of GDP at market prices)

	1991	*1992*	*1993*	*1994*	*1995*	*1996*	*1997*	*1998*
Total revenue including grants	15.8	18.0	20.3	16.7	15.0	16.7	15.9	16.4
Total revenue excluding grants	12.3	11.2	11.9	11.7	12.6	13.5	11.8	11.5
Private savings	21.4	21.0	8.3	17.0	7.3	4.8	8.3	1.2
Net flow of private savings into the financial market	5.5	4.7	−9.5	−0.5	−8.8	−8.2	−2.7	−11.2
Government savings	−9.7	−8.3	−7.0	−5.0	−3.4	1.6	5.1	5.5
Current account deficit	−4.2	−3.6	−16.5	−5.5	−12.1	−6.6	2.3	−5.7

Notes: Government savings defined as government expenditures (Table 9.2) subtracted by total revenue including grants (Table 9.3).

infrastructure, could have the effect of lowering the productivity of private investment.[5]

Since the mid-1990s Tanzania has made considerable progress in restoring fiscal discipline (Table 9.3), but the drastic expenditure cuts have had a negative impact in most sectors. To some extent, priority sectors such as education, health, water, roads and agriculture have been protected through additional resources made available through the Multilateral Debt Fund (MDF) facility.[6] Still, expenditures remain low, which is a reflection of the low domestic revenue base in Tanzania. Despite a change in the tax structure, the revenue–GDP ratio was fairly constant in the 1990s, hovering around 12 per cent of GDP. In conjunction with the tight fiscal policy the authorities have followed a strict monetary policy. Since 1993 the money supply–GDP ratio has been falling.

In April 2000 the IMF and the World Bank agreed to support a comprehensive debt reduction package for Tanzania under the enhanced HIPC Initiative. Total relief from all of Tanzania's creditors is worth more than US$2 billion, which is equivalent to more than half of the net present value (NPV) of total debt outstanding after the full use of traditional debt relief mechanisms.

The debt reduction operation will translate over time into debt service relief of US$3 billion, or about one-half of Tanzania's debt service obligations for fiscal years 2001–03 and about one-third of Tanzania's debt service obligations thereafter. The debt service–fiscal revenue ratio is expected to decline from 15 per cent to 9 per cent during 2000–09. Thus, even though the HIPC Initiative makes some additional resources available the amount is not excessive.

Macroeconomic developments in Zambia

The Movement for Multiparty Democracy (MMD) won the elections in 1991 on a liberal platform. As soon as elected, MMD introduced its economic reform programme (ERP) with the goal of arresting the economic decline. The donors responded to the government's efforts by resuming their support to Zambia (Table 9.4). During the first two years there was rapid liberalization of the external trade and payments system, and a move towards a market-determined exchange rate. Over a period of five years, all licensing and quantitative restrictions on imports and exports were removed, and the tariff structure was rationalized, and by 1994 Zambia had one of the most liberal foreign exchange regimes in Sub-Saharan Africa (SSA).

The reform programme has implied a tighter fiscal and monetary policy. The most important part of the budget balancing process was expenditure reduction, which was virtually unmatched in Africa. A cash budget was introduced in 1993, but budgetary discipline is still a problem. In 1998 more than 10 per cent of funds were spent on expenditures that were made in violation of the budget regulations. Financial liberalization meant that interest charges on domestic debt increased.

Apart from the cash budget, the government has also attempted to balance the budget by increasing revenue. In 1993, a revenue board was introduced, with a value-added tax (VAT) put in place in July 1995, while user fees have been introduced for most social services. The Zambia Revenue Authority has increased resource mobilization in the form of taxes, while non-tax revenue collection still remains weak.

The most important strategic error in Zambia was the mishandling of the earlier engine of growth, i.e. the copper mines, which were nationalized in the 1970s. Surpluses were not reinvested in the mines, but were diverted to politically more important uses outside the copper sector. There was inadequate supervision and management of the mines, where political considerations often outweighed economic

Table 9.4 Zambia: revenue 1990–2000 (% of GDP)

	1990	*1991*	*1992*	*1993*	*1994*	*1995*	*1996*	*1997*	*1998*	*1999*	*2000*
Total revenue (including grants)	24.6	32.9	33	26.3	30.2	29.0	26.8	24.8	24.9	25.5	26.7
Grants	4.3	14.2	14.7	10.5	10.1	9.2	6.1	5	6.5	7.9	8.4
Grants/total	17.5	43	44.5	40	33	31.7	22.3	20	26	31.8	31.5

Sources: CSO (Quarterly Statistics from various years); IMF (2001).

considerations. This neglect meant that copper production fell from 825,000 tonnes in 1969 to 250,000 tonnes at the end of the millennium. It was this decline in output that caused the income decline and not so much the price changes. The privatization of the copper parastatal (Zambia Consolidated Copper Mines) ZCCM was not concluded until March 2000. The drawn-out process for the privatization of the loss making mines had serious negative consequences for the economy.

GDP growth has been uneven during the reform period (Table 9.5). There was drought, which affected agriculture, while the removal of protection, the monetary squeeze, low internal demand and the parastatal reforms have impacted on manufacturing output. *Per capita* incomes fell by more than a quarter between 1990 and 2000. The mining industry declined throughout due to ZCCM's production problems. Terms of trade developments have shown a declining trend, largely driven by the negative changes in copper prices.

Finally, we can also note that there has not been any significant recovery of investment in Zambia (Table 9.6). Since this was one of the

Table 9.5 Zambia: GDP and sector growth rates, 1990–2000 (change in %)

	1990	*1991*	*1992*	*1993*	*1994*	*1995*	*1996*	*1997*	*1998*	*1999*	*2000*
Total GDP	−3.4	−0.6	2.1	−0.2	−8.6	−2.3	6.6	3.3	−1.9	2.0	3.5
Non-agriculture	−2.5	−1.4	7.4	−6.6	−12.3	−7.8	8.2	5.1	−2.0	2.2	5.5
Non-mining GDP	−2.4	1.4	−0.1	1.8	−12.5	2.8	7.2	3.5	1.2	6.3	5.6
Real GDP *per capita* index	100	96.4	95.6	92.6	81.6	73.6	76.5	77.5	73.6	72.8	72.9

Sources: CSO (Quarterly Statistics from various years) and Zambia (2001).

Table 9.6 Zambia: GDP, by type of expenditure, 1990–2000 (% of GDP at current prices)

	1990	*1991*	*1992*	*1993*	*1994*	*1995*	*1996*	*1997*	*1998*	*1999*
Consumption:										
Public	14.8	16.2	17.9	13	13.1	15.5	18.3	17.5	15.8	13.4
Private	68.7	75.4	82.8	75.8	79.5	72.3	76.4	73.2	80.3	87.7
Investment including change in stock	17.3	11	11.9	15	8.2	15.9	12.8	14.6	14.8	17.5
Trade balance	−0.7	−2.6	−12.6	−3.8	−1.0	−3.8	−7.5	−5.2	−12.5	−18.6

Sources: CSO (Quarterly Statistics from various years) and Zambia (2001b); new series from 1994.

Table 9.7 Zambia: debt service paid and external flows, 1990–99

	1990	*1991*	*1992*	*1993*	*1994*	*1995*	*1996*	*1997*	*1998*	*1999*
Debt service paid, (US$ million)	290	655	354	326	409	1584	319	217	147	136
Debt service paid (% of exports of goods and non-factor services)	21.6	56.0	29.6	31.2	34.8	120.4	28.7	17.6	18.0	16.2
Debt service paid (% of GDP)	7.7	19.4	10.7	10.0	12.2	45.7	9.7	5.6	4.6	4.3
Debt service paid (% of government revenue)	38.2	103.7	58.3	63.2	60.9	230.2	47.1	27.9	24.4	24.5
Gross external inflows (including rescheduling)	–	–	1,106	795	550	1,816	510	401	297	511
Net external flows (official)	–	–	752	469	141	232	191	184	150	375

Source: IMF and IDA (2000: 19).

aims of reform process, this is a major setback. The government has not been able to establish a credible reform environment, and the heavy burden of debt is certainly a part of the explanation for this. It is clear that the debt burden is a serious threat to the economy (see Table 9.7), but acceptance into the HIPC programme should go some distance towards solving this problem.

Zambia reached the decision point in December 2000, and the first interim relief started flowing in January 2001. At the end of 1999 Zambia had US$6.5 billion in total foreign debt. After the predicted Paris Club forgiveness and various other debt relief measures, the debt stock is about US$5.5 billion. It is estimated that 63 per cent or US$3.8 billion of the 5.5 billion debt is to be written off.

As of January 2001, Zambia started to receive interim relief from the World Bank, IMF and eventually also from the African Development Bank (ADB) and others. With these relief measures, Zambia, between 2001 and 2005, will lower its contracted debt service costs by US$260 million per year and during the period 2006–15 by roughly US$130 million per year. Compared to the actual debt service paid during 2000, however, Zambia will save only US$30 million per year up to 2015 years. Between 2001 and 2003, when the completion point is expected to be reached, the Bank will provide US$61 million of the total write-off of US$885 million that it plans to provide on the total debt stock of US$1.7 billion. In order for Zambia to reach the floating completion point, certain key objectives and reforms have to be achieved.

Model frameworks

On page 182 we discussed some of the ways in which debt relief may affect the economy. In this section we outline the methodological framework used to analyse the impacts of debt relief in Tanzania and Zambia. A key question for the evaluation of the impact of debt relief concerns the effect of government expenditures on growth, productivity and overall economic welfare. Gemmell (2004), surveying the recent literature on fiscal policy variables, taxes, public expenditures and budget deficits on growth, found that results from earlier studies ought to be treated with extreme caution both because of their failure to deal correctly with budget constraint issues and because cross-section econometrics is now considered questionable with regard to reliability. Second, due to excess short-term noise existing, sufficient doubts remain over the reliability of the fiscal–growth effects in developing countries, hindering effective policy advice.

Still policy makers need to make economic policy decisions that affect issues such as allocation of resources and the distribution of income. Some form of numerical model is implicit in the actions of any policy maker. One strand of numerical models is computable or applied general equilibrium (CGE or AGE) models which have been applied to the analysis of policy issues in both developing and developed countries.[7] CGE models have been used to evaluate a wide range of policy issues, including changes in the tax structure, trade policy, income redistribution and public investments. Policy packages typically involve simultaneous changes in the variables under the control of the government, such as taxes and public expenditures. Using CGE models not only has the advantage that general equilibrium effects are taken into account but also that the interaction of different policy measures can be studied. Perhaps most importantly, when used in recursive dynamic mode, the CGE models make it possible to evaluate lagged effects of policies, in particular of public investment. The results from simulation runs with alternative packages can then be compared in terms of various welfare measures. Although model results are not precise because of data and other problems, they can help policy makers by making explicit the implications of alternative courses of action. The credibility in policy debates is greatly enhanced when a variety of different approaches and models are applied, and there is a consensus about the results (Devarajan and Robinson, 2002).

In AGE models typically the government uses the proceeds of taxation to finance its own public consumption, debt obligations and the remainder is redistributed as transfers to either households or the private sector. Households are consuming a public good where utility is determined, as with other goods, by how much income is spent on it. In models run under a comparative static mode, the impact of government investment is often limited to changes in the demand for investment goods.

External effects of public expenditures have so far been limited in AGE models, which severely limit the possibilities of welfare economics for change in public policies. Still, some studies have looked at how the composition of government expenditures affects sectoral productivity, and hence labour demand and household income. For example, Feltenstein and Ha (1999) discuss the impact of infrastructure investments on the Mexican economy. They developed a dynamic intertemporal model to analyse the correlation between levels of public infrastructure and economic growth and found that an increase in the public provision of infrastructure may initially increase the productivity of private capital, but increased interest rates, because of increased public spending, may later dampen private investment. Fargeix (1990) developed a recursive dynamic model where total factor productivity (TFP) growth in each sector is a function of private investment in the sector and the amount of public investment, both of them normalized by the sectoral capital stock. Thus, depending on the amount invested, both private and public, TFP changes in the following period.

Other studies have looked at how changes in the supply of public services, particularly education, have impacted on a household's possibilities to acquire human capital. For example, Heckman, Lochner and Taber (1998) and Davies and Whalley (1989) looked at the role of human capital formation examining individual intertemporal decisions on the time invested in acquiring different levels of skills. Government investment in education can, for example, influence an individual's lifetime decision on accumulation of human capital. Using a dynamic general equilibrium (DGE) model with overlapping generations Dabla-Norris, Matovu and Wade (Chapter 11 in this volume) found that poverty and growth objectives are enhanced if resources are targeted to primary and secondary levels of education.

Jung and Thorbecke (2001) constructed a recursive dynamic general equilibrium model specifying the mechanism through which public expenditure on education affects the production of human capital. The simulation results suggest that increased public spending on education can increase growth and reduce poverty. However, a sufficiently high level of physical investment is needed to maximize the benefits from education.

We now describe the two models used in this study to analyse the impact of debt relief in Tanzania and Zambia. Both the Tanzanian and the Zambian models are of a fairly standard neoclassical type, although they have somewhat different characteristics.

The Tanzania model[8]

There are three sectors in the model: agriculture, manufacturing and services. The trade and production structure in the model is specified as a multi-level nest of different functional forms. At the highest level of aggregation the Armington (1969) specification is used, which defines a composite commodity for each sector as a constant elasticity of substitution (CES) function of commodities produced domestically and imported from abroad. Output in each sector is either sold on the domestic market or exported. A constant elasticity of transformation (CET) framework allocates domestic output between exports and domestic sales. Sectoral gross output is a CES function of aggregate labour and composite capital, while demand for intermediate goods is given by a Leontief technology. Composite capital in the agricultural sector is defined as a CES function of capital, land and aggregate labour. Aggregate labour is a set of nested CES functions for five different labour categories: highly skilled, skilled, semi-skilled, unskilled and casual labour. CES functions allow for imperfect substitution at each level. In a nested production structure, producers will choose the optimal mix of primary factors at each stage in the production process. At any level, primary factors are demanded up to the point where factor prices, inclusive of sector-specific differentials, equal marginal value product of the specific factor.

The model is based on the assumptions of a mobile labour force and fixed sector-specific capital augmented by investment in each period. In the labour market it is assumed that each sector initially has a specific combination of labour categories. Total supply of each category is assumed to be constant and demand varies with changes in each category's wage rate. Factor incomes of capital and land are distributed to two institutions: enterprises and proprietors of land. Enterprises keep a fixed proportion of capital income, net of taxes, as retained earnings while the remaining share is distributed to households. In the agricultural sector, factor income from land plus a government transfer is allocated directly to households. Sectoral factor incomes of the various labour categories, as well as other sources of income such as remittances from abroad and government transfers, are distributed in fixed proportions to various households. Households pay a direct tax to the government, while a fixed proportion of household disposable income is saved. Finally, consumer demand of the various households in the model is given by a Stone–Geary linear expenditure system (LES).

Besides direct taxes, government derives revenue from import tariffs on goods, transfers from abroad (aid) and indirect taxes levied on domestic output. Government savings equal revenue less current expenditures on goods and services, transfers and interest payments on foreign loans. Adding savings from households, enterprises and foreign savings equals total savings in the economy. Government investment is exogenous in the model, while aggregate private investment is assumed to be endogenous. At the sectoral level, private investment is determined by fixed coefficients. Goods demanded for investment purposes from the private sector are derived with the help of a capital-coefficient matrix. Fixed expenditure shares also determine government demand for investment goods.

The model incorporates complementary productivity effects of both private and public investments in sectoral production functions. TFP growth in each sector is a function of private investment in the sector and public investment, both normalized by the sectoral capital stock.[9] Thus, depending on the amount invested (both private and public) TFP changes in the following period.

The final bloc in the model defines equilibrium in the markets for factors, commodities and foreign exchange. Given behavioural and institutional constraints (elaborated upon above), there is a set of prices in the model solution that represents market equilibrium. Domestic prices for imports and exports are products of world prices (exogenously given) multiplied by the 'nominal' exchange rate, adjusted for tariffs. The price of the composite good is the sum of total values of domestic sales out of total output and values of imports divided by total output of the composite good. In a similar way the sectoral output price is defined as the value of domestic sales and exports divided by total output. Price of value-added or the net producer price is equal to the output price, adjusted for indirect taxes, less the cost of intermediate inputs per unit of output. The price of a unit of capital is defined as a weighted average of the prices of capital goods by sector of origin. A weighed producer price index is defined as the numéraire in the model. Given the numéraire and assuming exogenous capital inflows, movement in the exchange rate equilibrates the external account. An increase in the exchange rate would increase tradable prices, relative to non-tradable prices, leading to a real depreciation. This will increase exports and reduce imports.

The Zambia model

This model is a Walrasian type of general equilibrium model with a dynamic specification.[10] The main purpose of the modelling strategy was to build a model that was suitable for the analyses of investment changes resulting from various policy changes. The model incorporates different ways of modelling endogenous investment and capital formation in a dynamic setting with several linked time periods. Since the capital stock – and thus productive capacity – depends on investment, we have chosen a neoclassical type of production function approach in order to have a direct two-way link between investment and other economic variables.

The economy is divided into seven sectors or commodities. The supply of each commodity is determined by domestic production and imports. Essentially, production is determined by the amount of capital available in each sector and the amount of skilled and unskilled labour involved in the production process of each sector. With a relatively high price of a commodity, domestic production is larger than at a lower price. Furthermore, with a high domestic price of a good, imports also tend to be high. That is to say, supply increases with the price of the commodity.

Demand is determined by the demand for intermediate goods in the production process, by private and public demand, investment demand and export. Demand decreases as prices increase. Prices in the model are determined in such a way that demand equals supply of each commodity. Furthermore, wages are found for which labour supply equals labour demand.

Investment depends on savings and the marginal efficiency of capital in each sector. An increase in capital stock, i.e. investment, is undertaken as long as it yields profitable production. This induces changing capital stocks over time and determines the growth of production and GDP. Due to financial constraints of the economy, the model uses a balance of trade condition, meaning that net borrowing from abroad is limited. Financial aid can thus be modelled as a lowering of the balance of trade constraint, yielding fewer exports and an increase in imports.

This has a tendency to increase domestic demand and to increase domestic prices and profits, which in turn will increase investment and growth. A decrease in savings, which may be the consequence of increased consumption, may have a tendency to lower investment.

Foreign aid can also be modelled as an increase in capital stocks interpreted as 'gifts' of productive capital. With an increase in capital stock, there is also an increase in growth. Supply will increase and lower prices and profits, which will have a dampening effect on further investment. Reducing debt service makes it possible to increase public demand and public investment. In the model simulations it is assumed that an increase of capital stock in the production of public services is composed of imported capital goods in excess of imports subject to the balance of trade constraint. Reduced debt service is thus partly replaced by increased imports.

Simulation results

To say something about the magnitude of the impact of debt relief, we use the two CGE models presented previously for simulations. The models are not exactly the same, which means that we have to be cautious about comparing the results across countries. We are more confident in comparing different scenarios within one country. However, by applying two models with somewhat different designs on similar cases, we can get an indication of the extent to which the results depend on the model specification.

Results of simulations with the Tanzania model

As described above, the Tanzania model is slightly different from the Zambia model. The model runs over four periods, capturing the amount of resources expected to be released during 2000–05.[11] In the baseline scenario we have assumed that the economy grows on average by 4.5 per cent over the period. In the various experiments we look at the impact of a foreign interest payment reduction combined with four different policy scenarios. In the first scenario we assume, as in the Zambian case, that half of the resources released are used for public consumption. In the second experiment we add a 'human capital' effect of increased public current expenditures. The number of labourers in the skilled labour categories increases by 2.9 per cent per year while the growth rate of those regarded as unskilled is reduced to keep the overall growth rate at 2.5 per cent.[12] In the third scenario we assume, as in the Zambian case, that half of the resources released by HIPC are used to increase public sector investment. In the fourth experiment we assume that public sector investments also have an effect on private sector productivity. In the final experiment we add the second and the fourth experiment, assuming both human capital and productivity effects of increased public spending.

Table 9.8 shows the result of the various scenarios. Compared to the Zambian results, we note the impact is rather similar with one notable exception, the impact of productivity effects. The impact of increased public spending is rather modest regardless of whether it is public consumption or investment that is increased (simulation (1) and (3)). In these two experiments the impact of public spending is limited to either increased demand for investment goods (if capital expenditures are increased) or a higher wage bill (if current government expenditures are increased). Thus, just looking at HIPC resources as additional resources to stimulate demand would not generate any substantial gains.

What would be the impact if public resources were used to accumulate human capital in the economy? As in the Zambian case, this is modelled in a rudimentary manner assuming that the number of skilled labourers increases relative to the unskilled. The GDP growth rate would increase by 0.1 percentage units in the first period and 0.16 percentage units in the last period, which is quite close to the Zambian results. However, the impact is still modest. What would be the impact of increased public investment combined with improved productivity? The impact in the first period is modest, as productivity gains materialize in the following periods, but thereafter growth rates increase and at the end of the period the GDP growth rate is 2.4 percentage units higher than the baseline.[13]

Table 9.8 Growth impacts of HIPC-financed policy interventions in Tanzania (percentage units difference from baseline scenario)

	Period 1	*Period 2*	*Period 3*	*Period 4*
(1) Increase in public consumption	0.01	0.04	0.05	0.05
(2) Increase in public consumption + accumulation of human capital	0.10	0.14	0.15	0.16
(3) Increase in public investment	0.01	0.04	0.05	0.05
(4) Increase in public investment + productivity effects	0.01	0.10	1.30	2.42
(5) (2) + (4)	0.10	0.05	1.21	2.28

In the final experiment we combine, as in the Zambian case, simulation (2) and simulation (4) to get the combined effects of increased public spending, accumulation of human capital and changes in productivity. Compared to the baseline, GDP growth rates increase in all periods and particularly towards the end of the periods simulated. Thus, if resources were targeted to human capital accumulation and succeeded in inducing productivity changes, the impact on real GDP could be quite substantial. In period 4, GDP growth rate would be 2.3 percentage units higher compared to the baseline growth rate. However, as in the Zambian case, our model specification is not based on any detailed assessment of the 'true' impact of human capital accumulation and changes in productivity. This is illustrated by comparing experiment (4) and (5). Adding human accumulation to public investment plus productivity effects actually *lowers* the growth rates, as increased public consumption crowds-out private investments. Although there is a positive impact of accumulation of human capital and public investments, there is a net loss as private sector investments decline. Whether productivity changes, as a result of lower private investments, outweigh the positive impact of higher public spending is an important issue to consider. Thus, as highlighted earlier, it is important to undertake a more detailed analysis of the impact on public spending. Particularly important are complementarities between public investments and developments in the private sector. Moreover, the analysis would certainly benefit if public spending could be disaggregated into health, education and infrastructure spending, for example. Another potentially important aspect that is missing from the model is the monetary sector. Debt relief would certainly impact on financial markets, which would be an important channel to investment and future growth.

Results of simulations with the Zambian model

The simulations with this model are presented for two periods only, but this is sufficient to show how rates of growth and investment levels change. We have a base solution that assumes that nothing has happened with regard to debt service. We follow the approach previously outlined, and assume that the HIPC Initiative reduces interest and amortization payments of the government. In our simulation we assume that the HIPC Initiative annually releases resources for the government corresponding to 1 per cent of GDP. This is based on an estimate of how much actual payments change relative to the preceding years. Relative to contractual obligations the debt reduction represents a reduction in debt service of about 10 per cent of GDP.

Next we assume that the resources are used to increase public spending and/or reduce taxes in the Zambian economy.[14] We introduce the changes in a step-wise fashion, to see how much of the effect of the full package derives from each ingredient:

(1) In the first step we simply increase public consumption demand by 0.5 per cent of GDP, that is we use half the resources released to increase public consumption.
(2) In the second step we add a secondary effect of increased public expenditures. We assume that the HIPC-related increase in expenditures is focused especially on education, and we simulate the impact of this by increasing the number of labourers in the skilled labour category by 0.5 per cent per year and we reduce the number in unskilled labour to the same degree.[15] This productivity-enhancing effect of public expenditure in the real economy would take an extended period of time before it is realized, but we assume that it has an impact already in period 1 and 2. We thus try to capture the more long-term effects within the framework of our limited model.
(3) In this step we assume that 0.5 per cent of GDP in period 1 is used to increase public sector investment (but changes (1) and (2) are not included here).
(4) In this step we assume that public sector investment also has an effect on public sector productivity. We thus add to step (3) an increase in public sector productivity of 0.5 per cent in period 1 and this effect is maintained in period two.[16]
(5) Then we combine experiments (2) and (4), that is, increase in both public consumption and public investment with their assumed indirect effects.
(6) We add an attempt to simulate the effect of a tax reduction. Since we do not have taxes explicitly in the model, we simulate a tax reduction by assuming higher savings in the economy.
(7) Finally, we add the tax reduction effect to simulation (5) to get the effect of a complete package. The sums of our changes in public consumption and public investment are equal to 1 per cent of GDP, while the simulated tax cut comes on top of that. We do not have an easy way of measuring the size of the tax cut required to create this increase in savings and investment, so this final step is even more hypothetical than the previous ones.

It should be noted that our numbers for the magnitude of some of these effects are hypothetical, and much research is needed to provide a solid underpinning for the estimates. The uncertainty of those effects also translates into uncertainty regarding the effects of debt reduction estimated here. The growth results from our simulations are shown in Table 9.9. The full results of experiment (5) are provided in Appendix Table 9A.1.

The results show that the impact of a debt reduction of the type implemented in Zambia will have rather limited growth effects. We simulate the impact of a combined increase in public consumption and investment corresponding to 1 per cent of GDP. If we also assume certain indirect productivity effects, we do get an increase in the growth rate of around 0.2 per cent (experiment (5)). This is not insignificant, but by itself it is not going to change the situation in Zambia in any dramatic way. In the simulation, the capital stock is expanding and with a capital–output ratio of say 1–2 the increase in GDP seems a bit low. One reason is that changes in the composition of demand affect investments in the various sectors and this will have an impact on GDP. Investments in sectors with 'low' productivity will dampen GDP growth. When we add in our attempt to simulate a tax cut, we do get a slightly larger effect in year 2 but this experiment is a bit hard to evaluate. We also refer to another experiment in n. 12, where we assume that public sector infrastructure investments increase productivity throughout the economy. Then we do get a more dramatic increase in output, but since

Table 9.9 Growth impacts of HIPC-financed policy interventions in Zambia (percentage changes relative to baseline)

Experiment	*Growth in year 1 relative to the base solution (%)*	*Growth in year 2 relative to the base solution (%)*
(1) Increase of public consumption by 0.5% of GDP	0.07	0.07
(2) (1) + accumulation of human capital	0.11	0.14
(3) Increase in public investment by 0.5% of GDP	0.04	0.04
(4) (3) + increased productivity in the public sector	0.07	0.07
(5) (2) + (4)	0.19	0.21
(6) Tax reduction	0.00	0.00
(7) (5) + (6)	0.19	0.25

we do not have any empirical basis for our assumption in the experiment, we will not draw far-reaching conclusions from it.

The restrictions of an analysis of this sort are rather obvious. Due to the nature of the model, there are some effects that cannot be taken into account. For example, if capacity utilization is restricted because of a shortage of imported inputs, debt reduction may make it possible to increase capacity utilization. This is not dealt with in this model. There are also factors such as political will and ability that we do not take into account at all (see Bigsten and Kayizzi-Mugerwa, 2000; and Bigsten, 2001).

Conclusions

This chapter discusses some issues on how to evaluate the impact of HIPC debt relief in the case of Tanzania and Zambia using two CGE models. Both countries are among the poorest and most indebted countries in the world. In the year 2000 both Zambia and Tanzania qualified for debt relief under the HIPC Initiative. There is a strong emphasis that the budgetary resources released by debt relief should be used for poverty reduction and social sector development. In both countries the debt burden is a serious threat to the economy, but acceptance into the HIPC programme should go some distance towards solving this problem.

Within our model framework, the macroeconomic impact of debt relief seems modest. In the case of Zambia, where we combine debt relief with increased public spending and lower taxes, the GDP growth rate increases by about 0.2 per cent. In the case of Tanzania, a combination of debt relief, increased public spending and accumulation of human capital would increase real GDP by 0.2 percentage units. One reason for this relatively modest effect is that the annual injection of additional resources relative to current actual debt service is small in both cases, which implies that the impact of debt relief *per se* would be expected to be modest. However, as illustrated in the case of Tanzania, the impact could be considerably higher if additional public investment succeeds in improving private sector productivity.

Still, our approach fails to incorporate certain factors that link increased public spending to growth, productivity and overall economic welfare. For example, increased access to education and health services would have a positive impact on the stock of human capital and productivity of individuals, and investments in infrastructure would lower transaction costs, which would have a positive impact on production activities and investment and hence income. We also fail to allow for the fact that the countries will now be meeting their contractual debt service obligations, which should make them more credible as investment destinations. In the future, the analysis needs to take these aspects into account.

Appendix 1: results from the Zambian model

Appendix Table 9A.1 Results from the Zambia model: experiment 5

	Agri-culture	*Mining*	*Food*	*Manufac-turing*	*Construc-tion*	*Private services*	*Public services*
				Period 1			
Production	–0.40	0.10	–0.38	0.14	1.37	0.05	2.35
Consumption	–0.30		–0.40	–0.44	0.00	–0.64	0.00
Public demand							2.80
Investment demand	0.00			0.26	0.00		
Exports	0.00	0.11	0.00	0.00		0.00	
Imports	0.00	0.00	–1.89	0.23		0.00	
Sector GDP	–0.48	–0.24	–0.62	0.00	3.13	–0.10	1.61
Investment by sector	0.00	0.00	–1.85	0.00	2.50	0.00	–2.17
Market price	–0.10	–0.11	–0.10	–0.10	0.21	–0.10	–0.21
Producer price	–0.10	–0.11	–0.10	0.00	0.21	0.00	–0.21
Capital stock	0.26	0.09	0.14	0.12	0.53	0.10	2.43
Marginal productivity of capital	–0.78	–0.23	0.00	0.00	2.47	–0.47	0.00
Real GDP	0.19	Consumption value		–0.54			
Trade balance	0.00	Government income		0.00			
Skilled wage	–0.10	Unskilled wages		–0.20			
Skilled employment	0.59	Unskilled employment		–0.14			
Wage incomes	0.08	Disposable profits		0.00	Disposable income		0.00
Savings	0.30	Investment		0.21			
				Period 2			
Production	–0.25	0.10	–0.35	0.26	1.34	0.10	2.54
Consumption	–0.56		–0.38	–0.42	0.00	–0.30	0.00
Public demand							2.80
Investment demand	0.00			0.51	1.49		
Exports	0.00	0.11	0.00	0.00		0.00	
Imports	0.00	0.00	0.00	0.22		0.00	
Sector GDP	–0.23	–0.26	–0.59	0.25	0.00	0.00	1.69
Investment by sector	–3.03	0.00	0.00	1.14	0.00	0.60	0.00
Market price	–0.10	–0.11	–0.10	–0.10	0.00	–0.10	–0.42
Producer price	–0.10	–0.24	–0.10	–0.10	0.00	–0.20	–0.42
Capital stock	0.00	0.09	0.00	0.12	0.50	0.06	2.32
MP of capital	–0.78	–0.27	–4.35	0.00	1.45	0.00	–3.03
Real GDP	0.21	Consumption value		–0.46			
Trade balance	0.00	Government income		0.00			
Skilled wage	–0.41	Unskilled wages		0.20			
Skilled employment	0.95	Unskilled employment		–0.42			
Wage incomes	0.00	Disposable profits		0.00			
Savings	0.44	Investment		0.21	Disposable income		0.00

Appendix 2: application of the Zambian model

The model has been applied to Zambian data together with some assumed parameter values. The applied model has the following seven sectors: agriculture, mining, food, manufacturing, construction, private services and public services.

In our numerical examples we have used a fairly moderate growth rate of the labour force. We have assumed that both skilled and unskilled labour grow by 2.5 per cent per year. We have assumed that average annual depreciation of the capital stock is 5 per cent. In our base case, this implies that capital grows by about 1 per cent per year. Furthermore, productivity grows by 2.5 per cent per year.

In this case, real GDP grows by an annual 4.2 per cent. With a balance of trade constraint, domestic production prices decline in comparison to world market prices by 2 per cent per year. Growth in GDP means growth in import demand, which must be paid for by exports, a fact which can be accomplished only with improved terms of trade. There is an increase in total real private consumption of about 4.2 per cent per year. Investment increases by 4.4 per cent.

Nominal wages decline by about 1 per cent per year and there is also a slight decline in (nominal) marginal productivity of capital. The corresponding decrease in real wages is due to the larger growth rate of the labour force in comparison to the growth rate of capital. Net savings out of GDP is 14 per cent.

Notes

1. The IMF is the largest creditor followed by Japan and the World Bank. Multilaterals provide some 53 per cent, bilaterals 46 per cent and commercial sources 1 per cent of the money.
2. Some HIPC assistance may not immediately show up in the fiscal accounts. For example, IMF HIPC assistance would reduce the burden of debt service paid by the Central Bank. A special account is then needed to identify HIPC assistance and when the assistance is provided, transfers would be made to the budget as grants (in the absence of a special account the transfer would show up as a profit transfer to the budget with a lag). In a similar way, HIPC assistance in the form of write-downs of public enterprise debt guaranteed by the government will not be included in the budget unless arrangements are in place to ensure that the assistance is passed on to the budget.
3. While the empirical evidence about the extent of aid fungibility is mixed, the experiences of SSA show that aid may have unintended effects on expenditure patterns (Devarajan and Hussain, 1998).
4. Without going into details, this opens up numerous possibilities. The tax system could be designed to provide incentives for private sector development. Tax holidays and various investment tax incentives are instruments now commonly used to attract foreign direct investments (FDI). However, promoting investments through such policy measures may have some disadvantages. They may lead to greater revenue loss than increases in investments.
5. For example, poor infrastructure and deficient public services in Uganda significantly reduced investments of private firms (Reinikka and Svensson, 1999).
6. The funds are used for Tanzania's debt service to multilateral institutions, including the World Bank, IMF, ADB and African Development Fund. By the

end of December 1998 US$44.7 million, equivalent to TZS23.6 billion, was disbursed into the MDF and TZS18.2 billion was absorbed in the budget under the principle of protecting social sectors.

7. For a detailed description of computable general equilibrium models, see Dervis, de Melo and Robinson (1982), Showen and Whalley (1992) and Ginsburgh and Keyzer (1997).
8. This model follows the approach popularized by Dervis, de Melo and Robinson (1982) and the Social Accounting Matrix (SAM) used in this study is a modified version of the Tanzanian 1992 SAM developed by Wobst (1998).
9. See Fargeix (1990) for more details.
10. The model used is presented in full in Andersson, Bigsten and Persson (2000).
11. The debt service–government revenue ratio is assumed to decline from 15 to 10 per cent. The amount of resources 'saved' from debt relief amounts to 4.4 per cent of GDP, which is distributed for each year as follows: 0.7, 1.0, 1.2 and 1.5 per cent of GDP, respectively.
12. In the baseline scenario all labour categories are assumed to grow by 2.5 per annum. The 'education effects' of increasing the growth rate to 2.9 per cent among skilled categories are based on estimates from Jung and Thorbecke (2001).
13. Note that productivity changes as a result of an increase in both public and private investment.
14. Increased public investment is modelled by increasing productivity in the production of public services by 0.5 per cent in year 1. Increased public consumption is assumed to increase the supply of skilled labour. Skilled labour increases by 0.5 per cent above the population growth rate while unskilled labour reduces its share.
15. Jung and Thorbecke (2001) endogenize the production of new human capital in a more sophisticated way, but also they assume that it has an impact already in the first period after the base period in their two-period model.
16. As an alternative experiment we assumed that increased investments in the public sector infrastructure increase the profitability of investments throughout the economy. The productivity in all sectors is therefore increased by 0.5 per year over and above what is implied in the base solution. If the impact of infrastructure investments were as large as that, we would get a very substantial impact on the economy. The growth rate in period 1 increases by 0.52 per cent and in period 2 by 1.00 per cent. This is by far the largest effect we have got in any of our simulations, but since we are very uncertain about the practicality of this simulation, we relegate it to this footnote.

References

Adam, C., P.-Å. Andersson, A. Bigsten, P. Collier and S. O'Connell (1994). 'Evaluation of Swedish Development Co-operation with Zambia: A Report for the Secretariat for Analysis of Swedish Development Assistance'. SASDA, Ds 1994: 114. Stockholm: Ministry of Foreign Affairs.

Adam, C., A. Bigsten, P. Collier, S. O'Connell and E. Julin (1994). 'Evaluation of Swedish Development Cooperation with Tanzania: A Report for the Secretariat for Analysis of Swedish Development Assistance', SASDA, Ds 1994: 113, Stockholm: Ministry of Foreign Affairs.

Andersson, P.-Å., A. Bigsten and H. Persson (2000). 'Foreign Aid, Debt and Growth in Zambia', Research Report, 112. Uppsala: Nordiska Afrikastitutet.

Armington, P. S. (1969). 'A Theory of Demand for Products Distinguished by Place of Production', *IMF Staff Papers*, 16: 159–78.

Bigsten, A. (2001). 'Policy Making in Resource Rich Countries: Lessons from Zambia', *World Economics*, 2(3), 139–53.

Bigsten, A. and S. Kayizzi-Mugerwa (2000). 'The Political Economy of Policy Failure in Zambia', Working Paper in Economics, 23, Gothenburg: Department of Economics, Gothenburg University.

CSO (Central Statistical Office) (various years). 'Quarterly Statistics', Lusaka: CSO.

Davies, J. and J. Whalley (1989). 'Taxes and Capital Formation: How Important is Human Capital?', NBER Working Paper Series, 2899, Cambridge, MA: National Bureau of Economic Research.

Dervis, K., J. de Melo and S. Robinson (1982). 'General Equilibrium Models for Development Policy', Washington, DC: IBRD.

Devarajan, S. and S. I. Hussain (1998). 'The Combined Incidence of Taxes and Public Expenditures in the Philippines', *World Development*, 26(6): 963–77.

Devarajan, S. and S. Robinson (2002). 'The Influence of Computable General Equilibrium Models on Policy', IFPRI Discussion Paper, 98, Washington, DC: International Food Policy Research Institute.

Fargeix, A. (1990). 'Growth and Poverty in Stabilization Programs: A General Equilibrium Model with Financial Markets for Ecuador', UMI Dissertation Services.

Feltenstein, A. and J. Ha (1999). 'An Analysis of the Optimal Provision of Public Infrastructure: A Computational Model Using Mexican Data', *Journal of Development Economics*, 58: 219–30.

Gemmell, N. (2004). 'Fiscal Policy in a Growth Framework', in T. Addison and A. Roe (eds), *Fiscal Policy for Development: Poverty, Reconstruction and Growth*, Basingstoke: Palgrave Macmillan for UNU-WIDER.

Ginsburgh, V. and M. Keyzer (1997). *The Structure of General Equilibrium Models*, Cambridge, MA: MIT Press.

Heckman, J., L. Lochner and C. Taber (1998). 'Accounting for Heterogeneity, Diversity and General Equilibrium in Evaluating Social Programmes', NBER Working Paper Series, 6230, Cambridge, MA: National Bureau of Economic Research.

IMF (International Monetary Fund) (1999). *International Financial Statistics*, Washington, DC: IMF.

IMF (International Monetary Fund) (2000). Tanzania: Statistical Annex', IMF Staff Country Report, 00/122, Washington, DC: IMF.

IMF (International Monetary Fund) (2001). 'Zambia: Review of the Second Annual Program and Request for the Third Annual Program under the Poverty Reduction and Growth Facility', Washington, DC: IMF, Africa Department.

IMF (International Monetary Fund) and International Development Association (IDA) (2000). 'Decision Point Document for the Enhanced Heavily Indebted Poor Countries (HIPC) Initiative', 20 November, Washington, DC: IMF and IDA.

Jung, Hong-Sang and E. Thorbecke (2001). 'The Impact of Public Education Expenditure on Human Capital, Growth, and Poverty in Tanzania and Zambia: A General Equilibrium Approach', IMF Working Paper 01/106, Washington, DC: IMF.

Reinikka, R. and J. Svensson (1999). 'How Inadequate Provision of Public Infrastructure and Services Affects Private Investment', WB Policy Research Working Paper, 2262, Washington, DC: World Bank.

Showen, J. B. and J. Whalley (1992). *Applying General Equilibrium*, Cambridge: Cambridge University Press.

Wobst, P. (1998). 'A 1992 Social Accounting Matrix (SAM) for Tanzania', TMD Discussion Paper, Washington, DC: International Food Policy Research Institute.

Zambia (2001). 'Economic Report 2000', Lusaka: Ministry of Finance and Economic Development.

Part III
Poverty Effects of Debt Relief

10
Public Spending and Poverty in Mozambique

Rasmus Heltberg, Kenneth Simler and Finn Tarp

Introduction

Poverty reduction and investment in human capital are important concerns of the government of Mozambique. Following independence in 1975, substantial expansion of basic education and health services took place. Enrolment rates went up and mortality declined. These gains, however, were soon undermined by war and economic collapse (Tarp and Arndt, 2000). During the 1980s, the Renamo (*Resistência Nacional de Moçambique*) rebels systematically targeted education and health infrastructure for destruction, and teachers were often killed. The ceasefire in 1992 and peace in 1994 made it possible to turn attention to economic recovery and reconstruction, including the restoration and renewed expansion of basic health, education and economic infrastructure, often with the assistance of foreign donors. Towards the end of the 1990s basic rehabilitation was more or less complete. Macroeconomic stability had also been attained. Nevertheless, poverty remains extremely high, even by African standards. The national poverty headcount ranges from 69 to 82 per cent, depending on the method used (Tarp *et al.*, 2000). With such levels of poverty, little can be achieved from redistribution alone, so the key development challenge faced by Mozambique in the coming years is determining how to move on from stabilization and reconstruction to high, sustained and equitable economic growth.

Poverty reduction is the central objective in both the Five-Year Development Plan for 2000–04 and in the Interim Poverty Reduction Strategy (GoM, 2000a, 2000b). However, achieving equitable growth is far from easy. Historically, services – particularly transport and shipping – are a major component of the Mozambican economy, yet these sectors yield few direct benefits to the majority of the population (Addison, 2003).

The same goes for the largest export activity, prawn fishing. Another challenge is the low level of education of the poor that makes it difficult for them to be absorbed by the relatively more dynamic urban sector. A third constraint relates to the high prevalence of subsistence farming. Estimates vary, but it appears that less than half of the farmers sell agricultural output in any given year, primarily due to high transport costs (even after the post-war reconstruction of infrastructure) and low productivity in traditional peasant farming without modern inputs (Heltberg and Tarp, 2001). In this situation, public and donor budgets perform many important direct and indirect functions necessary for human development, equitable growth and poverty reduction, as explicitly recognized by the government of Mozambique.

In response to this background, public spending in education, health, water, sanitation and social welfare has been increasing since the early 1990s, particularly after the end of the war. For example, there has been a rapid increase in the availability of schools, clinics and other facilities in the social sectors and expanded coverage of services. Between 1994 and 1997, the number of lower primary, upper primary and basic post-primary schools increased by 66, 56 and 69 per cent, respectively. These rates of growth were achieved through huge public investments in infrastructure, teacher training and teaching materials, and the budget share of social sectors is quite substantial. According to official budget figures, education and health alone have accounted for 26–28 per cent of central government spending from 1998–2000, and all social sectors combined (defined here as education, health, social action, labour, social security and water) constitute around a third of total spending. Yet, although it is clear that spending on social sectors has been growing, there is limited knowledge about the extent to which this spending is targeted towards the poor and is helping to narrow the disparities within the country. This is the motivation of the present study. We focus on the incidence of public expenditures in education and health, which are arguably the main fiscal vehicles for improving the welfare of the poor.

Regional distribution is an important dimension of the incidence of public spending. There are clear regional differences in the popular political support for the ruling Frelimo (*Frente de Libertação de Moçambique*) government and the opposition party Renamo. The government gets a majority vote in southern Mozambique, while Renamo is stronger in the central and northern provinces. Traditionally, the south (including the capital city, Maputo) seems to have benefited in relative terms more from public investment and development than elsewhere. During the war regional disparities were maintained and exacerbated. The southern provinces were the safest, leading to concentration of government and donor investment in the south, in particular in Maputo. Using public expenditures to reduce regional gaps in income and in access to infrastructure and public services remains important for conflict avoidance (Addison, Chowdhury and Murshed, 2004). The incidence of public spending is also a concern to the donor community. Mozambique is one of the most aid-dependent countries in the world, and donors support public budgets directly in the case of debt relief under the HIPC Initiative as well as through untied budget support that is by definition fungible.[1] There is also scope for fungibility in the case of tied project or sector programme aid (McGillivray and Morrissey, 2004). This further motivates this study.

In sum, the objective of the present analysis is to assess the extent to which public expenditure on social sectors constitutes a targeted, efficient and powerful instrument for poverty reduction and human development. This may help underpin analysis of the social impact of debt relief and generate recommendations for a (more) pro-poor allocation of resources. The next section briefly summarizes the sources of data, followed by a section devoted to methodology and a number of important caveats. Results are presented in the next two sections (on participation and on distribution of monetary benefits). We conclude in the final section.

Data sources

Two types of data are necessary for benefit-incidence studies: household-level data on participation in public services and information on the unit costs (or benefits) of those services. Whereas participation in public services can be determined quite reliably from the nationally representative household surveys now available for many developing countries, information on the unit costs of service provision is often less reliable, insufficiently disaggregated, or both (see also McKay, 2004).

The source of data concerning participation in and access to public services is the first Mozambican national household survey of living conditions, conducted in 1996–97 by the National Institute of Statistics (INE).[2] The household survey, hereafter referred to by its Portuguese acronym, IAF, covered both rural and urban areas in all provinces of the country. A total of 8,289 households was included in the original sampling frame, and 8,250 had information on daily consumption over a seven-day period. The sample design was a three-stage stratified cluster sample. It was designed to be representative at the national and provincial levels (treating the capital city of Maputo as a separate province); it was also representative along the rural–urban dimension. Data collection occurred throughout the year within the rural sample of each province to assure coverage during the different seasons of the year (Cavero, 1998).

Two household-level components of the IAF data set were used here, the principal questionnaire and the daily household expenditure questionnaire. The principal questionnaire covered a broad range of data, including individual-level information on topics such as demographic characteristics, migration history, health, education and employment status. For health and education, the questionnaire included questions on the use of facilities and on current enrolment in schools at all levels. At the household level, additional information was obtained on land holding, agricultural production, livestock and tree holdings, dwelling characteristics, types of basic services (water and power), asset ownership, major non-food expenditures during a three-month period, regular non-food expenditures during the past month, transfers in and out of the household and basic sources of income. A daily consumption module collected information on consumption of food items and common non-food items (charcoal and matches) consumed during a seven-day period. Each household was interviewed three times during the seven-day period.

In addition to data collected at the household level, there were two instruments administered once during the survey period at higher levels of aggregation. First, within each village, a community-level survey was conducted soliciting information on available infrastructure, major improvements in infrastructure carried out, access to services and general community characteristics. Unfortunately, equivalent data were not collected in urban areas. Second, detailed market price information was collected in the major market for each *bairro* (urban areas) or *localidade* (rural areas), taking into account non-standard measurement units.

For unit costs, we rely on government budget data made available by the ministries of education and health. These include budget figures disaggregated by province, and unit costs calculated using statistics on the number of students in each province. Two important cautions should be noted regarding these data. First, the amount of funds received by a province can be quite different from the amount originally programmed for it. Unfortunately, fiscal accounts were not available. Second, because more disaggregated data were not available, we assume a uniform distribution of the budget within each province – i.e. the expenditure per student at a given educational level does not vary within a province.

Our analysis – and policy making more generally – could potentially be greatly improved if investment were undertaken to produce and publish disaggregated fiscal accounts.

Methodology

In this chapter we estimate the distribution or incidence of public spending by socio-economic status of recipients using the non-behavioural social benefit incidence approach (van de Walle and Nead, 1995). In essence, this means that data on costs of service provision are combined with client information to assess how costs are distributed among the various population sub-groups. Specifically, we undertake the following steps:

(i) Identify the households that receive (benefit from) *public services*.
(ii) Rank all households (recipients and non-recipients alike) by level of *welfare*. The welfare indicator used here is daily total household consumption *per capita*.[3]
(iii) Graph concentration curves that show the *cumulative distribution of total consumption plotted against cumulative participation in public education* and *health services*, as well as the distribution of new rural infrastructure.
(iv) Place a *value on services received*. This is taken to be the unit cost of service provision, disaggregated by type of service and province whenever possible.
(v) Plot concentration curves that show the *cumulative distribution of benefits across households*. The concentration curves may be compared to the cumulative distribution of expenditures (often referred to as the Lorenz curve).
(vi) Test for *statistically significant differences* among the concentration curves, also known as welfare dominance tests.
(vii) Conduct *supplementary descriptive data analysis* to help identify the sources of inequality in education.

Thus, in this study we follow the standard procedure where the monetary valuation of the benefits an individual receives from using a certain public service is not based on any behavioural information such as opportunity cost or willingness to pay.[4] Instead, all those who used the service are assigned the same monetary value of benefits received. This value is the unit cost of providing the service. As such, the term 'benefit incidence' is really a misnomer in the present context. Rather than measuring the exact value to recipients of government-sponsored services, we are looking at the distribution of beneficiaries from those services. It follows that *beneficiary incidence* would be a more precise term for this kind of study.

The main advantage of the non-behavioural benefit-incidence methodology is its simplicity and the relatively modest data requirements. A potential problem occurs when the quality of the service varies systematically with the level of welfare. If poorer individuals receive lower-quality services, the results will be biased in the direction of finding progressive results. Since the war resulted in massive destruction of infrastructure in remote and rural areas, there are good reasons to expect the quality of public service delivery to vary extensively across the country; these expectations are reinforced by observations in the field. This potential problem can be handled in various ways. Most important is to use data for the unit costs of service provision that are as disaggregated as possible. In this way, variation in the quality of service may be captured (to the extent that quality variation shows up in the unit costs), and bias will be reduced.[5] We therefore obtained unit costs at levels that are disaggregated by both province and kind of service provided, as discussed further below. As a form of sensitivity test, one may complement the analysis using direct information on the quality of public services that can be obtained, for example, from participatory techniques or from outcome data such as student pass rates, grades attained and, to some extent, mortality and morbidity rates.[6]

Before proceeding, a further caveat should be noted. We study the incidence of average public spending. It is not known whether *average* spending is different from the *marginal* spending that donors, for example, are funding directly (through untied aid and debt relief) or indirectly (through fungibility). Lanjouw and Ravallion (1999) have argued, using data from rural India, that marginal spending affects the poor more than average spending because when programmes are expanded or reduced, the composition of beneficiaries tends to change. Thus, expanding programmes may increase coverage of the poor, and likewise contraction may hurt the poor relatively more. Hence, benefit-incidence studies based on *average* incidence are likely to underestimate the impact of marginal fiscal changes including those induced by debt relief on poverty. This may also hold true for Mozambique. Reconstruction started in the relatively more accessible and high-potential areas, and it is likely that the expansion of coverage over time will gradually improve access for the poor to those services. This effect will tend to make marginal benefits more pro-poor than average benefits. In this study, we seek to shed light on marginal incidence by analysing the distribution of recent rural infrastructure investment and by assessing the gains from the expansion of education during the 1990s by looking at variations in cohort-specific schooling experience.

The identification of the utilization of services was based on the IAF data. In the survey data we identified those individuals who reported that they were enrolled in a school during the survey period or who had consulted any health service during a period of one month prior to the date of the interview. Ideally, we should include in the analysis only benefits from public services and, to the extent possible, private services (such as *curandeiros*, or traditional healers) were excluded from the analysis. Unfortunately, the survey does not allow complete identification of whether the health service or school in question is public or private. This introduces a potential bias in the direction of finding benefits to be regressive to the extent that the non-poor are more likely to attend private facilities. However, as private health and education services are extremely limited (apart from *curandeiros*), this does not appear to be a serious problem.[7]

More generally, the strength of this survey-based approach to identifying beneficiaries of public services is that the data come directly from the household survey, and hence is unlikely to have been tampered with by political processes. The drawback is that only a fraction of total public expenditures can be assessed. This is because the household survey does not identify the beneficiaries of many categories of spending, including administration, military spending and, within the education sector, university spending.[8] The omitted spending categories are likely to be less progressive than those categories of services we include, and our results may therefore not be representative for overall public spending. An additional limitation, along the same lines, is that the intensity of the use of health services – that is, the number of visits during the reference period and the type of treatment received – is not captured in the survey data.

As already mentioned, the unit cost of service provision was calculated, by province and type of service, by dividing the total expenditures for providing the service by the number of individuals who used the service. For education benefits, we used the 1997 budget data provided by the department of finance and administration of the Ministry of Education (1997a, 1997b) to obtain the cost of service provision and 1997 *Annual Statistics* produced by the planning department of the Ministry of Education to obtain the number of students enrolled in public schools, by level of education and by province. We followed the same procedure for the health sector, where the budget and the health services utilization data were provided by the planning department of the Ministry of Health. The data were disaggregated by province and by type of facility (health posts, health centres and hospitals). One should note that average unit cost is only a rough approximation for value of service provided. For example, for the same level of service quality, unit costs are likely to be higher in more sparsely populated areas. We are also aware that actual distribution of service provision can be quite different from that estimated using budget unit costs (as done for this study). Hence, the results for the distribution of monetary benefits have to be interpreted with caution. Nevertheless, this caveat does not apply for the participation results, which make no attempt to assign a monetary value to services received, thus implicitly assuming that all participants receive the same level of benefit. All analysis was done using the individual (not the household) as the unit of analysis, with the application of sampling weights so that the results are representative at the national and provincial levels.

Finally, it is worthwhile to define the concepts of progressivity used in what follows. We say that the distribution of benefits is 'progressive' if it is more equal than expenditure – that is, if the concentration curve for benefits everywhere lies above the Lorenz curve for expenditures. In this case, public benefits are helping to equalize the distribution of welfare. Furthermore, if the distribution of benefits is such that the poor receive more *per capita* in absolute terms than the non-poor, we say that the distribution is *per capita* progressive (also referred to as absolute progressivity). Graphically, *per capita* progressivity appears as a concentration curve of benefits above the 45-degree line. *Per capita* progressivity indicates successful targeting of benefits towards the poor. If benefits are distributed more unequally than expenditures (i.e. the concentration curve lies below the Lorenz curve), services are said to be regressive. When curves cross, no determination of progressivity or regressivity can be made using the Lorenz criterion, although one could resort to other welfare measures – such as the Gini coefficient, Atkinson index, or generalized entropy measures – for a complete ordering.

Participation in public services

The empirical results are presented in three parts. In this section, results for participation or utilization are reported, measuring incidence as a binary variable that indicates whether or not an individual utilized a given type of service. This approach is less demanding of the data, but is limited in that no allowance is made for the level of expenditure related to the benefit received. In the next section, the analysis is done using the unit costs of each type of service. This approach takes account of the level of public expenditure, and allows to some extent for variations in service quality as discussed above. The following section explores the education results in greater depth to gain a better understanding of the underlying reasons for inequality in education.

The Lorenz curve (or expenditure–consumption concentration curve) that is shown in Figures 10.2–10.9 plots the cumulative distribution of *per capita* household expenditure. By inspecting Figure 10.2, for example, it may be seen that the poorest 50 per cent of households account for only about 24 per cent of total expenditure. However, compared to many other African countries, Mozambique is not an especially unequal society. In South Africa, the poorest 50 per cent account for less than 10 per cent of total expenditures. In Côte d'Ivoire, Guinea, Madagascar, Uganda and Madagascar the poorest half account for less than 20 per cent, while in Ghana and Tanzania the share of the poorest half of the population is around 25 per cent (Sahn and Younger, 1998; Sahn, Younger and Simler, 2000). The present high rates of economic growth may well result in rising inequality, as the market-oriented growth process is likely to reward those relatively few Mozambicans who possess human and physical capital of any magnitude. The large majority of people, virtually without assets and with minimal education risk not sharing in economic growth, at least in the absence of equalizing government action (Wuyts, 2000).

Education

The education system in Mozambique is divided into the following levels and age groups:

- **EP1** Lower primary school (*ensino primário de primeiro grau*), from 1st through 5th class, which is intended to correspond to the ages of 6–11, but in practice also takes in many children who are much older, because they have started school late, had interruptions in their schooling, repeated grades, or some combination of these. Naturally, this also has an impact on the ages of students in subsequent levels of schooling.
- **EP2** Upper primary school (*ensino primário de segundo grau*), 6th and 7th class and intended for those aged 12–13 years.

- **ES1** Basic post-primary technical or lower secondary school (*ensino técnico básico and ensino secundário geral, primeiro ciclo,* ESG1), intended for those aged 14–16 years.
- **ES2** Intermediate post-primary technical or upper secondary school (*ensino técnico médio and ensino secundário geral, segundo ciclo,* ESG2), intended for those 17–18/19 years old.[9]

Enrolment data are presented in Table 10.1. The enrolment rates shown are the proportion within each age group currently studying at level of schooling. Hence, the data pertain to a certain age group, not to a specific level of schooling. Nationally, 54 per cent of boys and 45 per cent of girls aged 6–11 years are enrolled in schools according to the survey,[10] while 36 and 13 per cent of males and females aged 17–18 years attend school. Enrolment rates are highest among those in the age range of 12–13 years. Enrolment rates of boys (but not girls) 14–16 years old are almost equal to those for the 6–11 years old. As further discussed below, to a large extent this does not reflect enrolment in secondary education, but is rather an indication of starting school late and delays in passing through primary school. Enrolment is highest in Maputo City, which has a more developed infrastructure and higher incomes, followed by the rest of the southern provinces. Gender gaps in enrolment are smallest in Maputo City for all age groups. However, if we leave aside for a moment the unusual case of Maputo City, we note that in the youngest age group, inter-regional differences are greater than within-region gender differences. For example, the largest male–female enrolment rate gap in the 6–11 group is 11 percentage points in the central region; this compares with south–central gaps of 19 and 24 percentage points for boys and girls, respectively. In older age groups the pattern is reversed, with girls leaving school faster than boys in all regions. A particularly striking gender feature is that enrolment rates for girls drop

Table 10.1 Gross enrolment rates, by age group, region and sex

	Age 6–11		*Age 12–13*		*Age 14–16*		*Age 17–18*	
	M	*F*	*M*	*F*	*M*	*F*	*M*	*F*
North	0.50	0.40	0.61	0.46	0.52	0.25	0.25	0.06
Central	0.48	0.37	0.59	0.42	0.48	0.33	0.41	0.13
South excl. Maputo City	0.67	0.61	0.71	0.68	0.53	0.42	0.33	0.15
Maputo City	0.87	0.83	0.82	0.88	0.73	0.71	0.45	0.37
Total	0.54	0.45	0.63	0.53	0.52	0.37	0.36	0.13

sharply at age 14 in all provinces, perhaps reflecting parents' unwillingness to send daughters to secondary schools that are often located at some distance from home. The analysis of equity in schooling is pursued in greater depth later.

Figure 10.1(a) and 10.1(b) plots the age-specific enrolment rates for each decile of real *per capita* consumption for boys and girls, respectively. Enrolment in the education system increases markedly with

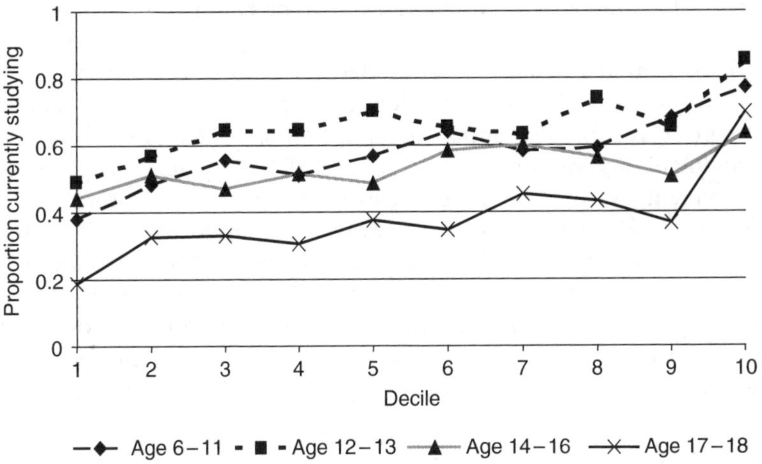

(b) Enrolment for girls, by age and decile

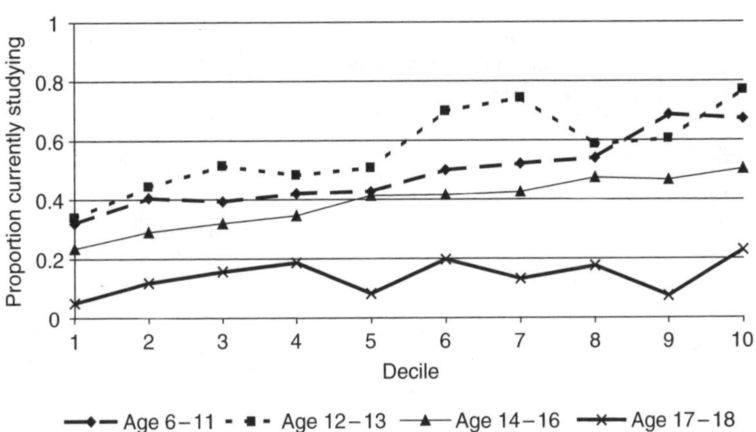

Figure 10.1 Enrolment

expenditure for all age groups and for both boys and girls. For example, among children aged 6–11, in the 1st decile only 38 and 32 per cent of boys and girls, respectively, are currently enrolled in school as compared to 77 and 67 per cent of boys and girls in the 10th decile. Among those 12–13 years old, 49 and 34 per cent of boys and girls, respectively, in the 1st decile are currently enrolled, against 85 and 77 per cent in the last decile. With few exceptions, boys have higher enrolment rates than girls within the same decile. However, from some perspectives the level of consumption appears to be a more significant factor than gender. For example, non-poor girls are more likely to be enrolled than poor boys across all age groups.

Participation in education is plotted using concentration curves in Figure 10.2. This shows that the lower the level of education, the more progressive is the distribution of its utilization. The figure shows that enrolment in primary education (EP1 and EP2) is progressive, i.e. school enrolment is distributed more equally than expenditure. Lower primary education, EP1, has the most progressive distribution, closely following the 45-degree line, but as it crosses the 45-degree line we cannot say it is *per capita* progressive. The EP1 and EP2 results are cases of Lorenz-dominance, i.e. the concentration curve for lower primary education everywhere lies above other levels of education, meaning that access to lower primary education is more equal than access to other education

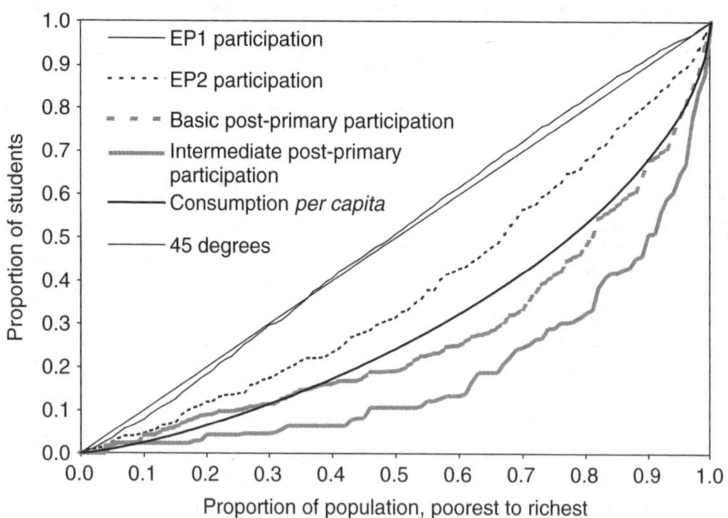

Figure 10.2 Education participation

services.[11] Participation in upper primary education is also progressive, and more equally distributed than post-primary education.

The concentration curves for post-primary basic and intermediate education cross the Lorenz curve, meaning that they are neither progressive nor regressive by the Lorenz criterion. However, post-primary intermediate education crosses the Lorenz curve at 0.1 on the horizontal axis, and lies well below the Lorenz curve for the rest of the distribution, so it would be considered regressive by most other criteria. From the concentration curves it might be observed that the poorest 50 per cent of school-age children constitute 50 per cent of all students enrolled in lower primary education (EP1) and 32 per cent of students in upper primary education (EP2). At higher levels, participation by the poor drops drastically with the poorest half accounting for only 19 per cent of students in post-primary education and 11 per cent of students in the intermediate post-primary category.

The pattern observed in Figure 10.2 cannot be explained by the fact that the poor tend to have more children. The calculations are done on an individual (rather than household) basis. Hence, the effect coming from higher demand from poor households due to more children has been removed by scaling the concentration curves to individuals. The observed trend has to be explained by the relatively easy access to lower primary education in the areas where the poor live, and conversely by constraints (in terms of access, financing and other) for the participation of the poor at higher levels of education, a fact which we return to below. From this comes the fact that to enter higher levels of schooling, an individual must first pass through lower levels.

Health

In the analysis of the distribution of benefits from public health services, the following types of health service utilization are considered:

(i) Children from 0 to 5 years old, who were vaccinated at least once.
(ii) Women who were pregnant at least once and received antenatal care.
(iii) All individuals who accessed health services (hospital, health centre, or other medical facility) during the month preceding the interview, seeking treatment for an illness or accident.

The results are presented in the concentration curves in Figure 10.3 for preventive care (i.e. item (i) and (ii) above) and in Figure 10.4 for

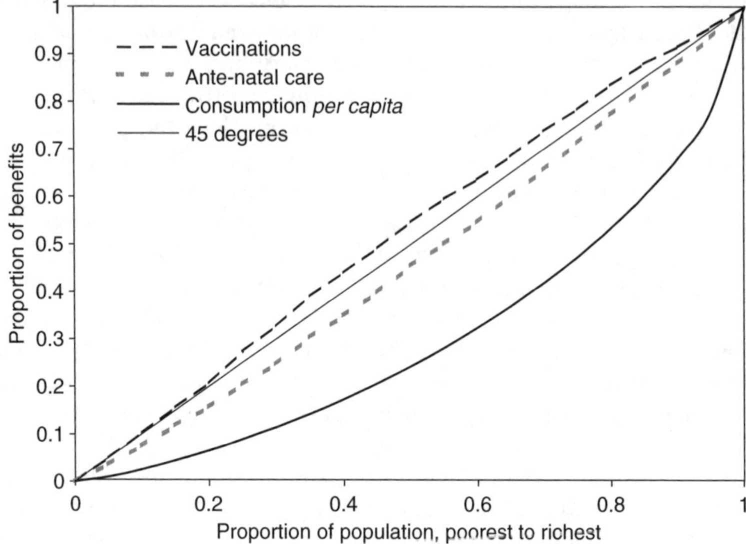

Figure 10.3 Use of preventive health care

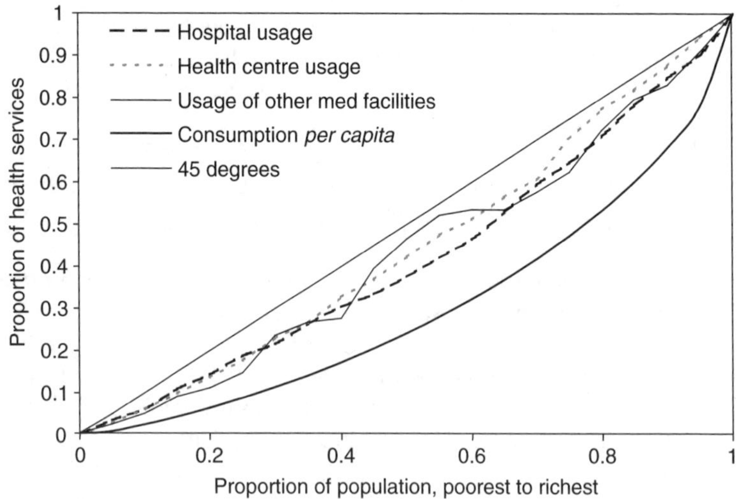

Figure 10.4 Use of curative health care

curative care (item (iii)), allowing comparison with household consumption expenditure. The participation of infants and pregnant women in basic preventive health care is progressive and appears particularly progressive for infant vaccinations. For most of the distribution, the curve for infant vaccinations lies above the 45-degree line; vaccinations cannot be classified as *per capita* progressive because it crosses the 45-degree at about the 5th percentile. The dominance testing of these preventive health services finds that the curve for infant vaccinations statistically dominates both antenatal care and the Lorenz consumption curve. Access to basic preventive care helps to equalize the income distribution curves, although the caveats previously noted apply here as well. The data show that among the group of children who have received at least one vaccination, 54 per cent come from the poorest 50 per cent of children – i.e. the poor are disproportionately represented in this group. For antenatal services, the poorest 50 per cent of pregnant women account for 45 per cent of those who receive at least some antenatal care.[12]

Figure 10.4 plots concentration curves for visits to curative health services by people who were ill during the month prior to being interviewed. The curves for hospital and health centre utilization are both situated between the Lorenz curve for consumption expenditure and the 45-degree line. This implies that access to these levels of health care is progressive, but not *per capita* progressive. The curve for other health services largely follows the same pattern, except that it crosses the Lorenz curve near the origin. Subject to the qualification already noted in n. 12, we observe that 38 per cent of those who were hospital patients, and 42 per cent of those who attended health centres, come from the poorest 50 per cent of the population. In comparison, the poorest 50 per cent account for only 24 per cent of total consumption. Dominance tests show that both the hospital and health centre curves dominate the consumption curve and neither of these two services dominates the other.

Rural infrastructure

As previously mentioned, the IAF questionnaire had a section designed to collect community data regarding construction and rehabilitation of public infrastructure during the two years prior to the survey. We linked this community data with data on consumption expenditure on individual households residing in the community and then identified those communities (rural villages) that received new investment (for rehabilitation or construction of infrastructure), classified by the level of well-being of individuals in the respective villages. This analysis is (as discussed earlier) useful, as it allows an incidence analysis of *marginal* (investment) spending, whereas the analyses of education and health services are concerned only with *average* incidence.

Table 10.2 shows the proportion of rural households whose villages have received various types of public infrastructure investment, broken down by expenditure tercile and region. We see that due to the rapid post-war reconstruction and rehabilitation of Mozambique, there is a fairly large proportion of the population whose communities have recently benefited from public investment. The most common investment received by rural communities is a new or rehabilitated school, followed by roads and health facilities. Investments in all types of public infrastructure appear to be more widespread in the southern regions

Table 10.2 Percentage of households in villages that benefited from rehabilitation or construction of infrastructure (health, education and roads), by terciles of household expenditure

Regions	*Construction and improvements of schools*			
	1st tercile	*2nd tercile*	*3rd tercile*	*Total*
National	20	22	23	21
North	13	16	19	16
Centre	18	20	20	20
South	32	37	41	37
	Construction and improvement of health infrastructure			
	1st tercile	*2nd tercile*	*3rd tercile*	*Total*
National	8	9	10	9
North	13	9	9	10
Centre	5	7	9	7
South	9	16	18	14
	Paving and improvement of roads			
	1st tercile	*2nd tercile*	*3rd tercile*	*Total*
National	14	17	17	16
North	24	20	25	23
Centre	11	14	7	11
South	8	17	21	25

than in the other regions. In the education sector, in particular, big regional differences in the incidence of fresh investment are apparent.

Differences in the incidence of recent infrastructure investments among expenditure terciles appear to be small. It should be kept in mind that this analysis is confined to rural areas due to data limitations, but it appears that rural public investment is fairly evenly spread across income groups, but not across regions.[13] This line of analysis is further pursued, using concentration curves, in Figure 10.5. This figure confirms that construction and rehabilitation of public infrastructure is progressive and close to the equality line. This means that recent public investments in rural areas have gone more or less to the poor and the non-poor in the same proportion. A key fact underlying this result is the observation that the majority of inequality in Mozambique is within-village.[14] In other words, it is not especially useful to categorize rural Mozambique into 'poor areas' and 'non-poor' areas, because the poor and the non-poor live side by side in the same villages.

Our understanding of the optimal geographic distribution of infrastructure is still limited. From a poverty reduction perspective, an even spread of investment is unlikely to be desirable. The social return to infrastructure investment may be higher in areas with relatively good

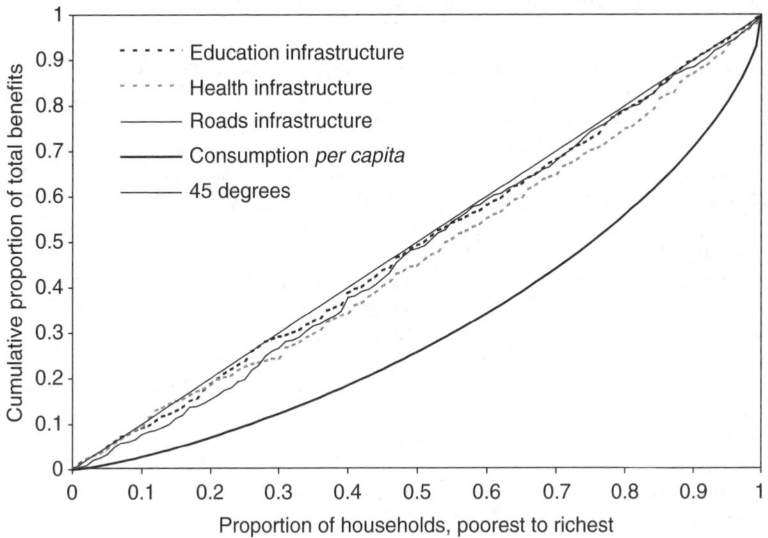

Figure 10.5 Benefits from rehabilitation or construction of infrastructure, education, health, roads

agro-ecological characteristics and market access. However, there is no assurance that the benefits of this investment will reach the poor in these high-potential areas, much less those situated in marginal areas or more isolated locations.[15] Conversely, infrastructure investment in remote, low-potential and relatively poor areas is not always the most efficient way of combating poverty. Spending on education and health, however, remains warranted also in low-potential areas. The benefit-incidence approach is not well suited to capture the indirect effects of public spending, say on agricultural prices or employment. Other work exploring these issues in more detail include Arndt *et al.* (2000) using a Social Accounting Matrix (SAM)-based approach.

Incidence of monetary benefits

Unit costs

Table 10.3 provides the unit costs of education services by level of education and by province (whenever available).[16] In general, the cost of providing education increases as we move from lower to higher levels of education. The second cycle of general secondary education (ESG2) is particularly costly. The major reasons for these variations in unit costs are that teachers at upper levels of education have higher qualifications and receive higher wages than those at lower levels and that classes tend

Table 10.3 Unit costs of education and health services (1,000 MT)

	Hospital care	*Other health care*	*EP1*	*EP2*	*ESG1*	*ESG2*	*Basic technical*	*Intermediate technical*
Niassa	1,159	253	167	307	1,578	3,064	959	–
Cabo Delgado	993	517	101	462	1,932	2,407	3,859	–
Nampula	1,682	141	153	598	1,256	1,901	2,815	–
Zambézia	891	251	138	441	598	5,009	1,762	–
Tete	1,701	652	135	384	1,094	–	2,057	–
Manica	1,254	314	112	215	1,101	2,379	1,475	–
Sofala	1,784	408	138	397	695	5,172	995	–
Inhambane	509	258	110	318	446	3,486	2,092	–
Gaza	294	1,314	100	160	585	1,972	1,636	–
Maputo Province	–	–	100	186	1,174	4,312	1,372	–
Maputo City	–	–	144	253	645	3,782	1,392	–
National	–	–	128	325	901	3,400	1,567	4,807

Notes: EP1 is lower primary (grades 1–5); EP2 is upper primary (grades 6–7); ESG1 is lower secondary (grades 8–10), and ESG2 is upper secondary (grades 11–12).

to be of smaller sizes at higher levels. Most of the variation in unit costs across provinces at the same level of education can be explained by a combination of variations in the qualifications of teachers and their salaries, variation in student–teacher ratios and in the provision of pedagogical materials. It was not possible to place a separate monetary value on preventive care, and the same goes for investment in new infrastructure. As in the education sector, there is substantial variation in the cost of service provision across provinces. These variations are a combined result of the professional qualifications and salaries of personnel in each province, the level of demand of services by the population and the type of services available in each province. Thus, the higher the ratio of hospitals to basic care facilities in a given province, the higher the average qualifications and average salaries of health personnel. The same holds for maintenance costs. This means that variation in unit costs are likely to be linked to differences in the type of facility and quality of service, and that the provincial breakdown of unit costs as carried out here is highly relevant to the analysis.[17]

Concentration curves for monetary benefits

Figure 10.6 shows the concentration curves that result from matching the unit costs of provision with the household data on participation in education. The pattern found for participation remains intact once we

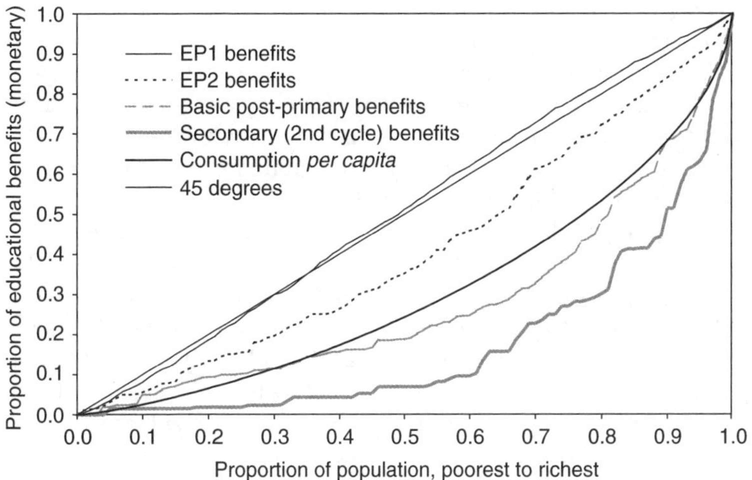

Figure 10.6 Education benefits

look at monetary benefits. Thus, the lower the level of education the more equal its distribution, with primary education being clearly progressive. For lower primary education (EP1), there is an almost equal distribution with the exception of the poorest 25 per cent of the population, who receive slightly less. Despite this very equal distribution the EP1 concentration curve does not dominate the other curves because the confidence intervals overlap within the first 5 per cent of the poorest. Yet overall, EP1 benefits in Mozambique are progressive. For example, the poorest 50 per cent receive around 51 per cent of all expenditures on EP1 education, whereas they account for only around 24 per cent of total consumption expenditures.

For upper primary education (EP2) a progressive trend can be noted, and the EP2 curve statistically dominates the consumption curve. However, except for a crossing at the poorest tail end of the distribution, EP2 is less progressive than EP1 with the poorest half receiving 35 per cent of all EP2 education expenditures. The curve that represents the benefits of post-primary basic education crosses the consumption distribution, so the Lorenz criterion cannot indicate whether this kind of education is progressive or regressive. The poorest 50 per cent of the population receive less than 19 per cent of expenditures on basic post-primary education (general and technical) and the richest 10 per cent receive more than 32 per cent. Note also that upper (second cycle) secondary education is distributed especially unequally. As already noted, the data are weak when it comes to the post-primary intermediate technical and university categories, which therefore had to be left out of the analysis both here and in what follows below.

An analysis of total benefits of education (all benefits added together except the post-primary intermediate technical category) shows a progressive situation in relative, but not in absolute terms, as EP1 is strongly progressive. We estimate that the poorest quintile receives 14 per cent of total education spending, the poorest half receives 36 per cent of public spending in the education sector, while the richest quintile receives 33 per cent. Compared to other African countries surveyed by Castro-Leal *et al.* (1999), this distribution is (i) more unequal than in Kenya, Ghana and Malawi, (ii) roughly comparable to Côte d'Ivoire, Tanzania, Uganda and South Africa, and (iii) more equal than in Madagascar and Guinea.

Figure 10.7 shows the concentration curves for the incidence of benefits associated with public health expenditures. In broad terms, there is little difference in the incidence of hospital and other health care medical facilities, but both types of expenditure are clearly progressive in the sense that they dominate the Lorenz curve. It is common for benefit-incidence

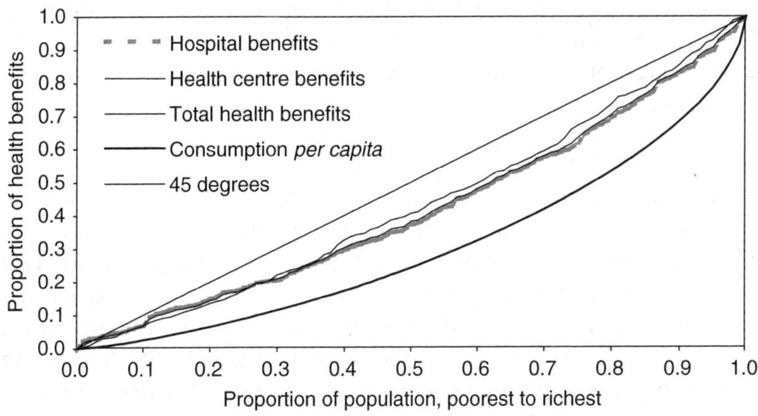

Figure 10.7 Incidence of health benefits in monetary value

studies undertaken in other developing countries to find non-hospital facilities to be more progressive than hospitals, so the degree of progressivity of hospital benefits in Mozambique is remarkable.

From Figure 10.8 it is seen that the incidence of 'total' education and health benefits (i.e. the total of primary education, part of secondary education and curative health care), while not *per capita* progressive, is

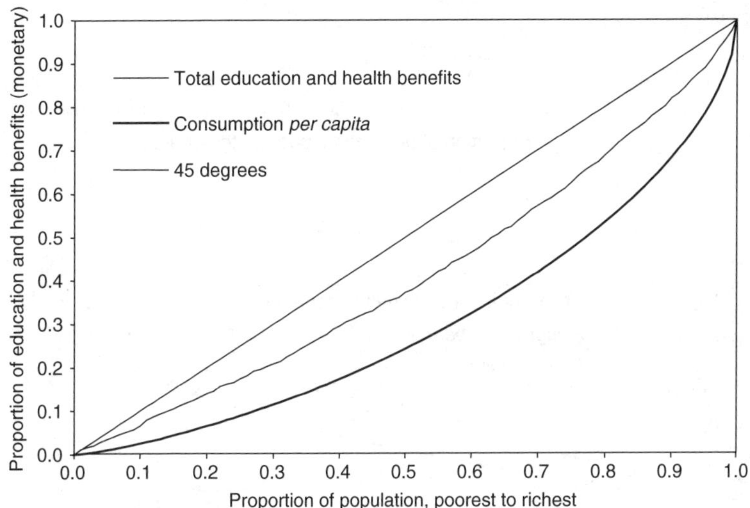

Figure 10.8 Total education and health benefits

clearly progressive in the relative sense that public spending on these items is more equally distributed than *per capita* consumption. The 'total' education and health benefit line everywhere lies above the Lorenz curve.

Regional analysis

We next analyse how benefits are distributed within each region. In Figure 10.9(a)–10.9(c) the concentration curve for 'total' education and health benefits (with the same omitted categories as before) is plotted for each region. It can be seen that total benefits are distributed most equally in the north, where the curve lies slightly above the 45-degree line. Benefits are still very equal in the central provinces while the distribution of benefits is least equal in the south, where the benefits curve crosses the Lorenz curve near the lower tail of the distribution. These results are caused in large part by higher enrolment in post-primary education

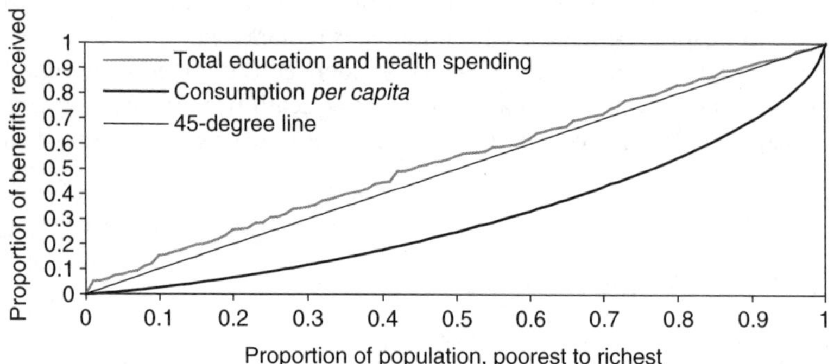

B CENTRAL

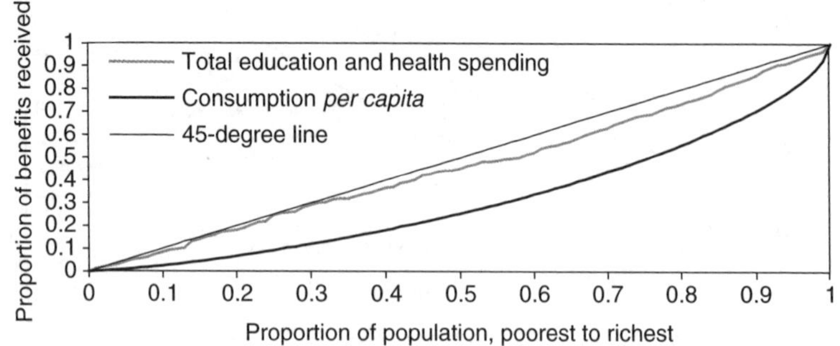

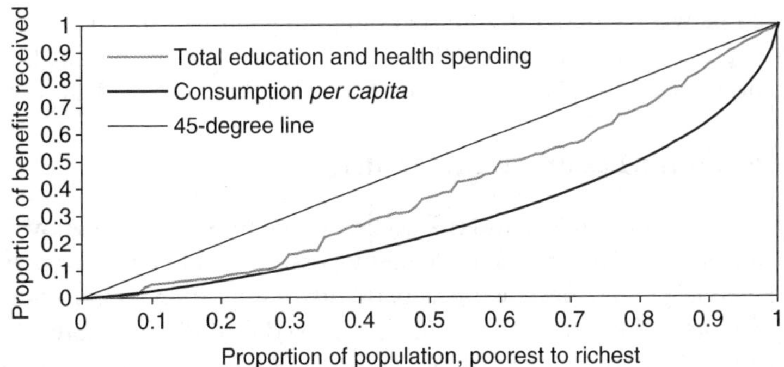

Figure 10.9(a)–10.9(c) Total education and health benefits by region

the further south one moves. Hence, above-primary education, which is less progressive, gets a higher weight in the total picture as one moves south.[18] Several caveats apply: the present analysis has captured only a fraction of total public expenditure and even among those services that we have in fact been able to analyse, there is potential for biases in the unit costs on which the analysis is based.

The distribution of benefits across regions is, as already mentioned, an issue of considerable political interest. Table 10.4 shows the population share and the proportion of public service benefits (those we are able to measure) of each region. The most striking observation is that the capital city, Maputo, receives almost a third of the benefits, yet accounts for only 6 per cent of the population. Part of this is because Maputo provides services such as secondary schools and hospitals that serve a wider catchment area throughout the southern region. Even so, the share of benefits received by the southern region excluding Maputo is roughly in proportion to its population, leaving the northern region and especially the central region under-served when measured as

Table 10.4 Regional distribution of population and monetary benefits

Share (%)	*North*	*Centre*	*South, excl. Maputo*	*Maputo City*	*Total*
Population	32.5	42.6	18.8	6.1	100
Education	18.8	26.2	22.7	32.2	100
Health	27.3	30.0	10.9	31.8	100
Total benefits	23.0	28.1	16.8	32.0	100

per capita benefits received. Given the regional imbalances already referred to and the political differences from one region to the next, it would be wise to design future spending programmes carefully so as to avoid tension and conflict (Addison and Murshed, 2003), and maximize the human and social impact of social spending financed by debt relief.

Education: what drives the results?

It is important to understand the decline in progressivity as we move up the educational ladder. There are many possible reasons, and for policy to be appropriately designed it is particularly important to understand the factors causing inequalities in access to education. The more widespread availability of lower primary schools (EP1) in rural areas and the supply of education materials to all students benefit poorer groups. For other levels of education, there are much greater barriers in terms of access (long distances to schools) that increase with the level of education. This is especially the case for rural areas where the incidence of poverty is higher. Furthermore, family work obligations that increase with age may be a particularly important constraint for children from poor and rural households from completing primary school and undertaking further study; and students need to pass primary exams before entering secondary school.

In the following, we address a different but related question: at which step in the educational ladder do the poor drop out? If education is to become more egalitarian, it is important to know at which level of schooling the constraints on the poor and girls are most binding. Additional data analysis was therefore undertaken in order to help pinpoint the location of inequalities within the education system. For example, it was observed in the previous sections that participation in and benefits from upper primary education (EP2) are much less progressive than basic lower primary education (EP1). The reason for this decline in progressivity may be located either at the EP2 or at the EP1 level: either the poor do not enrol in or do not pass EP2, or the poor are less likely to complete EP1 and hence do not qualify for admission into EP2, or both. Policy implications depend on which of the two factors are at work.

Table 10.5 describes the schooling experience of all sampled individuals 10 to 20 years old, inclusive. For each level of schooling and tercile of real total consumption, it shows the percentages of those who completed the level in question, are still studying, or did not complete (either never enrolled at that level or enrolled and then subsequently left school before completing). The main insight from the table is that

Table 10.5 School experience, by tercile and gender (%)

	Tercile			*Gender*		
	1	*2*	*3*	*Male*	*Female*	*Total*
Ever went to school						
Yes	59.4	69.7	74.1	73.2	58.8	66.2
No	40.6	30.3	25.9	26.8	41.2	33.8
Total	100	100	100	100	100	100
EP1 status						
Passed EP1	16.8	25.1	34.2	24.1	24.3	24.2
Still studying EP1	58.2	52.2	42.5	55.6	47.3	52.0
Did not pass/enrol	25.0	22.7	23.3	20.3	28.4	23.8
Total	100	100	100	100	100	100
EP2 status						
Passed EP2	19.7	18.1	35.2	25.4	24.2	24.9
Still studying EP2	33.9	40.2	37.8	39.9	34.5	37.6
Did not pass/enrol	46.3	41.7	27.1	34.7	41.3	37.5
Total	100	100	100	100	100	100
Post-primary status						
Passed post-primary	2.9	3.7	4.5	5.1	2.4	4.4
Still studying post-primary	32.7	47.1	58.3	48.1	52.4	50.4
Did not pass/enrol	64.4	49.3	37.1	46.8	45.3	45.2
Total	100	100	100	100	100	100

inequalities are present at all levels of education. The first row looks at the proportion of each tercile that replied in the affirmative to the question whether they ever went to school. A marked difference is found, as expected. In the first tercile, 59 per cent of this age group have gone to school, compared to 74 per cent in the third tercile. Next, the table shows the proportion of those who went to school that either (i) passed EP1, (ii) is still enrolled in EP1 or (iii) did not pass EP1. It may be noted that students from the third tercile are much more likely to have passed EP1 than others. Students from the first two terciles are more likely to remain at the EP1 level at age 10–20, because of late school start and/or delays in passing through the relevant grades (1–5). Family work obligations keeping the children of the lower terciles away from school part of the time and low quality of schooling services provided in relatively poor areas may account for this.

This pattern continues up through the education hierarchy. Table 10.5 goes on to show the status of students with respect to EP2, conditional on already having passed EP1, for each tercile. Students from the third tercile are almost twice as likely as students from the first and second terciles to have passed EP2 (given they previously passed EP1). This difference is not due to delays: the proportion still enrolled in EP2 is the same across terciles. The difference is entirely attributable to the fact that those students from the two lower terciles who qualify either never enrolled in upper primary school, or they enrolled in EP2 and then dropped out. The analysis is repeated for all post-primary education, combining general secondary education with post-primary technical education. In the third tercile 63 per cent of those students who passed EP2 are enrolled in post-primary education or have already passed it, compared to 36 per cent in the first tercile.

Turning next to gender inequalities, a similar picture of cumulative inequality appears. Table 10.5 shows that gender imbalance arises from early on – boys are more likely than girls to have gone to school. Compared to boys, those girls who actually did get to school are somewhat more likely to drop out before completing EP1, and those who pass EP1 are more likely to drop out from or never enrol in EP2. Hence, it is concluded that inequalities arise at all levels of schooling, starting from the most basic levels and accumulate up through of the school system. It is therefore the accumulated effects of inequalities at all previous levels that make intermediate and higher education regressive, as well as unequal in the gender dimension.

Next we analysed, as shown in Table 10.6, differences in schooling across age cohorts, based on the question: 'Did you ever go to school?'

Table 10.6 Education experience, by cohort and gender

	Proportion that ever went to school (%)							
	Age 20–28				*Age 13–14*			
	Tercile				*Tercile*			
	1	*2*	*3*	*Total*	*1*	*2*	*3*	*Total*
By gender:								
Males	68	76	82	76	71	82	87	78
Females	43	52	58	51	54	73	76	64
By region:								
North	61	64	67	64	64	70	71	68
Central	42	52	60	51	58	79	72	66
South, excl. Maputo City	58	70	86	70	70	79	96	79
Maputo City	95	96	99	97	88	96	97	95
Total	**53**	**62**	**69**	**61**	**63**	**78**	**82**	**72**

The highest rate of 'yes' was found for those aged 13–14, at 72 per cent. This contrasts markedly with the schooling experience of those aged 20–28, which is only 61 per cent. Those aged 20–28 at the time of the survey were of school age during the worst period of the war in the mid- and late 1980s, and they suffered from massive displacements and destruction of schools. Comparing the cohort aged 13–14 with the cohort aged 20–28 gives an indication of the impact of the massive school investment and reconstruction programme that took place starting in the early 1990s.

The results of the cohort analysis in Table 10.6 are disaggregated by gender, tercile and region.[19] Women have enjoyed the largest increase in schooling – i.e. the expansion of educational opportunities has led to a more rapid growth in the enrolment of females than in the enrolment of males. Growth has been sharpest for girls in the 2nd and 3rd terciles, with an increase in enrolment of 21 and 18 percentage points, respectively. Part of this is because of the simple fact that because they had lower enrolment rates in earlier years, females had more scope for increasing enrolment than males.

Regionally, the largest gains in schooling occurred in the central and the southern (excluding Maputo City) regions, where the first and second terciles enjoyed substantial increases in the likelihood of receiving schooling. In the other two regions, schooling exposure remained lower (north) or stagnated at a fairly high level (Maputo City) and inequality in schooling access appeared to increase.

Conclusions

The 'conventional wisdom' of the benefit-incidence literature is that spending on primary health care and primary education are the most progressive items on developing country public sector budgets, particularly if spending is targeted to rural areas. Nevertheless, previous studies conducted in other African countries indicate that public spending may not be very progressive due to the high budget shares of non-primary education and health services (Sahn and Younger, 1998; Castro-Leal *et al.*, 1999). The objective of the present study was to provide additional country case evidence on these issues based on budget allocation practices in Mozambique.

Poverty is widespread and deeply rooted in Mozambique, and poverty reduction is a fundamental goal of fiscal policy and debt relief. This implies there are two basic challenges for debt relief: (i) to help spur rapid economic growth, and (ii) to ensure that economic growth is distributed in a fair and equitable manner. The analysis in this chapter focused on the second point, and most of the public services we were able to measure have a progressive distribution. Mozambique is poor, but is not a very unequal society, and most of the public services analysed seem to reduce inequality relative to the distribution of consumption. The major exceptions at the national level are (i) upper secondary school benefits, which are less progressive than consumption expenditure, and (ii) university training, on which we have no data, but which is almost certainly highly regressive. Moreover, inequalities in public spending are to some extent, more of a regional nature. On this basis, we conclude that regional imbalances need to be addressed carefully in future spending programmes. Imbalances are important and can fuel conflict, so not addressing them in time may have undesirable human and political implications.

The analysis revealed that inequalities in school education and attainment accumulate up through the educational ladder, resulting in increasingly unequal distribution. This does not in itself constitute an argument for scaling back post-primary education. Instead, those factors that constrain poor students from fully sharing in education or advancing up through the system need to be addressed, for example, by expanding coverage and improving quality of services in rural and other less-advantaged areas. This way, the incidence of public spending can become more progressive, yet it will require more fiscal resources, including those yielded by debt relief, devoted to education at all levels.[20]

Other barriers for access by the poor to further education should also be addressed. For example, at present there are great difficulties in recruiting and attracting qualified teachers for primary schools in many areas, constraining the continued expansion (and quality improvement) of primary schooling. This problem is related to the poor state of secondary education. Hence, even if secondary education is not particularly progressive, it requires attention. It would be unwise to place exclusive emphasis on primary education because of immediate equity arguments as this would compromise long-run growth by not addressing the need for people with higher levels of education. In this context, an economy-wide perspective on bottlenecks in skills and education is required to better guide investments in education. In addition, it has been shown in Mozambique that the presence of a secondary school nearby has a positive impact on enrolment rates at the primary level (Handa and Simler, 2000).

With reference to the health sector, even hospital care appears to be distributed progressively, and hence should not be scaled back on equity grounds *per se*. What appears more relevant is to highlight that there are possibilities for directing welfare benefits to poor people through well-designed public interventions in the health area, and the same goes for the access of poor people to health, education and road infrastructure.

In sum, in the case of Mozambique we find the incidence of public services to be fairly progressive, and cautions relating to data and methodology were noted. In particular, we had to assume that the benefit from a given service is uniform throughout a province. This ignores the heterogeneity of quality that no doubt exists on the ground. To the extent that poorer individuals receive lower-quality services, the progressivity of benefits is diminished unless the quality of services in these areas is improved. Investments in better data generation, especially proper fiscal accounts, are necessary to improve future analyses and better guide budget priorities. However, it appears safe to assert that alleviating fiscal constraints in Mozambique (through debt relief) is likely to have significant poverty-reducing effects and help poor people access public services in one of the poorest countries in the world. The implications for the donor community of the present study would therefore certainly seem to suggest that debt relief is warranted. This is even more so if the marginal impact of public services is higher than the average.

Notes

1. For example, of Denmark's annual US$25 million aid to Mozambique, around a quarter is untied budget support, and what happens to this money once it enters the fiscal system is beyond the direct control of Danida.
2. The *Inquérito Nacional aos Agregados Familiares Sobre as Condições de Vida*, or National Household Survey of Living Conditions.
3. Total expenditures are the sum of food and non-food consumption expenditures. The food expenditures include all items consumed by the household (from purchase, own production or donation) and the non-food expenditures include all non-food items, such as clothing, house rents, cooking fuel, durable goods, transport, education, etc. as well as imputed values for rents if the household lives in owner-occupied housing.
4. For an example, see Younger (1999), who estimated monetary benefits based on estimated demand functions for public services.
5. To the extent that quality variation is not captured in the cost data – e.g. because of systematic variation in teacher absenteeism between the poor and the non-poor (which is plausible) – bias in the direction of finding progressivity still prevails. Alternative methods for adjusting for differences in the quality of services delivered are necessary but difficult to identify.
6. Strictly speaking, one cannot attribute all differences in outcomes (pass rates, health status, etc.) to differences in the quality of services, as other factors inevitably come into play. A health service in a poor area with inadequate

public sanitation is likely to be associated with inferior outcomes when compared with an identical service located in an area with good public sanitation.

7. For example, according to the IAF data, only 1.4 per cent of those who sought medical treatment for an illness or accident went to a private clinic (Lindelow, 2000).
8. The proportion of university students in Mozambique is too small for that category to be adequately represented in the survey.
9. Regular secondary education is intended to end at 18 years of age while technical education is intended to end at age 19, although as with primary education, students are often older than this. Lower and upper secondary school is sometimes referred to as secondary school, first and second cycle, respectively.
10. According to other, more recent data, primary enrolment is now above 60 per cent. However, this is the gross enrolment rate, which includes children of higher age who are still enrolled in primary education, and hence is not directly comparable to the figures used here.
11. Preliminary tests show that EP1 and EP2 both statistically dominate *per capita* consumption. Here, and elsewhere in this chapter, we say that one curve dominates if the ordinates at the 5th, 10th, 15th,..., 95th percentiles of *per capita* consumption are all statistically significantly different from one another at the 5 per cent significance level. This is a more stringent test than is usually found in the literature, so it is difficult to find results of statistical dominance (Sahn, Younger and Simler, 2000). All tests allow for the dependence between the distributions; however, they do not incorporate the effects of the stratified cluster sample design. Other analysis shows the cluster design to have a significant effect on computed standard errors (MPF, 1998). As such, the significance of dominance in our dominance tests is likely to be overstated. Thanks are due to Steve Younger and Jean-Yves Duclos for providing Gauss programmes for statistical dominance testing.
12. A data limitation should be kept in mind in the discussion of health service utilization. The operative variables at the individual level are binary, indicating whether or not a person accessed a given service during the reference period of the survey. However, multiple visits for antenatal services, and multiple vaccinations, are possible; indeed, they are recommended. Thus, there is a degree or intensity of participation that is not captured in the results reported here. For example, while it is estimated that 45 per cent of women who received some antenatal care were from the bottom 50 per cent of the income distribution, one cannot infer from this that same group of women accounted for 45 per cent of all antenatal care visits.
13. This result may obtain in part because of the two-year time reference period for the data, compounded by the inherent 'lumpiness' of infrastructure investments.
14. We have calculated a Theil index of inequality from the IAF data. It is 0.255 for rural Mozambique, which may be decomposed into 0.145 within-village and 0.110 between-villages. Put differently, approximately 60 per cent of rural inequality in Mozambique is within-village inequality.
15. Poor people living in low-potential areas can also benefit from investment in relatively better-endowed areas, for example, through migration to areas where new opportunities for paid employment arise.

16. Regionally disaggregated unit costs are not available for the intermediate post-primary technical education category. This group is therefore left out of the monetary analysis of total educational benefits as discussed further below.
17. As we noted above the household survey does not have complete information on the number of visits and the specific services received. Within each province we therefore had to assign the same benefit to anyone who utilized the service during the reference period. To the extent that better-off individuals made more visits and/or received more costly services than poorer individuals, the results reported here may over-state the progressivity of the benefit incidence.
18. Disaggregated analysis (not shown here) confirms that lower primary education closely follows the 45-degree line in each of the three regions.
19. Terciles are measured with respect to expenditure *per capita* today, not at the time education took place.
20. For expanded schooling to be most effective, it will also be necessary to take actions that reduce the opportunity costs of sending children to school.

References

Addison, T. (ed.) (2003). *From Conflict to Recovery in Africa*, New York: Oxford University Press for UNU-WIDER.

Addison, T., A. Chowdhury and S. M. Murshed (2004). 'The Fiscal Dimensions of Conflict and Reconstruction', in T. Addison and A. Roe (eds), *Fiscal Policy for Development: Poverty, Reconstruction and Growth*, Basingstoke: Palgrave Macmillan for UNU-WIDER.

Arndt, C., H. T. Jensen, S. Robinson and F. Tarp (2000). 'Marketing Margins and Agricultural Technology in Mozambique', *Journal of Development Studies*, 37(1): 121–37.

Castro-Leal, F., J. Dayton, L. Demery and K. Mehra (1999). 'Public Social Spending in Africa: Do the Poor Benefit?', *The World Bank Research Observer*, 14(1): 49–72.

Cavero, W. (1998). 'Inquérito Nacional aos Agregados Familiares Sobre Condições de Vida: Relatório de Missão', Maputo: National Institute of Statistics, mimeo.

GoM (Government of Mozambique) (2000a). *Interim Poverty Reduction Strategy*, Maputo: GoM.

GoM (Government of Mozambique (2000b). *Plano Quinquenal do Governo 2000–2004*, Maputo: GoM.

Handa, S. and K. R. Simler (2000). 'Human Capital, Household Welfare, and Children's Schooling in Mozambique', Washington, DC: International Food Policy Research Institute (IFPRI), Draft Research Report.

Heltberg, R. and F. Tarp (2001). 'Agricultural Supply Response and Poverty in Mozambique', Paper presented at the WIDER conference on Growth and Poverty, 25–26 May 2001, Helsinki: UNU–WIDER.

Lanjouw, P. and M. Ravallion (1999). 'Benefit Incidence, Public Spending Reforms, and the Timing of Program Capture', *The World Bank Economic Review*, 13(2): 257–73.

Lindelow, M. (2000). 'Health Care Demand in Mozambique: Evidence from the 1996/97 Household Survey', Washington, DC: International Food Policy Research Institute, Unpublished report.

McGillivray, M. and O. Morrissey (2004). 'Fiscal Effects of Aid', in T. Addison and A. Roe (eds), *Fiscal Policy for Development: Poverty, Reconstruction and Growth*, Basingstoke: Palgrave Macmillan for UNU-WIDER.

McKay, A. (2004). 'Assessing the Impact of Fiscal Policy on Poverty', in T. Addison and A. Roe (eds), *Fiscal Policy for Development: Poverty, Reconstruction and Growth*, Basingstoke: Palgrave Macmillan for UNU-WIDER

Ministry of Education (1997a). Education Statistics. Schools Survey; Maputo: Planning Department of the MoE.

Ministry of Education (1997). Budget Execution Plan 1997, Maputo: Administration and Finance Department of the MoE.

MPF (Ministry of Planning and Finance), Eduardo Mondlane University, International Food Policy Research Institute (1998). *Understanding Poverty and Well-Being in Mozambique: The First National Assessment (1996–97)*, Maputo: Ministry of Planning and Finance.

Sahn, D. E. and S. D. Younger (1998). 'Fiscal Incidence in Africa. Microeconomic Evidence', Ithaca, NY: Cornell University, unpublished report.

Sahn, D. E., S. D. Younger and K. R. Simler (2000). 'Dominance Testing of Transfers in Romania', *Review of Income and Wealth*, 46(3): 309–27.

Tarp, F. and C. Arndt (2000). 'Facing the Development Challenge in Mozambique: An Economywide Perspective', Draft IFPRI Research Report.

Tarp, F., K. Simler, C. Matusse, R. Heltberg and G. Dava (2000). 'The Robustness of Poverty Lines Reconsidered', Copenhagen: University of Copenhagen, Unpublished manuscript.

van de Walle, D. and K. Nead (eds) (1995). *Public Spending and the Poor: Theory and Evidence*, Baltimore, MD: Johns Hopkins University Press.

Wuyts, M. (2000). 'Aid Dependence, Fiscal Policy, and Pro-Poor Growth', Paper prepared for the UNU–WIDER project on New Fiscal Policies for Growth and Poverty Reduction, Helsinki: UNU–WIDER.

Younger, Stephen D. (1999). 'The Relative Progressivity of Social Services in Ecuador', *Public Finance Review*, 27(3): 310–52.

11

Debt Relief, Demand for Education and Poverty

Era Dabla-Norris, John M. Matovu and Paul R. Wade

Introduction

It is widely asserted that debt relief for heavily indebted poor countries (HIPC) could create and sustain a virtuous circle of poverty reduction and growth, primarily by providing additional fiscal resources for poverty alleviation. Debt relief targeted for human capital accumulation through increased public spending on education is viewed as a critical component of this link.[1] Low overall educational attainment, stagnant school enrolment rates, along with high estimated returns to schooling in many HIPCs, are often cited as justification for increased public investment in education (Table 11.1). As a result, explicit targets for expanding school enrolment rates and other performance criteria for education expenditures have been set in HIPC programmes.

A widely accepted policy recommendation for HIPCs with less than universal basic education has been to shift priorities in resource allocation away from higher education and in favour of primary schooling. This suggested reallocation of resources within the education sector is based on equity considerations and on the large estimated differentials in the rates of return to primary relative to higher levels of schooling (Psacharopoulos and Patrinos, 2002). However, the precise mechanism through which public intervention in different levels of schooling influences household life-cycle behaviour, growth and poverty reduction has been largely unexplored.[2]

Using a life-cycle perspective, this chapter examines the differential impact on household schooling decisions and human capital accumulation of utilizing debt relief savings for augmenting government spending on different levels of education – primary, secondary and tertiary – and of spending targeted by income groups. We develop a

Table 11.1 Countries with primary gross school enrolment ratios below 90 per cent, 1996

Enrolment between 50 and 90%			*Enrolment below 50%*		
Region and country	*Gross enrolment rate*	*HIPC*	*Region and country*	*Gross enrolment rate*	*HIPC*
Sub-Saharan Africa			Sub-Saharan Africa		
Benin	78	yes	Burkina Faso	40	yes
Burundi	51	yes	Djibouti	39	
Chad	57	yes	Ethiopia	43	yes
Gambia, The	77	yes	Mali	49	yes
Ghana	79	yes	Niger	29	yes
Guinea-Bissau	62	yes			
Kenya	85	yes	South Asia		
Mauritania	79	yes	Afghanistan	49	
Mozambique	60	yes			
Senegal	71	yes			
Tanzania	66	yes			
Uganda	74	yes			
Middle East and North Africa					
Morocco	86				
Oman	76				
Qatar	62				
Yemen	79	yes			
Latin America and Caribbean					
Guatemala	88				
East Asia and Pacific					
Papua New Guinea	80				
South Asia					
Pakistan	82				

Source: UNESCO.

dynamic general equilibrium model of sequential human capital investment with indivisible human capital and heterogeneous skill formation. In this framework, we examine how additional government spending for different levels of education influences parental decisions to invest in child human capital and physical assets over their lifecycle.

Our theoretical framework is a dynamic general equilibrium model of overlapping generations of long-lived and heterogeneous agents in the spirit of Auerbach and Kotlikoff (1987). Agents in the model are differentiated by their age–earning profiles. In contrast to much of the literature on human capital accumulation where each individual makes his own educational decisions, we explicitly model the intertemporal trade-off in the contribution of the child to household income and the parental choice of schooling involved, as in Glomm (1997).We assume that parents make schooling decisions for children and there are fixed and varied costs to different levels of schooling which are partially financed by parents. In many HIPCs, despite basic education being obligatory and free, in practice, schools collect contributions from students to supplement government subsidies and parents bear costs of uniforms and books. For instance, Canagarajah and Coulombe (1997) find that *per capita* costs of publicly provided primary education in Ghana accounted for more than 15 per cent of household mean *per capita* expenditures in 1994. For Uganda, Mackinnon and Reinikka (2000) note that parents on average contributed 60 per cent of total primary education spending.

Our model – calibrated to Ghana – yields important insights into the qualitative and quantitative effects of utilizing debt relief savings for targeting 'broad' and 'narrow' expenditures.[3] Specifically, the government in our model utilizes debt relief savings to provide transfer payments and public investment for different levels of education.[4] Our simulation results suggest that reducing the private costs of primary schooling has the largest impact on growth and poverty reduction in the short run. This result follows because in the presence of fixed schooling costs, human capital accumulation exhibits increasing returns over some range. As a result, altruistic households invest in child human capital at the expense of physical asset accumulation. A higher subsidy for basic (primary and secondary) education allows lower-income households to forgo child earnings and increase investment in child human capital while accumulating more assets for future consumption over their life-cycle. For households in the higher income classes, a reduction in schooling costs simply serves to increase their asset accumulation profiles over their lifetime, resulting in a higher aggregate physical capital stock in the economy. Therefore, both aggregate human and physical capital accumulation increase.

The growth and poverty effects of an increase in the subsidy for tertiary education are not as substantial, for several reasons. First, such policies do not affect the asset accumulation decisions of households earlier in their working lives and, hence, result in lower life-cycle asset accumulation. In addition, this policy has little impact on the marginal schooling decisions of low-income households as their optimal schooling choices typically involve lower levels of schooling. We also find that the impact of a targeted transfer on the life-cycle behaviour of households depends on the magnitude of the transfer. With a sufficiently large transfer, a significant improvement in growth and poverty reduction can be obtained.

The chapter proceeds as follows: the next section describes the analytical framework. Then we describe the calibration and parameterization of the model economy and present the policy experiments and the results of the sensitivity analysis. The final section concludes.

Theoretical framework

Demographic structure

The model economy population consists of households that comprise parents and their children. Households have identical preferences and each *j*-type generation born at a specific date contains 17 lifetime earnings groups distinguished by their level of schooling. The first group refers to individuals with no schooling (unskilled). Groups for the primary skilled range from 1 to 6 years of education attainment, for secondary skills range from 7 to 12 years and tertiary education ranges from 13 to 16 years.

Agents in the model live for 55 periods, consistent with figures for life expectancy at birth in Ghana. Individuals are children up to 22 years of age (the end of the schooling phase) when they consume as part of their parent's households. At model age 23, each agent gives birth to one child. They also enter the formal work force on their 23rd birthday and work through age 50. Between the following ages, the child is expected to be at the schooling levels shown in Table 11.2.

Table 11.2 Age and schooling level

Age		*Level of schooling*
Child	*Parent*	
7–12	30–35	Primary education
13–18	36–41	Secondary education
19–22	42–45	Tertiary education

We assume stationary population growth with the number of births per period equalling the number of deaths. While this assumption may be unrealistic for many HIPCs in Sub-Saharan Africa (SSA), it is adopted for analytical tractability.

Schooling attainment

Schooling decisions are sequential, and each household decides the fraction of time its child will spend in school each period, $s^j_{i,t} \in [0,1]$. For analytic tractability, we assume that once a child leaves school, s/he cannot return. To derive the aggregate educational attainment of an individual, that is the total number of years spent in school, we sum over the per-period optimal schooling time obtained from the household optimization decision. The total schooling attainment of a child of household *j* as of time *t* can then simply be written as:

$$S^j_{i,t} = \sum_{k=0}^{t} s^j_{i,k}$$

Preferences and household budget constraints

Each *j*-type agent beginning its economic life at calendar date *t* chooses a perfect-foresight consumption path $c_{i,t}$ and child time in school $s^j_{i,t} \in [0,1]$ to maximize a time-separable utility function of the form:

$$U^j_t = \sum_{i=23}^{55} \beta^{i-23} u\left(c^j_{i,t+i-23}\right) + \beta^{21} \mu\left(h^j_{45,t+21}\right) \qquad (11.1)$$

where U is strictly concave and increasing and β is the subjective discount rate. At the end of the schooling phase, households leave a child human capital stock $h^j_{45,t+45}[t+21]$, the value of which is given by an increasing concave function μ.[5] That is, we assume that parents have 'warm-glow' preferences over their child's human capital. We ignore leisure, both of the child and of the parent.

Define $a^j_{i,t}$ as the stock of physical capital held by an agent with schooling *j*, of age *i*, at time *t*. If children are not in the schooling phase, maximization of (11.1) is subject to a sequence of budget constraints given by:[6]

$$a^j_{i+1,t+1} = (1 + r_t - \delta)a^j_{i,t} + w^j_t H^j_i - (1 - \tau^c_t)c^j_{i,t} + z^j_{i,t} \text{ for } s^j_{i,t} = 0 \qquad (11.2)$$

If children are in the schooling phase, the relevant budget constraint is:

$$a^j_{i+1,t+1} = (1 + r_t - \delta)a^j_{i,t} + w^j_t H^{jP}_i - (1 - \tau^c_t)c^j_{i,t} + \left[\bar{w}h^j_{i,t}\left(1 - s^j_{i,t}\right) - s^j_{i,t}(1 - \phi_{i,t})e_i\right] + z^j_{i,t} \text{ for } 0 < s^j_{i,t} \leq 1 \qquad (11.3)$$

where r_t is the returns to savings, δ is the rate of depreciation of physical capital, $z^j_{i,t}$ are direct transfers received from government and τ^c_t is the tax rate on consumption. Household income has two components, parental income and child earnings. We assume that the labour income of a parent is the wage payment received, distributed according to the human capital efficiency levels of the parent (captured by his/her human capital stock, H_i^{jP}). Thus, $w^j_t H_i^{jP} + r_t a^j_{i,t}$ is total parental income at time t, where w^j_t is the rate of return for effective labour differentiated by skill level of the parent at time t.

The cost of attending school is forgone production or earnings and school fees, $s^j_{i,t}(1 - \phi_{i,t})e_i$.[7] The price of child time is assumed to be equivalent to the unskilled wage in the labour market, $\bar{w}$, multiplied by child human capital. We assume that all schooling is publicly provided, but is not entirely 'free'. Parents have to pay upfront fees and other costs e_i, where e_i includes school fees, books and other related education materials such as school uniforms. Education costs are exogenously fixed for each level of schooling (primary, secondary and tertiary) and the government subsidizes schooling costs at the rate $\phi_{i,t}$.[8] We assume that:

$$e_t^{primary} < e_t^{secondary} < e_t^{tertiary}$$

that is, fixed schooling costs increase across the education cycle.

Schooling time $s^j_{i,t}$ augments the child's beginning-of-period stock of human capital $h^j_{i,t}$, where the superscript j denotes the schooling level of a child with parent age i. Human capital of the child evolves according to:

$$h^j_{i+1,t+1} = \gamma_0 h^{\gamma_1}_{i,t} s^{\gamma_2}_{i,t} + (1 - \delta_h) h^j_{i,t} \tag{11.4}$$

where δ_h is the rate of depreciation of human capital, $0 \leq \gamma_1 \leq 1$, $0 < \gamma_2 < 1$, and γ_0 captures the innate ability of the child or school quality. This functional form is used widely both in the empirical literature and the literature on human capital accumulation.[9] However, this specification ignores the productivity of government education spending and its implications for human capital accumulation. In reality, the productivity of government education spending in many developing countries can have an important bearing on household demand for education.

The optimal consumption, schooling time and assets profile of individuals at different ages can be derived by reformulating the problem as a recursive structure via the value function:

$$V_{i,t}^{j}\left(a_{i,t}^{j}, h_{i,t}^{j}\right) = \max_{a_{i+1,t+1}, a_{i,t}, s_{i,t}} U\left(c_{i,t}^{j}\right) + \beta V_{i+1,t+1}^{j}\left(a_{i+1,t+1}^{j}, h_{i+1,t+1}^{j}\right) \quad (11.5)$$

subject to the constraints (11.3) and (11.4) when children are in the schooling phase and subject to (11.2) before children start schooling ($i = 23, \ldots 29$) and when children quit schooling permanently ($i = 45, \ldots 55$). The agent solves a life-cycle optimization problem given initial stocks of human and physical capital. At the end of the terminal period, we assume that the household's assets are zero.

In this framework, given $(1 - \phi_{i,t}^{1})e_i > 0$ and the ability to borrow imply that the optimal per-period solution for schooling will be a corner one, either $s_{i,t}^{j} = 0$ or $s_{i,t}^{j} = 1$. That is, the child never attends school part-time. Therefore, each household maximizes its expected lifetime discounted utility by choosing the optimal time to interrupt child schooling and for the child to enter the labour market.

The solution to the dynamic schooling problem is as follows. Working backward from T, the end of the schooling phase, the value of going to school for an additional year and the value of stopping schooling and entering the informal labour market can be characterized using backward recursions. The value function associated with the decision to remain in school, $V_{i,t}^{S}(a_{i,t}, h_{i,t})$ (dropping cohort-specific superscripts j) given that an individual was in school the previous period is given by:

$$V_{i,t}^{S}(a_{i,t}, h_{i,t}) = \max_{a_{i,t}} U(c_{i,t}) + \beta V_{i+1,t+1}|_{S_t=1} \quad (11.6)$$

where $V_{i+1,t+1}^{j}|_{S_t=1}$ denotes the value of following the optimal policy next period (either to obtain schooling or enter the informal labour market). The relevant constraints for the household are:

$$\begin{aligned} a_{i+1,t+1} &= (1 + r_t - \delta)a_{i,t} + w_t H_i^P - (1 - \tau_t^c)c_{i,t} - (1 - \phi_{i,t})e_i + z_{i,t} \\ h_{i+1,t+1}^{S} &= \gamma_0 h_{i,t}^{\gamma_1} + (1 - \delta_h)h_{i,t} \end{aligned} \quad (11.7)$$

Notice that by choosing $s_{i,t} = 1$, the household reduces its current disposable income (by $\bar{w}h_{i,t} + (1 - \phi_{i,t})e$) but increases labour income of the child and future household consumption if the child leaves school in subsequent periods as well as child human capital at the end of the schooling phase.

The value of stopping schooling in period t, $V^{NS}_{i,t}(a_{i,t},h_{i,t})$, is the value of entering the informal labour market this period and not accumulating any additional human capital in the future. That is:

$$V^{NS}_{i,t}(a_{i,t},h_{i,t}) = \max_{a_{i,t}} U(c_{i,t}) + \beta V_{i+1,t+1}|_{s_t=0} \tag{11.8}$$

The household now faces the constraints:

$$\begin{aligned} a_{i+1,t+1} &= (1+r_t-\delta)a_{i,t} + w_t H^P_i - (1-\tau^c_t)c_{i,t} + \bar{w}h_{i,t} + z_{i,t} \\ h^{NS}_{i+1,t+1} &= (1-\delta_h)h_{i,t} \end{aligned} \tag{11.9}$$

A household, therefore, chooses $s_{i,t}=1$ when $V^S_{i,t}(a_{i,t},h_{i,t}) > V^{NS}_{i,t}(a_{i,t},h_{i,t})$ and zero otherwise.

Given that the schooling decision is independent of the asset accumulation decision, the Euler equation for assets still holds, such that:

$$\frac{U'(c_{i+1,t+1})}{U'(c_{i,t})} = \beta(1+r_{t+1}-\delta) \tag{11.10}$$

This equation is standard: the household equates the cost of forgone consumption at time t to the benefit of acquiring an additional unit of capital at time $t+1$.

Since sending a child to school reduces current consumption more for those households that choose more education, the desire to smooth consumption over the life-cycle results in differential demand for schooling by high-income, skilled parents and poor, unskilled parents in our model. This is because, even in the absence of credit constraints, for sufficiently high fixed costs over the schooling phase, parents with lower life-cycle earnings may optimally choose lower levels of schooling than high-income, skilled parents. It is not the higher income itself that makes it easier for skilled parents to choose more schooling, but the availability of this income to forgo the child's contribution to household income and pay the fixed costs during the schooling phase while allowing the household to accumulate more assets for retirement.

Firms

Output in the model economy is produced by identical competitive firms using a neoclassical, constant returns to scale production technology. Letting λ^j be the fraction of j-type agents in each generation, aggregate capital K_t is obtained from household asset accumulation decisions as:

$$K_t = \sum_{j=1}^{17} \lambda^j \sum_{i=23}^{55} a_{i,t}^j \tag{11.11}$$

Labour types are differentiated by their years of schooling attained. For tractability, we aggregate the 17 years of schooling into four types of labour: unskilled, primary-educated, secondary-educated and higher-educated (or tertiary), where:

$$L_t^U = \sum_{j=1}^{50} \lambda^j \sum_{i=23}^{50} H_{i,t}^{jP} + \sum_{j=1}^{17} \lambda^j \sum_{i=7}^{22} h_{i,t}^j \Big|_{s_{i,t}=0}$$

$$L_t^P = \sum_{j=2}^{8} \lambda^j \sum_{i=23}^{50} H_{i,t}^{jP}$$

$$L_t^S = \sum_{j=9}^{14} \lambda^j \sum_{i=23}^{50} H_{i,t}^{jP}$$

$$L_t^T = \sum_{j=15}^{17} \lambda^j \sum_{i=23}^{50} H_{i,t}^{jP} \tag{11.12}$$

Note that the unskilled labour demanded, L_t^U is simply the summation of the individual human capital stocks of unskilled parents and children who have dropped out of school as of period t.[10]

The technology of the firm producing output y_t is:

$$y_t = F(K_t, L_t^U, L_t^P, L_t^S, L_t^T) \tag{11.13}$$

where $F(.)$ is a neoclassical production function exhibiting positive but diminishing marginal productivity in its arguments. Since households make the investment choices, the firm's problem is static and it chooses effective labour to maximize profits. Physical capital evolves over time according to:

$$K_{t+1} = (1 - \delta_k)K_t + I_t \tag{11.14}$$

where δ_k is the depreciation rate.

Government

The role of government in the model is to collect taxes and spend revenues on transfers, government consumption and education. We assume that in some periods the government runs unbalanced budgets and borrows. Total government expenditure (excluding interest costs on government debt) in period t is given by:

$$G_t = \sum_{j=1}^{17} \lambda^j \sum_{i=23}^{45} \phi^j_{i,t} e_{i,t} + \sum_{j=1}^{17} \lambda^j \sum_{i=23}^{55} z^j_{i,t} + \Gamma_t \tag{11.15}$$

where Γ_t is other government consumption.

The evolution of public debt b_t is given by the following:

$$b_{t+1} = (1 + r_t)b_t + \sum_{j=1}^{17} \lambda^j \sum_{i=23}^{55} \tau^c_t c^j_{i,t} - G_t \tag{11.16}$$

We assume that all public debt is foreign-owned and the government does not borrow from the domestic market since capital markets are typically not well developed in HIPC countries. The government is subject to the following intertemporal budget constraint, which imposes the condition that at the terminal date, with debt relief being granted, the discounted value of government debt is zero:

$$b(0) + \int_0^\infty Ge^{-rt} dt = \int_0^\infty Te^{-rt} dt \tag{11.17}$$

where $T = \sum_{j=1}^{17} \lambda^j \sum_{i=23}^{55} \tau^c_t c^j_{i,t}$

Equilibrium

A competitive equilibrium is a set of processes for individual allocations, $\{a^j_{i,t}, c^j_{i,t}, s^j_{i,t}\}$, aggregate inputs, $\{K_t, L^U_t, L^P_t, L^S_t, L^T_t\}$, prices for the factors of production, $\{w^j_t, r_t\}$ such that:

(i) $\{a^j_{i,t}, c^j_{i,t}, s^j_{i,t}\}$ solves the representative household's problem,

(ii) $\{K_t, L^U_t, L^P_t, L^S_t, L^T_t\}$ solves the firm's problem,

(iii) $H_t = \sum_{j=1}^{17} \lambda^i \sum_{i=7}^{22} h^j_{i,t} + \sum_{j=1}^{17} \lambda^i \sum_{i=23}^{50} H^{jP}_{i,t}$

(iv) $K_t = \sum_{j=1}^{17} \lambda^i \sum_{i=23}^{55} a^j_{i,t}$

(v) $a^j_{i+1,t+1} = (1 + r_t - \delta)a^j_{i,t} + w^j_{i,t} H^{jP}_t - (1 - \tau^c_t)c^j_{i,t} - (1 - \phi_{i,t})e_{i,t} + z^j_{i,t}$ for $s = 1$

(vi) $a^j_{i+1,t+1} = (1 + r_t - \delta)a^j_{i,t} + w_t H^{jP}_t - (1 - \tau^c_t)c^j_{i,t} + \bar{w}h^j_{i,t} + z^j_{i,t}$ for $s = 0$

(vii) $b_{t+1} = (1 + r_t)b_t = \sum_{j=1}^{17} \lambda^j \sum_{i=23}^{55} \tau^c_t c^j_{i,t} - G_t$

Poverty

We extend the above model to consider poverty issues by adopting the Foster, Greer and Thorbecke (1984) poverty measures. We assume that $m = (m_1, m_2, \ldots m_n)$ is a vector of agents' incomes in increasing order, and assume that the poverty line given by $\Phi > 0$ is predetermined. If $g_i = \Phi - m_i$ is the income shortfall of the ith household, q is the number of households having income less than the poverty line and the total number of households is N, the poverty measure used is given by:

$$P_\alpha = \frac{1}{N}\sum_{i=1}^{q}\left[\frac{g_i}{\Phi}\right]^\alpha \tag{11.18}$$

where P_0 is the headcount ratio while P_1 is the renormalization of the income gap measure. The value of α is a measure of poverty aversion and a higher value gives greater emphasis to the poor.

Calibration and parameters

The experiments reported in the next section share a common set of parameters and an initial steady-state equilibrium in Table 11.3. We choose all the parameters for both the consumers and producers so that

Table 11.3 Parameters

α_0	Production efficiency parameter	1.01
α	Capital factor share	0.31
α_U	Unskilled labour factor share	0.20
α_P	Primary labour factor share	0.25
α_S	Secondary skilled labour factor share	0.15
α_T	Tertiary skilled labour factor share	0.09
δ_K	Physical capital depreciation	0.05
β	Discount factor	0.95
σ	Elasticity of substitution	0.25
δ_h	Human capital depreciation	0.03
γ_1	Human capital investment parameter	0.67
γ_2	Parameter on human capital accumulation	0.15

our model economy mimics as closely as possible the main Ghana economic statistics:

(i) *Factor shares and production efficiency parameter*: Both the factors share α and the efficiency parameters α_0 are derived from a cross-section study by Senhadji (2000). These parameters are obtained from a human capital index which is derived by weighting education levels attained using relative earnings of different types of labour.
(ii) *Real rate of return*: A value of 10 per cent is assumed. In an overlapping-generations setting, economic theory does not impose any restriction on the size of the discount factor.[11] The value of the households' discount factor that implements the targeted rate of return is $\beta = 0.95$.[12]
(iii) *The human capital depreciation rate* is assumed to be 0.025. Driffill and Rosen (1983) use a value of 0.01, while Lord (1989) employs values of 0.08 and 0.12; some empirical studies report values as high as 0.10 for certain categories of labour.
(iv) For the *parameter* γ_1 and γ_2 which are in the investment function of human capital, values of 0.67 and 0.33 are used. Previous estimates of the parameter γ_1 in the literature lie in the range of 0.5–0.8. (See Heckman, 1999.)

Years of schooling attainment of adults in Ghana were obtained from Barro and Lee (2000) and enrolment rates for children at different levels of schooling were taken from Blunch and Verner (2000). We utilize the following functional form to estimate the Mincerian returns to human capital using the 1999 Ghanaian Living Standard Measure Survey (LSMS) survey:

$$\ln EARN_{it} = \alpha_0 + \alpha_1 SCHOOL_{it} + \alpha_3 AGE_{it} + \alpha_4 (AGE_{it})^2 + X_{it}\beta + \varepsilon_{it}$$

where i is the index for the individual, t is the time period of the cross-section in hand, ε_{it} is the error term capturing any unobserved factors, ln *EARN* is the natural logarithm of total earnings, *SCHOOL* is the years of schooling, *AGE* is the age of the individual approximating his/her years of experience, X is a set of controls and β is a set of parameters. The controls include demographics and reference characteristics of the individual. We obtain a coefficient of schooling of 0.067, close to the value of 0.085 found by Glewwe (1996). Using this estimate, we simulate earnings ability profiles for agents.

The benchmark equilibrium

The benchmark steady state is calibrated to the 1999 Ghanaian national accounts, distribution and poverty data. Government expenditure on education is set at 4 per cent of national output, while education expenditures as a share of total government expenditure are set at 11.4 per cent. The shares of education expenditures across education categories are set at 41 per cent for primary education, 38 per cent for secondary education and 21 per cent for tertiary education. The out-of-pocket primary education expenditures by the parents are taken from a study by Demery *et al.* (1995). They find that the annual per-student costs of primary, secondary and higher education borne by the family are US$17, US$56 and US$228, respectively.

Given our parameter choices, the model generates the consumption and investment output ratios, wage rates and poverty indices described in Table 11.4. The wage rate for labour with tertiary education is normalized to one and wages for other education categories are obtained relative to the tertiary wage.

Figure 11.1 shows the optimal life-cycle asset accumulation profiles for different generations. The human capital efficiency profiles start when an individual joins the labour force, and reach their peak at age 50. The shapes of the simulated age–earnings profiles for individuals with different skills are not very different from what is found in cross-section household surveys, with incomes rising with age and starting to fall at about mid-working age. As can be seen from Figure 11.1, such a concave age–earning profile is less conducive to saving in the early years and just before retirement.

Figures 11.2(a), 11.2(b), 11.2(c) and 11.2(d) provide a general introduction to the nature of policy generated by the model. All parents

Table 11.4 Baseline

Capital	5.6430
Output	1.5970
Consumption	1.1230
Aggregate human capital	1.3240
Return on capital	0.0460
Unskilled wage rate	0.3650
Primary wage rate	0.7610
Secondary wage rate	0.9690
Tertiary wage rate	1.0000
Poverty (headcount ratio)	0.5350
Poverty (P_1)	0.2431
Poverty (P_2)	0.0832

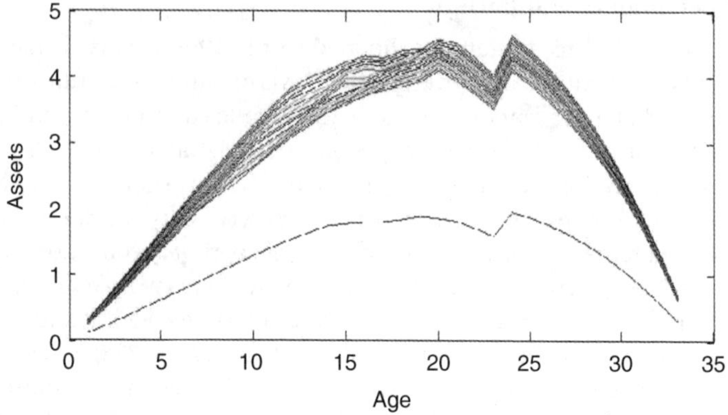

Figure 11.1 Baseline household age–earning profiles[a]
Note: [a] Household age 1 denotes the year the parent enters the labour market.

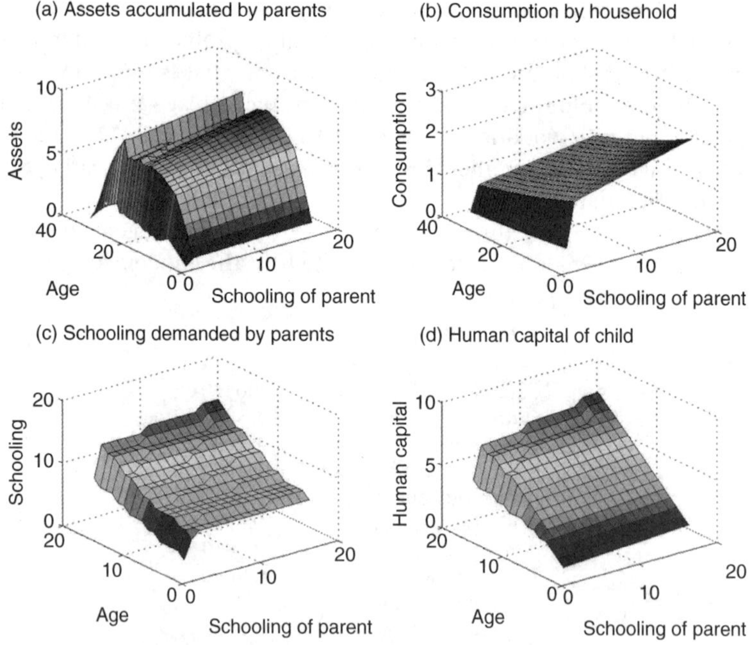

Figure 11.2 Baseline scenario[a]
Note: [a] Household age 1 denotes the year the parent enters the labour market.

choose between asset accumulation and child schooling to smooth lifetime consumption. However, given indivisibilities in human capital accumulation, physical and human capital accumulation decisions of households vary with the parents' age and level of schooling attainment. As can be seen from Figure 11.2(a), the rate of asset accumulation declines for most households during the schooling phase of the child. This decline is most significant for low-income, unskilled households as they increase investment in child human capital at the expense of asset accumulation, particularly during their early working years. Accordingly, as is demonstrated in Figure 11.2(c), unskilled households demand less schooling for their child than do more educated parents, and child labour is more likely for low-income households, consistent with the link between child labour and poverty in the literature. Since children of more educated parents have higher human capital than children of parents with low educational attainment (Figure 11.2(d)), our model can explain inter-generational persistence in lifetime earnings inequality.

Policy experiments

The policy experiments described in this section examine how the government should allocate its debt relief savings so as to achieve both growth and poverty objectives. In all simulations, additional fiscal resources available from debt relief are used to increase education expenditures on primary, secondary and tertiary education. Table 11.5 provides a comparison of the various steady-state macroeconomic aggregates and poverty levels relative to the benchmark case.

Increase in government subsidy for primary, secondary and tertiary education

The first policy experiment examines the intertemporal effects on growth and poverty when debt relief savings of 2 per cent of GDP are used to further subsidize primary, secondary or tertiary education.[13] In contrast to the baseline steady state, Table 11.5 indicates that output is higher if resources are devoted to primary and secondary education due to higher aggregate physical and human capital accumulation.

The increase in primary education spending results in the most significant increase in the physical and human capital stock and, hence, output. Two reasons account for this. First, a reduction in the costs for primary education affects households' marginal schooling decisions by lowering their opportunity costs of schooling. As a result, lower-income

Table 11.5 Steady-state results

Simulation	*(1)*	*(2)*	*(3)*	*(4)*	*(5)*
Capital	5.8553	3.0701	1.2567	1.8238	4.0823
Output	2.3267	1.2286	0.4910	0.7273	1.6317
Consumption	1.2435	0.8765	0.3541	0.5643	1.4220
Aggregate human capital	1.8954	1.2341	0.8932	0.5438	1.1011
Return on capital	−3.3912	−1.8149	−0.7319	−1.1010	−2.3985
Unskilled wage rate	2.1324	1.2286	0.4910	0.7273	1.6317
Primary wage rate	2.5408	0.0012	0.0018	0.7942	1.7818
Secondary wage rate	1.5634	1.5026	0.0009	0.8895	1.9956
Tertiary wage rate	1.0932	1.0452	1.4354	0.9073	2.0355
Poverty (headcount ratio)	0.4321	0.5185	0.5272	0.4537	0.4235
Poverty (P_1)	0.2212	0.2654	0.2699	0.2323	0.2168
Poverty (P_2)	0.0612	0.0734	0.0747	0.0643	0.0600

Simulation (*1*) Increasing primary education spending.
(*2*) Increasing secondary education spending.
(*3*) Increasing tertiary education spending.
(*4*) Lower direct transfer to households.
(*5*) Higher direct transfer to households.

households that previously had optimally chosen very little schooling for their child now increase their investment in child human capital. Given the sequencing of schooling decisions, this enables households to choose higher levels of secondary and tertiary schooling in subsequent periods, leading to a higher accumulation of human capital in the steady state.

Second, higher primary education spending serves to smooth household lifetime asset accumulation profiles. Figures 11.3(a)–11.3(d) illustrate the effects of such a policy on household asset accumulation decisions. Note that for all households, a reduction in primary schooling costs results in higher asset accumulation over their lifetime. Lower schooling costs during the beginning of the schooling phase (the early working years) enables low-income, unskilled households, to forgo child earnings and increase investment in child human capital while accumulating more assets in subsequent periods for future consumption.[14] For skilled households (with higher life-cycle earnings), a reduction in primary schooling costs also allows for a larger accumulation of assets earlier in life. Therefore, increasing primary education spending shifts the household life-cycle asset accumulation curve upwards for all skill types. This increase is more significant for primary education spending than for secondary and tertiary spending, as in the latter cases parents are already

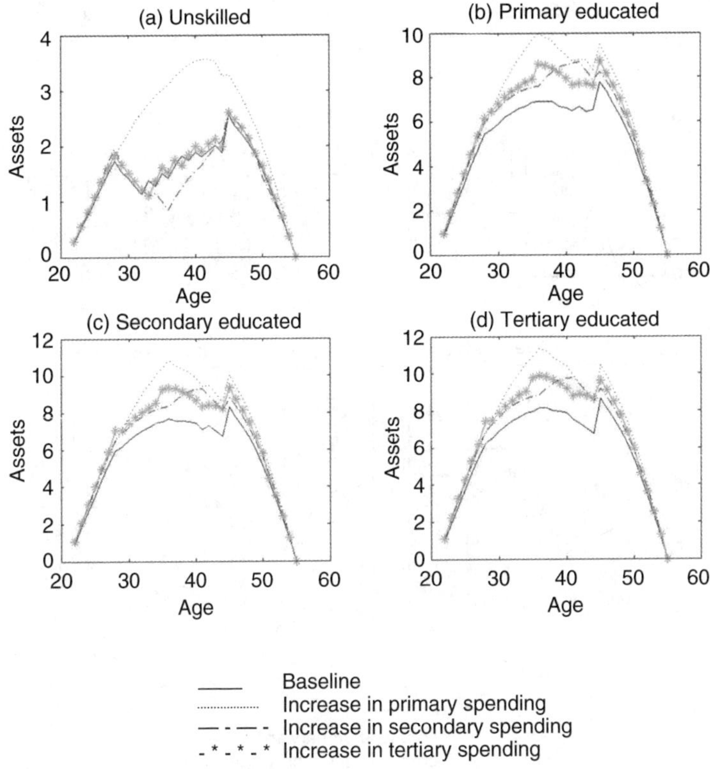

Figure 11.3 Impact of increasing education spending on asset accumulation, by skill types in the steady state

in their prime working years (between ages 36 and 45) when these policies come into effect. The higher asset accumulation profiles translate into a larger aggregate capital stock and to higher levels of output.

With a higher capital stock, the return to labour of all skill types increases. The price of unskilled labour exhibits a significant increase relative to the baseline, by over 2.2 per cent, as more parents choose to keep their children in school, thereby reducing the pool of unskilled labour in the economy. The large increase in the primary wage rate, of 2.5 per cent, results from older cohorts (with higher age–earning profiles) demanding higher levels of secondary schooling for their children. Figures 11.4(a)–11.4(d) illustrate the demand for schooling by households of different ages. As a result, the supply of primary educated labour in the economy declines, which increases the

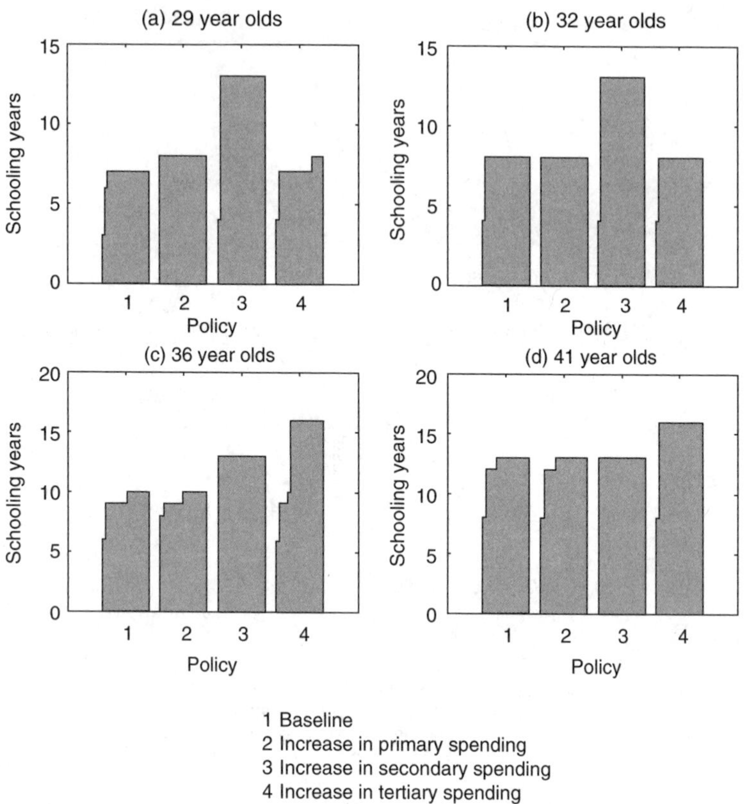

Figure 11.4 Demand for schooling, by age and skills of households in the steady state

price of such labour. The skilled–unskilled wage differential is reduced relative to the baseline as the supply of skilled human capital in the economy increases while the number of unskilled and primary-educated workers falls.

As discussed above, the growth effects of an increase in secondary education spending are reduced as households benefit from such a policy only in the middle of their working life. Moreover, as shown in Figure 11.3(a), unskilled households increase investment in child human capital at the expense of asset accumulation, leading to lower lifetime asset accumulation profiles relative to the baseline. Therefore, aggregate physical and human capital stocks are lower than in the previous case. Given the sequencing of schooling decisions, an increase in government subsidy on tertiary education benefits only those households which demanded secondary education in the baseline (the high-income, skilled groups). This policy stance has no impact on the marginal schooling decisions of low-income households as their optimal schooling choices typically involve much lower levels of schooling. As a result, an increase in the government subsidy for tertiary education leads to lower physical and human capital accumulation and, hence, output relative to increases in primary or secondary education spending.

Table 11.5 also reports the impact on poverty of alternative education policies. The decline in the headcount ratio is most marked when primary education spending is increased relative to secondary or tertiary spending. Two reasons account for this: the first is the higher household disposable income at the beginning of the schooling phase. Second, there is an increase in lifetime asset accumulation profiles of low-income households in response to the policy change. As discussed above, the increase in aggregate human and physical capital accumulation is most significant for an increase in primary education spending, resulting in the sharpest reduction in the headcount ratio. The severity of poverty is also shown to decline as indicated by the lower poverty indices, P_1 and P_2.

The transition effects of the policy changes on macroeconomic aggregates are illustrated in Figures 11.5(a)–11.5(d). Notice that the growth effects of higher primary and secondary education spending are more important in the short run. However, in the long run, an increase in tertiary education results in the largest aggregate capital stock and, hence, output, due to the higher productivity of such labour. This result suggests that the policy currently advocated in developing countries of increasing primary and secondary education spending at the expense of tertiary education may be detrimental to the long-term growth prospects of these countries. It suggests that countries should not ignore tertiary education, given its importance for long-run growth.

Targeting transfers

Two types of targeting of public resources are typically advocated in the literature. The first, 'broad targeting', involves an allocation of debt relief savings on social services which are directly beneficial to both the rich and the poor, with no attempt made to identify individuals who are most needy. The simulations in the previous section fit this description. The second approach, known as 'narrow targeting', requires identifying groups according to their income levels or geographical

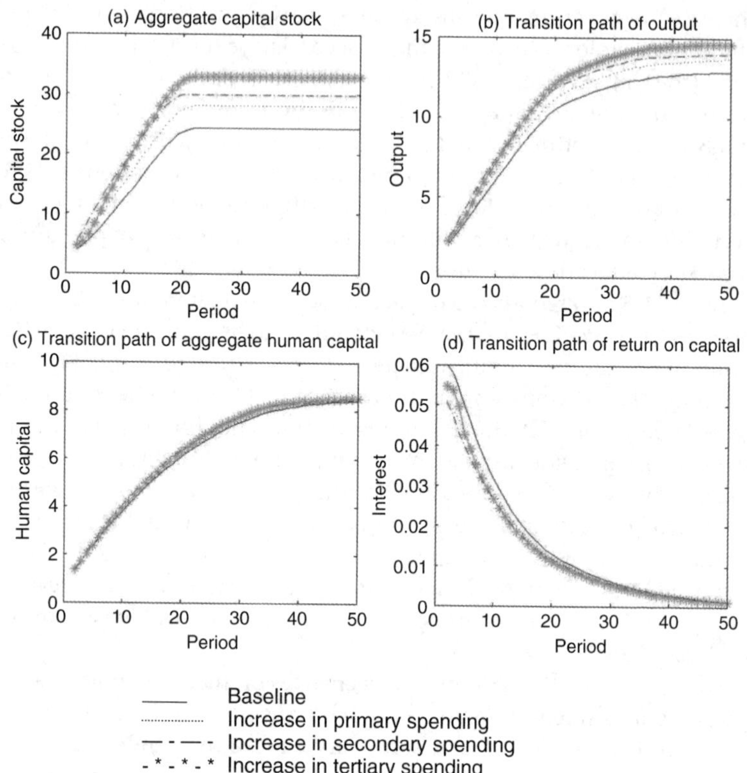

Figure 11.5 Transition effects

location. In the latter case, the government supplements household income with directed transfers or subsidies.[15]

The policy experiments reported in this section examine the implications of narrow targeting of government expenditures on household demand for schooling, growth and poverty reduction (columns (4) and (5) in Table 11.5). Households below the poverty line are assumed to be targeted through two types of transfers: a 'low' type, equivalent to the costs of primary education, and a 'high' type, equivalent to the costs of secondary education.[16] As expected, the actual impact of the transfers on the life-cycle behaviour of households depends upon the relative size of the transfer. The 'low' transfer lowers the opportunity cost of schooling and results in a higher demand for primary schooling by low-income (unskilled) households as households forgo child earnings to increase

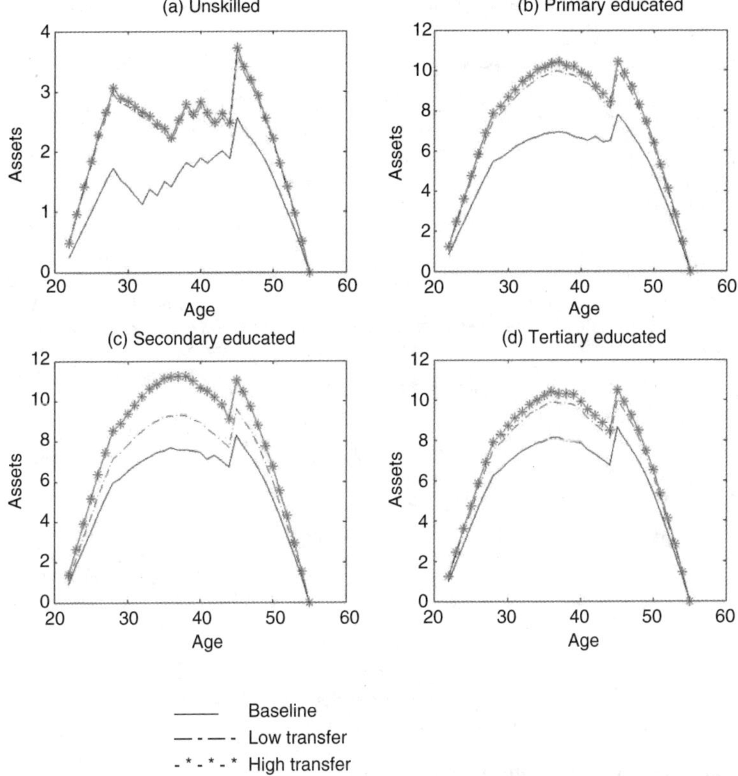

Figure 11.6 Impact of transfers on asset accumulation, by skill types in the steady state

investment in child human capital. In addition, this policy results in a higher life-cycle asset profile (Figure 11.6(a)). However, the household's lifetime asset accumulation profile is not smoothed as parents are forced to substitute physical assets for investment in human capital at higher levels of schooling.

A higher transfer allows households to increase investment in child human capital and demand more primary as well as secondary schooling, leading to an increase in the aggregate human capital stock. Aggregate physical capital is also higher in this case as households of all types increase asset accumulation over their life-cycle. The impact on poverty in the steady state also depends on the size of the transfer. If the transfer results in a substitution of human capital accumulation for asset

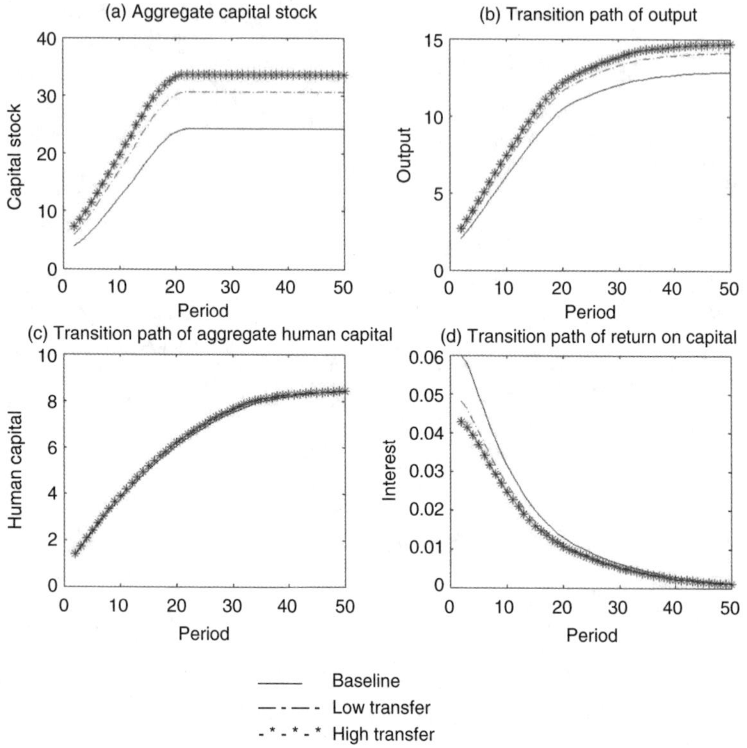

Figure 11.7 Transition effects of transfers

accumulation, poverty levels may not be significantly improved relative to the baseline. With a sufficiently large transfer, however, poverty levels are significantly lower than in the baseline. As in the steady state, the transition paths of physical capital stock and output are higher the larger the transfer (Figures 11.7(a)–11.7(d)).

Sensitivity analysis

In this section, we briefly summarize the sensitivity of the results of the preceding sections to the parameters employed. In particular, we experiment with different values of the elasticity of substitution, the subjective discount rate and the elasticity of human capital accumulation with respect to an increase in years of schooling. As shown in Table 11.6, it turns out that the conclusions from the previous sections are robust to alternative parameter specifications.

Table 11.6 Sensitivity

	Low sigma $\sigma - 0.001$	*High sigma* $\sigma + 0.001$	*Low beta* $\beta - 0.001$	*High beta* $\beta + 0.001$	*Low gamma* $\gamma 1 - 0.001$	*High gamma* $\gamma 1 + 0.001$
Capital	−0.1131	0.1269	−0.1068	0.1370	−0.1194	0.1382
Output	−0.0442	0.0496	−0.0417	0.0535	−0.0466	0.0540
Consumption	−0.0319	0.0358	−0.0301	0.0386	−0.0336	0.0390
Aggregate human capital	−0.0804	0.0902	−0.0759	0.0974	−0.0849	0.0983
Return on capital	0.0659	−0.0739	0.0622	−0.0798	0.0695	−0.0805
Unskilled wage rate	−0.0442	0.0496	−0.0417	0.0535	−0.0466	0.0540
Primary wage rate	−0.0388	0.0436	−0.0367	0.0470	−0.0410	0.0474
Secondary wage rate	−0.0468	0.0525	−0.0442	0.0567	−0.0494	0.0572
Tertiary wage rate	−0.1292	0.1450	−0.1220	0.1565	−0.1364	0.1579

Conclusion

A key element in the policy discussion for HIPCs involves the allocation of external debt savings across different levels of schooling to meet the country's growth and poverty reduction objectives. This chapter adopts a life-cycle perspective to examine the implications of increased narrow and broad targeting of education expenditures financed by debt relief savings. In an environment in which altruistic parents make schooling decisions for their children and there are fixed costs to different levels of schooling, we find that the macroeconomic and poverty reduction benefits of increasing the subsidy for primary and secondary education in countries with less than universal basic education can be substantial. However, public spending on tertiary education has important implications for long-run growth. We also find that targeting of transfers to households below the poverty line can have non-trivial growth effects. The precise quantitative impact on growth and poverty alleviation, however, depends upon the magnitude of the transfer. This result suggests that appropriate targeting of transfers for education can serve as an important policy tool for achieving the twin objectives of growth and equity.

Some simplifying features of the model should be kept in mind when interpreting the quantitative effects of the policy changes. First, we assumed that credit markets are perfect, which results in households optimally choosing higher levels of schooling than would be the case if borrowing constraints were binding. While this assumption may be unrealistic in a developing country context, incorporating credit market imperfections will probably compound the effects of polarization of educational attainment by rich and poor households but will not change the qualitative nature of our results. Second, the study ignores the interaction between fertility and human capital accumulation decisions which are particularly relevant in the case of developing countries. Finally, the chapter does not explicitly trace the impact of debt relief savings on social and economic outcomes for HIPCs. Instead it focuses on the implications of utilizing debt relief savings for a key social spending policy, namely education policy for augmenting human capital accumulation. Future work could focus on incorporating these factors in a fuller analysis of debt relief and social sector and poverty outcomes.

Notes

1. For cross-country studies that emphasize the importance of schooling for economic growth, see Barro (1991), Collins and Bosworth (1996) Hanushek (1996), and Judson (1998). Some examples of studies that focus on the connection between schooling and labour market outcomes include Card and Krueger (1992) for the United States, Behrman and Birdsall (1983) for Brazil and Duflo (2002) for Indonesia. Other studies focus on the relationship between schooling and income distribution (Psacharopoulos *et al.*, 1992).
2. In an empirical study, Judson (1998) finds that countries whose allocations of education are inefficient gain little in output and growth from their investments. However, she ignores the impact of public education policies on household schooling decisions.
3. In this chapter we abstract from expenditures on health, and focus on education spending, although there clearly are complementarities between the two.
4. Ghana is used as an illustrative case and similar results can be derived by applying the model to other HIPCs with less than universal basic education.
5. For simplicity the value of the child's final human capital enters into the parent's utility function at the parent's age 45 when the child completes tertiary education and enters the workforce. In cases where children drop out of school, this assumption tends to under-estimate the value of the child's primary and secondary education in the parent's utility function.
6. Note that this is the budget constraint faced by households for $i = 23, \ldots 29$ and $i = 45, \ldots 50$. The relevant schooling decisions are made between the ages of 30 and 44, the time at which the child first starts school to the point when the child can quit school permanently.
7. While it may be more realistic to assume that the same school fees are paid for full-time and part-time schooling, for analytical tractability, we assume that overall schooling costs are lower with part-time schooling.
8. Note that the level of subsidy provided can vary with the age of the parent and the commensurate level of education of the child. Since schooling costs net of the subsidy therefore vary across education levels, different cohorts face different environments.

9. See Ben-Porath (1967) and Heckman (1999). New human capital can also be produced through formal or informal job training or as a product of experience (learning-by-doing). We abstract from these considerations by focusing on human capital accumulation through schooling.
10. The present model implicitly assumes that the labour markets for the four types of labour are segmented. That is, the higher-educated workers cannot enter the market for primary-educated or non-educated workers and vice versa. In many developing countries, it is not unusual to find underemployment, whereby more educated workers decide to enter the market for less skilled activities. While this would result in a greater 'crowding-out' of unskilled workers and, hence, a larger differential between skilled and unskilled wages, the basic thrust of our results will continue to hold.
11. See Deaton (1991) for a discussion of restrictions on the subjective discount factor in economies with infinitely lived agents.
12. Recent empirical evidence on the value of β suggests that a subjective discount factor greater than unity is plausible (Hurd, 1989).
13. Since education costs are fixed, we assume that when government increases its contribution to education parents pay less in education expenses.
14. In contrast with the baseline, unskilled parents do not have to deaccumulate assets (borrow) earlier in life to finance schooling for their child.
15. While, in principle, the latter approach is a more appealing and effective way of achieving equity objectives, these schemes are usually associated with high administrative costs to identify those who qualify. Narrow targeting can also distort the incentive structure facing agents as they may change their behaviours in order to qualify for these programmes.
16. These transfers can take the form of school lunches for the poor or directed subsidies for education in the form of free textbooks or school fees.

References

Auerbach, A. and L. Kotlikoff (1987). *Dynamic Fiscal Policy*, Cambridge: Cambridge University Press.

Barro, R. (1991). 'Economic Growth in a Cross Section of Countries', *Quarterly Journal of Economics*, 105(2): 407–43.

Barro, R. and J. Lee (2000). 'International Data on Educational Attainment: Updates and Implications', NBER Working Paper Series, 7911, Cambridge, MA: National Bureau of Economic Research.

Behrman, J. and N. Birdsall (1983). 'The Quality of Schooling: Quantity Alone Is Misleading', *American Economic Review*, 73: 928–46.

Ben-Porath, Y. (1967). 'The Production of Human Capital and the Life Cycle of Earnings', *Journal of Political Economy*, 84: 449–72.

Blunch, D. and N. Verner (2000). 'Revisiting the Link Between Poverty and Child Labor: The Ghanaian Experience', World Bank Working Paper, 2488, Washington, DC: World Bank.

Canagarajah, S. and H. Coulombe (1997). 'Child Labor and Schooling in Ghana', World Bank Policy Research Working Paper, 1844, Washington, DC: World Bank.

Card, D. and A. Krueger (1992). 'Does School Quality Matter? Returns to Education and the Characteristics of Public Schools in the United States', *Journal of Political Economy*, 100: 1–40.

Collins, S. and B. Bosworth (1996). 'Economic Growth in East Asia: Accumulation versus Assimilation', *Brookings Papers on Economic Activity*, 2: 135–203.

Deaton, A. (1991). *Understanding Consumption*, Oxford: Clarendon Press.

Demery, L., S. Chao, R. Bernier and K. Mehra (1995). 'The Incidence of Social Spending in Ghana', PSP Discussion Paper, 82, Washington, DC: World Bank.

Driffill, E. and H. S. Rosen (1983). 'Taxation and Excess Burden: A Lifecycle Perspective', *International Economic Review*, 24: 671–83.

Duflo, E. (2002). 'The Medium Run Effects of Educational Expansion: Evidence from a Large School Construction Program in Indonesia', NBER Working Paper Series, 8710, Cambridge, MA: National Bureau of Economic Research.

Foster J., J. Greer and E. Thorbecke (1984). 'A Class of Decomposable Poverty Measures', *Econometrica*, 52(3): 761–6.

Glewwe, P. (1996). 'The Relevance of Standard Estimates of Rates of Return to Schooling for Educational Policy: A Critical Assessment', *Journal of Development Economics*, 51: 267–90.

Glomm, G. (1997). 'Parental Choice of Human Capital Investment', *Journal of Development Economics*, 53: 99–114.

Hanushek, E. (1996). 'Schooling, Labor Force Quality and Economic Growth', NBER Working Paper Series, 5399. Cambridge, MA: National Bureau of Economic Research.

Heckman, J. (1999). 'Accounting for Heterogeneity, Diversity and General Equilibrium in Evaluating Social Programs', NBER Working Paper Series, 6230, Cambridge, MA: National Bureau of Economic Research.

Hurd, R. (1989). 'Issues and Results from Research on the Elderly', NBER Working Paper Series, 3018(1–3), Cambridge, MA: National Bureau of Economic Research.

Judson, R. (1998). 'Economic Growth and Investment in Education: How Allocation Matters', *Journal of Economic Growth*, 3: 337–59.

Lord, W. (1989). 'Transitional from Payroll to Consumption Receipts with Endogenous Human Capital', *Journal of Public Economics*, 38: 53–73.

Mackinnon, J. and R. Reinikka (2000). 'Lessons from Uganda on Strategies to Fight Poverty', World Bank Working Paper, 2440, Washington, DC: World Bank.

Psacharopoulos, G. and H. A. Patrinos (2000). 'Returns to Investment in Education: A Further Update', World Bank Working Paper, 2881, Washington, DC: World Bank.

Psacharopoulos, G., S. Morly, A. Fiszbein, L. Haeduck and B. Wood (1992). *Poverty and Income Distribution in Latin America: The Story of the 1980s*, Washington, DC: World Bank.

Senhadji, A. (2000). 'Sources of Economic Growth: An Extensive Growth Accounting Exercise', *IMF Staff Papers*, 47(1): 129–57, Washington, DC: IMF.

12
Making Debt Relief Conditionality Pro-Poor*

Oliver Morrissey

Introduction

Debt relief is a form of aid, and one that is becoming increasingly important for poor developing countries. From the perspective of donors, funds allocated to debt relief are attributed to the aid budget. From the perspective of developing countries, debt relief reduces debt servicing costs. As with aid, it represents an increase in funds available to government. Furthermore, as with aid, eligibility for debt relief is conditional on implementing specified economic policy reforms. The literature on aid conditionality should therefore be informative regarding the appropriate form of conditionality for debt relief. Furthermore, debt relief is intended to have a poverty-reducing effect. Although relief in itself will not affect poverty, the way in which the government funds that are freed through relief are used can reduce poverty. In other words, and this is the argument of the chapter, it is the funds associated with debt relief that can reduce poverty (if allocated to pro-poor expenditures). The flaw in current debt relief conditionality is that the conditions relate to *policies* (that should be pro-poor) rather than to the *use* of these funds, which are released only after the conditions have been met. We argue that pro-poor expenditures can and should be disbursed independently of, and if necessary prior to, full compliance with policy conditions.

The economic study of the effectiveness of aid is like a very large jigsaw. Theory gives us insights into how the pieces fit together, and cross-country studies provide a vague outline of what the picture looks like. However, each country is different, in both the nature of the economic interactions that determine the effects of aid and, at least as importantly, in terms of the underlying policy process. Policy clearly influences economic performance, and thus mediates the effectiveness of aid, but there is a debate regarding the mechanism by which policy influences effectiveness (contrast Burnside and Dollar, 2000 with Hansen and Tarp, 2001). A separate issue, on which current understanding is limited, is whether and how aid influences policy, the aspiration behind conditionality. World Bank (1998) seems to take the view that conditionality does not work, and it is certainly true that tight conditionality is not an effective instrument to get governments to do something they do not want to do (White and Morrissey, 1997). However, this may be going too far. For example, many African countries have implemented significant economic policy reforms since the 1980s, and aid has clearly played an important role, both encouraging and supporting reform.

This chapter addresses the latter issue – in what ways aid, in the form of debt relief, can influence policy reform. Being the policy that is now foremost among donor objectives, the focus is on poverty reduction. Donors have established the adoption of poverty reduction policies, as represented through a country's poverty reduction strategy paper (PRSP), as a criterion for aid – and, more specifically, debt relief under the HIPC Initiative. The question addressed here is whether this has increased the policy leverage of aid as an instrument of poverty reduction and whether there are lessons for the design of conditionality associated with HIPC debt relief. We adopt a political economy approach, being concerned with the interface of politics and economics – the political factors that influence the economic policy process rather than political systems *per se*.

It is useful to distinguish pro-poor *policies* from pro-poor *expenditures*. First, we consider how liberal economic policy reforms, those associated with structural adjustment and stabilization, can be made pro-poor. Our concern is not with the detail of reform areas, such as trade or exchange rate policy, but with the broad implications. The desirability of some liberalization is accepted, the question is how to protect the relatively poor (those who are either poor, or are in danger of being pushed into poverty). This leads to an emphasis on complementary policies that, in an environment of liberalization, make the reform process pro-poor. Second, we elaborate the notion of compensatory policies in respect to the policy reform conditions associated with debt relief under HIPC. Such compensatory policies comprise pro-poor expenditures that target and protect the poor and vulnerable.

In general, it is *easier* (but by no means easy) to identify and implement pro-poor expenditures than it is to implement complementary policies that make a reform process pro-poor, especially if the reform process is relatively complex and wide-ranging. Macroeconomic, liberal, policy reform is a pre-condition for eligibility for debt relief under HIPC. There is considerable debate, however, regarding the effect of such reforms on the poor, and thus on the appropriate pro-poor complementary policies. The design and implementation of pro-poor policies is demanding of policy makers, whose potential is conditioned by the policy environment – the political and administrative constraints on policy. The design and implementation of pro-poor expenditures is somewhat easier. A central argument of this chapter is that, given the policy environment, the objective of poverty reduction can be more effectively promoted through pro-poor expenditures than by *requiring* pro-poor policies. Less 'up-front' conditionality should attach to the broad economic reforms and more emphasis should be given to the composition of expenditures.[1]

The next section considers the role of external influences, channelled through aid and debt relief, in the policy process – how policy preferences combine with the political capacity of a government to adopt policy and create a commitment to reforms that can be implemented. The following section considers debates on the impact of economic reform on the poor, discusses the policy context of debt relief under HIPC and identifies the features of the policy environment for poverty reduction. The relationship between economic policy, aid and poverty reduction is an issue of increasing research activity and policy interest, although current knowledge is limited. The final section concludes with some implications for HIPC conditionality and how aid can be targeted on poverty reduction via support for PRSP processes and pro-poor expenditures.

Aid and external influence on the policy process

This section presents a framework for analysing the nature of the policy process in a country with a view to identifying the appropriate ways in which external agencies, in this context aid donors, can influence the process so as to promote pro-poor policies. Some comments on terminology are in order. 'Government' refers to the set of ruling politicians who are policy makers (and may include senior civil servants and advisors). This chapter is not concerned with the political process by which policy makers are selected. 'Administration' refers to the civil service and other institutions that implement policy. We wish to draw a clear distinction between *policy making* – the choice, design and advocacy of policy – and *implementation* (acknowledging that implementation experience should feed back to policy making).[2] Policy making will depend on the way in which government functions, the strength of opposition and the quality of technocrats involved in the process (the same individuals may also be involved in administration, but that is a distinct function). This is our principal concern. We recognize the importance of implementation capability, especially insofar as limitations constrain policy choice, but are not concerned with issues relating to administrative or institutional reform.

It will be helpful to locate this chapter within the emerging literature on the politics of pro-poor policy, although that is peripheral to our main concern. Much of this literature starts from the premise of 'assuming that governments are willing to pursue pro-poor policy' and concentrates on three issues (Johnson and Start, 2001: 9). First, how to identify activities and target beneficiaries. Second, how to ensure communication and satisfaction of needs and priorities for such activities within the public sector. Third, the politics of the interface between public sector providers and beneficiaries (such as devolving accountability, promoting local democracy and involving civil society). Johnson and Start (2001) review this literature in some detail. Although we comment on the first issue (as central to the identification of pro-poor expenditures), the concern here is with the premise. What role do external influences, in particular donors, play in encouraging governments to adopt and implement pro-poor strategies?

Morrissey (1999) proposes a framework for analysing the factors influencing governments' choices of which policies to adopt, and the presentation here builds on this. The government has to have a *preference* for the particular policy or reform (as elaborated below, this is distinct from the notions of 'commitment' and 'ownership' that are prevalent in the literature). Preferences in this context are policy-specific. A government may wish to retain the status quo or may perceive the need for change. If the latter, there is a preference for reform (with a particular aim), but this does not imply that the government knows what are the most appropriate policies to achieve the reform (this is where external influences come into play).[3] Aid, in itself and as a manifestation of donor views on what are appropriate policies, can play a role in shaping preferences. There is no reason why aid, or donors, should have an immediate effect. It takes time to shift preferences, although is easier when there is a policy vacuum to fill (and when governments are receptive). While the aid financing acts as a carrot, effort should be made to convince recipients that the policies proposed are indeed appropriate (made easier if, in fact, they are – a point we return to later).

To a large extent preferences are shaped by internal factors. At one extreme, ideological regimes will tend to have relatively fixed and inflexible preferences, although these can change over time. At the other extreme, liberal technocratic regimes will be inclined to search for the most appropriate policy and tailor it to internal political needs (their technocratic nature implies an ability to do this). Most governments are somewhere in between: they have a set of preferences, but these can be altered or refined in the face of a changing internal or external environment. Our focus is on the influence of the external environment and external actors; internal politics is, in effect, treated as a constraint (this is not to claim that change may not arise internally). That is, we take internal factors as shaping initial preferences and then consider how external influences can alter these. We begin by elaborating these factors.

A core concept is that of 'political capacity' – the ability of the political system to institute policy evolution and policy change. This will depend on the nature of decision making within the government itself, and the relative strength of constituencies that support or oppose the direction of policy. Morrissey (1999) considers four types of political regime in the context of how this shapes willingness to adopt new policies. Two are mentioned here. Established regimes tend to have vested interests they will want to protect; this combined with hysteresis renders them less willing to change preferences and adopt new policies. New regimes may find that they have power before they have formed policies and may be encouraged to become reformist.

The political difficulty with pro-poor reforms is that they require *redistribution*. On the one hand, this implies that there will be opposition to reform (from the rich, who are the powerful). On the other, there is the possibility that redistribution will, at least in the short run, slow the rate of growth. Alesina and Rodrik (1994) develop a dynamic endogenous growth model with production as a function of capital, labour and production services offered by governments and financed by a capital tax. The capital tax captures the redistributive policies of government. Growth is a result of investment in capital and therefore investment and growth are lower the higher the tax rate on capital. Thus, redistribution 'is conducive to the adoption of growth-retarding policies' (Alesina and Rodrik, 1994: 465). This would be of concern to governments as growth is often the most important determinant of the sustainability of policy reform. More can be attempted and support is greater during a period of growth, whereas reforms that are perceived as reducing growth increase opposition. 'Popularly elected governments realize that political survival depends upon good economic performance' (Sandbrook, 1996: 6).

Much of the discussion of policy reform in developing countries has been concerned with the concepts of 'ownership' and/or 'commitment' (e.g. Killick, 1995; Sandbrook, 1996; Leandro, Schafer and Frontini, 1999; Dijkstra and Van Donge, 2001), with ownership seen as necessary if policies are to be implemented successfully and sustained. The implication that ownership is a necessary, albeit not sufficient, condition for effective reform may be too strong. Typically, the concept of 'ownership' is not clearly defined and is used in a loose sense, frequently indistinguishable from commitment. Sandbrook, for example, argues that 'ownership', which is not defined, is necessary for commitment, apparently defined as requiring that 'the executive authority must be [cohesive and] firmly convinced of the necessity of [reform]' (Sandbrook, 1996: 5). Leandro, Schafer and Frontini (1999: 288) acknowledge that no clear and unambiguous definition of ownership appears in the literature, and consider it some combination of commitment and capacity to 'conceive, negotiate and implement reforms'. Thus, if a government supports a particular policy, has chosen that policy itself (although it is never fully clear how it was chosen), and openly expresses its commitment to the policy, then it is claimed to own the policy. This may be an acceptable definition of ownership, but it is unlikely to be a necessary condition for effective reform. The focus here is on commitment as the necessary condition, rather than ownership. In other words, we are not concerned with where the policy originated,[4] but simply with whether the government accepts (chooses) the policy.

Commitment, defined as the explicit adoption of a specific policy, can be seen as comprising two elements – *preferences* and *political capacity*. Preferences for reform are a sufficient condition to ensure an attempt at implementation (irrespective of ownership), but do not guarantee successful implementation, nor do they guarantee that the government will make its intentions public.[5] Preferences and capacity give rise to commitment to reform, but the ability to implement successfully will then depend on administrative capability and institutional structures. In this sense, we define commitment as revealed preference. If a government favours a particular reform and believes it has the political capacity to advocate and try to implement the reform, it is willing to declare the commitment. If a government has a preference for reform but capacity is weak, it may choose not to declare its commitment (it will be implicitly, but not explicitly, adopted). If there is no preference for the reform, there is no commitment by this definition (irrespective of what the government may declare).[6]

While preferences and capacity are necessary and sufficient for commitment, this does not imply ownership – the government could simply choose to implement a set of policies 'off the shelf' (from, for example, donors). A meaningful concept of ownership, as suggested above, would require that the policy originates with the government. This requires considerable policy making and policy analysis capacity, often beyond that available to most developing countries (at least in respect of complex issues where policy knowledge is not well known, such as poverty reduction). This is a strict definition of ownership, and neither necessary to ensure that reform is attempted nor that it is successful. Although ownership as defined *is* desirable in its own right, it is not at all evident that ownership rather than simply commitment is *necessary* to ensure that reform programmes will be advocated, implemented and sustained.

The discussion above is summarized in Table 12.1 which also indicates the various stages at which external influences can come into play. If policy making within government is relatively open and based on dialogue there is scope for developing new policies and the government

Table 12.1 External influences on the policy reform process

Political dimension	*Donor influences*
A Preferences	*The government is in favour of the reform*
• Placing specific concerns high on the agenda	
• Policy advice and knowledge transfer	
• Evidence of how policy has worked elsewhere	
B Capacity	*Ability to advocate policy and move to implement*
• Taking responsibility for unpopular policies	
• Providing evidence to build support	
• Assistance for policy advocacy	
• Poverty monitoring and analysis*	
C Commitment	*Preference revealed because capacity is adequate*
• Financial support for adopting policies	
• Building policy making capability	
• Technical assistance on policy design and analysis	
D Administration	*Process of implementing the policy*
• Technical support and assistance	

Notes: Basic structure taken from Morrissey (1999: Table 4.1). The aim is to identify the 'entry routes' of external influences on the politics of policy reform. A definition of the political dimension is provided in italics.

* These contribute to policy making and therefore enhance capacity, but are also elements in implementing effective policy, and therefore contribute to administrative capability.

will be receptive to external influences. External influences are often most important in shaping preferences. Donors can encourage governments to give particular issues more priority on the policy agenda, or try to convince governments that there is 'new' policy knowledge and experience that they should recognize. Disseminating 'good' policy experiences is one of the most effective ways to influence preferences. If a government is presented with evidence of policies that have worked elsewhere, they are more likely to be convinced that the policy is appropriate for them (i.e. external agencies can influence beliefs over the efficacy of policy alternatives).

Donors can also support political capacity – providing evidence to counter opposition and assistance in policy advocacy, for example. When political capacity is weak but governments accept the desirability of reform, external agencies can be 'blamed' for requiring governments to adopt unpopular policies. If responsibility for the adverse effects of the reform is not attributed to the government, but to external actors, then opposition has less to attack (Frey and Eichenberger, 1994). More generally, the government may support the objectives, but may have limited capacity to advocate an appropriate policy and mobilize support for it. The type of evidence that influences government preferences is essentially the same as that which supports policy advocacy, although dissemination modes differ. The former should be designed to appeal to policy makers (accentuate the positive) whereas the latter should appeal to the public and interest groups (e.g. deflecting or countering opposition arguments). In these ways, donors can fill the gap where preferences are pro-reform but capacity is weak. This implies working with or even for government.

Once commitment exists, external agencies can help to strengthen it, directly with financial support (to offset costs of implementation) or more generally with advice and help in policy design. Commitment implies the government has advocated the policy and is moving to implementation. External assistance at this stage should be directed on appropriate policy design, such as resolving problems of targeting in pro-poor expenditures. Some see such technical assistance as contributing to ownership (e.g. Leandro, Schafer and Frontini, 1999). This is true in a dynamic sense, if support for capacity now contributes to enhanced policy making capacity in the future. However, technical assistance for implementing specific reforms should not be considered as promoting ownership of that reform – it is too late. Similarly, such assistance does not establish commitment, rather it assists the process of acting on commitment.

Increasing administrative capability is an essential part of effective policy reform, relevant not only to implementation but also to political capacity itself. 'However difficult and politically risky it is to decide to introduce a reformist initiative, the process of implementing and sustaining that decision is likely to be even more fraught with difficulty and risk' (Grindle and Thomas, 1991: 121). The problem in many African countries is that bureaucrats were 'captured' by the elite. 'Political patrons secure positions in the civil service and parastatals for clients, who then owe loyalty to those patrons rather than their hierarchical superiors. These transorganizational factions advance the interests of their members – often to the detriment of the public they are supposed to serve' (Sandbrook, 1996: 8). This captures the inherent interaction of administrative capability and political capacity. A more capable and independent bureaucracy can contribute to effective policy making as it strengthens capacity (and promotes ownership), whereas weak capabilities undermine implementation and political capacity. Donors can contribute via technical assistance in administration and implementation.

Elements of a poverty reduction strategy

This section places pro-poor policies within the framework developed above. First, we consider how liberal economic policy reforms, those associated with structural adjustment and stabilization, can be made pro-poor. Our concern is not with the detail of reform areas, such as trade policy, but with the broad implications for protecting the relatively poor. This requires complementary policies that ensure a pro-poor effect and compensatory policies that minimize or offset adverse effects on the poor (these include pro-poor expenditures). We elaborate the notion of compensatory policies in respect to the policy reform conditions associated with debt relief under HIPC. This allows us to identify some problems with HIPC conditionality as practised and to identify pro-poor expenditures. This is then related to the discussion of the previous section to identify the policy environment for poverty reduction. Given the policy environment prevailing in a country, what types of pro-poor policies and expenditures should be promoted?

The impact of economic policy reform on the poor

Kanbur (2001) provides a seminal discussion of the current state of debate on the effects of economic policy reform on poverty (or, more accurately, on the poor). He identifies three areas of disagreement over whether or not 'liberal' economic policies are pro-poor – aggregation, time horizon and market structure. The source of disagreement due to aggregation is explained clearly by an example. Economic measures of poverty mostly focus on what is happening to national headcount poverty (the percentage of households or individuals living below some poverty line). Those who work at the grassroots tend to invoke personal experience of what is happening to particular households (in, for example, a study village or region). It is therefore not unusual for the first group to argue that poverty (overall) is declining whereas the second group counters that, in their experience, poverty has increased. Both may be right, as they are talking at different levels of aggregation. It may even be the case that the percentage of the poor in poverty may decline while the absolute number increases (given population growth).

Economists (and those who could be said to adopt the 'economists' view') tend to think in terms of the effect of economic policy over a medium time horizon (say, 5–10 years). That is, they are concerned with what is likely to be the outcome when the economy has adjusted to the economic policy reform. This is not to say that economists ignore adjustment costs and the fact that some will suffer (on the contrary, many emphasize the need for social safety nets and the role of compensatory policies), rather that they look beyond these costs. Others, again especially those at the grassroots, are concerned precisely with those among the relatively poor who are suffering the costs of adjustment. To such people, 'short-run survival trumps medium-run benefits every time, if the family is actually on the edge of survival' (Kanbur, 2001: 1089). Thus, the proponents of liberalization argue that reform is necessary for economic growth and this offers the opportunity for future poverty reduction, accepting adjustment costs as a 'no gain without pain' sacrifice. The critics of liberalization counter that they see the pain, but where's the gain? As with aggregation disagreements, there is truth in both sides of the argument. The common ground is that both sides recognize the need for policies to protect the poor from the *costs of adjustment* (although they may disagree on the detail).

The greatest disagreement is over perceptions of the underlying distribution of economic and political power. While most economists recognize the problems of imperfect competition and the need for regulating the behaviour of monopolistic firms, economists tend to base their arguments on an assumption of competitive markets. In other words, competitive efficiency is the analytic norm, and excessive market power is a distortion or exception. Critics, and the 'anti-globalization' protesters are an example of this, are more likely to see concentrated market power as the norm, and inequality in the distribution of power as increasing. Competitive markets are an academic concept at variance with what is observed in the real world. This disagreement is important and intense, and an important area for future work. For example, there is increasing recognition of the need to address the behaviour of multinationals in the context of multilateral (WTO) trade liberalization (e.g. Morrissey, 2002). However, this is beyond the scope of the current analysis.

These sources of disagreement have important implications for the design of pro-poor policies, and are thus relevant to our consideration of conditionality for debt relief. At stake is getting the right balance between adjusting the reform policies to make them pro-poor and including targeted expenditures to benefit the poor during periods of reform. The issue of aggregation relates to whether one concentrates on the effects for particular groups (typically the poor) or on the economy overall (allowing that there are winners and losers, the issue is whether the net gain is positive and whether the losers are compensated). Policies that promote economic growth are generally good for the poor on aggregate, and are desirable for this reason. Specific groups will suffer, and these are likely to be the relatively poor, implying a need for additional, compensatory policies targeted at those groups. Provided this is acknowledged, there is nothing inconsistent with advocating broadly liberal economic policy reforms and having a poverty reduction objective.

Debt relief and pro-poor policies

The HIPC II scheme, agreed in 1999, is based on conditionality linking debt relief to policies for poverty reduction (the Introduction to this volume provides an overview). Stated briefly, countries are required to establish a good record of implementing economic and social policy reform and prepare a PRSP indicating how they will tackle poverty reduction. In the terminology above, PRSPs include pro-poor complementary policies and compensatory expenditures. However, it is the record on implementing broad economic reform, not the PRSP or pro-poor policies, that determines eligibility for HIPC relief, the timing of the decision point and the triggers for reaching completion. The funds made available by debt relief would be then channelled into poverty reduction, typically through a poverty action fund (PAF) that identifies pro-poor expenditures. Thus, there is incoherence insofar as the pro-poor element of the package does not 'kick in' until after compliance with liberal economic reforms (this is discussed again in the conclusions). A number of observations are in order with respect to this process.

As with HIPC I, to qualify for debt relief countries must demonstrate their ability for sound economic management through satisfactory compliance with and implementation of policy reforms over three years under IMF and World Bank programmes. This is the condition on which selectivity is based. Yet 'satisfactory compliance' inevitably implies judgement, and even governments trying to comply may find themselves thrown off course by external shocks (such as the increasingly frequent and calamitous weather shocks). The inherent problem with selective conditionality is that it is the donors, specifically the international financial institutions (IFIs, the World Bank and IMF), that both stipulate conditions and judge compliance and their criteria are not transparent.

Unlike HIPC I, to qualify under HIPC II countries must also draw up a PRSP (this is where pro-poor policy enters in). The PRSP process should include consultation with civil society and other interested parties. While commendable *prima facie*, involving affected parties in the design of poverty reduction strategies, this is a highly demanding condition. On the one hand, as elaborated above, there is no consensus on what actually constitutes a 'pro-poor growth strategy' while the impact of economic policies on poverty is not well understood. On the other hand, 'consultation with civil society' is a politically sensitive topic.

The Fund and Bank must endorse and assess the PRSP. They will then agree with the government a policy reform and macroeconomic management programme to be followed during the HIPC period. Consequently, there will be some degree of cross-conditionality (Killick, 2000). The poorest countries, almost by definition countries with weak policy making and implementation capacity, are being required to design and implement a sophisticated programme of linked policies. This is likely to stretch political capacity and may undermine commitment.

Performance criteria, monitoring and review will be applied regularly and relief will be disbursed in tranches. The timetable will depend on how well the government complies with the PRSP and policy programmes agreed. Upon completion, which requires implementation of the PRSP for at least a year, debt relief is provided without conditions. The inherent defect with this approach is that the resources to fund pro-poor expenditures are not released fully until the end of the process. The problems experienced with conditional lending in the past remain. The effectiveness of HIPC II will depend on the time-frame and severity with which implementation is evaluated.

A major criticism of HIPC I was its excessive reliance on conditionality (Killick, 2000). Campaigners for debt relief have argued that conditionality can be used by donors to avoid granting the promised relief. If the conditions for macroeconomic stability and policy reform are demanding, it will be difficult for debtor countries to qualify for relief. Furthermore, the debt burden itself may be one reason why the debtor has difficulty meeting the conditions. HIPC II, in requiring a PRSP to be drawn up by the country that meets Fund/Bank requirements may make eligibility more difficult to achieve for the poorest countries. The severity of conditionality is a major concern in any debt relief programme. HIPC II, by appearing to increase the conditions required, and by making these a criterion for pre-selection, is very demanding of poor countries.

Another difficulty arises in trying to make the process pro-poor. One approach is to make the conditions pro-poor, by adapting the types of economic policies that constitute 'a good record of implementation' as defined by the IFIs. An alternative approach (that is not exclusive of the former) is to place the pro-poor policies in the PRSP. As this is in keeping with the argument for complementary and compensatory policies above, it is the approach discussed.

On the face of it, PRSPs are about listing the policy areas of specific concern to the poor and providing a list of proposed actions in these areas. As such, there appears something of a template that includes education, health, agriculture, water and security. Other areas may be included, but these are the core. Similarly, the policy detail (where there is any) may differ from country to country, but all will address these five areas. Of course, for most countries, especially HIPC ones, these areas encompass the issues of greatest importance to the welfare of the poor, especially if interpreted broadly. As our interest is in general principles rather than fine detail, discussion under these areas is appropriate.

The essential pro-poor policies in PRSPs can be considered under two headings – those relating to the provision of and access to public services and those relating to the rural sector, as the majority of the poorest in HIPCs are in rural areas. The former are mostly pro-poor expenditures while the latter are mostly pro-poor policies. Consumption of public services is an important element of the well-being (or real income) of the poor, usually omitted from income-based measures of poverty (Kanbur, 2001). The most important services are education, especially at the primary level, health (including nutrition) and water (sanitation and access to safe water). To maximize the consumption of the poor, it is necessary not only that public services are delivered but also that they are available for free (at least for the relatively poor). Charges for access to health or education (including implicit charges, such as for school uniforms, textbooks or drugs) bear disproportionately on the poor. Even if they do make efforts to meet these charges, and thus secure access, this implies a severe reduction in income available for food and other basic needs. Consequently, increased public spending on the provision of social services is a central element of PRSPs. The abolition of charges or the inclusion of specific targeting schemes provides the means of ensuring that such expenditures are pro-poor.

Policies to address poverty in low-income countries must address the rural dimension, especially the relevance of the agriculture sector that provides the livelihoods for most rural people. 'Seventy-five percent of the dollar-poor work and live in rural areas; projections suggest that over 60% will continue to do so in 2005' (IFAD, 2001: 15). Policies to address rural poverty must tackle four types of inequalities (IFAD, 2001). First, the rural poor have unequal access to physical and financial assets – distribution of land is highly concentrated and the poor are disadvantaged in access to irrigation, safe water, credit and productive assets. Second, the poor require access to technology and extension services to increase productivity. Third, markets tend to discriminate against the poor (this relates to the issue of market structure mentioned above). Fourth, institutions, political and financial, often fail to serve the poor. PRSPs typically contain a range of policies directed towards subsistence and smallholder farmers, intended to support a pro-poor agriculture policy.

The role of debt relief itself is to provide increased government resources to finance these pro-poor policies; the PAF details how savings on debt servicing will be spent and monitors expenditure. The conditionality associated with debt relief under the HIPC Initiative is intended to assist in two further ways. First, the record of sound economic policies should ensure that the country has in place pro-growth policies, including policies to reverse any bias against agriculture. Second, the PRSP process should ensure that the needs of the poor are recognized and pro-poor policies adopted by the government.

The policy environment for pro-poor policies

We have now identified some priorities in pro-poor policies. To see how these can be turned into policy actions, and to identify an effective role for donors, it is useful to place the 'pro-poor agenda' within the policy process, previously discussed. One way of summarizing the policy environment for poverty reduction is on two dimensions. Political commitment can be either low, where the desire and capacity to adopt pro-poor policies are weak, or high, where preferences and capacity are strong. Similarly, administrative capability can be weak, such that only a few fairly simple reforms are feasible, or strong, such that the reform programme can be more ambitious. An advantage of this approach is that specific types of pro-poor policies can be classified according to whether they are more demanding of political commitment or of administrative capability, or both. This can be represented in the four quadrants of Table 12.2 (following Morrissey, 1999, but here applied to poverty reduction policies). An appropriate objective in the design and sequencing of reforms is to keep the range of reforms narrow and increase complexity as commitment and capability are expanded. Successful implementation of even simple reforms can promote commitment and enhance the capability for attempting more complex reforms.

If a country has neither the desire nor means to commence reform (cell I) then only minimal reforms are likely. Countries with such an environment (e.g. where there is a strong bias against agriculture) are unlikely to embark on a PRSP process, as that requires commitment, so most poverty reduction will be embodied in donor projects (aid is used directly). Donor dialogue plays a role here to shift preferences towards poverty reduction, and initiating the PRSP process can be a central element of such dialogue. For a country initially in this position, shifting preferences and then supporting political capacity are the appropriate functions for external agencies.

High commitment, or at least preferences for poverty reduction, but low capability (cell II) is perhaps the most common case in Africa.

Table 12.2 Policy environment for pro-poor policies

		POLITICAL COMMITMENT	
		Low	High
ADMIN CAPABILITY	Weak	(Weak preference and capacity) **I (minimal)** donor dialogue donor projects initiate PRSP	(Strong preference and capacity) **II (incremental)** sector focus (e.g. SWAPs) technical assistance/PAF 'imposed' strategy
	Strong	**III (erratic)** interim PRSP targeted schemes dialogue	**IV (extensive)** consultative PRSP integrated budget 'owned' strategy

Note:
Basic structure taken from Morrissey (1999: Table 4.3), although that relates to trade liberalization policies. 'Admin Capability' relates to the administrative capacity of the government in respect of policy making (rather than administration).

Governments may have adopted and embarked on the PRSP process but administrative capability is the constraint that must be relaxed. Aid in the form of technical assistance can be very important here. Given the weak capability, it is inadvisable to attempt wide-ranging reform, so a sector focus is helpful. Donor initiatives in sector-wide approaches (SWAPs) are appropriate, and our earlier discussion suggests a focus on agriculture and social sectors (health and education). As policy making capacity is weak, ownership need not be emphasized (it is commitment that really matters) and appropriate policy strategies can be offered or even imposed.

As so few African countries have a strong administrative system, the case of strong capabilities but low commitment (cell III) is rare. Unfortunately, and for the same reason, the case of strong capability and high commitment (cell IV), where extensive reforms can be implemented successfully, is also rare. Nevertheless, cell IV is the objective and the notion of the policy environment cautions for gradual sequenced policies that build administrative capability and political commitment. Donors can do much to assist in capacity-building. In practice, it may be more meaningful to interpret cell III as representing an intermediate point between a 'minimal' and 'incremental' policy environment. As preferences are shifted and administrative capability is strengthened, political capacity becomes stronger. However, the underlying weakness in capacity suggests that such a phase is unstable and associated with 'erratic' policies, as policy reversals arise to placate strong opposition. It is because this phase is unstable that extensive reforms are not feasible; these require the establishment of adequate commitment and capability. Only then can one have a truly consultative PRSP process, an integrated budget (as donors trust the ability of the recipient to monitor spending) and, ultimately, pro-poor policies that are owned by the country.

Conclusions: implications for conditionality

The basic argument of this chapter is that the potential for implementing poverty reduction policies is conditioned by the policy environment in developing countries. Of central importance are government preferences for pro-poor policies and the political capacity to promote a pro-poor agenda. Taken together these create commitment. Persuasive economic arguments supported by relevant research can shape preferences while technical and financial support can enhance political capacity. Through such interventions donors can help to establish commitment to poverty reduction strategies. A poverty reduction strategy requires increased spending in certain sectors. Developing countries have limited capacity to reallocate spending from domestic resources to any significant degree, and limited ability to increase revenues. Aid can play here its traditional role of bridging a financing gap. More importantly, debt relief is vital to release resources for allocation to pro-poor expenditures.

The binding constraint on increasing pro-poor expenditures is resources, and donors can relax this (especially as new resources obviate the early need for domestic redistribution that can undermine reform and growth). Pro-poor policies, on the other hand, are more difficult to design and imply redistribution. They therefore require stronger political capacity and administrative capability. This problem is compounded by the disagreements and limited knowledge on the effects of economic reform on the poor. If the primary objective is poverty reduction, therefore, the prior policy is pro-poor expenditures, and this is a feasible implementation objective (conditional on the policy environment that prevails). Pro-poor policies, however desirable, are of secondary priority. They are more difficult to design and achieve, and external intervention can as easily be counter-productive as it is constructive. Pro-poor expenditures offer a first stage in building commitment and a foundation for pro-poor policies.

What are the implications for conditionality? The obvious implication is that the current approach to HIPC conditionality reverses these priorities. The resources for pro-poor expenditures are released only after a record of policy reform has been demonstrated and after the basis of a pro-poor policy is outlined. This is not necessary, and results from a misguided approach to conditionality. It is not that pre-selection is a misguided principle. Rather, the implication is that eligibility for the release of resources (aid and debt relief) should be based on pro-poor expenditure criteria. This is more simple, and more transparent, than eligibility criteria based on a package of economic reforms that interact in complex ways, are often contested regarding appropriateness and can be undermined by poor economic performance (not infrequently due to events beyond the control of governments). Support for broader economic reform may require eligibility criteria, but these could relate to pro-poor policies and should not be a pre-condition for release of funds for pro-poor expenditures.

There are at least two reasons why conditions may be attached to debt relief. First, the donors want to encourage policy reform in a particular direction. A distinction can be made between pro-growth reforms intended to enhance the opportunities for economic performance, about which there is some dispute, and specific pro-poor policies and expenditures, about which there is less dispute. The inherent problem with current HIPC arrangements is that the first set of conditions determines eligibility whereas the second comes into effect only once the PRSP is accepted and resources are released. This blurs the distinction, and can delay the implementation of pro-poor policies that do not require comprehensive economic policy reform. In particular, this approach delays the disbursement of pro-poor expenditures. Second, conditions are criteria for monitoring the compliance required, if aid flows are to be maintained or debt relief granted. In this sense, conditions (by stipulating what must be done) serve an enforcement role by triggering eligibility. This further blurs the distinction between types of reform.

It is important to note that these two 'roles' of conditionality may conflict. Typically, the extent of reform the donor wants to encourage will be broader and deeper than the minimum reform required to maintain aid flows. In other words, the level of reform required to continue receiving aid is less than the level of reform required to be eligible for debt relief. This conflict lies at the heart of the problems and ineffectiveness of conditionality, as it gives rise to a signalling problem. Recipients want to signal a commitment to reform in order to be eligible for debt relief. Whatever the level of genuine reform they wish to implement, recipients will see a need to meet only the minimum requirements. If the compliance conditions are set too high, even recipients that are genuinely trying to reform may be denied relief (there are many reasons other than intentional behaviour to explain failures in implementing reforms). Alternatively, if the conditions are set too low, insufficient reform is encouraged. Donors do not know how much reform a recipient really wants to implement, therefore may set the conditions at the wrong level (White and Morrissey, 1997, provide an exposition of this argument). A general resolution to this problem is to allow the recipients to set the target level of reform, and donors can decide whether this is acceptable. This is implicit in the spirit of HIPC selection criteria, but is not so evident in the application.

A related problem is how compliance is assessed. In the case of aid, it is the donor who decides the conditions and if compliance is satisfactory. A donor wishing to continue disbursing funds faces an incentive to tolerate more non-compliance than really desired. Consequently, levels of compliance (evaluated against the time-frame of the aid agreement) were often low without punishment being triggered. Allowing the recipient to in effect establish the conditions (the target level of reform) reduces the uncertainty and makes it more credible for the donor to assess acceptable compliance. The recipient wants to propose sufficient reforms to be acceptable to the donor, but not so much as to run the risk of non-compliance and punishment. This incentive structure encourages recipients to commit to a feasible level of reform. Donors, if they accept this as the minimum target, could still offer additional incentives for exceeding the target.

A similar line of argument can be extended to debt relief. To facilitate future fiscal and debt sustainability, donors (who are the creditors) are justified in desiring pro-growth reforms, hence such reforms have been the basis for eligibility. Donor emphasis on poverty reduction leads to the addition of pro-poor policies under the PRSP in HIPC II. These were not part of the eligibility criteria, and thus have implicitly been subject to 'softer' conditionality based on performance indicators rather than the implementation record. Pro-poor expenditures are in a sense an add-on, being activities that support implementation of pro-poor policies. However, although the PRSP allows the debtors to set the performance indicators for the PRSP (pro-poor policies and expenditures), the IFIs in effect set the tighter pro-growth conditions for eligibility. Thus, tighter conditions (with greater likelihood of unsatisfactory compliance) are applied to pro-growth policies than apply to pro-poor policies. By implication, countries that could implement pro-poor policies, especially expenditures, are being at least constrained, if not prevented, from doing so by being denied eligibility. Reversing these implicit priorities could enhance the provision and effectiveness of debt relief.

Four measures to reform HIPC conditionality to promote and support pro-poor policies are recommended:

- Aid resources should be deployed to support pro-poor expenditures, the only condition being the existence of an *expenditure strategy, monitoring arrangements and performance indicators*.
- Debt relief should be initiated subject only to a *PRSP plan being in place*. This facilitates the initiation of pro-poor policies. The minimum conditions for eligibility should not be very tight, otherwise countries trying to reform may be unfairly punished. 'Softer' conditions favour genuine reformers by allowing them to signal good intentions by exceeding the performance targets.
- *Debt relief can be accelerated* when an appropriate package of pro-growth policies is in place. The developing country should be allowed to establish the level of reform intended. The aim is to get countries moving in the right direction. In this way conditions can support or underpin government policy.

- Conditions should be part of a *negotiating incentive strategy* rather than as a coercive punishment strategy, and used to encourage rather than force policy reform. Conditions should be consistent and policy-coherent.

Has the PRSP process enhanced the capacity of aid to contribute to poverty reduction? The answer is an unequivocal 'yes', but there remains considerable room for improvement. In particular, the need to meet eligibility criteria has delayed the granting of debt relief, and hence delayed the release of funds for pro-poor expenditures. The requirements for broader economic policy reform, under our proposals, would be lessened and de-linked from initial debt relief. There is no necessary reason why this would undermine the reform process in any country. In fact, front-loading support for pro-poor policies is likely to enhance commitment to and potential for economic and social reform.

Policy advisors and donors, who tend to be the major proponents of poverty reduction strategies in developing countries, should show greater awareness of the prevailing policy environment, and work with it rather than against it. Donors can assist the policy making process through providing technical assistance and aid, to support the budgetary costs at the initial stage of moving to poverty reduction strategies and to support projects and sector programmes directed at helping the poor. Donors can also help to increase administrative capability; support for technical assistance and training is the most obvious mechanism. Technical assistance is equally important in contributing to policy making capabilities, also enhancing administration but perhaps at a higher level. In both contexts, but especially the latter, it is best if the assistance is in and through, rather than simply to, the government. Most importantly, implementing pro-poor policies should not be held hostage to judgements regarding the broader policy reform agenda.

Notes

* This chapter was originally prepared for the WIDER Development Conference on Debt Relief, Helsinki, 17–18 August 2001; useful comments were received from Maureen Were and participants. The research is part of a project on 'Poverty Leverage of Aid' funded by DFID (grant R7617). The views expressed here are those of the author alone.

1. A longer version of this chapter is available as Morrissey (2001) in which the arguments are illustrated with examples from Kenya, Tanzania and Uganda.
2. This is not to deny that implementation is integral to the policy process, but allows the focus to be on policy making. Grindle and Thomas (1991) provide

the seminal discussion of policy making and implementation in developing countries.

3. There are two issues here. First, donor and recipient preferences regarding reform may differ; this is the standard case of conditionality failure (White and Morrissey, 1997). Nevertheless, donors can influence preferences (Morrissey and Nelson, 2001 discuss how institutions such as the WTO can influence policy makers' *beliefs* and thus shape preferences for reform). Second, having chosen a specific policy, recipients may lack full information on design and implementation. This is where donors can play a directly constructive role, assuming there are shared preferences.
4. I am grateful to David Booth for suggesting this wording.
5. As should be clear from the context, preferences here do not mean that the government 'likes' the policy (although it may do). Preferences relate to *policy choice*, based on information on given objectives.
6. It should be admitted that political commitment is difficult to define in an operational way. Ideally, one needs to know the true intentions of the government rather than relying on revealed preferences (which may be opportunistic and politically, rather than policy, motivated). A government may declare an intention to reform simply to receive aid, and then renege on this 'commitment' (the source of aid conditionality ineffectiveness). In practice, stated policy preferences are the best available indicator of commitment.

References

Alesina, A. and D. Rodrik (1994). 'Distribution Politics and Income Distribution', *Quarterly Journal of Economics*, 109: 465–90

Burnside, C. and D. Dollar (2000). 'Aid, Policies, and Growth', *American Economic Review*, 90(4): 847–68.

Dijkstra, A. and J. Van Donge (2001). 'What Does the "Show Case" Show? Evidence of and Lessons from Adjustment in Uganda', *World Development*, 29(5): 841–64.

Frey, B. and R. Eichenberger (1994). 'The Political Economy of Stabilization Programmes in Developing Countries', *European Journal of Political Economy*, 10(1): 169–90.

Grindle, M. and J. Thomas (1991). *Public Choices and Policy Change: The Political Economy of Reform in Developing Countries*, Baltimore, MD: Johns Hopkins University Press.

Hansen, H. and F. Tarp (2001). 'Aid and Growth Regressions', *Journal of Development Economics*, 64(2): 547–70.

IFAD (2001). *Rural Poverty Report 2001: The Challenge of Ending Rural Poverty*, Rome: International Fund for Agricultural Development.

Johnson, C. and D. Start (2001). 'Rights, Claims and Capture: Understanding the Politics of Pro-Poor Policy', ODI Working Paper 145, London: ODI.

Kanbur, R. (2001). 'Economic Policy, Distribution and Poverty: The Nature of Disagreements', *World Development*, 29(6): 1083–94.

Killick, T. (1995). *IMF Programmes in Developing Countries: Design and Impact*, London: Routledge.

Killick, T. (2000). 'HIPC-II and Conditionality: Business as Before or a New Beginning?', Paper presented to the Commonwealth Secretariat Policy Workshop on Debt, HIPC and Poverty Reduction, 17–18 July.

Leandro, J., H. Schafer and G. Frontini (1999). 'Towards a More Effective Conditionality: An Operational Framework', *World Development*, 27(2): 285–300.

Morrissey, O. (1999). 'Political Economy Dimensions of Economic Policy Reform', Chapter 4 in M. McGillivray and O. Morrissey (eds), *Evaluating Economic Liberalization*, Basingstoke: Palgrave Macmillan.

Morrissey, O. (2001). 'Pro-Poor Conditionality for Aid and Debt Relief in East Africa', University of Nottingham, CREDIT Research Paper 01/15, available at: www.nottingham.ac.uk/economics/credit/.

Morrissey, O. (2002). 'Investment and Competition Policy in the WTO: Issues for Developing Countries', *Development Policy Review*, 20(1): 63–73.

Morrissey, O. and D. Nelson (2001). 'The Role of the WTO in the Transfer of Policy Knowledge on Trade and Competition', University of Nottingham, GEP Research Paper 2001/32, available at: www.nottingham.ac.uk/economics/gep/.

Sandbrook, R. (1996). 'Democratization and the Implementation of Economic Reforms in Africa', *Journal of International Development*, 8(1): 1–20.

White, H. and O. Morrissey (1997). 'Conditionality when Donor and Recipient Preferences Vary', *Journal of International Development*, 9(4): 497–505.

World Bank (1998). *Assessing Aid. What Works, What Doesn't and Why*, New York: Oxford University Press.

Index